Hobbes and the Democratic Imaginary

Hobbes and the Democratic Imaginary

CHRISTOPHER HOLMAN

SUNY PRESS

Published by State University of New York Press, Albany

© 2022 State University of New York

All rights reserved

Printed in the United States of America

No part of this book may be used or reproduced in any manner whatsoever without written permission. No part of this book may be stored in a retrieval system or transmitted in any form or by any means including electronic, electrostatic, magnetic tape, mechanical, photocopying, recording, or otherwise without the prior permission in writing of the publisher.

For information, contact State University of New York Press, Albany, NY
www.sunypress.edu

Library of Congress Cataloging-in-Publication Data

Name: Holman, Christopher, author.
Title: Hobbes and the democratic imaginary / Christopher Holman.
Description: Albany : State University of New York Press, 2022. | Includes bibliographical references and index.
Identifiers: LCCN 2022006877 | ISBN 9781438490434 (hardcover : alk. paper) | ISBN 9781438490441 (ebook) | ISBN 9781438490427 (pbk. : alk. paper)
Subjects: LCSH: Hobbes, Thomas, 1588–1679. | Democracy—Philosophy. | Natural law.
Classification: LCC JC153.H66 H597 2022 | DDC 320.1—dc23/eng/20220707
LC record available at https://lccn.loc.gov/2022006877

10 9 8 7 6 5 4 3 2 1

Contents

Acknowledgments	vii
Introduction	1
Democratic Non-Sense	2
Hobbes as Democratic Anatomist	6
Summary of Contents	8

Part I: Democratic Critique

Chapter 1	
Hobbes on the Madness of Democracy	17
The Multitude and the People in *The Elements of Law* and *De Cive*	19
Democracy and Its Administration	23
Democracy and the Hubris of the Many	31
Eloquence and the Democratic Inflammation of the Passions	36
Madness and Multitude in the Democratic Assembly	38
Chapter 2	
Civil Science against Democratic Normativity	45
Freedom and Democratic Participation in *The Elements of Law*	49
The Disarticulation of Freedom and Participation in *De Cive*	54
Authorization and Representation in *Leviathan*	59
The Disappearance of Democracy	66

Part II: Democratic Conditions

Chapter 3
Human Institution and Alterity ... 75
    Ontological Materialism and the Limits of Natural Knowledge ... 77
    Hobbesian Contingency ... 80
    The Philosophical Anthropology of Sensation ... 84
    Difference and the Passions ... 89
    Creativity and Social-Historical Alterity ... 95

Chapter 4
Hobbesian Equality-in-Difference ... 101
    Equality as Natural Law ... 106
    Natural Reason and the Equality of Intelligences ... 110
    The Plurality of Reasons ... 116
    Curiosity, Happiness, and the Limits of Practical Wisdom ... 122
    The Practice of Equality ... 126

Part III: Democratic Ethics

Chapter 5
Democracy and Natural Law ... 139
    Hobbes's Critique and Reconstruction of the Idea of Natural Law ... 143
    Politics and Antipolitics ... 149
    Liberty and Natural Power ... 154
    Natural Law and the True Liberty of the Subject ... 159
    The Reappearance of Participatory Desire in *Leviathan* ... 164
    Toward a Hobbesian Democracy ... 173

Summation ... 181

Notes ... 187

Bibliography ... 269

Index ... 299

Acknowledgments

Much of this book was written during the initial stages of the COVID-19 pandemic, which prevented the opportunity to travel in order to discuss the material with other scholars. I was able, however, to present some material in-person at the 2019 Canadian Political Science Association annual conference at the University of British Columbia, and virtually in the Yale-NUS Philosophy program's visiting speaker colloquium. I am grateful to the organizers and participants of these sessions for their questions and feedback. My largest debt is to the anonymous reviewers of the book, who read the initial manuscript extremely carefully, and provided me with exceptionally detailed feedback that improved the work enormously. My thanks are also due to all the staff at SUNY Press involved in the production of the book, and in particular Michael Rinella, who supported the project from the beginning and provided much valuable editorial guidance. Finally, thank you to all the usual friends, colleagues, and teachers with whom I have discussed democratic theory and the history of political thought over the years. I won't mention you by name, but by now you know who you are.

An earlier version of chapter 2 of this book appeared as " 'That Democratic Ink Must Be Wiped Away': Hobbes and the Normativity of Democracy," *Review of Politics* 83, no. 3 (2021): 305–28. Some material from chapters 3 and 4 was also published in "Hobbes and the Tragedy of Democracy," *History of Political Thought* 40, no. 4 (2019). Additional thanks are due to the referees of these pieces, which appear with permission.

The research for this project was financially supported by a Singapore Ministry of Education AcRF Tier 1 Grant.

Introduction

Within the history of ideas, few concepts have been subject to such a rapid and radical shift in the way that they have been normatively evaluated as that of democracy. It is a striking fact that although throughout the history of political thought the vast majority of so-called canonical thinkers have been explicitly anti-democratic, in the present day almost all political theorists and practitioners claim to be committed to democratic ideals. The content of these ideals, however, varies widely, democratic advocates affirming a wide range of distinct and often times mutually incompatible principles and values. There is thus little consensus on the necessary institutional physiognomy of the democratic regime, let alone the social and cultural background conditions that facilitate its effective reproduction, or the philosophical assumptions—such as those regarding human sociality and the source of fundamental law—that render it a political possibility. Universal ideological appeal to the language of democracy has thoroughly mystified the concept.[1] Although the most egregious of such mystifications are evident to most, certain others are more credible, yet nevertheless problematic. When, for example, democracy is considered in epistemic terms—as the discovery of specified procedures facilitating competent decision-making and culminating in the resolution of factually correct determinations—or in consensual terms—as looking toward the establishment of a realm of mutual understanding that mediates opinion so as to maximally enable the harmonization of interest—something fundamental about democracy's being and object is obfuscated.

It is this conceptual situation that renders the clarification of the nature of the democratic imaginary particularly urgent. In order to specify what should be seen as essential to this imaginary, I perhaps counterintuitively turn to the political thought of one of democracy's most notorious enemies, Thomas Hobbes. Despite his antipathy to democratic sovereignty in relation to its aristocratic and especially monarchical expressions, and the fact that he never elaborates a systematic account of democratic self-organization, I argue that Hobbes nevertheless exceptionally understands not only its fundamental characteristics and conditions, but also those risks embedded within it, risks that are covered up by most forms of contemporary democratic theory. At a first level of analysis, I show how Hobbes's engagement with democracy is absolutely central to the elaboration of his civil science, the democratic imaginary functioning as a negative counterfigure that perpetually menaces, and thereby orients, his political philosophy. At a second level, however, the reconstruction of the terms of this engagement deeply clarifies our understanding of (1) the essence of democracy as a form of regime, (2) the ontological conditions that structure democratic possibility, and (3) the normative ground upon which an ethical preference for democracy might be constructed. In the final instance, I suggest that even if we cannot imagine, contrary to some readers, a democratic Hobbes, we can nevertheless imagine a Hobbesian democracy, and that such can enrich contemporary democratic theory.

Democratic Non-Sense

The question of Hobbes and democracy is certainly one that has been explored before, and most especially recently. It is a curious feature of Hobbes's intellectual legacy that his body of work, one of the most enthusiastically anti-democratic within the history of political thought, has become a conceptual resource for the articulation of a variety of different normative defenses of democratic life. It is no doubt the case that some potentially democratic implications of certain Hobbesian principles were recognized immediately, both by Hobbes's critics and sympathizers alike. Hence, for example, the important contribution made by *De Cive* to the development of the Dutch republican tradition.[2] It was only within the latter half of the twentieth century, however, that a large percentage of Hobbes scholars began to appreciate the extent to which Hobbes's political thought was, although not in itself democratic, nevertheless capable of contributing to democratic thinking. Initially this democratic appropriation was firmly situated within the philosophical horizon of liberalism.[3] A variety of scholars argued that Hobbes could be seen—despite his anti-constitutionalism, his absolutism, and his preference for monarchy—as prefiguring, initiating, or participating in the modern liberal tradition.[4] Central to such readings was the issue of the voluntary consent of the contractors, *Leviathan*'s concept of authorization being seen to speak to a deliberate exercise of democratic will by individuals possessing a fundamental natural right.[5] Hobbes is interpreted as moving in a democratic direction through stressing the extent to which citizens in any form of regime must actively assent to sovereign rule after rational reflection on political necessity.[6]

Already here, however, we can observe what I will identify shortly as the fundamental error of Hobbes's democratic readers, those whom Kinch Hoekstra calls the "democratical Hobbesians."[7] As I will have occasion to note in chapter 2, Hobbes's entire theory of authorization is developed in an effort to think the possibility of political institution independently of the expression of democratic will. Specifically, Hobbes in *Leviathan* reconceptualizes political foundation as a process defined in terms of the simultaneous individual authorization of a set of representative relations on the part of each distinct natural person belonging to the multitude, as opposed to the collective self-activity of an already unified people capable of acting as one. Democracy for Hobbes, however, is defined precisely in terms of such latter self-activity. In short, the democratic Hobbesian content highlighted by his liberal readers is not democratic by Hobbes's own criterion.

This operation repeats itself it in subsequent and more robustly democratic readings of Hobbes, which attempt to either further supplement the liberal construal, or deploy Hobbes in the name of alternative democratic models. Here we can briefly identify several varieties of interpretation. Gianfranco Borrelli, for example, influentially locates in Hobbes the theoretical foundations for modern representative government, going so far as to write that Hobbes anticipates "the entire tradition of Western parliamentarianism and the history of the forms of modern political representation."[8] For David Runciman this anticipation is to be located specifically in Hobbes's recognition that the sovereign represents not each individual subject as a distinct natural person, but rather that corporate entity—the state—which their mutual authorization brings into existence, this conception ultimately suggesting a solution to the political problem of "how to reconcile the claims of representatives to take decisions on behalf of individuals with the rights of individuals to judge how well they are being represented."[9] On Richard Tuck's account, meanwhile, Hobbes is the first systematic theorist of modern representative democracy to the extent that his democratic polity does not require perpetual activity on the part of citizens, the sovereign person delegating the administrative business of government to various specialized offices and magistrates.[10] Hobbes, via the image of the "sleeping sovereign," thus provides us with a model of democracy without a democratic assembly, sovereignty inhering in a people that might only periodically awaken in order to express its will.

In addition to the representative democratic Hobbesians, there are also those we might label the liberal pluralist Hobbesians. The most important of such readers is Richard Flathman, who argues that Hobbes's thought provides us with the conceptual resources to think the possibility of a "duly chastened democratic politics."[11] Such a politics is constituted not through the instauration of a concrete political form in which self-actualization is achieved via active political participation, but rather the establishment of a social condition in which the power of government is institutionally moderated so as to maximize the scope of the individual pursuit of private goods. For Flathman and other such readers, Hobbes is a pluralist to the degree that he prescribes no single mode of being required for self-realization, the function of the body politic being the provision of security such that citizens may indulge their diverse and multiple ends.[12]

The last group of interpreters I will call attention to are the radical democratic Hobbesians, whose readings are often explicitly framed in opposition to liberal ones. Paul Downes, for example, argues that Hobbes can be seen to contribute to a post-Marxist theory of radical democracy that refutes the limits on democratic organization imposed on the latter by liberal and capitalist logics.[13] The effort to reclaim Hobbes as a forerunner of liberal democracy pacifies the former's civil science, ideologically deploying it in order to conservatively legitimate "a conventional liberal-capitalist version of democracy."[14] Radical democratic appropriations of Hobbes often frame themselves as being necessarily anti- or countersovereign in orientation. James Martel, for instance, proposes that Hobbes's nominalism suggests to us an alternative mode of reading that decenters the principle of textual authority, the latter being generated through the critical act of interpretation as opposed to being unilaterally sourced in the author.[15] Rereading Hobbes with this in mind allows us to imagine a concept of radical democracy that has successfully jettisoned the principle of sovereignty, which is always incapable of expressing that human diversity which radically democratic politics seeks to affirm.[16]

As creative and theoretically sophisticated as all of these democratic applications of Hobbesian political thought are, my suggestion is that most of them are in fact either not democratic, not Hobbesian, or neither. Such conceptions are examples of what Hobbes identifies as absurd speech, propositions in which the predicate is incapable of naming that which the subject does.[17] Hobbes would assert that the notions of a democracy without sovereignty,[18] or a democracy without absolutism,[19] or a democracy without a democratic assembly,[20] are as sensical as the notions "of a *round Quadrangle*; or *accidents of Bread in Cheese*; or *Immaterial Substances*; or of *A free Subject*; *A free-Will*; or any *Free*, but free from being hindred by opposition."[21] As opposed to mere error, to which all individuals are subject to from time to time—such as, for example, when they reckon without the use of words and fail to correctly identify a phenomenon's necessary consequents or antecedents,[22] or when they misapply a name to a thing which is incapable of being so subsumed[23]—absurdity occurs when reckoning with common words produces false determinations as a result of any of a certain number of causes. In *Leviathan* Hobbes identifies as the first, and for our purposes the most important cause of absurd conclusions, the failure of ratiocination to ground itself in and commence from the generally accepted signification of words.[24] Indeed, it is this failure that Hobbes associates with the greater part of scholastic philosophy, writing that "it is most true that *Cicero* sayth of them somewhere; that there can be nothing so absurd, but may be found in the books of Philosophers. And the reason is manifest. For there is not one of them that begins his ratiocination from the Definitions, or Explications of the names they are to use."[25] My suggestion is that the non-sense of the democratical Hobbesians results from their failure to accept what Hobbes sees as the necessary components of the democratic commonwealth, abstracting from them in such a way as to facilitate the mapping of their own particular conceptions onto the Hobbesian schema. Through such operations, though, they violate the logical structure of Hobbes's civil science. Any possibility of theorizing a normative preference for democratic modes of political life along Hobbesian lines must, on the contrary, be firmly rooted in Hobbesian signification, for "in the right Definition of Names, lyes the first use of Speech; which is the Acquisition of Science: And in wrong, or no Definitions, lyes the first abuse; from which proceed all false and senselesse Tenets."[26]

Hobbes as Democratic Anatomist

My argument in this book is not only that an understanding of democratic potentiality in Hobbes must begin from the terms of his own conception, but more importantly, that engagement with what Hobbes takes to be the core components of democracy sheds important light on features of the latter's mode of operation and conditions of being that are increasingly obscured in contemporary debates. Specifically, what Hobbes reminds us of is the fact that democracy is always a tragic regime. Here I borrow the characterization of democracy in terms of tragedy from Cornelius Castoriadis, whose analysis engages the problematic that emerges from the recognition that the political institution of the social world is always a specifically self-institution.[27] That is to say, there exists no extrasocial rule or law—be it "Nature, Reason, or History as ultimate 'principle' "[28]—that functions to structure or delimit political determination. The formal institutional configuration of democracies may vary widely, but what the latter all share is the effort to maximally facilitate the universal participation of citizens in the formulation of those legal norms governing communal life, through for example the construction of general assembly fora and the deployment of the modes of sortition and rotation for the distribution of political offices not requiring a special skill or knowledge. In this sense "democracy is not an institutional *model*, not even a 'regime' in the traditional sense of the term. Democracy is the self-institution of the collectivity by the collectivity, and this self-institution as movement."[29] To the extent, however, that there exists no transcendent law guiding this movement, any limitation on the instituting power, which is indeed absolutely necessary for the stabilization of social life, must be a specifically self-limitation.

What Hobbes perceives, and what worries him so deeply, is that there is no guarantee that the people will practice such self-limitation. Indeed, for Hobbes the very nature of deliberation in democratic assemblies, which is marked by the discursive confrontation of individual opinions in a process whereby speakers deploy eloquence in order to stimulate the passions of listeners for the sake of the cultivation of political support, is uniquely unsuited to fostering such restraint. It is this absence of self-limitation that constitutes the hubris of the people. Hubris speaks not to the transgression of established limits, but rather the very absence of self-limitation. To once more quote Castoriadis, the twentieth century's most astute analyst of this phenomenon: "It is the transgression of limits that have never been defined by anyone, and which in a sense will only be defined after the fact."[30] That the people as collective instituting power, in the face of the lack of transcendent constraints on the scope of their activity, fail to substitute for this lack their own autonomously formulated limits, is the intrinsic risk of democracy, and what constitutes its tragic dimension: "Democracy is the regime of self-limitation; therefore it is also the regime of historical risk—another way of saying that it is the regime of freedom—and a tragic regime."[31] Whereas the major part of contemporary democratic theory and practice occults this dimension of democratic being—through, for example, the effort to construct or model various national constitutionalisms or international regimes that are seen as giving a legal form to ostensibly prepolitical norms, such as so-called natural and universal human rights—Hobbes confronts it directly. Political history would seem to show that the transcendent basis of such mechanisms is always illusory, to the extent that, whatever legal function they might serve, this function does not include the capacity to definitively settle all political questions. Regardless of any ideological claims to the contrary, there exists no exterior source to ground and facilitate the perpetuation of the legal configuration, which is perpetually subject to transgression. Such a fact is one that we should be intimately familiar with in the present historical moment, given the multiplication of various authoritarian political movements and governments within liberal democratic regimes, movements and governments which often challenge and threaten the very constitutional context from which they emerge. What Hobbes argues is that popular hubris is always a possible source of such transgressions.

    Within the history of political thought Hobbes's conception of democracy is exemplary in capturing the above features of this form of society. His articulation of the constitutional attributes of democracy, however, does not exhaust his contribution to democratic theory. What I call Hobbes's democratic imaginary refers not only to his particular institutional anatomy of the form of the democratic regime, but also what it reveals to us about certain metaphysical conditions of democratic being, and, more subtly, the possibility of identifying an ethical ground for the normative preference for democracy in relation to other sovereign configurations. The three sections of this book correspond to what I take to be the three democratic images that collectively constitute the Hobbesian democratic imaginary. The constellation of these images not only clarifies our understanding of the social and political problematics suggested by the idea of democracy, but also the importance of this latter idea to the Hobbesian endeavor. Hobbes's reflection on democracy centrally informs significant elements of his political-philosophic project, such that his civil science is incapable of being completely grasped independently of consideration of the place of the democratic imaginary within it.

Summary of Contents

The first Hobbesian democratic image reveals this latter fact, it articulating the role that the idea of democracy plays in the construction of Hobbes's political thought. Democracy functions as a sort of ccounterimage imperiling the normative goals of his civil science.[32] I begin in chapter 1 by outlining the main features of Hobbes's critical anatomy of the democratic regime. Hobbes's strong aversion to democratic sovereignty is well established, and this despite the fact that he is perfectly aware that his civil science is incapable of definitively proving its inferiority in relation to other sovereign forms at a philosophical level.[33] As he concedes in *De Cive*, the preference for monarchy is "the only thing in this book which I admit is not demonstrated but put with probability."[34] Hobbes's argument against democracy must thus proceed through a historical investigation of what he intuits to be its intrinsically practical limitations. At the center of his critique is what he takes to be the problem of the multitude. As opposed to a people, a unified collective actor endowed with a singular will capable of initiating action, a multitude is a mere agglomeration of a multiplicity of distinct individuals that remain always nonidentical with one another, this natural nonidentity militating against the formulation of concerted and joint political deeds. Hence the need, if stable life in common is to be possible, to reduce the plurality of distinct wills to a single one through the creation of an entity whose will stands in for and expresses those of all. A commonwealth may be represented by either a monarch, an aristocratic assembly, or a democratic assembly. The superiority of monarchy, however, lies in the fact that the will of the sovereign representative is already unified in the natural being of the occupier of sovereign office. In assemblies such is not the case, and hence the need for the generation of an artificial unity through a process of deliberation among the multiple people occupying said office. Hobbes's critique of democracy is made on the basis of what he takes to constitute the formal mechanics of such deliberation within major assembly fora. Political deliberations in democratic assemblies are characterized by the confrontation between distinct individuals with unique normative conceptions, who deploy eloquence in an effort to persuade others of their positions. In this process, Hobbes thinks, the passions of assembly members are so enflamed as to render ratiocination impossible, reason being overwhelmed by emotion so as to allow for the generalization of antagonism between people on the basis of their differing interests and opinions. In short, Hobbes considers democracy to be an intrinsically paradoxical mode for generating a collective will, for it is governed by that very logic of multitude—the logic of difference, heterogeneity, and nonidentity—which the effort to construct a commonwealth was aimed at overcoming in the first place. Ultimately Hobbes concludes that democracy is, by its own institutional force, oriented toward uncertainty and instability, democratic citizens being incapable of practicing that rational self-limitation that stable political life depends upon.

After detailing Hobbes's critical anatomy of democracy in chapter 1, in chapter 2 I demonstrate the centrality of this opposition to democracy through philosophically contextualizing the overall elaboration of his political thought in light of it. I argue that Hobbes's opposition to democratic life constitutes a central frame through which we must understand various of the most important theoretical mutations that occur throughout the several expressions of his civil science. Specifically, key alterations that Hobbes makes in his political work from *The Elements of Law* to *Leviathan* should be interpreted as motivated by his antipathy to democracy, each new text being an effort to retroactively foreclose a substantive democratic normativity that the prior theoretical framework allowed for or suggested. In *The Elements* the potential source of this normativity is Hobbes's assertion of a unique type of civil liberty that is found only in democratic commonwealths, to the extent that the latter singularly facilitate shared participation in the formulation of law. Recognizing the extent to which such a conception of liberty might predispose citizens to preferring democratic bodies politic to monarchical or aristocratic ones, in *De Cive* Hobbes attempts to neutralize this source of normativity by, firstly, reconceptualizing liberty in terms of the mere absence of impediments to motion, and secondly, denying any intrinsic desire on the part of citizens to participate in political modes. *De Cive*, however, continues to think political foundation in terms of a necessarily originary democratic moment, individuals self-organizing themselves as a collective agent prior to definitively choosing, via democratic procedure, a final sovereign form. By the time of *Leviathan* Hobbes had realized the extent to which such a conception of foundation might be exploited so as to produce an ethical preference for democracy as the temporally earliest, and hence most natural of sovereign constitutions. Hence in *Leviathan* Hobbes reformulates political institution in terms of the mechanics of authorization and representation, in which citizens supposedly individually authorize sovereign representation without recourse to collective determination. Overall, then, Hobbes's opposition to democracy is so significant as to fundamentally structure core elements of his political philosophy, the very form of the account of political institution changing in response to the perception of democratic potentiality that it suggests.

In part 2 I turn to the second image constituting the democratic imaginary that can be found in Hobbes's thought. Just as Hobbes recognizes the necessary institutional form of democracy as the direct and explicit self-institution of the people via active participation in the formulation of law, he also recognizes those metaphysical conditions that render such self-activity a human possibility. In this section I thus turn to Hobbes's natural philosophy and philosophical anthropology in order explicate these conditions of democratic being. In chapter 3 I detail the extent to which Hobbes considers the natural world to be open to the type of autonomous self-institution that democracy depends upon. As noted above, he recognizes the fact that the instituting power is not constrained by any exterior limits, such as a law of nature or of history, that would structure or guide political determination. Hobbes's materialism certainly considers the emergence of phenomena in terms of necessity, but such necessitation is irreducible to any teleological principle, matter lacking an intrinsic purpose or essence that would direct its motion. Such applies to material human bodies as much as any other, and hence the impossibility of thematizing the human psyche so as to extract from it certain natural standards of sociality valid in every historical context. Thus for Hobbes we can observe within the world an overwhelming diversity of forms of human association, which are not systematically derived from any shared first principles beyond that directing us to institute some form of society for the sake of the preservation of our lives. Social-historical alterity ultimately reflects the radically creative human power to autonomously institute our world.

In chapter 4 I turn to the second ontological condition of democratic being. If the first condition speaks to the creative power to institute a social world lacking prior foundation, the second speaks to the equal capacity of members of society to so participate in such institution. Hobbes understands that what fundamentally defines democracy is the lack of all natural titles or qualifications to govern, access to offices of rule not being restricted to a part of the community on the basis of this part's supposed possession of a unique intelligence, skill, or knowledge exclusively identified with it. Hobbes's rejection of all such presumed competencies is revealed through his affirmation of a radical human equality. Most readers of Hobbes have difficulty dealing with this affirmation, some seeing it as existing in fundamental tension with his philosophical-anthropological nominalism, which asserts the absolute singularity and nonidentity of individual beings. Hobbesian equality, however, is not meant to conceptually represent a literal continuity of human characteristics or traits. It expresses, rather, a condition of equality-in-difference, each individual possessing an equivalent potential to adequately deploy practical reason in order to outline as far as possible the nature of their particular goods, and the effective modes to these goods' actualization. Natural equality thus does not deny difference, but rather reflects it. Hobbes's effort to refute democracy does not proceed through the denial of natural equality, but rather through the recognition of the consequences that result when such natural equality is given a concrete expression in democratic modes and orders. Whereas aristocratic thinkers deny that the majority of citizens possess the requisite rationality required to make informed determinations regarding technical political things, for Hobbes the danger of democracy lay in its effort to translate a very real natural equality into a political equality considered in terms of the right of all citizens to utilize their reason in deliberative contexts. Precisely because all individuals are different—possessing differing desires, opinions, normative conceptions, and so on—the realm of politics will always be conflictual, the individual deployment of equal reason for the sake of the advancement of particular values or ends inevitably meeting resistance from opposed projects. The potential for hostile antagonism is thus embedded within democracy's very logic, and given Hobbes's skepticism that political conflict may be institutionally moderated so as to facilitate self-limitation, this antagonism is bound to eventually destabilize the social order.

In the last part of the book I turn finally to the question of the ethics of democracy and whether Hobbes's political philosophy is capable of functioning as a conceptual resource for thinking a normative preference for specifically democratic sovereign forms. Needless to say, such an undertaking runs entirely counter to Hobbes's own intention, which was always to prevent the emergence of any such preference. The articulation of the third image constituting the Hobbesian democratic imaginary is thus one that is only latent within Hobbes's work. In order to present this image, in chapter 5 I switch methodological modes, attempting not a comprehensive reconstruction of the logic of the Hobbesian argument, but rather selectively deploying certain of Hobbes's concepts in relation with one another in order to generate conclusions about political life very different than Hobbes's own. The unexpected juxtaposition of particular Hobbesian categories in a unique way thus produces new ideas whose content might otherwise remain obscured. I suggest in this final chapter that the constellation of Hobbes's reformulation of the idea of natural law with his concept of the true liberty of subjects allows for the emergence of a theoretical basis to ethically prefer democracy, although counter to Hobbes's democratic readers noted above, on specifically Hobbesian grounds. Contrary to the classical natural writers in the Aristotelian-Thomist tradition, who assume that legal norms may be derived from the perception of transcendent moral principles of extrasocial origin, Hobbes's laws of nature specify only that minimal content that can be said to constitute the immanent tendencies of the natural human being, and the means to institute a political order capable of facilitating these tendencies' expression. This institution exists for the sake of the safety of the people, the actualization of which depends on the creation of a sphere of right that ensures the ongoing facilitation of that general human motion upon which all particular motion depends. It is precisely this facilitation that the so-called true liberties of the subject look toward. True liberty aims at the preservation of those truly universal human powers and faculties whose expression is ethically suggested by natural law as a basic prerequisite for the realization of the safety of the people. My suggestion is that *Leviathan*'s recognition, contrary to what is earlier claimed in *De Cive*, that all individuals have a natural desire for political participation—recognizing it as the most effective means for the pursuit of their particular good—combined with a rejection of the Hobbesian critique of the mechanics of democratic deliberation, allows us to reinterpret democratic self-activity as an important element for the realization of the safety of the people. To this extent, democracy can be rethought as that sovereign form that most adequately facilitates the self-preservation demanded by natural law.

PART I
DEMOCRATIC CRITIQUE

Chapter 1

Hobbes on the Madness of Democracy

One of the most striking features of Hobbes's analysis of democracy as a sovereign form is that on its surface it seems to devote far more attention to what are seen to be the social inconveniences that this form generates, as opposed to the fundamental characteristics and mechanics that define its mode of operation. The democratic regime, its particularity in relation to other sovereign constitutions, thus initially appears to be undertheorized.[1] Commentators on Hobbes have perhaps expectedly devoted their attention primarily to detailing what Hobbes considers to be these consequent inconveniences, glossing over the question of the actual dynamics of democratic political organization. The failure to undertake that task has obscured the content of what Hobbes sees as inherent to democracy and is perhaps a major factor in accounting for the manifold efforts of contemporary readers to map their own particular democratic conceptions—representative, liberal, anti-sovereign, and so on—onto the Hobbesian framework. These efforts, I argue, tend to cover up the profundity of the Hobbesian insights into democracy and its conditions, and contribute to the continued pacification of this particular idea of political life.[2] Before detailing the specific elements of Hobbes's critique of democracy, we should thus begin by calling attention to that minimal description of the necessary characteristics of democracy that Hobbes provides.[3]

In the next chapter I will trace out the alterations in the account of sovereign institution that Hobbes makes over his three major political works, attempting to explain the perception of the need to initiate such variation in terms of the effort to neutralize democratic potentiality. In this chapter, however, I will mostly abstract from this trajectory, recognizing the relatively consistent account of democracy's characteristics and inconveniences from *The Elements of Law* to *Leviathan*. As is well known, the general legal structure of sovereign power is identical regardless of the order of the regime, the marks, rights, and characteristics of sovereignty being articulated in the same form irrespective of the particular constitution of the political entity. The commonwealth is always characterized by the generation of a single and unitary will that is meant to overcome the plurality of wills that defines the multitude of natural persons, it standing in for each natural person to the extent that all are seen as its individual authors. That said, the concrete processes by which this activity of reduction is carried out are distinct in each particular case, the variation between forms of commonwealth being wholly expressed through the institution of sovereign office.[4] This criterion allows us to identify three distinct kinds of political society.[5] In *Leviathan* Hobbes writes that "the difference of Common-wealths, consisteth in the difference of the Soveraign, or the Person representative of all and every one of the Multitude. And because the Soveraignty is either in one Man, or in an Assembly of more than one; and into that Assembly either Every man hath right to enter, or not every one, but Certain men distinguished from the rest; it is manifest, there can be but Three kinds of Common-wealth."[6] These three kinds are monarchy, where the sovereign representative is one natural person; aristocracy, where it is an assembly of part of the people; and democracy, where it is an assembly of all the people. As Hobbes always stresses, contrary to those most well-known political typologies to be found in the history of political thought, these three species exhaust the range of political potentiality. Most notably, there are no correspondent forms that represent the negative counterimage of these regimes, as in for example that typology which identifies corrupt deviations from properly instituted forms. Tyranny and monarchy, for example, "are not the names of Formes of government, but of the same Formes misliked."[7] Individuals tend in their naming to denote not just external things but their affections, so that one who calls a democracy an anarchy refers us more to the desires of this one individual than it does to the governmental form: "For men not only indicate things by the names they use, but also their own *feelings*, e.g., *love, hatred, anger,* etc."[8] Differing names do not speak to differing forms, but to differing opinions among individuals regarding the normative value of each form or those occupying its offices: "It is not *different kinds* of commonwealth that are designated by these different names, but *different sentiments* on the part of the citizens about the ruler."⁹

Of Hobbes's major political works, *Leviathan*, for reasons that will be explained in the following chapter, contains the most abbreviated discussion of the specific mechanics of democratic sovereignty, its brief commentary mostly being confined to chapter 19. Hobbes nevertheless calls attention here to what is democracy's signature characteristic, stressing that political determinations formulated in this commonwealth are the result of a uniquely participatory type of self-activity. Democracy presupposes a political endeavor on the part of the people as a collective entity, the individuals constituting this entity sharing in decision-making: "When [a sovereign representative is] an Assembly of All that will *come together*, then it is a DEMOCRACY, or Popular Common-wealth."¹⁰ This feature of Hobbes's account of democracy is expanded on in more detail in *The Elements of Law* and *De Cive*. The crucial element that these texts outline is the extent to which democratic political life, to the degree that it is marked by generalized participatory activity, is governed by a particular logic of being that is primarily associated with the multitude, democracy representing a reappearance within the sovereign body of that mode of existence that the institution of the commonwealth was meant to overcome in the first place. The singular will of the people as a collective entity is generated via the conflictual confrontation of particular wills belonging to diverse natural persons, there thus existing a tension between, on the one hand, the result of the deliberative process—the production of an internally unified determination attributable to a single actor—and, on the other hand, the mode by which this process expresses itself, that is, via contestation between multiple actors with a plurality of divergent interests and opinions. Before detailing Hobbes's allegations regarding this operation, however, we must first briefly discuss the concept of multitude in terms of its negative relation to political endeavor.¹¹

The Multitude and the People in *The Elements of Law* and *De Cive*

That the problem of multitude is a central one within the Hobbesian project is recognized by many commentators.¹² As is the case with his interpretation of democracy most generally, Hobbes's hatred of multitude does not prevent him from providing one of the most penetrating analyses of its meaning and significance.[13] Hobbes's concept of multitude is meant to articulate the specificity that defines natural human relations, and the latter's inability to facilitate action in concert. The nature of these relations, and how they cannot be seen as assimilable to the types of spontaneous organization that are characteristic of the so-called social animals, will be discussed further in chapter 3. We note for now, however, that lacking the type of natural concord that structures animal association, any immediate concurrence of individual wills to one action must be interpreted as perpetually fragile and not sufficient for the maintenance of peace.[14] This fragility is a consequence of the radical singularity of individual natural persons, there existing no universal principle of being—be it theological, biological, psychological, and so on—that would naturally bind them all. Peace must be compelled by a common power that is capable of maintaining the identity of individual wills via their union, "the involving or including the wills of many in the will of One man, or in the will of the greatest part of any one number of men, that is to say in the will of one man, or of one COUNCIL."[15] Outside of such a union, which establishes a body politic or civil society characterized by the investment of one or a council with the common power—a sovereign wielding a sovereign authority—the collection of natural individuals remains a mere multitude.

In *De Cive* Hobbes defines a multitude as "not a *single entity* but a number of men, each of whom has his own will and his own judgement about every proposal."[16] This constitution of the multitude as a sum of discrete individuals who retain a private sensibility despite any communal relationships they may enter into, militates against the generation of collective subjectivity. Hobbes thus writes in the *Elements of Law* that, "for their persons they are many, and (as yet) not one; nor can any action done in a multitude of people met together, be attributed to the multitude, or truly called the action of the multitude, unless every man's hand, and every man's will, (not so much as one excepted) have concurred thereto. For multitude, though in their persons they run together, yet they concur not always in their designs."[17] A multitude lacks a sole will that belongs naturally to it, being composed instead of a plurality of irreducibly singular wills which are incapable of being immediately reconciled. The multitude is this agglomeration of individual wills, the conceptual representation of the insatiable and unconstrained motion of natural persons disunited. It would thus be a mistake to consider the multitude in terms of a static entity whose contours are capable of being determined and mapped, it existing in a state of perpetual becoming and flux, its form being displaced and reorganized in light of the constantly shifting movement of the individuals composing it.[18]

The multitude is hence a heterogeneity, a chaotic and disordered cluster of beings lacking objective structure and form. This privation of being prevents us from attributing to it action, which can only emanate from a self-identical subject capable of definitively willing for itself. It is in light of this recognition that Hobbes emphasizes the need to rigorously affirm the proper signification of the word *people*. Much confusion, and indeed much sedition, arises from the equivocal double meaning of this term in common political discourse.[19] In the *Elements* Hobbes notes how often the term *people* is incorrectly taken to refer simply to the sum of individuals occupying a defined geographic space, whereas it only rightly signifies a civil person that unifies the many through the incorporation of each particular will into its own singular one that stands for them all. When writers, for example, speak of the rebelliousness of the people and so on, they actually refer only to a dispersed multitude, within which the demand of each individual is simply their own, thus precluding the formation of any unified demand:

> They say the people rebelleth, or the people demandeth, when it is no more than a dissolved multitude, of which though any man may be said to demand or have right to some thing, yet the heap, or multitude, cannot be said to demand or have a right to any thing. For where every man hath his right distinct, there is nothing left for the multitude to have right unto; and when the particulars say: *this is mine, this is thine*, and *this is his*, and have shared all amongst them, there can be nothing whereof the multitude can say: *this is mine.*[20]

It is only possible for the multiplicity of individuals to speak of *theirs* collectively when they have been singularly united as a people in the proper sense of the term.

True action is achievable only to the degree that a body manifests this concurrence of action and will, a state of being that characterizes the formation of the body politic. The latter is created when the individuals of the previously divided multitude unite such that "they allow the wills of the major part of their whole number, or the wills of the major part of some certain number of men by them determined and named; or lastly the will of some one man, to involve and be taken for the wills of every man."²¹ As we know already, where the will of one person stands in for the wills of all, the government is a monarchy; where the major part of a certain number of individuals expresses the will of each particular, the government is an oligarchy or an aristocracy; and where the wills of all particulars are expressed through the major part of the whole number, or in those who actively choose to participate, the government is a democracy.²² The plurality of the individual wills characteristic of multitude are reduced to a singular common will when all individuals agree with each other to not resist the will of that person or council whose will is from there on taken to stand in for their own.²³ It not being a natural person, a multitude is only capable of being transformed into an artificial person through an act of contract whereby one will or the majority of a designated number of wills comes to express the will of all. Exclusively under such conditions are we justified in speaking of the existence of the people and of the action of the people. Hobbes thus writes:

> Whenever we say that a People or a number [of men] is willing, commanding or doing something, we mean a commonwealth which is commanding, willing and acting through the will of one man or through the wills of several men who are in agreement; and this can only happen in a meeting. But whenever something is said to be done by a number of men, great or small, without the will of that man or meeting, it means that it was done by a people as subjects, that is, by many individual citizens at the same time, and that it does not spring from one will but from the several wills of several men, who are citizens and subjects but not a commonwealth.²⁴

Hobbes here certainly acknowledges that individual natural persons are capable of socially coordinating activity independent of a single common will.²⁵ It is simply that no such activity can be properly considered an action that we ascribe to a subject, the multitude lacking the singular being capable of willing such action. In any apparent action of the multitude there is contained as many actions as there are individuals, the trajectory of whose desire or behavior may temporarily overlap without the establishment of a structural identity. As Hobbes consequently writes, "Whatever is done by a multitude must be understood as being done by each of those who make up that multitude," such that those who have not assented to the action cannot be considered as having done it.[26] Again, for such a situation to be overcome, for a will of all to be generated given the inherent lack of a natural coalescence of will, each individual must agree that the determinations produced by the designated one or assembly stand in for the will of one another, "for otherwise, a multitude will never have any will at all, since their attitudes and aspirations differ so markedly from one another."[27] Those who do not consent to the unification of wills are excluded from the city, with the city retaining the right of war against them.

Democracy and Its Administration

In the *Elements of Law* and *De Cive*, within the simple political typology identified by Hobbes democracy holds a unique place, at least with respect to "the nature of a commonwealth institutive."[28] Specifically, democracy necessarily precedes both monarchy and aristocracy temporally, the latter two forms being established only after the major part of a people assents to their institution via democratic procedure.[29] In *De Cive* Hobbes expands on the principle that he introduces in the *Elements* regarding the intrinsically democratic origin of the creation of all cities: "When men have met to erect a commonwealth, they are, almost by the very fact that they have met, a *Democracy*. From the fact that they have gathered voluntarily, they are understood to be bound by the decisions made by agreement of the majority. And that is a *Democracy*, as long as the convention lasts, or is set to reconvene at certain times and places."[30] Democracy is not instituted via contract between all particular natural persons and the people—for as we know there is no people prior to compact, but only a multitude of said natural persons—but via mutual compacts of particulars with one another. After the institution of the people, furthermore, individuals cannot contract with the former either, for it contains within its will the will of all particulars. Hobbes sums up the process in the following way: "Since therefore such agreements are understood to take place as a matter of necessity in the formation of a commonwealth, but (as has been shown) no agreement is possible between a *citizen* and a *people*, it follows that each of the citizens makes an agreement to submit his will to the will of the majority, on condition that the others also do likewise; as if each man said: *I transfer my right to the people, for your benefit, on condition that you transfer your right to the people for my benefit.*"³¹

Being so instituted, the originary democracy dissolves where the people fail to appoint fixed and regular times and places to assemble and convene with one another: "A people therefore retains *sovereign Power* only so long as a certain time and place is publicly known and appointed, on which those who wish may convene."³² If the meetings of the people be occasional or in diverse times and places, then the activity is factional, and the people has been dissolved into a multitude. If, furthermore, these conditions exist, yet intervals between meetings are too great to allow the people to deliberate on all necessary matters, then authority must be delegated to inferior bodies who assume responsibility for administration. Hobbes thus writes that "if a *People* is to retain *sovereign power*, it is not enough to have settled times and places for meeting. Either the intervals between the meetings must not be so long that something could happen in the meanwhile which (for lack of *sovereign Power*) would endanger the commonwealth, or the *People* must devolve at least the exercise of sovereign power on some *one* man or *one* assembly for the intervening period."³³ Hobbes here implicitly identifies the defining characteristic of democratic political organization: the generation of institutional spaces open to all citizens which, via the mediation of particular wills, facilitates deliberation over essential political questions, aiming ultimately at the production of legislative norms that orient and govern life in common. The active, participatory quality of democratic rule is affirmed through Hobbes's very definition of an assembly, a necessarily deliberative body. An assembly is "a group of several men deliberating about what is to be done or not to be done, for the common good of all."³⁴ A specifically democratic assembly would then generalize political participation to the degree that all citizens would have formal access to its deliberations.³⁵ Hobbes's perception, however, of the incapacity of democratic political organs to directly legislate on all matters pertaining to civil life, and hence on the practical need for the establishment of an organizational distinction between government and its administration, has led many commentators to occult the radical foundation of Hobbes's democratic considerations. The most well-known of such readings is that recently produced by Richard Tuck.

In Tuck's account, Hobbes considered democracy as a potentially adequately functional regime when government was separated from the administration of government, which would mean in practice democracy without a democratic assembly.[36] He sees Hobbes's discussion of the sleeping sovereign in *De Cive* as particularly revealing.[37] Here Hobbes distinguishes between sovereignty and administration, between the right and the exercise of sovereign power. Hobbes famously compares the periods between the citizens of an assembly convening to the periods when the monarch sleeps: "The intervals between meetings of the citizens may be compared to the times when a *Monarch* is asleep; for the power is retained though there are no acts of commanding."[38] If the sleeping people does not maintain for itself this power to meet, then the people dies, just as much as does the natural monarch who never wakes from their sleep:

> A king who is going to sleep for a while gives sovereign power to someone else to exercise, and takes it back when he wakes up; just so *a people, on the election of a temporary Monarch*, retains the right of meeting again at a certain time and place, and on that day resumes its power. A king who has given his power to someone else to exercise, while he himself stays awake, can resume it again when he wishes; just so a *people* which duly meets throughout the term set for a *time-limited Monarch* can strip him of power if it so wishes.[39]

Modern democracy, the contemporary argument suggests, can be seen as a manifestation of Hobbes's schema, the political apparatus identified with government—despite its command over legislation and the exercise of power—not actually being sovereign, but simply administratively exercising the authority that belongs to that sovereign who sleeps. Administration can here be executed via nondemocratic offices and institutions, and yet the regime remains democratic in that "some ultimate authority" is invested in the people. In Tuck's words, "The only condition which had to be met in order for a constitution to be democratic was that all the citizens could meet or otherwise declare their will on *at least one occasion* without being summoned by a monarch or aristocratic council."[40]

Tuck's reading is extremely important in that it calls attention to the crucial distinction between sovereignty and its administration. In general, though, it significantly obscures the fact that, despite the necessity of the sovereign delegation of administrative tasks to subsidiary bodies, democracy for Hobbes still requires a level of popular activity on the part of its citizens, as well as an absolute control over these administrative bodies, that modern representative democracies (which Tuck sees Hobbes as the first systematic theorist of)[41] simply do not allow for. Consideration of what Hobbes has to say about the limits of democratic administration reveals that modern democracies are incapable of being subsumed under Hobbes's category. It is perhaps relevant to begin by observing that Hobbes is explicit that the political relation he articulates between a sovereign people and its administrative apparatus within the democratic regime is not one that manifests within the social-historical context of his time. As he laments at the beginning of *De Cive*, "How many men have been killed by the erroneous doctrine that sovereign Kings are not masters but ministers of the multitude?"[42] Obviously the very existence of a unified people is no evidence of that people's possession of sovereignty, for every commonwealth is defined in terms of such a unification of the multitude. Although he would move away from the formulation in *Leviathan*, Hobbes perhaps does not help matters when he writes that the affirmation of the unity and singularity of the people should lead us to recognize that the people of necessity rules in all forms of city: "In every commonwealth the *People* Reigns; for even in *Monarchies* the *People* exercises power; for the *people* wills through the will of *one man*. But the citizens, i.e., the subjects, are a *multitude*. In a *Democracy* and in an *Aristocracy* the citizens are a *Multitude*, but the *council* is the *people*; in a *Monarchy* the subjects are the *multitude*, and (paradoxically) the *King* is the *people*."[43]

The more significant error that people tend to make according to Hobbes, however, is the presumption that it is natural to take the vote of the majority to stand in for the consensus of all. This presumption leads individuals to the conclusion that the sum of the wills of the majority of citizens may overwhelm the singular will of the sovereign person in nondemocratic contexts, thereby rendering a multitude superior to the city, allowing the supreme authority to be revoked after it is conveyed. The very procedural rule, though, is for Hobbes a conventional one that derives its being only through that process of institution which brings the civil person into existence:

> For most people believe that whether subjects are summoned by the authority of the commonwealth or gathered seditiously, the consent of all resides in the consent of the majority. This is in fact false; for it is not a natural rule that the consent

of the majority should be taken for the consent of all, nor is it true of seditious gatherings. Rather the rule has its origin in civil institution, and is only true when the *man* or *council* which has sovereign power, summons the citizens and in view of their large numbers decides that selected men should receive authority to speak on behalf of those who select them, and that a majority of speakers on the proposals he puts forward for discussion is to stand for all of them.[44]

The upshot of all this, of the fact that the majority does not naturally stand in for all and that it is inconceivable for there to be achieved a universal consensus of each particular on any matter, is that subjects cannot despoil the one of the supreme authority. The mere existence of a congress of the people, even a congress that is empowered to deliberate and resolve, is not an indication of a sovereign permission. One must scrutinize, rather, the particular circumstances of the association in order to determine if it meets the criteria of democratic right. We know that for Hobbes "government is a *capacity*, administration of government is an *act*."[45] We also know that because all forms of government have an equal power, a particular mode of a regime's conveniences or inconveniences cannot be grounded in consideration of the quality of power, but rather only in the administrative bodies and officers who act.[46] There is thus something essential to the administrative organization of particular regimes that must delimit the range and extent of political delegation in these particular regimes.

It is true that the indivisibility of sovereignty does not rule out the potential for the administration of public affairs to be carried out by subsidiary bodies with a wide variety of different forms. Hobbes thus writes in *The Elements of Law*: "But though the sovereignty be not mixed, but be always either simple democracy, or simple aristocracy, or pure monarchy; nevertheless in the administration thereof, all those sorts of government may have place subordinate. For suppose the sovereign power be democracy, as it was sometimes in Rome, yet at the same time they may have a council aristocratical, such as was the senate; and at the same time they may have a subordinate monarch, such as was their dictator, who had for a time the exercise of the whole sovereignty, and such as are all generals in war."[47] Despite the particular function of such latter offices, supreme sovereign authority always remains in that body that possesses the right to delegate administrative permissions, such ministers and magistrates being necessarily subordinate to this authority regardless of the particular gravity of their charge. For example, "As if a man should think, because the great council of Venice did nothing ordinarily but choose magistrates, ministers of state, captains, and governors of towns, ambassadors, counsellors, and the like; that therefore their part of the sovereignty is only choosing of magistrates; and that the making of war, and peace, and laws, were not theirs, but the part of such councillors as they appointed thereto; whereas it is the part of these to do it but subordinately, the supreme authority thereof being, in the great council that choose them."[48] Implicit in Hobbes's example here is the affirmation of the fundamental and necessary characteristic of democratic sovereignty, the perpetuation of an institutional space that is able to mediate generalized participation in public affairs, and which maintains an absolute power over its magistrates, however the range of such participation is demarcated via the delegation of administrative responsibilities. In the words of Luc Foisneau, "it is an etymological truism" that that there is no democracy without a demos that exists through its self-activity in a constituted assembly.[49] As Hobbes puts it in *De Cive*, Tuck's primary source, democracy is the regime "in which *of course* everyone manages public business."[50]

This democratic prerequisite is highlighted in all of Hobbes's discussions of the distinctions between government and administration. Elsewhere in *The Elements of Law*, for example, Hobbes notes that after the originary democratic institution, a sovereign form is not established unless the power of the people is dissolved by the decree of the latter to transfer sovereignty to a new organ, a transfer assented to via a plurality of votes.[51] If the sovereignty of the people is maintained, the body that is created, an apparent king for example, is just a minister, as in the case of the Roman dictator: "For it is to be understood, when a man receiveth any thing from the authority of the people, he receiveth not from the people his subjects, but from the people his sovereign. And farther, though in the election of a king for his life, the people grant him the exercise of their sovereignty for that time; yet if they see cause, they may recall the same before the time."[52] The people may also elect a limited sovereign executor on the basis of a conditional principle, "As for example: for so long as he shall observe such and such laws, as they then prescribe them."[53] In both of these instances, the people must declare its intent to retain sovereignty by maintaining its right to periodically assemble at determinate times and places. Hobbes thus writes,

"If in electing him, they reserved to themselves a right of assembling, and appointed certain times and places to that purpose, then are they sovereign still, and may call their conditional king to account, at their pleasure, and deprive him of his government, if they judge he deserve it, either by breach of the condition set him, or otherwise."[54] In short, the concretely specified active participation of the people remains a condition of democratic rule, and includes an absolute right of recall of all administrative officials.

De Cive provides similar analyses. Consider again the case of the creation of a monarchy via a popular transfer of authority. Hobbes cautions us that in such instances we must be careful to interrogate the quality of such creation through consideration of the limiting conditions placed on the so-called monarch, distinct governmental forms being differentiated from one another by the nature of this limitation or nonlimitation. Specifically, "*M*onarchs who exercise sovereign power only for a time are not actually monarchs buts *ministers* of the commonwealth."[55] If the people create a temporary "monarch" while reserving for itself the right to meet at certain appointed times, the people retain supreme command, the monarch being their chief administrator: "If after the election of a *time-limited Monarch*, the *people* has departed from the council with the understanding that it would hold meetings at fixed times and places while the term set for the Monarch is still running, (as *Dictators* were appointed among the Romans), such a one is not to be regarded as a *Monarch* but as the first minister of the *people*."[56] To the degree that this designated individual remains a mere officer of the civil person who maintains supreme authority in the city, the latter may deprive the former of their office at any time and for any reason. This right remains for Hobbes a clear and necessary consequence of the absolute nature of political command: "The reason is that it is unthinkable that a man or assembly which has direct and immediate power of action should hold power in such a way that it cannot actually give any commands; for power is simply the right to give commands whenever it is possible by nature."[57] If, however, the people create the monarch without providing occasion for itself to assemble independently of the will of this monarch, then the latter becomes absolute and a monarch in the true sense of the term, while the sovereign people is dissolved.

Hobbes is explicit that the perpetuation of the integrity of the sovereign office is a requirement for the maintenance of absolute sovereign power. For Hobbes democracy is no less an absolute form of regime than any other.⁵⁸ The hatred of the language of absolutism that manifests among certain individuals prevents them from grasping that a democratic assembly is just as absolute an authority as an aristocratic assembly or monarch. Hence Hobbes provides as an example here individuals who, to avoid absolutism, go about constructing a city in which citizens convene in order to deliberate on legal articles, determine punishments for violation of laws created, appoint ministers to assume necessary offices, and yet maintain authority to redistribute magistrates as they would like. As Hobbes asks, "Who does not see that in a commonwealth so organized, the group which gave these instructions had *absolute power?*"⁵⁹ One of the main causes of the dissolution of the democratic state, as it is of all commonwealths, is the failure to affirm its absolute character. In *Leviathan* Hobbes refers to the loss of democratic potential in Rome as an example of such a movement, sovereignty being forfeited precisely where the people were alienated from their sense of the ultimate authority of popular institutions in relation to nonsovereign offices: "For whereas the stile of the antient Roman Common-wealth, was, *The Senate, and People of Rome*; neither Senate, nor People pretended the whole Power; which first caused the seditions, of *Caius Gracchus, Lucius Saturninus*, and others; and afterwards the warres between the Senate and the People, under *Marius* and *Sylla*; and again under *Pompey* and *Caesar*, to the Extinction of the Democraty, and the setting up of Monarchy."⁶⁰

In the final instance, as long as the people in a democratic regime "remains in being, or holds meetings from time to time on set days at set places, its *power* will be continuous."⁶¹ The lack of popular ownership of this right in the political societies of Hobbes's time demonstrates clearly that the people do not hold sovereign power. Hobbes's schema similarly does not allow us to interpret modern representative governments as democratic governments in his sense, given that the latter require (1) a *concrete* and *universally accessible* assembly, that (2) meets at *determinate* times and places, and which (3) possesses an *absolute* right of political recall of subordinate magistrates. Even if Hobbes contends that the self-activity of a democratic people cannot attend to all civic concerns, they being unable to deliberate on all necessary matters, he is more than clear that they must be active with respect to some necessary matters at settled times and places, this action being carried out within an institutionalized assembly space whose contours are fixed and recognized. That no identifiable assembly fora—however they might be uniquely specified in light of social-historical facts structuring their potential—exist in order to facilitate the expression of the authority of the people in extant commonwealths would seem to clearly suggest that the people in these societies lack the institutional prerequisites for the possession of sovereign power. Established modes of political engagement in modern liberal societies do not meet Hobbes's criteria for democratic participation. As Leon Craig has suggested, Hobbes would classify these societies not as democracies, but as elective aristocracies.[62] Indeed, Hobbes recognizes, like Aristotle before him, that the generalization of election as the primary expression of this engagement is an indicator of aristocratic political organization.[63] Hence in *De Cive*, after noting the emergence of aristocracy from the democratic form via the people's conveyance of authority to a minor council, Hobbes specifies election as a fundamental characteristic of an aristocracy. Here "certain men who are distinguishable from the rest by name or family or some other mark are put before the *people* and elected by a majority vote, and the total right of the whole *people*, or of the commonwealth, is transferred to those who have been elected, with the effect that the *council* of elected *optimates* may now rightly do what the *people* could rightly do before."[64] In any case, it is only once we comprehend that Hobbes sees generalized popular political participation as the condition of democratic sovereignty that we can fully grasp the essence of his critique of democracy as a sovereign form.

Democracy and the Hubris of the Many

Although all commonwealths are bound to be home to various inconveniences, as we have already noted, Hobbes formally maintains that the range of variance with respect to the quantity and intensity of these inconveniences are not to be found in any differences in the structure of power, which is deployed in the same manner in each. These inconveniences, furthermore, are in any case negligible in relation to the inconveniences that would result in the absence of a commonwealth: "The estate of Man can never be without some incommodity or other; and that the greatest, that in any forme of Government can possibly happen to the people in generall, is scarce sensible, in respect of the miseries, and horrible calamities, that accompany Civil Warre."[65] Nevertheless, if there are no differences in the structure of power instituted in unique governmental forms, there are differences with respect to the "Convenience, or Aptitude to produce the Peace, and Security of the people."⁶⁶ It is on the basis of the perceived variation in the constitution of forms of sovereign office that Hobbes produces his critique of the internal mechanics of democracy, labeling it the most undesirable expression of political authority. The main contours of Hobbes's critique of democracy are well known.⁶⁷ Certain commentators have even gone so far as to assert that not only does Hobbes prefer nondemocratic commonwealths—monarchy in particular—but that his political philosophy, despite the formal identification of the legal equivalence of regimes, does not logically and/or practically permit of the institution of democratic sovereignty.⁶⁸ Before examining the centrality of the critique of democracy to his entire civil science, through tracing the extent to which alteration in various of his theoretical formulations must be read as responses to certain facts implying democratic normativity, in what remains of this chapter I will briefly outline what Hobbes sees as the central problem of major assembly political organization.

That the main outlines of Hobbes's critique of democracy remained consistent throughout his life was confirmed in both Hobbes's prose and verse biographies. In both "The Prose Life" and "The Verse Life" he reaffirms his early judgment on Thucydides's critique of democratic life. He writes in "The Prose Life" that "of all the Greek historians, Thucydides was his source of particular delight . . . In [his history] the weaknesses and eventual failures of the Athenian democrats, together with those of their city state, were made clear."⁶⁹ While in "The Verse Life" he reflects that "there's none that pleas'd me like *Thucydides*. / He says Democracy's a Foolish Thing, / Than a Republick Wiser in one King."⁷⁰ We should thus begin by briefly examining Hobbes's introduction to his translation of Thucydides, paying particular attention to what he sees as fundamentally defining the latter's characterization of the Athenian people, before then locating the source of this mode of popular being in the unique features of assembly organization.⁷¹ Summarizing Thucydides's apparent hostility to democracy, Hobbes writes:

> For his opinion touching the government of the state, it is manifest that he least of all liked the democracy. And upon divers occasions he noteth the emulation and contention of the demagogues for reputation and glory of wit; with their crossing of each other's counsels, to the damage of the public; the inconsistency of resolutions, caused by the diversity of ends and power of rhetoric in the orators; and the desperate actions undertaken upon the flattering advice of such as desired to

attain, or to hold what they had attained, of authority and sway amongst the common people.[72]

Here we find the main elements of Hobbes's critique of democracy. The question of demagoguery will be discussed in the following chapter, in relation to Hobbes's sporadic characterization of democracy as a *de facto* aristocracy of orators, while here we emphasize the significance of the nature of the discursive "diversity of ends," and its contribution to the production of a perpetual "inconsistency of resolutions" that tends to affirm "desperate actions."

What Hobbes thinks essentially defines the democratic person is its hubristic nature. The Athenian people are characterized in terms of their perception of their own power and ability, they opining that they possessed "the facility of achieving whatsoever action they undertook."[73] It was this opinion of their own capacity that generated within them a will to constantly affirm risk, as they lent their support to "the most dangerous and desperate enterprises."[74] Those Athenians who were cautious and prudent in their reasonings were incapable of gaining support within this environment, political life being monopolized by actors who were capable of manipulating and playing on the hubris of the people. In the end "it came to pass amongst the Athenians, who thought they were able to do anything, that wicked men and flatterers drove them headlong into those actions that were to ruin them; and the good men either durst not oppose, or if they did, undid themselves."[75] What the Athenian people lacked was that which Hobbes always considered essential to the art of governing: a capacity for self-limitation, an ability to temper, moderate, or sublimate one's desire.[76] With respect to Agrippa, for example, he thus writes in his discourse on Tacitus that "the Art that he is principally taxed to want, seems to have been the Art of conforming to times, and places, and persons, and consists much in a temperate conversation, and ability upon just cause, to contain and dissemble his passions, and purposes; and this was then thought the chief Art of government."[77] Although in his later work Hobbes would go on to reject the very idea that under certain conditions a sovereign monarch might act so as to violate or despoil their subjects, here Hobbes nonetheless notes that "it is a great misfortune to a people, to come under the government of such a one, as knows not how to govern himself."[78]

In any case, Hobbes always thought it true that it was much easier for a monarch to practice this self-limitation than an assembly, contra those critics of monarchy who would maintain that this form of rule always contains the acute threat of the occupier of sovereign office eschewing their responsibility in order to oppress their subjects. Indeed, Hobbes is consistently concerned with demonstrating that many of what are taken to be the specific inconveniences of monarchical government are not only not unique to monarchy, but in fact more pronounced and threatening in a democracy. With respect to this question of the oppression of subjects, while acknowledging that it is a possibility for a monarch to violate and transgress the laws of nature through attacking and killing their citizens, such a possibility is common to all political forms. In Hobbes's account, such "fault is the Ruler's, not the Régime's. Not all the deeds of *Nero* are of the essence of *Monarchy*."[79] As one would expect, Hobbes ultimately claims that this common potential for oppression is exacerbated in a democracy, and this because "where there is *popular control*, there may be as many *Neros* as there are *Orators* who fawn on the *people*. For every Orator wields as much power as the *people* itself, and they have a kind of tacit agreement to turn a blind eye to each other's greed (*my turn today, yours tomorrow*), and to cover up for any of them who put innocent fellow citizens to death arbitrarily or because of private feuds."[80]

Similarly, individuals often complain that a sovereign monarch may tend to bestow special privileges on familiars and flatterers, arbitrarily enriching some subjects at the expense of others. While Hobbes concedes such a possibility, he maintains that this risk is greater in major assembly contexts, for "in a *Democracy* the large number of *Demagogues*, i.e., the orators who have influence with the people (and there are a lot of them and new ones come along every day), are so many men who have *children, relatives, friends* and *flatterers* to be enriched."[81] Unlike in a monarchy, this abundance of flatterers is incapable of being satisfied, Hobbes thinks, without the oppression of certain citizens. Not only then is the potential for determinations to be influenced by flattery greater in an assembly, but also, contrary to in a monarchy, a flatterer's interventions may only harm and never help others: "Whereas the Favorites of Monarchs, are few, and they have none els to advance but their owne Kindred; the Favorites of an Assembly, are many; and the Kindred much more numerous, than of any Monarch, which cannot as well succour his friends, as hurt his enemies: but Orators, that is to say, Favourites of Soveraigne Assemblies, though they have great power to hurt, have little to save."[82]

Daniel Kapust has recently identified Hobbes's account of flattery as principal to his preference for monarchy.[83] Hobbes's distaste for assembly rule, in both its aristocratic and democratic variants, is seen as rooted in its deployment of rhetoric for the sake of flattery, this mode of expression rendering impossible the proper ratiocination upon which Hobbes's civil science depends. For Kapust, "Hobbes's analysis and defense of monarchy in light of flattery has a distinctive institutional and psychological quality: Hobbes reduces political deliberation to the reason of one individual, taking counsel in isolation. Hobbes's monarch resists flattery most effectively because he reasons alone."[84] Kapust here calls attention to the primary issue at stake in Hobbes's differentiation between sovereign configurations: that of the singularity or plurality of the composition of the legislative body. Recall that every commonwealth, regardless of the form of sovereign office, is defined in terms of the unification of the social field through the reduction of a multiplicity of distinct wills to a singular will attributable to a self-identical person. The particular modes through which this process of unification is achieved and self-identity realized, however, vary significantly, a monarch already possessing a unitary form in their natural body. More specifically, unlike in assemblies the sovereign in a monarchy has two bodies, bearing both the person of the people as well as their own natural person. There is thus the closest possible coalescence between private and public interest in a monarchy, the latter being advanced most adequately here: "Where the publique and private interest are most closely united, there is the publique most advanced. Now in Monarchy, the private interest is the same with the publique. The riches, power, and honour of a Monarch arise onely from the riches, strength and reputation of his Subjects."[85]

When the determination of the collective will emanates from an assembly, even if union and thereby unanimity is ultimately produced, the literal agreement of individual wills is never realized. Hobbes hence writes that "the *will of an Assembly* is understood as the *will of the greater part* of the men who make up the assembly."[86] Political determination here, in other words, is characterized by the active mediation of different particular wills.[87] Indeed, the participatory quality of assembly rule, which I have already emphasized, is affirmed through Hobbes's very definition of an assembly as a necessarily deliberative body. The problem of assemblies is that their unity needs to be achieved, a goal that is not required with respect to the unity of natural persons. To this extent, a monarch acts with much greater ease, a political determination in a monarchy not needing to be preceded by a "lengthy and potentially divisive process of deliberation."[88] To the extent that a sovereign is supposed to represent unity as opposed to diversity, a people as opposed to the distinct individual persons constituting a multitude, a monarch functions intrinsically more efficiently than an assembly, its natural person being already so unified.[89]

Eloquence and the Democratic Inflammation of the Passions

The lack of a natural unity among the constituent elements of the democratic person thus means that unity must be artificially created, the sovereign will being generated through a concrete process by which the individual wills of the assembly members are negotiated for the sake of the eventual production of a singular determination. Hobbes's main problem with democratic deliberation lay in his perception of the nature of the specific mechanics of this negotiation, specifically, its reliance on techniques of eloquence that aim at persuasion and its tendency to enflame passion through the commingling of distinct subjectivities.[90] The hubristic nature of a democratic people, as noted in the previous section, is partially facilitated by its correct perception of a specifically human capacity, the ability to legislate absolutely in a world lacking transcendent limits on action.[91] Hubris, however, can be neutralized through a willingness to place limits on one's actions, to autonomously regulate behavior in light of rational consideration of social and political conditions. The potential for such rational consideration, though, is closed off in major assemblies as a result of the deployment of rhetorical modes as techniques for attracting adherents to one's particular position, which one ultimately hopes will, through democratic mediation, come to stand in for the will of the collective entity.

For Hobbes the place of a particular type of rhetorical expression in democratic decision-making renders it inherently impulsive and unstable.[92] As he writes in *Behemoth*, "Impudence in Democraticall assemblies . . . does almost all that's done, 'tis the Goddesse of Rhetorick, and carries proofe with it."[93] In *De Cive* Hobbes distinguishes between two distinct practices of eloquence.[94] The first "is a lucid and elegant exponent of thought and conceptions, which arises partly from observation of things and partly from an understanding of words taken in their proper meanings as defined."⁹⁵ The second, however, far from being deployed in the service of reason, is considered as "an agitator of the passions," where metaphorical speech is deployed to influence the immediate desires of the listener such that the opinions propagated be affirmed independently of reasoned consideration.⁹⁶ Whereas the first mode is an art of logic, the second is of one of rhetoric, the latter being utilized to irrationally stir up the passions of the people. Needless to say, Hobbes considers democratic deliberation to be marked by the second mode, democracy tending to the production of long and excessive speeches for expressing opinion, participants deploying the latter eloquence in the effort to persuade listeners.⁹⁷ Such rhetorical techniques elide the production of genuine knowledge via proper ratiocination: "However much reasoning they put into it, they do not begin from true principles but from ἐνδόξοις, i.e., from commonly accepted opinions, which are for the most part usually false, and they do not try to make their discourse correspond to the nature of things but to the passions of men's hearts. The result is that votes are cast not on the basis of correct reasoning but on emotional impulse."⁹⁸

Hobbes seems to suggest that the mode of expression characteristic of communication within large bodies of people is inevitable given the plurality characterizing the latter. Hence, for example, in his discussion in *Leviathan* of the distinction between command and counsel, he notes that a particular form of the latter—exhortation or dehortation—is appropriate only in these contexts given the dynamics internal to them. These two terms, *exhortation* and *dehortation*, are defined as "Counsell, accompanied with signes in him that giveth it, of vehement desire to have it followed; or to say more briefly, *Counsell* vehemently pressed."⁹⁹ Hobbes suggests that the vehemence of urging that characterizes these modes should be taken as evidence that the counsel is in the interest of the counselor, which thus violates the principle of counsel, which should tend to the realization of "the good of him, to whom [the counselor] giveth [the counsel]."¹⁰⁰ Those who exhort or dehort are thus corrupt counselors. That being said, Hobbes qualifies his account by maintaining that there is one legitimate use of these modes: they are appropriate in speaking with a multitude, which, as a multiplicity of singular individuals bearing a diversity of desires and opinions, is incapable of functioning as a rational interlocuter: "The use of Exhortation and Dehortation lyeth onely, where a man is to speak to a Multitude; because when the Speech is addressed to one, he may interrupt him, and examine his reasons more rigorously, than can be done in a Multitude; which are too many to enter into Dispute, and Dialogue with him that speaketh indifferently to them all at once."[101] Hence even if this type of counsel is legitimate in engaging a multitude, in the final instance it should not even be identified as counsel at all strictly speaking, for counsel must take the form of rational speech. This is because the primary job of the counselor is the revelation of the consequences of action, proper ratiocination being demanded whenever we deal in the realm of cause and effect.[102] It is thus no surprise that Hobbes explicitly notes that counsel is much better received by individuals than by assemblies. In an assembly, and most especially in a democratic assembly, the tendency is for a speaker to attempt to persuade their audience as opposed to educate it, which they attempt to do through the stimulation of their passions, utilizing rhetorical trickery to render more visible their own opinion in relation to their competitors. Hence speakers are inclined "to give their advice in long discourses, which may, and do commonly excite men to action, but not to governe them in it."[103] Consistent with the critique of democratic deliberation found in *De Cive*, Hobbes again blames eloquence for manipulating any advice given to the assembly, this rhetorical tool when utilized by diverse speakers arousing many via the generation of a surplus of passion: "For the Passions of men, which asunder are moderate, as the heat of one brand; in Assembly are like many brands, that enflame one another, (especially when they blow one another with Orations) to the setting of the Common-wealth on fire, under pretence of Counselling it."[104] In short, whereas in taking advice alone one may discuss with and interrogate a counselor in a rational mode, such is difficult in an assembly, and to a greater degree the greater its size. Hence Hobbes's conclusion is that in the final instance "no great Popular Common-wealth was ever kept up; but either by a forraign Enemy that united them; or by the reputation of some one eminent Man amongst them; or by the secret Counsell of a few; or by the mutuall feare of equal factions; and not by the open Consultations of the Assembly."[105]

Madness and Multitude in the Democratic Assembly

It is the tendency of the deliberative relation—intensified in major relative to minor assemblies—to stimulate passion to excess so as to upset the equilibrium necessary for rational determination that leads Hobbes to conceptually associate democracy with madness. What characterizes madness, a "principal defect of the mind,"[106] is the unregulated flux of desires and images without direction or order of any kind. In *Leviathan* Hobbes calls it "to have stronger and more vehement Passions for any thing, than is ordinarily seen in others."[107] Madness, this "too much appearing Passion,"[108] produces within the subject of madness "strange and unusuall behaviour,"[109] the symptoms of which most closely resemble the effects that alcohol has on the body. The lowering of inhibitions allows the passions to externalize themselves independently of moderation: "For the variety of behaviour in men that have drunk too much, is the same with that of Mad-men: some of them Raging, others Loving, others Laughing, all extravagantly, but according to their severall domineering Passions: For the effect of the wind, does but remove Dissimulation; and take from them the sight of the Deformity of their Passions."[110] The surplus of passion that is madness thus takes a multiplicity of forms depending on the particular passion that is expelled, this surplus itself being determined by a variety of sources: "Sometimes the extraordinary and extravagant Passion, proceedeth from the evil constitution of the organs of the Body, or harme done them; and sometimes the hurt, and indisposition of the Organs, is caused by the vehemence, or long continuance of the Passion. But in both causes the Madnesse is of one and the same nature."[111] In detailing madness as an incapacity to moderate or place limits on passion, Hobbes explicitly associates it with democratic politics. The excesses of democracy are conceptually related to the excesses of passion characteristic of madness, Hobbes suggesting that democracy is in fact the mad regime. He writes of the behavior of certain individuals within the democratic assembly in the following way: "When many of them conspire together, the Rage of the whole multitude is visible enough. For what argument of Madnesse can there be greater than to clamour, strike, and throw stones at our best friends? Yet this is somewhat lesse than such a multitude will do. For they will clamour, fight against, and destroy those, by whom all their life-time before, they have been protected, and secured from injury. And if this be Madnesse in the multitude, it is the same in every particular man."[112]

Madness is thus an interruption of reason, the actualization of the latter being blocked as a result of the expulsion of a surplus of passion. This surplus does not, however, have a biological root, the organization of passion, as we will see in chapter 3, having its foundation in various contingent social facts, such as differing modes of education and life trajectories. Madness and rationality are intrinsic potentialities that the individual bears within themself simultaneously. Hence Hobbes characterizes emotions in *De Homine* as "*perturbations* of the mind" that interfere with the exercise of rational faculties, as opposed to operate without impediment as a result of the lack of the latter.[113] Mónica Brito Vieira is thus correct to point out the extent to which madmen, unlike natural fools, do not lack a capacity for reasoning, but are rather those who are overwhelmed by their passions so as to distort the material of ratiocination: "Madmen appear in Hobbes's texts, not as men deprived of intellectual faculties, but rather as those who, by the violence of their passions, or any other such disturbance, take their fancies for truth, and make what are often the right inferences from distorted first premises."[114] Democratic modes of political self-organization are presented by Hobbes as precisely one of those sources that tend to reconfigure the relationship between passion and reason, the amplification of the former that results from the structure of deliberation militating against the consistent and stable exercise of the latter. If it is true that all individuals are subject to the vicissitudes of their affects and passions, it is nevertheless the case that the inconveniences that arise from this fact are multiplied in an assembly. Hobbes hence writes in *The Elements of Law*, "And because an aristocracy consisteth in of men, if the passions of many men be more violent when they are assembled together, than the passions of one man alone, it will follow, that the inconvenience arising from passion will be greater in an aristocracy, than a monarchy."[115] These inconveniences are only further exacerbated in a specifically democratic assembly, given the increase in the number of inherently passionate individuals occupying sovereign office and the generalization of eloquence as a rhetorical mode of expressing opinion.

What becomes apparent in emphasizing these elements of Hobbes's critique of democracy is that its mechanics, its deployment of its specific institutional and organizational form, are in tension with its end, the generation of a unified and singular collective will. The latter is produced only through a conflictual process by which a multiplicity of particular natural persons, with their own unique interests, opinions, and appetites, confront one another in an attempt to negotiate this diversity.[116] The democratic assembly, in other words, seems to be governed by the very logic of multitude that it is designed to overcome. Hobbes's dislike for democracy is grounded in the extent to which its internal dynamics represent a reemergence within the commonwealth of the logic of multitude, democratic deliberation prior to the formation of sovereign will reproducing the chaotic nonstructure of human relations that adheres between a mere agglomeration of individuals.[117] As Mikko Jakonen reminds us more generally, the multitude as a human reality does not disappear after the institution of the state, to the degree that it "is the key term that defines the ongoing confusion and tumult in human community."[118] Its disruptive potentiality emerges from the fact that individuals, even when subjects or citizens, remain still natural persons, subject to their internal endeavor and the flux of their own desire. The multitude is thus a perpetual political problem that always threatens the stability of the instituted order, this threat taking on a concrete form of existence in the institution of a democratic assembly, which rather than containing and quieting the minds of its members, stimulates and enflames them.[119]

Given the association of the democratic assembly with multitude, it is thus no surprise that Hobbes identifies the trajectory of the former with that of the latter, highlighting the predisposition of democracy to encourage the formation of faction, that which increases the risk of civil war. In *Leviathan* he identifies the multiplication of psychic inconstancy that results from the confrontation of a multiplicity of individual minds with the emergence of civic strife. He writes that "the Resolutions of a Monarch, are subject to no other Inconstancy, than that of Human Nature; but in Assemblies, besides that of Nature, there ariseth an Inconstancy from the Number. For the absence of a few, that would have the Resolution once taken, continues firme (which may happen by security, negligence, or private impediments,) or the diligent appearance of a few of the contrary opinion, undoes to day, all that was concluded yesterday."[120] As I have emphasized, despite the singularity of the people as civil person, the process by which the will of the people is formed in a democracy is inherently conflictual, it involving deliberation and negotiation between necessarily distinct natural persons with unique goods, desires, and wills. The result of such processes is social instability, as the flux of passion constantly stimulates efforts to reorganize the legal order of the polity independent of rational consideration of necessity. Law is always precarious, this precarity originating in the fact that law derives its force and legitimacy from the existing sovereign, having no inherently customary foundation in past history or tradition.[121] Although the sovereign is free to make and unmake law as it sees fit, such a capacity certainly does not suggest that a sovereign thereby ought to. It is necessary for any polity to possess institutional mechanisms for changing law when objective circumstances require; however law should not be altered due to subjective variation in the passions of the mind: "It is necessary that such a power be, that the laws may be altered, according as men's manners change, or as the conjuncture of all circumstances within and without the commonwealth shall require; the change of law being then inconvenient, when it proceedeth from the change not of the occasion, but of the minds of him or them, by whose authority the laws are made. Now it is manifest enough of itself, that the mind of one man is not so variable in that point, as are the decrees of an assembly."[122]

Ultimately these conditions render the democratic regime more susceptible to the development of faction and, ultimately, civil war. Hobbes articulates the relation between legal inconstancy and faction in democracies in *De Cive*, writing that: "It follows from this that where the supreme power to make laws is lodged in such assemblies, the laws are unstable, and are not changed to follow an alteration in the state of affairs or a change of sentiment, but according to whether a larger number of men from one *faction* or the other has found its way into the council."[123] Faction is a potential by-product of the ontological condition of human difference. It is a reflection of the nonidentity of the individuals that collectively constitute the sovereign representative and emerges as a result of the tendency of these individuals to politically self-organize themselves on the basis of their particular shared normative conceptions, which will always be varied given the radical diversity characteristic of human existence. The risk of civil war is intensified in a democratic regime to the extent that it facilitates the public expression of the divergent multiplicity of opinion emanating from distinct clusters of citizens. As Hobbes writes in *The Elements of Law*, "For where the union, or band of a commonwealth is one man, there is no distraction; whereas in assemblies, those that are of different opinions, and give different counsel, are apt to fall out amongst themselves, and to cross the designs of commonwealth for one another's sake."[124] Like Machiavelli before him, Hobbes grasps the inherent connection between tumult and democracy, the latter taking a necessarily conflictual form given that it is characterized by the confrontation between individuals and groups with always distinct desires, interests, understandings, and so on.[125] Hence, for example, in his critique of what he takes to be Aristotle's and other's false identification of liberty and democracy, Hobbes writes: "And by reading of these Greek, and Latine Authors, men from their childhood have gotten a habit (under a false shew of Liberty,) of favouring tumults, and of licentious controlling of the action of their Soveraigns; and again of controlling these controllers, with the effusion of so much blood; as I think I may truly say, there was never any thing so deerly bought, as these Western parts have bought the learning of the Greek and Latine tongues."[126] What Hobbes understands is the intrinsically disputatious nature of democracy, and hence his characterization of the teaching of his own civil science in terms of the neutralization of the multiplicity of opinion, the democratic contestation over meaning that assembly deliberation between particulars implies being the source of so much seditious activity.[127]

Chapter 2

Civil Science against Democratic Normativity

Contrary to those readers who suggest that the Hobbesian concept of democracy prefigures modern representative political forms, I suggested in the previous chapter that Hobbes's critique of democracy is only comprehensible to the degree that we recognize its radical and direct form: major assembly organization is disparaged to the extent that it, through providing a space for the confrontation of a plurality of distinct wills expressing a plurality of distinct normative conceptions, intensifies a form of antagonism which has the potential to destabilize the political regime. In this chapter I highlight how seriously Hobbes takes this democratic threat to be, through demonstrating the centrality of the critique of democracy to the overall articulation of Hobbes's political philosophy. In particular, I attempt to show how certain key changes in the structure of this political philosophy are stimulated by the imperatives of the democratic critique. The most well-known such change is Hobbes's new account of the mechanics of sovereign institution that is developed in *Leviathan*.[1] The earlier model, presented in both *The Elements of Law* and *De Cive*, considered the establishment of the commonwealth in terms of an alienation or relinquishment of right proceeding through two temporally distinct moments: an originary constitution of a democratic assembly that functions as an initial corporate body and this assembly's subsequent institution of a definitive sovereign form. In *Leviathan* this two-step process is replaced with a simplified one, in which each subject simultaneously authors a set of representative relations, creating through this process the artificial persons of the state and the sovereign representative that bears it. Whereas the earlier description thinks the creation of the commonwealth in terms of a seemingly passive alienation or relinquishment of right,[2] *Leviathan* establishes a more positive relationship between the subject and the sovereign, to the degree that the subject no longer merely renounces a private will but, via a correspondingly revised account of the dynamics of representation, expresses it through the authorship of the sovereign's actions.[3] As will be examined in more detail below, each subject conveys the use of right to the sovereign, who is no longer a merely natural person (or group of natural persons) retaining their own private right (or rights) of nature, but rather an artificial person representing both the subjects as individuals, who in this transfer have each authorized the representative relations, and the commonwealth as a collective body, the latter through this process assuming an identity as a fictional artificial person.[4]

In light of the so-called contextual turn in the study of the history of political thought, numerous Hobbes scholars have attempted to explain the adoption of the new terminology and framework of sovereign institution through situating it in relation to the historical accounts of political representation that were prominent immediately prior to and during the English Civil War.[5] Contrary to the claims of Hanna Pitkin and others, Quentin Skinner, the most influential such reader, notes that Hobbes was hardly the first English theorist of political representation.[6] Indeed, for Skinner, Hobbes in *Leviathan* is responding specifically to contemporary parliamentarian theorists of representation, attempting to develop a philosophy of the latter while denying the supposedly democratic conclusions of the former group.[7] Whereas prior to *Leviathan* Hobbes does not extensively engage with the English parliamentarian writers, whose works were mainly produced after or at the same time as *The Elements of Law* and *De Cive*, the third major political text is an entirely different matter: "By contrast, it would scarcely be an exaggeration to say that Hobbes's entire theory of representative government in *Leviathan* takes the form of a critical commentary on the parliamentarian arguments."[8] The innovation in conceptual language characteristic of this book is precisely the evidence of the extent of this engagement, Hobbes strategically deploying his opponents' terminology and certain of their premises in order to repudiate the conclusions that they draw. Most notably for Skinner, Hobbes adopts the parliamentarian discourse of representation and authorization in order to attempt to demonstrate how the parliamentarian writers are confused with respect to the political status of the people. The people are not an original sovereign subject that maintains a superior right against the artificial sovereign, thus legitimating the negotiation or resistance of the conditions of the latter's sovereignty, but in fact lacks any existence prior to its unification and representation in the commonwealth. Sovereignty cannot naturally lie in the body of the people, for the body of the people does not exist by nature: the people comes into being only with the creation of the state, which the sovereign represents and acts for. In the final instance Hobbes accepts "the basic structure of their theory without endorsing any of the radical implications they had drawn from it."[9]

In this chapter I attempt to supplement this contextual argument through revealing that the theoretical innovation that characterizes Hobbes's presentation of the mechanics of authorization and representation in Leviathan is merely one manifestation of a more general theoretical strategy that can be identified as the source of key mutations in the trajectory of his political thought, the latter being irreducible entirely to historical contextual circumstances.[10] Tracing out the logic of the development of Hobbesian political theory from The Elements of Law to Leviathan is a notoriously difficult task. Deborah Baumgold has highlighted this difficulty through her account of the problems that emerge as a result of Hobbes's process of serially composing works, specifically those of "an amorphous text; continuity and discontinuity among his political-theory texts; and the issue of consistency between and within works."[11] Hobbes's tendency to regularly add new material to existing discussions certainly introduces ambiguity and inconsistency into the work, but such inconsistency is not one that is incapable of being resolved by the commentator so long as the latter adheres to certain principles of textually plausible interpretation.[12] In attempting to explain a set of definite theoretical movements that we can observe in the development of Hobbes's civil science, I take as my starting point what I see to be a relatively uncontroversial historical fact: Hobbes's consistent hostility to democratic sovereignty relative to other sovereign forms. Despite the evident conceptual variation that I will note as occurring throughout his three major political works, the critique of democracy remains constant and formally identical within each one. I argue that the specific variations I discuss should be interpreted within the context of the philosophical critique of the logic of democracy and that this allows us to plausibly account for seeming inconsistencies both across and within particular works. Most simply, each conceptual alteration that I call attention to can be read as an effort to retroactively foreclose the possibility of the emergence of a substantive democratic normativity that the prior theoretical framework allows for or suggests. Hobbes's political philosophy wants to ward off any ethical preference for democracy as a sovereign form, and Hobbes in his subsequent modifications of his civil science after *The Elements of Law*, in both *De Cive* and *Leviathan*, addresses a content that can be seen to generate just such a preference.[13]

In each of the two modifications that I will examine, the issue of generalized political participation—which in the previous chapter I identified as the key characteristic defining the specificity of the democratic regime—is fundamental. In the first section of the chapter I examine Hobbes's early articulation in *The Elements of Law* of the specificity of the democratic regime in terms of the popular realization of liberty, citizens being free only in this type of city to the extent that it uniquely facilitates their participation in the formulation of law. I also detail Hobbes's account of how democracy devolves precisely when this facilitation is no longer feasible given the institutional failure to preserve popular spaces of participation. In the second section of the chapter I turn to *De Cive*, which attempts to address the possible democratic imperative that *The Elements of Law* implicitly affirms through its account of civic freedom. In this text the effort to delegitimize democracy takes the form of the disentanglement of the concept of liberty from active citizen participation in government, and the subsequent redefinition of liberty in terms of the absence of impediments. In the third section I examine *Leviathan*'s effort to address the leftover democratic problem of *De Cive*. This occurs through the denial of the logical and practical necessity of an originary democratic moment, and hence of a participatory endeavor that can be read as potentially natural. Finally, in the fourth section I note how, after the relinquishment of this originary moment from the process of sovereign institution, be it real or merely apparent, the language of democracy has been definitively purged from the account of political foundation. Overall, consideration of the textual elements that I highlight allows us to plausibly conclude that Hobbes's opposition to democracy motivates him to fundamentally reformulate key elements of his political philosophy. Contrary to the dominant historical contextualist interpretation of Hobbes, on my reading the alterations that Hobbes makes to his civil science are not only discrete reactions to existing political debates, but rather expressions of an autocritique that takes democratic normativity as its object.

Freedom and Democratic Participation in *The Elements of Law*

I suggested in the previous chapter that the main elements of Hobbes's critique of democratic political organization remained relatively consistent throughout his philosophical career, a fact noted by Hobbes himself in both his "Prose Life" and "Verse Life," via his reaffirmation of the legitimacy of what he perceives to be Thucydides's assessment of democratic decision-making in major assemblies. Within the early humanist context, the essential component of this critique—the association of popular desire with inconstancy—is articulated clearly in the "Discourse on the Beginning of Tacitus." Here the fickleness of the people in the ancient Roman case is revealed in the oscillation between political forms that occurred after the elimination of rule by kings, the people manifesting a perpetual dissatisfaction with newly instituted forms: "After the people had delivered themselves from the authority of Kings, and came themselves to undergo the cares of government, they grew perplexed at every inconvenience, and shifted from one form of government to another, and so to another, and then to the first again."[14] In this instance, however, Hobbes specifies that the character of the people's behavior takes the capricious mode that it does to the degree that they fear the privatization of power by some, who would deploy authority not to advance the popular interest, but rather their own. He thus writes how "they were jealous of their liberty, and knew not in whose hands to trust it, and were often at the point to lose it."[15] Hence, "after the Decemvirate they returned again to Consuls: they were not long content with them, but bestowed the same authority on Tribunes of the soldiers; and weary of these, they had recourse unto the Consulship."[16] For our purposes in this chapter, the essential thing to note in this early discussion is the place of the concept of liberty, the content of this concept being reaffirmed in Hobbes's first major effort to outline a systematic political philosophy in *The Elements of Law*. Specifically, in this discourse Hobbes's account of popular fickleness is grounded in that which he would go on to attempt to repudiate in *De Cive*, that is, a popular desire on the part of the people for liberty, liberty here, and again consistently with the *Elements*, being seen as actualizable only in a specific type of regime.[17]

The specificity of Hobbes's early definition of liberty in the *Elements of Law*, and its general place within the overall conceptual movement of the category throughout the development of the Hobbesian oeuvre, is well known.[18] Here Hobbes maintains that the democratic regime is a unique form of body politic, precisely to the extent that it is the only one capable of generalizing the realization of liberty. Within a civil society, only the sovereign can be said to have freedom, to the extent that it is the sovereign that monopolizes legislative authority. Democracy, meanwhile, is that commonwealth in which the concrete actualization of freedom via positive participation in government is extended such that all individual subjects have access to various modalities of such participation. Hobbes thus writes: "Now seeing freedom cannot stand together with subjection, liberty in a commonwealth is nothing but government and rule, which because it cannot be divided, men must expect in common; and that can be no where but in the popular state, or democracy. And Aristotle saith well (lib. 6, cap 2 of his *Politics*), *The ground or intention of a democracy, is liberty*; which he confirmeth in these words: *For men ordinarily say this: that no man can partake of liberty, but only in a popular commonwealth.*"[19] In thinking the realization of liberty in terms of collective self-government Hobbes again refers us to the crucial issue of political participation, in particular its essentiality as a constituent marker of democratic life. Such is clearly revealed in the *Elements* through Hobbes's account of the originary institution of the body politic in time.

Hobbes notes that of democracy, aristocracy, and monarchy, "The first in order of time of these three sorts is democracy, and it must be so of necessity, because an aristocracy and a monarchy, require nomination of persons agreed upon; which agreement in a great multitude of men must consist in the consent of the major part; and where the votes of the major part involve the votes of the rest, there is actually a democracy."[20] As we have already noted in a previous discussion, democracy is characterized primarily by the creation of a space of assembly which all citizens may enter in order to provide a vote regarding public matters, the outcome of this decision process being taken to represent the will of the people. Indeed, the people here, as opposed to the multitude of discrete individuals, emerges as a singular entity—and in this case a sovereign person—only through this activity of reduction. As Hobbes explicitly recognizes, the very etymology of the word *democracy* refers us to the Athenian invention and its definition in terms of popular political access and self-activity: "And this is that which giveth being to a democracy; wherein the sovereign assembly was called by the Greeks by the name of *Demus* (*id est*, the people), from whence cometh democracy. So that where, to the supreme and independent court, every man may come that will and give his vote, there the sovereign is called the people."²¹ Hobbes, though, is careful to clarify that in a democracy the right of sovereignty and its use are typically located in different places, the people as a whole formally possessing the right, but the use being deployed in practice only by some.²² It is this observation that grounds Hobbes's general strategy, within the *Elements*, to neutralize the potential for the development of a democratic normativity rooted in democracy's singular facilitation of popular participation.

Hobbes asserts that in general it is not possible for all subjects to actively participate in the deliberations characteristic of major assembly activity, hence the predisposition of the assembly to become dominated by particular speakers: "In a multitude of speakers therefore, where always either one is eminent alone, or a few being equal amongst themselves, are eminent above the rest, that one or few must of necessity sway the whole; inasmuch, that a democracy, in effect, is no more than an aristocracy of orators, interrupted sometimes with the temporary monarchy of one orator."²³ Several commentators pick up on Hobbes's characterization here of democracies as de facto aristocracies of orators: the very nature of deliberation in democratic assemblies is seen to promote a form of demagoguery in which the few are able to deploy their unique rhetorical skills in order to cultivate popular support for the sake of the advancement of their private benefit.²⁴ Such readings, however, in attributing to Hobbes a typology that posits a strict identity between the two regimes on the basis of the restriction of activity within the institutional space to a distinct minority, are not properly sensitive to Hobbes's recognition of the particular background conditions that mediate the establishment of such an identity. Consider Hobbes's language in the above quotation: it is not that a multitude of speakers necessarily comes to be dominated by a few, but that such remains a possibility under certain undefined circumstances. Democracy is not intrinsically an aristocracy, although independently of legal moderation, it seems to tend toward it. Although Hobbes himself does not speak on the matter, one might speculate on any number of particular organizational strategies that could function to militate against the concentration of assembly authority in the hands of a few, through limiting and restraining the influence of ambitious elites. Indeed, generally when Hobbes critically discusses this feature of democracy—its tendency to devolve into an aristocracy of orators—it is the latter group of elites that remains his primary object of reproach.

Such is revealed most clearly through his discussion of the so-called "democratical gentlemen" of *Behemoth*.[25]

One of the principal groups of antagonists in *Behemoth* are those apparently democratically oriented individuals schooled in the classical tradition, who harbored exclusive love for the ancient name of liberty (a name perhaps sharing much with Hobbes's definition of the concept in the *Elements*, which by the time of *Behemoth* was long since discarded, as will be noted in the following section). Hobbes writes that they "had been so educated, as that in their youth hauing read the bookes written by famous men of the ancient Græcian and Roman Commonwealths concerning their Policy and great actions, in which books the popular gouernment was extolled by the glorious name of Liberty, and Monarchy disgraced by the name of Tyranny, they became thereby in loue with their forms of gouernment."[26] In Hobbes's account these so-called "men of the better sort" formed a large part, and perhaps a majority, of the House of Commons and were able to exert a significant influence on the rest through their skilled use of eloquence, the significance of which to democratic persuasion we noted in the previous chapter.[27] Hobbes is careful to specify, though, in line with his contention that in practice so-called democracy is often merely an aristocracy of orators, that the democratical gentlemen who seduced and misled the people "by their Harangues in the Parliament, and by their discourses and communication with people in the Country," were not truly committed to the popular liberty they affirmed in speech, but desired to appropriate authority for themselves alone.[28] Esteeming their own intellectual ability above all others, the belief in their rational superiority was compounded by their education in the universities, thereby producing a perception of a special privilege to rule: "For 'tis a hard matter for men who do all thinke highly of their owne wits (when they haue also acquired the Learning of the Vniursity) to be perswaded that they want any ability requisite for the Gouernment of a Commonwealth; especially, hauing read the glorious Histories, and the Sententious Politicks of the ancient Popular gouernments of the Greeks and Romans; amongst whom Kings were hated and branded with the name of *Tyrants*, and *Popular gouernment* (though no Tyrant was euer so cruell as a Popular assembly) passed by the name of *Liberty*."[29]

Hobbes is explicit in maintaining that the greater part of parliamentary leaders, even well before the outbreak of war, had wished not for democracy but for aristocracy. They "desired the whole and absolute

Soueraignty, and to change the Monarchicall gouernment into an Oligarchie, that is to say, to make the Parliament consisting of a few Lords and about 400 Commoners absolute in the Soueraignty for the present, and shortly after to lay the House of Lords aside."[30] And indeed, after the execution of the king and the marginalization of the House of Lords, the commonwealth was transformed not into a democracy as it might first appear, but an oligarchy. Hobbes's characterizations here are particularly interesting, as throughout *Behemoth* he chooses to privilege the utilization of the language of oligarchy over that of aristocracy in describing the parliamentarian cause. Such would appear to be an element of a deliberate rhetorical strategy designed to produce particular emotional affects in his readers, an effort which is perhaps in tension with his otherwise persistent emphasis on the conceptual identity of the two designations.[31] This fact takes on a special importance in light of Quentin Skinner's observation that Hobbes's well-known deployment of rhetorical techniques in *Leviathan* for the sake of the strengthening of the persuasive character of the presentation—an effort rejected in his earlier works, which attempted to develop a purely demonstrative political science grounded in reasoning from fixed definitions—was specifically the result of witnessing the demagogues of the English Civil War's ability to persuade the people of absurd and irrational notions.[32] In any case, Hobbes would maintain as well that the Rump Parliament was "doubtlesse an Oligarchy," and this simply because not all had access to the sovereign assembly: "For the Supreame Authority must needs be in one man or in more. If in one, it is Monarchy, the Rump therefore was no Monarch. If the Authority were in more then one, it was in All, or in Fewer then All. When in All, it is Democracy, four euery man may enter into the Assembly, which makes the Soueraigne Court. Which they could not do here. It is therefore manifest that the Authority was in a Few, and consequently the State was an Oligarchy."[33] In declaring that they wanted to enact a free state, the Rump really meant that they wanted the people to be ruled by its members as opposed to by the king.[34]

With respect to our interrogation of the Hobbesian account of democracy, what is essential to *Behemoth* is Hobbes's argument that the experience of the civil war provides evidence of the irrationality that results from the intersection of individual minds, emerging via the dynamics that result from the combination of particular natural persons within deliberative assembly contexts. Unlike certain other revolutionary factions opposed to the project of the parliamentary oligarchs, the democratical gentlemen never instituted, nor had any desire to institute, a democracy in the proper Hobbesian sense. The problems of assembly nevertheless emerged in a minor form within the oligarchic parliamentary structures. Democracy is not identical with aristocracy, although it exponentially exacerbates aristocracy's problems as a result of its generalization of the quantity of persons who participate in assembly activities, and although democracy may be transmuted into aristocracy given the mechanics of deliberative decision-making, and in particular given the place of rhetoric in political persuasion.

At this point, then, we may return to *The Elements of Law* and note the manner in which Hobbes transitions from the discussion of democracy to that of aristocracy. Hobbes notes that the emergence of the latter from the former is stimulated by the decline in the desire for the very political participation on the part of the individual members of the people that they were seemingly not willing or able to actualize within the body politic as a result of its specific, although in no way necessary, organizational form, that is, the de facto aristocracy of orators. This suggests that even though in a democratic assembly the majority of citizens may not manifest an intensity of participation on par with the leading orators, they nevertheless must be seen as participators in some substantive sense, and that they indeed originally are so. For democracy to be preserved in time they must remain, that is, invested in active political participation. Aristocracy is instituted precisely once subjects become no longer devoted to democratic rule: "When the particular members of the commonwealth growing weary of attendance at public courts, as dwelling far off, or being attentive to their private businesses, and withal displeased with the government of the people, assemble themselves to make aristocracy."[35] It is this diagnosis of the nature of political desire that Hobbes will refine in *De Cive*, its reformulation, along with the more well-known reformulation of the concept of liberty, constituting the main elements of the anti-democratic innovation within this work.

The Disarticulation of Freedom and Participation in *De Cive*

The at least originary popular desire for political participation and the actualization of liberty via a mode of social institutionalization that is capable of facilitating said participation constitute the potential ground of democratic normativity that *De Cive* must overcome. Hobbes undertakes a multipronged strategy on this front: liberty and participation are first of all disentangled through the redefinition of liberty in terms of the absence of impediments, while any ethical basis for participation grounded in a consideration of human desire is rejected through the perception of a lack of participatory interest among the commonality of citizens. No longer is it the case that the desire for political participation among the plurality of subjects is one that is lost—for example, through the constitutional failure to construct and maintain deliberative spaces that are able to ensure the perpetual integration of common citizens in legislative modes, while warding off capture by elites who are able to deploy disproportionate resources in order to monopolize authority—but rather it is one that never existed in the first place.

On his eventual rejection of the *Elements'* claim that liberty is the ground of democracy, David Gauthier does not exaggerate in noting that "Hobbes rarely shows such a marked change of opinion in his political writings."[36] As scholars have observed, Hobbes's later concepts of liberty were formulated specifically in order to close the possibility of the language of freedom being utilized in order to legitimate a positive ethical imperative for self-government.[37] In *De Cive* Hobbes takes a significant first step forward in this project that culminates in his mature definition of liberty, defining it here as "the *absence of obstacles to motion*," the degree of liberty enjoyed being proportional to the scope of the space for movement enjoyed, such that "the more ways one can move, the more *liberty* one has."[38] Hence one may be free even when one is a subject or servant, for one who is not "in bonds or in prison" may still move to some measurable extent.[39] The specific concept of civil liberty must be grasped within this general context: "And this is what civil *liberty* consists in; for no one, whether *subject* or *child* of the family or *slave*, is prevented by the threat of being punished by his *commonwealth* or *father* or *Master*, however he may be, from doing all he can and trying every move that is necessary to protect his life and health."[40] Although seemingly suggesting that subjection to law does not impinge upon freedom to the degree that resistance to law is always an option, Hobbes concedes on a point that he will expand upon in much greater detail in *Leviathan*: that contrary to the complete yet unproductive liberty possessed outside of government, "once a commonwealth is formed, every citizen retains as much liberty as he needs to live well in peace, and enough liberty is taken from others to remove the fear of them."[41]

In the civil state individuals retain liberty to the degree that the laws do not legislate behavior within the totality of the spheres of human activity within which they move. Liberty is thus, in *De Cive*'s account, the part of natural right that remains to the subject after the institution of the civil laws: "Since all the movements and actions of the citizens have never been brought within the scope of law, and cannot be because of their variety, the things that are neither commanded nor forbidden must be almost infinite; and each man can do them or not at his own discretion."[42] Laws thus do not abolish movement, but rather guide and orient it: "For laws were invented not to extinguish human actions but to direct them; just as nature ordained banks not to stop the flow of the river but to direct it."[43] And indeed, it is the moral duty of rulers to legislate no more laws than are necessary for the maintenance of public peace and good.

For Hobbes now, political misapplications of the language of liberty derive primarily from a failure to comprehend this proper signification. Individuals tend to be especially confused regarding the meaning of civil liberty as a consequence of the fact that, within a democracy, the many share in creating the laws by which they are all bound. This feature, the fact that citizens in a democracy are themselves the authors of the limits on their movements via their legislative self-activity, does not render such citizens any more free than those in alternative forms of regime. To the extent that liberty is now defined as absence of hindrances to motion, one cannot be any less free in a monarchy than in a democracy. It is the unique articulation of the relation between the subject and the law within democratic regimes that causes the confusion, subjects failing to grasp that their authorship of that which is intended to restrict their movement does not alter the fact that they are thereby restricted, and hence lacking a surplus of freedom specific to the popular commonwealth. As Hobbes puts it in *De Cive*, "What gives the impression that they [are more free in a democracy] is equal *participation* in public offices and in power. For where Power belongs to the *people*, individual citizens participate in it insofar as they are part of the sovereign *people*. And they participate equally in public offices in so far as they have equal votes in electing magistrates and public ministers."[44] To think a differentiation in the scope of freedom in distinct regimes is thus to confuse the concepts of liberty and sovereignty.[45]

In the final chapter of this book I will examine Hobbes's discussion of the nature of liberty in *Leviathan* in a different context, although we should briefly note here the slight alteration in the definition of the term in that work, an alteration that Quentin Skinner has traced back to 1645, it being formulated within the context of Hobbes's debate with John Bramhall on the question of so-called freedom of the will.[46] Clarifying his characterization of liberty in terms of the absence of impediments, in *Leviathan*, unlike in *De Cive*, Hobbes specifies that liberty refers particularly to the absence of external hindrances to motion, there being a distinction between extrinsic and intrinsic limitations on action, the former taking away our liberty, the latter on the contrary our power.[47] Despite the conceptual innovation, it remains true that in *Leviathan* Hobbes makes the same effort as he did in *De Cive* to detach this category from the collective activity of generating binding legal norms for the political community. Within the commonwealth civil laws function as artificial bonds regulating the movement of citizens, the specific liberty of subjects being articulated within the context of these external legal impediments. In addition to retaining a natural liberty that only imprisonment takes away, every commonwealth has some space of civil liberty, given the extensive range of human behavior and the impossibility of the sovereign legislating the totality of this range: "For seeing there is no Common-wealth in the world, wherein there be Rules enough set down, for the regulating of all the actions, and words of men, (as being a thing impossible:) it followeth necessarily, that in all kinds of actions, by the laws praetermitted, men have the Liberty, of doing what their own reasons, shall suggest, for the most profitable to themselves."[48] The liberty of the subject, then, is seen as located within these domains in which the law is silent, which Hobbes in the contemporary case perhaps ahistorically generalizes from through his apparent positing of the universality of the following: "The Liberty of a Subject, lyeth therefore only in those things, which in regulating their actions, the Soveraign hath praetermitted: such as is the Liberty to buy, and sell, and otherwise contract with one another; to choose their own aboad, their own diet, their own trade of life, and institute their children as they themselves think fit; & the like."[49]

As he was in *De Cive*, Hobbes in *Leviathan* is concerned with repudiating that republican conception of freedom characteristic of the classical tradition, and which he himself affirmed in *The Elements of Law*. In attempting to make sense of the political phenomenon that the ancient writers uniformly perceive yet mischaracterize, he claims that the liberty referred to by the latter is meant not to signify the freedom of subjects, but rather cities: "The Libertie, whereof there is so frequent, and honourable mention, in the Histories, and Philosophy of the Antient Greeks, and Romans, and in the writings, and discourse of those that from them have received all their learning in the Politiques, is not the Libertie of Particular men; but the Libertie of the Common-wealth."[50] Specifically, cities are free to the degree that they retain the absolute right to judge the means to their own self-preservation in an anarchic international order that lacks the capacity to regulate their relations via reference to a common standard of just and unjust. If commonwealths retain this freedom, however, the citizens that occupy them certainly do not, remaining each one equally bound: "The *Athenians*, and *Romanes* were free; that is, free Common-wealths: not that any particular men had the Libertie to resist their own Representative; but that their Representative had the Libertie to resist, or invade other people. There is written on the Turrets of the city of *Lucca* in great characters at this day, the word LIBERTAS; yet no man can thence inferre, that a particular man has more Libertie, or Immunitie from the service of the Commonwealth there, than in *Constantinople*. Whether a Common-wealth be Monarchical, or Popular, the Freedome is still the same."[51]

Regardless of the form of regime, civil laws deprive people of liberty in an equivalent manner, our obedience to them being the means through which our obligation and subjection to the sovereign is expressed.[52] Aristotle is thus wrong in the *Politics*, again contrary to Hobbes's judgment on this issue in the *Elements*, to maintain that it is only within a democratic polity that individuals have liberty. The classical writers who follow Aristotle simply deploy the language of freedom in an effort to legitimate or excuse the many inconveniences of democracy, this form of regime appearing most natural to them to the degree that they were socialized within it. As we have already noted in the previous chapter, the pernicious effects of this conceptual operation are still felt in the present, Hobbes in the Latin *Leviathan* going so far as to blame the perpetuation of Aristotelian thought for the civil wars and unrest in early modern Europe: "Whence have arisen these civil wars about religion in Germany, France, and England, if not from the philosophy, ethics, and politics of Aristotle, and of those Romans who followed Aristotle?"[53]

Let us at this point again return to *De Cive*. After rejecting the idea that democracy may be ethically preferred to other forms of city to the extent that it allows for the realization of a more expansive civil liberty, Hobbes turns to the question of whether democracy may be preferred on the basis of its generalization of participation in political decision-making. If participation in legislative activities is not a mode for the actualization of a unique condition of freedom, why would individuals have an interest in it? Specifically, Hobbes interrogates the question of whether political participation may allow for the actualization of a certain type of intrinsic pleasure, rendering it desirable for the majority of persons: "But for this reason perhaps someone will say that the *popular state* is immensely preferable to *Monarchy*, because in that state, in which of course everyone manages public business, everyone has been given leave to publicly display his prudence knowledge and eloquence in deliberations about matters of the greatest difficulty and importance; and because the love of praise is innate in human nature, this is the most attractive of all things to all those who surpass others in such talents or seem to themselves to do so."[54] Hobbes flatly denies any such argument, suggesting that outside of a small minority of individuals there is no evidence of such participatory desire, citizens generally preferring to attend to their own private as opposed to public business. Exclusion from deliberative activities in council contexts is thus no hardship: "I will tell you. To see the proposal of a man whom we despise preferred to our own; to see our wisdom ignored before our eyes; to incur certain enmity in an uncertain struggle for empty glory; to hate and be hated because of differences of opinion (which cannot be avoided, whether we win or lose); to reveal our plans and wishes when there is no need to and to get nothing by it; to neglect our private affairs. These, I say, are disadvantages."[55] Contrary to what a reader might have intuited based on the conceptual articulation of the form of relationship between the categories of freedom and participation in *The Elements of Law*, Hobbes is now explicit that there is no reason for the typical subject to prefer living under a democracy than any other type of political regime.

Authorization and Representation in *Leviathan*

In *De Cive* Hobbes thought he had successfully neutralized the ground of any source of democratic normativity through the redefinition of the concept of liberty and the rejection of a generalized participatory desire. What would become clear, however, is that it was possible to construct an ethical defense of democratic preference based on the consideration of the temporality of political institution, that is to say, if—as was still the case in *De Cive*—democracy was considered to necessarily precede all sovereign constitutions as a logical and practical moment. As was the case in *The Elements of Law*, in the subsequent text Hobbes continues to insist on the originary democratic origin of all civil states, writing that "when men have met to erect a commonwealth, they are, almost by the very fact that they have met, a *Democracy*."[56] It could plausibly be argued, then, that on this basis democracy was the most natural of constitutions. And indeed, shortly after Hobbes produced the book there emerged within the context of the political and ideological dynamics of the civil war a flourishing of revolutionary texts that implicitly affirmed such a position. Even if the democratical gentlemen were not democrats, there certainly existed some revolutionary actors and factions opposed to the parliamentary oligarchs, actors and factions who harbored democratic sympathies that were often expressed in the language of natural law. For example, a characteristic feature of much Leveller political thought was the insistence that the people possessed an inherent and natural sovereignty that predated any instituted political form, be it a monarchy or a parliament.[57] Such was given an early expression in "England's Miserie and Remedie," where it is asserted that the people possess an original "sovereign or legislative power" which is only "lent" to the representative for the sake of the advancement of the former's well-being.[58] Sovereign power inheres not in a king, a parliament, or any representative body whatsoever, the latter needing to be considered as a mere executor of the more fundamental substance from which it draws life.[59] That being said, it remains the case that a popular parliamentary government retains an ethical privilege relative to others, to the extent that it most adequately expresses natural political right. As the Levellers note in the "Large Petition," "no government is more just in the constitution than that of the parliaments—having its foundation in the free choice of the people."[60]

That Hobbes's introduction of the schema of authorization in *Leviathan* is intended to foreclose the possibility of thinking the existence of a "fundamental popular sovereignty"[61] revealed through the necessarily democratic foundation of all political societies is suggested by many readers.[62] With the new model the singularity of democracy is annulled, each particular form of commonwealth deriving its authority from the same source and through the same process.[63] The first step in this movement is the reclarification of the language of personhood and personation. In his earlier work Hobbes had referred to the body politic as an artificial civil person. In *De Cive* it is written that in their submission each individual "transfers to that other the *Right to his strength and resources*," and in possession of these strengths and resources the one can "use the fear they inspire to bring the wills of individuals to unity and concord."[64] Such a union is known as a commonwealth, civil society, or civil person: "A COMMONWEALTH, then, (to define it) is *one person*, whose *will*, by the agreement of several men, is to be taken as the *will* of them all; to make use of their strength and resources for the common peace and defence."[65] The individual or council to whom all particulars have subjected their will, and for whose will stands in for them all, possesses supreme power or dominion, every other citizen standing as a subject in relation to this entity. Note that the relation here between the sovereign and the civil person as commonwealth is still somewhat unclear, it not yet being explicitly specified that these are two distinct entities, the former being that artificial person who represents the latter. Monarchy is just as much a city as a democracy, the city simply being "contained in the person of a King."[66] Such is because the will of the sovereign is identical with the will of the city, and contains within itself the wills of all particular citizens.[67]

The more refined account of personation in *Leviathan* clarifies the nature of the plurality of forms of person, as well as the distinct modes of representation. The theory of sovereign institution rooted in authorization emerges from this examination.[68] Hobbes will here, as he will do in a slightly amended account later in *De Homine*, emphasize the theatrical root of the concept through highlighting the Latin signification of the term *persona*, the origin of the English word: "*Persona* in latine signifies the *disguise*, or *outward appearance* of a man, counterfeited on the Stage."[69] In the theater the actor assumes a persona through the articulation of speech understood to not belong to them: "For in the theatre it was understood that the actor himself did not speak, but someone else, for example, Agamemnon, namely the actor playing the part of Agamemnon in a false face who was for that time, Agamemnon; nevertheless, afterwards he was also understood without his false face, namely being acknowledged as the actor himself rather than the person that he had been playing."[70] A person is thus one who produces significations which may be attributed either to themselves or to an other whom they act for, this other being ultimately responsible for the significations of the one who acts. As he puts it in *Leviathan*, a person is "he, *whose words or actions are considered, either as his own, or as representing the words or actions of another man, or of any other thing to whom they are attributed, whether Truly or by Fiction.*"[71] Note that Hobbes introduces a further distinction here: all representatives are artificial persons, but these persons may represent either "*Truly* or *by Fiction*," the former occurring in instances where the author is the represented and the latter where they are not. Importantly, Hobbes thus maintains that things lacking natural personhood may be represented, even if they cannot give authority to their representative: "Inanimate things, as a Church, an Hospital, a Bridge, may be personated by a Rector, Master, or Overseer. But things Inanimate, cannot be Authors, nor therefore give Authority to procure their maintenance, given them by those that are Owners, or Governours of those things."[72] In a sense, through this process the inanimate thing gains the capacity for animation, acquiring a will through the representation.[73]

Hobbes is concerned mostly to explore the political consequences of the nature of that form of representation that characterizes the actor's assumption of a role whose movements are attributed to someone else: whereas a natural person is one whose words or actions are considered their own, an artificial person is one whose words or actions are considered to represent the words or actions of another.[74] Hobbes uses the idea of authorization in order to attempt to clarify with precision the mechanics through which an artificial person is capable of such representation. Once more the theatrical image is meant to clarify the potentialities of personhood and in particular the ability of a person to act so as to personate or represent the being of a separate author: "So that a *Person*, is the same that an *Actor* is both on the stage in in common Conversations; and to *Personate*, is to *Act*, or *Represent* himself, or an other; and he that acteth another is said to beare his Person, or act in his name."[75] An actor is thus an artificial person whose words and actions are owned by those that they represent, the latter in this process of representation retaining ownership of the words and actions performed by the former. Needless to say, any one actor has not the right to act for any one author, the legitimacy of the relation being constituted through a duly enacted process of contractual exchange. An author is ultimately defined as one "*that hath declared himself responsible for the action done by another according to his will.*"[76] Authority is generated when an author charges an actor to act on their behalf, the actor being authorized to exercise that right of action belonging to the author: "So that Authority, is always understood a Right of doing any act; and *done by Authority*, done by Commission, or Licence from him whose right it is."[77] One has authority when one is empowered to act for another, "For unless he that is the author hath the right of acting himself, the actor hath no authority to act."[78] As a consequence it arises that when a legitimately authorized actor makes a covenant the author is just as bound to respect it as if they made it themself: "From hence it followeth, that when the Actor maketh a Covenant by Authority, he bindeth thereby the Author, no lesse than if he had made it himself; and no lesse subjecteth him to all the consequences of the same."[79]

After outlining in general terms the nature of the process of authorization, Hobbes turns to examine the degree to which it elucidates the nature of political institution. As was the case in both the *Elements of Law* and *De Cive*, the problem of this institution is identified with the need to transform a mere multitude into a unified entity endowed with a capacity for action. As we know already from the earlier texts, a multitude is not a self-identical subject capable of willing substantive determinations regarding common life. The radically singular individuals of the multitude each possess a range of interests and opinions specific to them, there existing no natural mechanism capable of resolving this discursive plurality so as to allow for consensus in decision-making. Hence there is perpetual dispute regarding what is and what is to be done: "And be there never so great a Multitude; yet if their actions be directed according to their particular judgements, and particular appetites, they expect thereby no defence, nor protection, neither against a Common enemy, nor against the injuries of one another. For being distracted in opinions concerning the best use and application of their strength, they do not help, but hinder one another; and reduce their strength by mutuall opposition to nothing."[80] If such determinations could be made by a multitude, commonwealths would not be required in any time or place: "For if we could suppose a great Multitude of men to consent in the observation of Justice, and other Lawes of Nature, without a common Power to keep them all in awe; we might as well suppose all Man-kind to do the same; and then there neither would be, nor need be any Civill Government, or Common-wealth at all; because there would be peace without subjection."[81] Social interaction between human beings, however, is not characterized by the type of spontaneous correlation of interest that marks the association of the so-called political animals, Hobbes providing various reasons why humankind is not capable of this type of self-organization.[82]

Given the lack of a homogeneity of opinion or interest, the particular wills of the disunited multitude are only capable of being reduced to a unity through being personated.[83] Specifically, "a Multitude of men, are made *One* Person, when thay are by one man, or Person, Represented; so that it be done with the consent of every one of that Multitude in particular. For it is the *Unity* of the Representer, not the *Unity* of the Represented, that maketh the Person *One*. And it is the Representer that beareth the Person, and but one Person: And *Unity*, cannot otherwise be understood in Multitude."[84] The becoming one of the multitude is thus achieved not through the literal identification or fusion of the particular wills of those natural persons composing it, but rather through the representation of each of these wills in a unified artificial person expressing a single will.[85] In this situation every particular natural person, as a unique singularity, must specifically authorize the institution of the representative relation, the multitude again being incapable of forms of coordinated action attributable to a single author. Hobbes thus writes: "And because the Multitude naturally is not *One*, but *Many*; they cannot be understood for one; but many Authors, of every thing their Representative saith, or doth in their name; Every man giving their Common Representer Authority from himself in particular; and owning all the actions the Representer doth, in case they give him Authority without stint: Otherwise, when they limit him in what, and how farre he shall represent them, none of them owneth more, than they gave him commission to Act."[86]

In Hobbes's account in *Leviathan*, then, the commonwealth is generated through the reduction of the plurality of wills to a single one via a process of authorization, the multiplicity of authors each consenting to be represented by an artificial person whose acts will henceforth be attributed to them all. In his words,

> The only way to erect such a Common Power . . . is, to conferre all their power and strength upon one Man, or upon one Assembly of men, that may reduce all their Wills, by plurality of voices, unto one Will: which is as much to say, to appoint one Man, or Assembly of men, to beare their Person; and every one to owne, and acknowledge himselfe to be Author of whatsoever he thath beareth their Person, shall Act, or cause to be Acted, in those things which concerne the Common Peace and Safetie; and therein to submit their Wills, every one to his Will, and their Judgements, to his Judgement.[87]

Only in this way can the multitude of individuals be combined in a genuine substantive unity, not through the merely accidental concordance of distinct wills, but through the artificial generation of a singular and internally self-identical will that represents all: "This is more than Consent, or Concord; it is a reall Unitie of them all, in one and the same Person."[88] The one person through which the multitude is unified is called the commonwealth. But as Hobbes's language above suggests, the personhood of the commonwealth is only capable of being animated through the concentration of authority in an entity that is able to bear this commonwealth, that is to say, "one Man, or Assembly of men." The sovereign, ultimately, to the degree to which it "carryeth this Person," is the one authorized by each individual to act for it, as "the Common-wealth is no Person, nor has capacity to doe any thing, but by the Representative, (that is, The Soveraign)."[89] Thus within the sovereign "consisteth the Essence of the Common-wealth; which (to define it,) is *One Person, of whose Acts a great Multitude, by mutuall Covenants one with another, have made themselves every one the Author, to the end he may use the strength and means of them all, as he shall think expedient, for their Peace and Common Defence.*"[90]

As David Runciman has cautioned, readers must be careful here not to conflate the distinct places of authorization and representation in this process.[91] When Hobbes speaks of authorization he refers to relations between individual subjects, but when he speaks of representation he refers also to a relation between the sovereign and the subjects as a whole, to the degree that that which the sovereign represents is not just each of the multiplicity of natural persons who authorize it, but the commonwealth, that is, the people as a singular corporate entity.[92] It is precisely the authorization of the sovereign by the multitude of individuals that allows for the representation of the state by the former. In *Leviathan* the act of covenanting, then, brings into existence two new persons: the sovereign, who each member of the multitude authorizes to act and speak in each's name, and the commonwealth or state, an artificial person that unites the multitude under a single will, thereby converting the former into a people proper, and which the sovereign represents by fiction. The state is ultimately an artificial person that achieves its personhood through being fictionally represented by a distinct sovereign whose actions are attributed to it. Recall that the nature of personation differs in the case of the representation of inanimate things because objects cannot authorize representative relations themselves, thus introducing the need for a third term to mediate the representative relation: one needs not just the object to be represented and the representative, but a third party who authorizes the actor to act for the object. In the political case, the sovereign is authorized by the multitude to speak and act in the name of the state, for the benefit of the good of the people who are united through the person of the state.[93] Even if the commonwealth cannot authorize or perform the acts of the sovereign itself, it can still have acts attributed to it via the mechanics of representation.[94]

We are now in a position to note what implications emerge out of Hobbes's description of political institution in *Leviathan* from the standpoint of democratic theory. If the development of the schema of authorization and representation constitutes the major theoretical innovation in *Leviathan*'s account of political institution, this addition is accompanied by a major theoretical subtraction. Specifically, the language of democracy disappears from *Leviathan*'s account. In the following section I suggest that the fact that this terminology is expunged from Hobbes's text, even when the earlier account of political foundation as having an originally democratic foundation seems to reemerge in a later chapter, reveals Hobbes's motivations. In asserting that the neutralization of civil strife and faction, the latter being associated with the democratic contestation over meaning and value, can only be achieved through a concerted pedagogical effort against "the writers of heathen politics and philosophy," Hobbes in the Latin *Leviathan* demands that "that democratic ink must be wiped away by preaching, writing, and arguing."[95] Far from being merely a prescription for the instructors in the schools and universities, this imperative is one that Hobbes sees as applying to himself, the "democratic ink" of his earlier political philosophy being "wiped away" in *Leviathan*.

The Disappearance of Democracy

Recall that in his earlier writings, Hobbes posited that a multiplicity of natural persons became a people through self-organizing into a city by way of the constitution of an originary democracy.[96] The people so constituted only afterward became either a monarchy or an aristocratic assembly depending on the next form of sovereign authority the existing democratic assembly wished to institute. It has been pointed out that Hobbes's reformulation of the mechanics of political institution in *Leviathan* in terms of authorization is meant to eliminate this temporal priority of democracy as a sovereign form. A democratic assembly is no longer needed to choose the form of government at the point of institution, the process of authorization both establishing obligation as well as determining the structure of the person to whom each is obliged.[97] If previously the institution of the commonwealth was seen as taking place in two steps—the covenanting of individuals so as to form a civil society via unanimous agreement, and the selection of a sovereign via majority vote—*Leviathan* is intended to simplify this process through reducing it to a single step of authorization, thus jettisoning the originary democratic moment. Unlike in the earlier model, there is here no communal entity—the initial democratic assembly—that precedes the sovereign. The sovereign must come into being co-temporally with the commonwealth to the degree that the commonwealth is defined in terms of the possession of a single unified will, and the sovereign is precisely that representative capable of expressing this will through its words and actions. Unity is immediately achieved through the figure of the sovereign person and not before. Political self-activity on the part of the people as a collectivity, in other words, as a presovereign democratic assembly, is not only not necessary, but not practically nor logically possible.[98]

On the basis of the new model, therefore, Hobbes believes he has definitively foreclosed the possibility of reading into the act of institution a democratic normativity grounded in the fact of an obligatory popular participation, an obligatory popular participation that could be theoretically transmuted into an image of natural popular sovereignty.[99] The parliamentarian writers who attempt to initiate this latter theoretical move are thus thwarted: political institutions cannot be seen as representative of a prior popular community that retains supremacy within the commonwealth, to the degree that such a community only comes into existence through the artificial generation of sovereignty. Parliament cannot represent the people in the sense that the parliamentarians think, for the people is only created through the act of sovereign institution, human diversity precluding the spontaneous formation of any such prior collective entity.[100] As was always the case, the unity upon which the being of the people rests is not a natural fact, but must be constructed. Now, however, such construction proceeds via the simultaneous generation of a representative which personates the commonwealth in order to immediately express the former's singularity, this second reduction—which is the creation of the sovereign—no longer necessarily relying on a preceding democratic moment.

What Hobbes's new schema of representation is trying to demonstrate is that political foundation does not proceed through the popular activity of a people. That being said, it would certainly remain the case that within a specifically democratic commonwealth such activity would still characterize the deliberative mechanics of the government. Philip Pettit is correct to therefore emphasize the extent to which the nature of personation in a democracy must be unique, the procedural operation of the representative person being characterized, regardless of the range of potential variation to be located within distinct such persons, by a political endeavor lacking in other sovereign forms: "Clearly, the personator group associated with democracy would be of a different sort of people, a different sort of civil person, from the personatee group envisaged in a monarchy; it would have an *active, participatory* character."[101] Pettit speculates that Hobbes deliberately deemphasizes this singularity to the degree that it would render democracy more appealing to individuals than other sovereign forms: "While insisting on the contrast between a multitude and a people, he downplays the difference between the passive mode in which a people comes to be constituted under a monarchy or an aristocracy, and the active form that it achieves under a democracy."[102] Recall that it was the necessary origin of the civil person in such self-activity that was identified as the major conceptual ambiguity of *De Cive*, from the anti-democratic perspective. Now that this element has been overcome, Hobbes sees no reason to call particular attention to this democratic singularity, although crucially, as I will note in the final chapter, the language of participatory desire thereby returns in *Leviathan* in a new mode.

Historical contextualist readers are correct to see this conceptual innovation as Hobbes's response to parliamentarian theorists who attempt to interpret political foundation as an expression of a natural popular sovereignty. The innovation, however, is just one manifestation of a larger philosophical effort, the recognition of which becomes acute when we consider not only *Leviathan*'s addition of the language of authorization and representation, but also a certain linguistic subtraction. Philosophical-textual analysis helps us explain why, even when in *Leviathan* Hobbes reverts to his earlier model of institution—which had been explicitly framed as democratic—the language of democracy does not consequently reappear. A variety of readers have questioned whether *Leviathan* does provide a real alternative form of political institution, the independence of the one-stage authorization process being complicated by the apparent reemergence of the two-stage process in the book's eighteenth chapter.[103] Here Hobbes is explicit that the institution of the commonwealth entails a multitude initially coming together and assembling as a corporate body, while subsequently conferring sovereign power as a collective entity.[104] Already in chapter 17 Hobbes had let slip that the reduction of the plurality of wills to a single unified will takes place "by plurality of voices."[105] The implication of this conception becomes clear in the subsequent chapter, where it seems that the very capacity to perform the constructive operation depends upon the existence of an assembly that is already itself sovereign.[106] As Arash Abizadeh writes, "If there were any doubt that assembling together with the intention of establishing a commonwealth in itself constitutes a multitude as a democratic sovereign assembly, Hobbes dispelled it in chapter 18's fifth paragraph. He did so by repeating the argument he had given in *De cive* for why an instituted commonwealth always begins as a democracy, namely, that merely to assemble with the intention of establishing a commonwealth is tacitly to covenant to abide by majority rule."[107]

Consider Hobbes's concise overview of the institution of the commonwealth and the sovereign representative in the chapter in question:

> A *Common-wealth* is said to be *Instituted*, when a *Multitude* of men do *Agree*, and *Covenant*, *every one*, *with every one*, that to whatsoever *Man*, or *Assembly of Men*, shall be given by the major part, the *Right* to *Present* the Person of them all, (that is to say, to be their *Representative*;) every one, as well he that *Voted for it*, as he that *Voted against it*, shall *Authorise* all the Actions and Judgements, of that Man, or Assembly of men, in the same manner, as if they were his own, to the end, to live peaceably amongst themselves, and be protected against other men.[108]

If the result of this particular decision process obliges both those who voted for and against the institution, then it would seem that this presumes a prior unity existing before sovereign enactment, individuals agreeing to participate in an assembly on the question of the establishment of a representative, the determination of which they will be bound to regardless of the vote to the degree that they each accept the legitimacy of the particular procedure. That is to say, in giving assent to the legitimacy of the procedure they act as a people prior to the institution of the commonwealth. This ambivalence is suggested in an even more explicit way when Hobbes identifies the third of the rights and capacities of the sovereign that derive from institution. Here he maintains that the minority of individuals is bound to the decision of the majority in this movement of political foundation: "Because the major part hath by consenting voices declared a Soveraigne; he that dissented must now consent with the rest; that is, be contented to avow all the actions he shall do, or else justly be destroyed by the rest. For if he voluntarily entered into the Congregation of them that were assembled, he sufficiently declared thereby his will (and therefore tacitly covenanted) to stand for what the major part should ordayne."[109] Significantly, this procedural logic mirrors that which applies to decision-making within commonwealths in which sovereignty inheres in an assembly. If the actor that each author authorizes to represent them is composed of many individuals, that is if it is a council, the determinations are made via plurality vote, or as Hobbes says, "And if the Representative consist of many men, the voyce of the greatest number, must be considered the voyce of them all."[110]

Readers of Hobbes have provided a range of differing interpretations regarding what they see as the real or apparent tension introduced by chapter 18 of *Leviathan*.[111] My suggestion is that the textual situation of this chapter within the context of Hobbes's critique of democracy can help us more adequately explain the ambivalence. In particular, it helps us understand why Hobbes implicitly reverts to the earlier model while failing to explicitly acknowledge as much.[112] In chapter 17 Hobbes wants to provide a general philosophical alternative to the earlier account of political foundation through that of individual authorization, one that is seemingly intended to apply to commonwealths by both institution and by acquisition.[113] Chapter 18 reveals, however, that such an alternative cannot be plausibly applied to the former type, the practical exigencies of political institution necessitating collective coordination between always distinct beings who lack the natural homogeneity of interest characteristic of the political animals. Human difference, which in chapter 17 is identified as that which makes the commonwealth necessary in the first place, therefore seems to itself militate against the literally simultaneous authorization of distinct individuals. Such an authorization would depend on the unrealistic establishment of an a priori consensus preceding the political act. In chapter 18 Hobbes concedes the unfeasibility of reaching this consensus, and hence the recourse to majority vote as a procedural mode. Hobbes must have recognized the conceptual proximity between the presentation of political foundation here and the accounts given in *The Elements of Law* and *De Cive*. The fact that even within chapter 18 Hobbes refuses to characterize institution in terms of an originary democratic moment—despite the fact that the earlier works repeatedly and unequivocally make a point of emphasizing this essential characteristic—should be interpreted as a deliberate linguistic strategy. Hobbes refuses to acknowledge what seems immanent to the logic of foundation, which would thereby reintroduce into his framework a ground that could be exploited by those partisans of democracy who would argue that this form of regime remains the most natural.

Regardless of whether or not we accept that Hobbes has fully emancipated himself from his earlier account of political institution as possessing an inherently democratic origin, what seems clear at least is that he recognized the degree to which such a conception potentially endowed democratic sovereignty with a unique normative legitimacy in relation to other constitutions. My suggestion has been that we can read certain significant changes in Hobbes's political philosophy as being motivated by the need to overcome such legitimacy, both *De Cive* in relation to *The Elements of Law* and *Leviathan* in relation to *De Cive*, looking to neutralize a democratic potential that could be located in the antecedent variant. The substance of Hobbes's critique of democracy remained consistent throughout his life, the refinement of certain aspects of his political theory being undertaken in light of the philosophical perception of elements of his framework that might be exploited so as to construct an ethical defense of democratic rule. On this reading, then, the alterations in Hobbes's thought that I have highlighted cannot be explained exclusively through historical contextual analysis, even if it is essential to aiding us in the identification of the sources that revealed to Hobbes the fundamental philosophical problems, as, for example, did those contemporaneous authors who extrapolated from the temporality of the logic of originary democracy a fundamental popular sovereignty. My argument has been that a richer understanding of the shift in the framework and terminology of Hobbesian political institution requires not just historical contextual analysis, but also the theoretical situation of this movement within Hobbes's uninterrupted opposition to democratic rule most generally. This political commitment shapes the contours of Hobbes's philosophy in fundamental ways, it having to be transformed if it can be perceived as allowing for a normative preference for democratic life.

PART II
DEMOCRATIC CONDITIONS

Chapter 3

Human Institution and Alterity

In chapter 1, I outlined the main contours of Hobbes's anatomy of democracy, stressing in particular the sovereign's major assembly composition and the extent to which the internal dynamics of the latter tend to render the democratic regime perpetually unstable. In chapter 2, I traced out several major alterations made to Hobbes's political philosophy that emanated from the perception of a ground of democratic normativity that could be theoretically located in the former variants of his civil science, suggesting that such revealed the centrality of the critique of democracy to the overall Hobbesian project. Hobbes's undertaking on this front can be seen as all the more urgent once we consider certain elements of his natural philosophy and in particular his philosophical anthropology. In the following two chapters I will discuss what I have elsewhere identified as the two ontological conditions of democratic being that Hobbes's philosophy affirms, conditions which are essential for the practical instauration of democratic life: first, the lack of a transcendent source of fundamental law that places essential limits on the scope and range of legislative potential; and second, a natural human equality that asserts an equivalent capacity of all individuals to participate in legislative modes.[1] Despite the fact that his political science is largely oriented toward maligning democratic sovereignty, his philosophy uniquely articulates, very much unlike the greater part of contemporary democratic theory, the ontological preconditions required to render the idea of democracy thinkable.

In *De Corpore* Hobbes defines philosophy as "*such knowledge of effects or appearances, as we acquire by ratiocination from the knowledge we have first of their causes or generation: And again, of such causes or generations as may be from knowing first their effects.*"[2] In this work Hobbes simplifies his earlier systematic account of the structure of philosophical investigation, which was grounded in a metaphysical *philosophia prima* dealing with the science of being itself, and which was subdivided into natural philosophy or physics (that branch dealing with the motion of natural bodies), moral philosophy (that branch dealing with the motion of human beings), political philosophy (that branch dealing with the operation of political life), and mathematics (that branch dealing with "the relations of space to space, time to time, figure to figure, number to number").[3] There are now just two broad categories of philosophy, each corresponding to two types of bodies: natural philosophy deals with the motion of natural objects, while civil philosophy (famously no older than *De Cive* itself, in Hobbes's account) deals with the commonwealth, an artificial body created via the agreement of individuals. Civil philosophy is itself subdivided into two parts: ethics, "which treats of men's dispositions and manners," and politics, which concerns civil duties and obligations.[4]

In this chapter I will begin with a brief account of some of the features of Hobbes's natural philosophy as consideration of the motion of bodies—the essential attribute of which is extension, a body being "any thing that hath a being in itself, without the help of sense"[5]—that reveal the first ontological condition of democracy: the openness of the world to the generation of genuinely new determinations, that is to say, determinations that are irreducible to the movement of a teleological process from which they must inevitably emerge. It is only to the extent that the world is open to such emergence that it is possible to think the institution of society as a specifically self-institution, an institution carried out autonomously by individuals who are free to act independently of a transcendent source delimiting their activity. What Hobbes's materialism reveals is that the basis of social institution can only be individuals themselves, their existing no extrasocial source—whether identified as God, natural law, laws of history, and so on—that functions as a fundamental ground from which the establishment of social norms proceeds.[6] Now, if this nongrounding characterizes all modes of social institutionalization, what is singular about democracy is the achievement of consciousness of this fact. The particularly democratic form, regardless of the specificities of the regime's institutional configuration, is defined in terms of the generalization of participation in the legislative process, all citizens being empowered to freely partake in the formulation of those legal rules that bind them together in a discrete political community. Democracy depends on the clear comprehension of the capacity of the individuals within society to collectively institute and reinstitute the system of law that governs their life in common, without reference to any exterior sources that would structure or regulate this political self-expression. In short, in democracy the openness of the world to human intervention takes on, through the lucid recognition on the part of citizens of their legislative capacity, a unique significance. As I noted in chapter 1, it was the potential for hubris that resulted from this recognition that so worried Hobbes. Indeed, the instability of the Athenian democracy resulted from fact that the citizens of the regime "thought they were able to do anything."[7] Such a thought is only possible in a democracy, in which the fact of social innovation is explicitly affirmed.

Ontological Materialism and the Limits of Natural Knowledge

I have suggested that in the first instance democracy depends on the reflective recognition of the openness of the world to its creative reorganization, independent of reference to foundational schemata or models that would delimit the range and scope of the human capacity to institute the norms that regulate social life. We should thus begin by saying something about Hobbes's own recognition of this openness. His natural philosophy articulates the condition through a materialist account of the perpetual motion of the always singular objects of the world, which exist in a complex web of mutual determination that forecloses the possibility of the systematization of worldly movement. For Hobbes anything that exists is either substance or accident, the latter not existing without the former to the degree that it is that whose being is contained in another, all accidents inhering in a substance which they cannot be extracted from. In the language of *De Corpore*, if a body *"is that, which having no dependence upon our thought, is coincident or coextended with some part of space,"* an accident is *"the manner of our conception of a body,"* which we can consider from the standpoint of the object—as "that faculty of any body, by which it works in us a conception of itself"—or the subject— as "the manner by which any body is conceived."[8] For the time being we will bracket the issue of the means by which a subject conceives of a body, noting only the extent to which consideration of any body is irreducible to the appropriation of a perpetual content that defines its essential being. Indeed, Hobbes redefines essence as "that accident which we give a certain name to any body, or the accident which denominates its subject."[9] Essence thus simply speaks to a particular mode of conceiving a thing, as opposed to some intrinsic principle or rule governing this thing's existence.

An accident is thus not a substance or a part of the natural object: it is not a property inherent in the thing that substantially participates in the latter's fundamental reality.[10] An accident rather is constituted through bodies' interactions with one another.[11] Bodies, as agents, act when they generate or destroy an accident within other bodies, or patients. In this motion the cause is all those accidents in both agents and patients necessary to produce the effect, the accidents in the former being called the efficient cause, and the accidents in the latter being called the material cause.[12] The power to act is thus the ability to produce an effect within the patient, the agent's requisite accidents reconfiguring those of the patient through the dynamic encounter of bodies.[13] It is this motion of bodies that constitutes the essential source of Hobbes's materialism, and indeed, as we will see eventually, of all possible knowledge.[14] Hobbes's conception of matter emphasizes its lack of an intrinsic purpose that directs its motion. Contra Aristotle, there exist not any natural kinds of objects whose being is structured by an internal telos.[15] As many commentators have noted, for Hobbes the empirical world lacks a teleological direction of any kind.[16] In Thomas Spragen's words, the world "has no order, no structure, no end or limitation. It is endless, aimless motion."[17] Hobbes's "dynamic ontology,"[18] articulating the productivity of the encounter between bodies whose motions are untraceable to a purposive source that germinally structures their mechanics, has thus led to the identification of his philosophical undertaking as an "*anti*foundational project"[19] and "nearly Heraclitian."[20]

The consequences for theoretical investigation that the basic principles of Hobbesian materialism impose upon human inquiry are obscured by those readers who suggest that Hobbes had totalizing pretensions to generate a systematic philosophy capable of accounting for the totality of the movement of natural and civic life.[21] Hobbes, on the contrary, quite consistently maintains that there are innumerable phenomena, even excluding those that pertain to the realm of the divine, that we can never hope to explain to the degree that we are incapable of acquiring adequate knowledge of them.[22] Consideration of the differentiation in the depth and breadth of understanding that discrete domains of reality or experience are open to is useful in articulating the issue at stake. We can note, for example, the much-discussed place of geometry within Hobbes's system and the certainty that it exclusively allows the researcher to approach.[23] The exclusivity of this investigative mode is crucial. Hobbes is explicit that there exists no universal method that is similarly valid in every sphere of investigation. On the contrary, the appropriateness of the method must be derived from careful consideration of the nature of the object of investigation. Hence, for example, the case of mathematics: "For though an arithmetical calculation be true in numbers, yet the same may be, or rather must be false, if the units be not constantly the same."[24] Confusion and inconstancy can only result if "the number is sometimes so many lines, sometimes so many planes, and sometimes so many solids."[25]

What must be emphasized in particular is the specificity of propositional truth. In his critique of Thomas White Hobbes identifies "true philosophy" with the "faithful, correct and accurate nomenclature of things," "right reasoning" consisting in the proper deployment of this nomenclature, that is, the correct combination of properly defined propositions in a subject-predicate form so as to yield necessary conclusions.[26] The truth of the proposition consists in the inclusion of the meaning of the subject within that of the predicate, such that truth always takes a hypothetical as opposed to a categorical form. Truth does not inhere in the demonstration of the being of the object, but rather in a demonstration of the logical ordering of words: "Demonstrable truth lies in logical inferences; and in every demonstration the term that forms the subject of the conclusion demonstrated is taken as the name, not of a thing that exists, but of one supposed to exist. A conclusion, therefore, has a force that is not categorical, but is merely hypothetical."[27] In view of such a conception, we can understand what Hobbes sees as the philosophical implications of the methods of geometry, given its correct use of definition. Geometry does not concern itself primarily with the being of natural objects, but rather fixed definitions set down by common consent, such consent neutralizing the potential for dispute: "Geometers, even before Euclid, never examined the rationale of lines, surfaces and bodies or argued about the properties of figures, save in one respect: the meaning of the terms used when we describe things as 'figures' and 'quantities.' Thus definitions were fixed at the start, with the aim of excluding wholly all ambiguous and metaphorical language."[28] When philosophers, on the contrary, attempt to investigate the qualities of objects themselves, irreconcilable disagreement is inevitable given the diversity of modes of sensuous appropriation, as will be detailed later in this chapter. Ultimately there is no possibility of individuals understanding the world in an identical way as a cause of their lack of direct access to the life of the object.

Because geometry works with elements that we construct and define ourselves, it allows for the achievement of a precision that eludes the study of natural objects, given the lack of certain knowledge regarding the latter's relevant causes.[29] As Hobbes writes in *De Homine*, "Since the causes of the properties that individual figures have belong to them because we ourselves draw the lines; and since the generation of the figures depends on our will; nothing is more required to know the phenomenon peculiar to any figure whatsoever, than that we consider everything that follows from the construction that we ourselves make in the figure to be described."[30] The potential efficacy of a specifically political science, and how that efficacy eludes other domains of study, is grounded in this technique of constructive definition. Like geometry, politics and ethics allow of an a priori demonstration, given our role in the initial definition of the objects of analysis. Such is very much not the case in the study of natural objects, given the latter's imperviousness to sensuous perception and immersion in an infinitely complex causal environment: "On the other hand, since the causes of natural things are not in our power, but in the divine will, and since the greatest part of them, namely the ether, is invisible, we, that do not see them, cannot deduce their qualities from their causes."[31] Ultimately Hobbes delinks knowledge from natural being, truth inhering not in an ontological order of things whose structure we have access to, but the systematization of logical discourse. Political science as a properly demonstrative science, then, depends in the first place on the liberation of politics from ontology, the objects of the former possessing perhaps a real being, but one that is artificial as opposed to natural.[32]

Hobbesian Contingency

Hobbes's warning is that our capacity to systematically order words should not deceive us into thinking that we possess an equivalent capacity to order nature: "We must take heed that we don't think, that as names, so the diversities of things themselves may be searched out and determined by such distinctions as these."³³ There is no possibility of developing an internally unified master science whose coherently integrated techniques would be capable of outlining the contours of the totality of material life. In Hobbes's account, we must give up the unrealizable hope of ever being able to acquire a complete understanding of the natural motions of the world, nature being far too diverse and complex for us to isolate or identify all of the relevant causes producing movement. Hobbes gives the example of the limitations of astronomy, noting how "owing to the countless umber and the imperceptibility of the stars' movements it is impossible to comprehend these influences; therefore the effect deriving from them is certainly not predictable."³⁴ We should abandon the unrealizable quest to totally schematize the operation of the natural world so as to allow for completely accurate causal prediction, regardless of the particular advances that the refinement of scientific technique might stimulate. On this point it is worth quoting Hobbes at length:

> Perhaps some advance estimates could be made concerning the changing of the air if someone had accurate commentaries in which were set forth, from a millennium ago to the present day, what kinds of weather occurred every day in every place on earth, i.e., whether the sky was cloudy or clear; where and when there was thunder, rain, hail, etc.; in what position any of the planets was on any single day, and at what aspect the planets were, both each to each and in relation to the place whose climate was being investigated. Perhaps the weather could be forecast, I say, for if it were constantly and frequently recorded that similar storms occurred at a similar position of the starts and place, surely by the same token a conjecture concerning a similar even in the future would be quite plausible. Since, however, these commentaries neither exist nor will exist, such predictions must be worthless.³⁵

Ultimately there is no objective order to the world that presents itself as discoverable and thereby thematizable by the human mind.

The impossibility of systematically outlining the form of the world, thus producing a closed order of natural being that could direct and regulate our lives, is perhaps most clearly articulated in Hobbes's concept of contingency.³⁶ The category of contingency is the conceptual representation, not of the emergence of phenomena independently of causal determination, but rather of the lack of knowledge of such determination. Hobbes writes that "the true and only reason why a man thinks that human affairs are ruled by chance seems to be this: he does not know their integral and necessary causes."[37] And, "all results are necessary because of their causes; consequently they seem fortuitous for no reason other than this: that we do not perceive all their causes."[38] The language of contingency, then, is generally deployed to refer to the inability to identify those causes that produce an effect in question. As Hobbes puts it in *De Corpore*, "men commonly call that *casual* or *contingent*, whereof they do not perceive the necessary cause . . . all propositions concerning future things, contingent or not contingent, as this, *it will rain tomorrow*, or this, *tomorrow the sun will rise*, are either necessarily true or necessarily false; but we call them contingent, because we do not yet know whether they be true or false; whereas their verity depends not upon our knowledge, but upon the foregoing of their causes."[39] It is to the contingent form of phenomena that the language of the miraculous speaks, individuals often interpreting as miracles those events that they find sufficiently strange and wondrous, not being able to imagine that they have a natural origin or explanation. Again, however, the inability to discover the natural operations that produce the occurrence is no evidence that such operations do not exist and that the occurrence is thereby supernatural.[40]

The significance of the concept of contingency is stressed particularly strongly in Hobbes's debate with Bramhall, where Hobbes maintains that "a *contingent agent* is the same with an *agent* simply. But, because men for the most part think those things are produced without cause, whereof they do not see the cause, they use to call both the agent and the action contingent, as attributing it to fortune. And therefore, when the causes are necessary, if they perceive not the necessity, they call those necessary agents and actions, in things that have appetite, *free*; and in things inanimate, *contingent*."[41] The failure to grasp that the concept of contingency refers only to our lack of knowledge of causes is characteristic of Bramhall's understanding, which assumes that the language of contingency captures some kind of phenomenal nonnecessity: "Then for *contingent*, he understandeth not what it meaneth. For it is all one to say it is *contingent*, and simply to say *it is*; saving that when they say simply *it is*, they consider not how or by what means; but in saying it is *contingent*, they tell us they know not whether necessarily or not."[42]

More generally, the presumption that a lack of knowledge of the integral causes of motion is a legitimate ground on which to affirm that no such causes exist is precisely the error of those natural philosophers in the Aristotelian tradition: "And in many occasions they put for cause of Naturall events, their own Ignorance; but disguised in other words: As when they say, Fortune is the cause of things contingent; that is, of things whereof they know no cause."[43]

The impossibility of schematically mapping natural causality results from both the complexity of the natural world and the epistemological limitations to inquiry that the dynamics of human sense-perception impose. Regarding the first, in "Of Liberty and Necessity" Hobbes specifies that every action is necessarily determined by a confluence of various causes: *"That which I say necessitateth and determinateth every action . . . is the sum of all things, which being now existent, conduce and concur to the production of that action hereafter, whereof if any one thing now were wanting, the effect could not be produced."*[44] That said, this confluence is not linearly ordered such as to be open to codification by an observing mind, but is rather a complex web of a multiplicity of causes that potentially overdetermine the production of the phenomenon.[45] If Hobbes's philosophy of motion interprets all being in terms of matter that exists in a shifting web of causal relation, this web is not systematized, lacking as it does an architectonic fixity of order.[46] Hobbes thus writes that "Nor does the *concourse of all causes* make one simple *chain* of concatenation, but an innumerable number of chains, joined together, not in all parts but in the first link God Almighty; and consequently the whole cause of an event, doth not always depend on one single chain, but on many together."[47] The relevant features of Hobbes's account of sense-perception, secondly, will be explored in more detail in the following section. For now, however, we can briefly anticipate this discussion through provisionally noting the incapacity of the human sensorium to penetrate to the being of the object, the greater part of its motions being ultimately imperceptible to us. As Hobbes writes in the "Decameron Physiologicum": "For you enquire not so much, when you see a change of anything, what may be said to be the cause of it, as how the same is generated; which generation is the entire progress of nature from the efficient cause to the effect produced. Which is always a hard question, and for the most part impossible for a man to answer to. For the alterations of the things we perceive by our five senses are made by the motion of bodies, for the most part either for distance, smallness, or transparence, invisible."[48]

To recapitulate, although all events or phenomena have their necessary efficient and material causes, such does not imply that we are thereby capable of isolating and identifying these causes so as to generate an exhaustive explanatory framework. Readers are thus incorrect to conclude on the basis of Hobbes's determinism that the world is open to complete methodical classification, the universal laws constituting the order of physical causality being ultimately discoverable by us.[49] Hobbes's emphasis on necessity and determination in no ways suggests the possibility of achieving a rational mastery of the world. Certain determinants will always remain unknown, as we can neither identify all total past causes of occurred action, nor predict with certainty future action on the basis of the analysis of anticipated factors. Samantha Frost thus notes that in the final instance, "Hobbes's determinism is so complex as to not be determinable."[50]

The Philosophical Anthropology of Sensation

As alluded to in the previous section, the constraint on the human potential to acquire comprehensive knowledge of the motions of the objects of the natural world is largely traceable to the characteristics of sensuous perception, characteristics that fundamentally structure the possibilities of any civil science. The significance of the analysis of the nature of sensation to political theory is revealed through Hobbes's inclusion of a detailed discussion of the former in both his initial and his most mature political treatise. For Hobbes, political philosophy must begin with philosophical anthropology, the Hobbesian account of human sensibility being fundamental to the direction and orientation of Hobbesian political thought.[51]

We have seen that for Hobbes every object that exists in the natural world is an absolute singularity, each particular thing existing only as that particular thing that it is, as opposed to a mere manifestation or reflection of a universal substance. As Hobbes puts it in the *Anti-White*, "Neither the nature of any celestial body nor of any body beneath the heavens is universal, nor is the nature of the whole world universal, for the nature of any single body would [then] be the same [as that of any other]."[52] Such goes just as much for human beings as any other natural object: "It is obvious that any individual thing is one, and singular. Like Peter and John, each man is an individual, and because there exists no man who is not one of a number of individuals, it follows that no man is universal. In the same way we prove that no stone, no tree and, in sum, no thing is universal."[53] When Hobbes suggests that there is no universal human essence, he means this in the sense that there occur no abstract essences having an incorporeal being existing independently of particular material bodies. In the final instance, then, "there is no 'universal nature' at all."[54] In the case of humans and other animate beings, such is revealed through the consideration of the mechanics of sensation and imagination, Hobbesian analysis starting from the embodied, material, and sensuous form of the living thing.[55]

The central fact for political theory deriving from the account of sense-perception is the incapacity of discrete natural persons to identically organize objects through a process of conceptual subsumption grounded in perceivable resemblances that generate similar internal motions. What in *The Elements of Law* Hobbes calls the cognitive or conceptive power— referring to the power of knowing or conceiving—is that faculty by which we produce imaginative representations of the qualities of things.[56] In the process of sensation the motion of objects is imaginatively marked through the production of various types of images. These images, however, are not of the things themselves, but are rather fantasies of the motion of the objects acting upon our senses. Such images must be produced precisely to the extent that these qualities do not naturally adhere in the objects of perception, but are apparitions generated by the mind in response to the movement or motion of the things. Sensuous perception occurs where an object external to the organism is impressed on one or more of this organism's sense organs, producing an internal counterimpression manifesting as a "*seeming*, or *fancy*, which we call sense."[57] The motions of the object, when impressed upon our sensoria, thus stimulate internal motions within us that generate sensible qualities.[58] Perception is just motion, specifically, the stimulation of the internal motion of an organism by the external motion of an object. The perceived qualities are not mere reproductions of the qualities of the object of perception, "For if those Colours, and Sounds, were in the Bodies, or Objects that cause them, they could not bee severed from them."[59] Hence ultimately "image and color is but an apparition unto us of that motion, agitation, or alteration which the object worketh in the brain, or spirits, of some internal substance of the head."[60] Hobbes calls this fact that the perceived qualities are not objective qualities of things, but mere apparitions stimulated by the motion of things, "the great deception of sense."[61]

Sensation is therefore not direct representation, there existing no quality internal to the object that immediately reflects the quality represented to us: "Yet still the object is one thing, the image or fancy is another. So that Sense in all cases, is nothing els but originall fancy, caused (as I have said) by the pressure, that is, by the motion, of externall things upon our Eyes, Eares, and other organs thereunto ordained."[62] As a result of these dynamics of perception, it inevitably will be the case that different individuals perceive in different ways, to the degree that the former are always and everywhere constituted as singular minds with unique sensoria.[63] In *The Elements of Law* Hobbes thus writes, "It is apparent enough, that the smell and taste of the same thing, are not the same to every man, and therefore are not in the thing smelt or tasted, but in the men."[64] This sensorial variety is also highlighted in the more mature *Leviathan*, where Hobbes again notes that "divers men, differ . . . in their Judgement on the senses, of what is pleasant, and unpleasant to the tast, smell, hearing, touch, and sight."[65] And furthermore, as we might expect given the discussion in the previous section, the multiplicity of modes of perception is configured not only by the uniquely constituted modes of sensuous appropriation, but also by the invariability of objective movement, the world not presenting to our sensoria identical motions. As Hobbes writes in the *Anti-White*, "Body or *materia prima* can be changed, and its parts moved in innumerable ways; and by means of motions of this sort it can arouse innumerable fantasies in the minds of percipient creatures, i.e., numerous kinds of images. Granted that it is impossible to know what motions the separate particles of the whole world have, it follows that we cannot know how many varieties of things there are and hence whether or not in the heavens bodies like ours."[66] There is not, in other words, any stable object whose fixity would allow individuals to perceive it identically, even if they were structurally inclined to via the possession of a shared sensorium.

Now, if these sensorial conditions characterize the nature of perception for all forms of animate life, what initially distinguishes humans from other beings capable of voluntary animation is humans' singular capacity for naming, the human experience of imaging exceeding that of animals to the extent that it may be mediated by the use of words. Just as much as any other animal, the human being can think, imagine, discourse, remember, and anticipate. Unlike nonhuman animals, however, humans can employ reason, and this because they are capable of utilizing names to preserve images and communicate conceptions. The persistence of the image of the object after its removal—which becomes increasingly weaker as time progresses—constitutes imagination, which Hobbes defines in terms of *"decaying sense,"*[67] and which we as humans are able to transform into understanding in a unique way through our capacity to organize our conceptions in speech, "the most noble and profitable invention of humanity."[68] Psychic expression is chaotic and disorganized, lacking a determinate trajectory or form.[69] There is no natural necessity to the direction of mental discourse given the diversity of the imagination, itself rooted in the diversity of sense. Hobbes writes, "Because in sense, to one and the same thing perceived, sometimes one thing, sometimes another succeedeth, it comes to pass in time, that in the Imagining of any thing, there is no certainty that we shall Imagine next; Onely this is certain, it shall be something that succeeded the same before, at one time or another."[70] Humans, however, via speech, have a singular ability to impose order on their mental discourse, their succession of one thought to another, and thereby relatively stabilize the flux of the mind.[71]

In light of the ability to impose direction on the succession of thought, we can distinguish between two general types of mental discourse: the first, unguided and without design, where "the thoughts are said to wander, and seem impertinent one to another, as in a Dream"[72]; and as already suggested, the second, a constant expression in which our mental discourse is in some sense regulated according to a plan. Here, "From Desire, ariseth the thought of some means we have seen produce the like of which we ayme at; and from the thought of that, the thought of means to that mean; and so continually, till we come to some beginning within our own power."[73] In the final instance, Hobbes contends that all uniquely human faculties and capacities not innately bound by nature, but which may be "encreased by study and industry," are dependent upon the invention of words and speech.[74] Speech is used to articulate verbally our mental discourse, thereby converting our train of thoughts into a train of words that is able to mediate the social intercourse upon which all human artifice depends. It consists of an order of words whose constituent parts are names, which function as both marks and signs of our thought: as the former preserving our conceptions in the face of the inconstancy of our minds, and as the latter communicating our acquired knowledge to others.[75]

Hobbes is clear in maintaining that names signify our conceptions of things and not the things themselves, although there nevertheless remains a relation between name and thing, even in those instances when that which we name lacks a concrete being, for example as a phantasm or a fiction or a nonexistent.[76] Hobbes writes that "seeing every name has some relation to that which is named, though that which we name be not always a thing that has a being in nature, yet it is lawful for doctrine's sake to apply the word *thing* to whatsoever we name; as if it were all one whether that thing be truly existent or be only feigned."[77] What is in any case true is that all names have a merely arbitrary origin, an origin with no connection to the qualitative substance of the object, for "how can any man imagine that the names of things were imposed from their natures?"[78] It is partly this dissociation of name and being that has led to Hobbes being identified as a "super-nominalist,"[79] "ultranominalist,"[80] or "radical nominalis[t]."[81] Whereas proper names are those singular to one thing, common names are those that denote multiple things, although necessarily in their singularity, each common name subsuming many particular objects on the basis of some perceived similarity of motion, not an essential homogeneity of being. In the latter case then, "every of which though but one Name, is nevertheless the name of divers particular things; in respect all of which together, it is called *Universall*; there being nothing in the world Universall but Names; for the things named are every one of them Individuall and singular."[82] In the final instance, universal names artificially or conventionally gather together a group of particulars, subsumption proceeding not via reference to an ontological participation of the object in some shared natural identity.

Even if the unique human capacity to name allows particular things to be grouped together under common categories, Hobbes wants to stress that these common categories can never exhaust or fully capture the being of the thing. It is thus that "the same thing has names almost beyond number. Anything that is compared with countless [other] things will resemble some in one respect, others in another. So the thing will have a name in common with each thing resembling it in every several comparison; it will therefore have as many names as there are ways in which it may be compared."[83] Such must be the case if universal names refer to objects which are all distinct singularities, there existing no natural unity to the things gathered under the universal name. What matters is the multiplicity of similarities perceived among the diversity of such things so as to allow us to imaginatively organize the singularities under a common name: "For the understanding of the extent of an universal name, we need no other faculty but that of our imagination, by which we remember that such names bring sometimes one thing, sometimes another, into our mind."⁸⁴ It is from the diversity of conceptions of things that there arises a diversity of names, one object generating multiple conceptions and names, while the same conceptions and names may be deployed in relation to differing objects. Ultimately it is the conventional universality of names that is the source of so much misunderstanding, this universality generally being confused with a fictional universality of the thing itself, the name thereby being mistaken for the object. Indeed, it is this failure to grasp the nominalistic character of signification that distinguishes vain from true philosophy, the former collapsing hypothetical and categorical analysis, failing to distinguish between definition, which signifies the relation of names and conceptions, and nature, the being of the objects themselves.⁸⁵

In sum, although Hobbes identifies four grounds upon which names may be generated, the radical singularity of both the objects of the world and the subjects of sense-perception necessitates a nonidentity of linguistic reference, common names lacking an objective basis for the conceptual subsumption of different conceptions of things, which individuals in any case appropriate uniquely as a result of the variance of bodily constitution and education. The inconstancy of signification is thus largely rooted in the diversity of individual beings: "The names of such things as affect us, that is, which please, and displease us, because all men be not alike affected with the same thing, nor the same man at all times, are in the common discourses of men, of *inconstant signification*."⁸⁶ Given the diversity of perception, there is no reasonable basis for expecting a commonality of naming to arise naturally: "For seeing all names are imposed to signifie our conceptions; and all our affections are but conceptions; when we conceive the same things differently, we can hardly avoyd different naming of them. For though the nature of that we conceive, be the same; yet the diversity of our reception of it, in respect of different constitutions of body, and prejudices of opinion, gives every thing a tincture of our different passions."⁸⁷

Difference and the Passions

Hobbes's nominalism can be philosophically extended so as to generate a multitude of political possibilities or imperatives, including democratic ones.⁸⁸ For our purposes here, the key thing to note is the extent to which it commits one to an ontological affirmation of an essential human difference, a nonidentity between individual beings that forecloses the possibility of producing normative standards of life grounded in the continuity of existential experience. In *The Elements of Law* Hobbes notes "the great difference there is in men, from the diversity of their passions."[89] We have seen how humans can attach universal names, which mark and signify conceptions of particular things, to the experience of the motions of these things. In this sense "'perception' is to do not with things themselves but with the words and terms by which we express our judgement about things."[90] We have also seen how the sensorial apparatus of the organism that is the subject of perception is itself singular. This results in the emergence of a diversity in the generation of sense, the motion of objects being appropriated differentially among individuals, ultimately stimulating unique sensible images. Far from being restricted to variation in substantive moral conceptions, which has characterized the greater part of the skeptical pluralist tradition,[91] human difference for Hobbes is traceable to the deep level of sensation, the substratum of human motion.

Such can be acutely revealed through considering Hobbes's discussion of voluntary movement in chapter 6 of *Leviathan* and its conditioning of individual judgment regarding the good and the bad. Here Hobbes distinguishes between two types of motion that can be attributed to animal beings. The first is what he calls vital motion, that "begun in generation, and continued without interruption through their whole life; such as are the *course* of the *Blood*, the *Pulse*, the *Breathing*, the *Concoction*, *Nutrition*, *Excretion*, &c; to which Motions there needs no help of Imagination."[92] The second, which does depend on the imagination, is voluntary motion, such "as to *go*, to *speak*, to *move* any of our limbes in such manner as is first fancied in our minds."[93] Hobbes reminds us that all sense is motion internal to our body generated by the impression made upon our sensoria by the motion of objects external to us. Fancy refers to the relics of such motion that remain after the disappearance of the object and its immediate impression of sense. It is precisely these fancies that stimulate voluntary motion: "And because *going*, *speaking*, and the like Voluntary motions, depend always upon a precedent thought of *whither*, *which way*, and *what*; it is evident, that the Imagination is the first internall beginning of all Voluntary Motion."[94] Although usually imperceptible, those initial motions which are the source of all visible external actions in the world are called endeavors, those oriented toward something that arouses them being appetites, and those oriented away from something being aversions. The presence of the object of our appetite or aversion is what we call love and hate. As Hobbes says, "That which men Desire, they are also said to LOVE: and to HATE those things, for which they have Aversion. So that Desire, and Love, are the same thing; save that by Desire, we always signifie the Absence of the Object; by Love, most commonly the Presence of the same. So also by Aversion, we signifie the Absence; and by Hate, the Presence of the Object."[95]

As is well known, the terms *good* and *evil* for Hobbes thus have relevance only in relation to the objects of desire of specific individual persons, speaking not to persons themselves, nor to any qualities naturally inhering in the object: "'Good, therefore, and 'evil' are applied relatively and *ad personam*. Hence, because the same things do not please or displease everyone, and because they are not the same thing to the same person on every occasion, the same things are not good or bad, beautiful or repellent to all."[96] To the extent that they lack a fixed context manifesting in each circumstance, nothing can be good or evil in itself, these concepts referring only to that which pleases or displeases particular people at particular times: "Since different men desire and shun different things, there must needs be many things that are *good* to some and *evil* to others; so that which is *good* to us is *evil* to our enemies."[97] In the final instance, the diversity of conceptions of good and evil is a natural result of the diversity of individual beings, which results from distinct modes of socialization and the multiplicity of forms of bodily constitution and modalities of sense-perception: "Men's desires differ, as their temperaments, habits and opinions differ; one may see this in the case of things perceived by the senses, by the taste, for instance, or by touch or smell, but it is much more so in everything to do with the ordinary actions of life, where what one man *praises*, i.e., calls *good*, the other *abuses* as *bad*."[98] Ultimately, differing trajectories of desire naturally produce differing patterns of naming, Hobbes asserting that "men give different names, to one and the same thing, from the difference of their own passions."[99] Such renders human passion intrinsically nonthematizable.[100]

Hobbesian difference, however, is irreducible to an external nonidentity of discrete beings, the latter remaining also nonidentical with respect to themselves. If appetite refers to the beginning of an endeavor toward a thing that pleases us, crucially for Hobbes, the trajectory of our appetite (and our aversion) is never determinately fixed given our perpetual internal motion, the flux of human desire thus structuring a continual process of psychic self-alteration. As Hobbes writes, "Because the constitution of a mans body, is in continuall mutation; it is impossible that all the same things should always cause in him the same Appetites, and Aversions: much lesse can all men consent, in the Desire of almost any one and the same object."[101] Not only, then, is there a nonidentity of desire between different organisms, but even within the same organism given the temporality of the appetites. Hobbes specifies this fact concisely in *De Homine*, where he stresses the extent to which pleasures and displeasures are subject to mutation via habituation: "Even if first experiences of something be sometimes displeasing, especially when new or rare, by habit they are rendered not displeasing, and afterwards pleasing; that much can habit change the nature of single men."[102] It is not just the case, then, that goods and evils are relative to the particular pleasures and displeasures of distinct individuals, but also to the same individuals at different moments and in different contexts, the mutability of pleasure producing displacements in any individual's conception of that which they perceive as the object of their good and bad. Hence "good is said to be relative to person, place, and time. What pleaseth one man now, will displease another later; and the same holds true for everyone else."[103] The upshot of such a conception is the recognition of the impossibility of the existence of a natural order of things that is capable of regulating good and evil, the former being simply the object of the appetite of a given person at a given point in time, the latter the object of aversion, subject to the same conditions: "For these words of Good, Evill, and Contemptible, are ever used with relation to the person that useth them: There being nothing simply and absolutely so; nor any common Rule of Good and Evil, to be taken from the nature of the objects themselves; but from the Person of the man (where there is no Common-wealth;) or, (in a Common-wealth,) from the Person that representeth it; or from an Arbitrator or Judge, whom men disagreeing shall by consent set up, and make his sentence the Rule thereof."[104]

Thus far we have been highlighting the internal sources of human difference emanating from the singularity of the organism's sensorium. This constitution, however, does not exhaust the production of such difference, contrary to the suggestion of certain readers. Tom Sorrel, for example, finds reason to doubt Hobbes's account of the extent of variation between persons regarding the good, to the extent that

Hobbes entirely reduces it to a subjectivist account of variation lacking external intervention: "He usually neglects the ways in which appetites and aversions are formed by training or conditioning; consequently, he seems to leave out of account the ways in which patterns of training can enforce a single pattern of values that prevails in a wider community."[105] Far from ignoring the productive effects of socialization on individual desire, however, Hobbes merely rejects the naïve possibility of a community already identical with itself, in which modes of being are rendered sufficiently homogenous so as to universally impose the same social and cultural standards or patterns on all subjects.[106]

Indeed, Hobbes is explicit that despite the arbitrary origin of names, it is not the case that we originate them ourselves as private subjects. The origin of speech is found in an initial imposition of names on conceptions of things through an act of will, those names accepted by others being customarily passed down through the generations. Hence some form of common assent grounds the order of words, which is subsequently perpetuated in time through instruction.[107] Associations of individuals, however, are not uniform, but traversed through by a variety of lines and strata. The self-organization of individuals into communal bodies, whatever their form, does not homogenously impress meaning on individuals in equivalent ways. Names are handed down to us from a variety of sources, often in conflict with one another, and hence the common equivocation and confusion that we see regarding meaning: "We are not the first to devise names; we received them from our nurses, our teachers, our friends, and our associates; and the majority of names have been applied neither accurately nor in a constant and fixed sense, but have been used figuratively and catachrestically."[108] Throughout his work, in fact, Hobbes persistently criticizes the extent to which individuals—and especially the supposedly most educated, such as moral, political, and theological thinkers—fail to deploy words that correspond to their established signification, uncritically adopting the idiosyncratic nomenclature of their marginal teachers and interlocuters. Typical in this respect is John Bramhall, of whom Hobbes writes: "I should wonder how any man, much more a doctor of divinity, should be so grossly deceived, but that I know naturally the generality of men speak the words of their masters by rote, without having any ideas of the things, which the words signify."[109] The inconstancy of language that results from the unreflective deployment of names whose signification is not properly grasped can only lead to general misunderstanding. Hobbes is ultimately led to conclude that "no man living can tell what a Schoolman means by his words."[110] There thus may exist any number of regimes of linguistic reference, rigorous or not, each of which define the meaning of words in their unique way. Human communities, in other words, given the extent of this plurality, are always internally divided, and hence the urgent task of the sovereign to impose an artificial universality on the natural difference, a difference irreducible to a mere methodological individualism.[111]

The role that socialization plays in the conditioning of human desire is revealed with special clarity in an important discussion in *De Homine*. Here Hobbes identifies six potential sources for human inclinations or dispositions toward particular things: the constitution of the body, experience, habit, good fortune, self-opinion, and the influence of authorities. Firstly, variation in the movement of the imagination produces two general divisions: "First, because some dispositions are more acute; whence some people are of a lively disposition, and others a slow one; secondly, of those that are of a quick disposition, because some let their thoughts wander over vast spaces, and some let them revolve around one thing; whence fancy is praiseworthy in some, while judgment is commendable in others."[112] With respect to the latter distinction, the second group has the disposition to excel at philosophy, while the former at "poetry and invention."[113] What is crucial to note, however, is that Hobbes does not affirm that these bodily constitutions are fixed. They are, rather, subject to change and mutation via their interaction with additional sources.[114] Secondly, although objects that are encountered at a first point in time may not please, individuals may become habituated to them through repetition, continued exposure generating a new appreciation for the effects of the thing. Thirdly, experience sharpens our dispositions through providing the opportunity for us to observe causal sequences: "For the human mind proceeds from its reasoning from the known to the unknown; and it cannot perceive the long-term consequences of things without knowledge from the senses, that is, without experience of many consequences."[115] Those who endure the consequences of their actions will be rendered more cautious in their dispositions. Fourthly, social, cultural, and economic factors intervene so as to mold dispositions in innumerable complex ways, beyond exhaustive categorization. For example, "From the goods of fortune, that is, from riches, nobility, or birth, and civil power it happens that dispositions are in some measure made various; for dispositions are frequently made more proud by riches and civil power; for those who can do more demand that they be allowed more, that is, they are more inclined to cause injuries, and they are more unsuited for entering into a society of equitable laws with those who can do less."[116] Fifthly, and closely related, individuals who esteem themselves highly tend not to be dispositionally oriented toward modesty and self-improvement. Such a character marks the aristocratic mind, which considers itself as naturally most appropriate to govern: "And so they judge a state to be badly governed which is not governed as they themselves wish."[117] And sixthly, if an authority who is followed is one who presents good precepts and examples, then the subject will develop a just and reasonable disposition, although if the precepts and examples are unsound the disposition will be ill-informed. Needless to say, the works of classical philosophy produced in ancient Greece and Rome are taken by Hobbes to be instances of corrupting authority, for they "are filled with both examples and precepts that make the people's dispositions hostile to kings."[118]

What *De Homine* ultimately reveals is that the only seemingly natural tendencies of the individual are strongly conditioned by their particular historical encounters.[119] The human being is one that is largely open, the desires of distinct individuals coalescing by nature around only a few tedious objects.[120] It is thus not surprising that many commentators assert that it is impossible to extract from Hobbes's anthropology a positive conception of human nature or psychology,[121] or that the latter is fundamentally receptive to transformation via our self-activity.[122] The Hobbesian conception of human being is best thought not in terms of an affirmative set of fixed traits or characteristics, but rather in terms of a bundle of active and dynamic capacities open to alteration and reconstitution.[123] The fact of social-historical alterity, of the staggering diversity of modes of collective life that we observe in the world, is ultimately grounded in this nondeterminate form of the natural person.

Creativity and Social-Historical Alterity

The fact of human difference, of the lack of a natural homogeneity between sensuous beings, forecloses the possibility of establishing a harmonious social existence grounded in the coalescence of human desire.[124] The lack of a natural principle of order that is capable of holding diverse individuals together so as to perpetuate a shared unity distinguishes human beings from the so-called political animals, whose communion is facilitated by a uniformity uncomplicated by the specificities of human psychology. Hobbes writes in *De Cive* that "it is true that among creatures who live by sense and appetite alone, *accord* of feelings is so long lasting that nothing but their natural appetite is needed to maintain it and thus to keep peace among them. But it is otherwise with men."[125] In this work and in *Leviathan* Hobbes identifies six facts that collectively constitute this difference: (1) animals do not compete over honor and status; (2) the natural appetites of the sociable animals are biologically shared, such that all particular interests coalesce in group interest; (3) lacking reason, animals have no basis to question or interrogate the common organization of life, whereas individuals often attempt to socially innovate on the basis of their estimation of their particular insight or intelligence; (4) lacking speech, animals are incapable of distorting their sensuous affections through attaching to them a moral valuation; (5) animals cannot distinguish between injury and harm, and thereby cannot attribute blame; and (6) to the extent that agreement between animals is natural as opposed to artificial, it requires no external guarantee of its perpetuation.[126] As we have already seen, the direction of all human wills to a common end can only be achieved if the diversity of wills is reduced to a single one that is taken to stand in for all, which "can only happen if each man subjects his *will* to the *will* of a *single* other, to the *will*, that is, of one *Man* or of one *Assembly*, in such a way that whatever one *wills* on matters essential to the common peace may be taken as the *will* of all and each."[127]

The presumption that it is possible to construct a political order grounded in the perception of certain natural principles of human sociality is characteristic of that group of individuals who in *The Elements* Hobbes labels the *dogmatici*, "they that take up maxims from their education, and from the authority of men, or of custom, and take the habitual discourse of the tongue for ratiocination."[128] The *dogmatici* are contrasted with the *mathematici*, learned individuals who derive their conclusions from rigorous logical demonstration, building up their conceptions through the reasoned evaluation of prior principles and their propositional relations: "They proceed from most low and humble principles, evident even to the meanest capacity; going on slowly, and with most scrupulous ratiocination (viz.) from the imposition of name they infer the truth of their first propositions; and from two of the first, a third; and from any two of the three a fourth; and so on, according to the steps of science."[129] Such a method is foreign to the *dogmatici*, including the moral and political philosophers, who far from reconciling controversy through the application of correct method, instead multiply it via the deployment of their particular idiosyncratic approaches, for "in their writings and discourses they take for principles those opinions which are vulgarly received, whether true or false; being for the most part false."[130] Traditional moral philosophy, then, proceeds dogmatically, asserting certain abstract ethical principles derived from particular contingent sources as natural and universal, and grounding subsequent reasoning in such baseless opinions, be they those of human nature, natural law, and so on.[131] Given the lack of a natural morality capable of regulating human passion, true moral philosophy can only refer to the articulation of notions of good and evil in social contexts organized by a determinate civil power: "For Morall Philosophy is nothing else but the Science of what is *Good*, and *Evill*, in the conversation, and Society of man-kind."[132]

What needs to be highlighted is that to maintain that human beings are not naturally directed to life in a specifically civil society is not to assert that they are not naturally inclined to sociality. Such is acknowledged by Hobbes in *De Cive*, where he writes that "I am not therefore denying that we seek each other's company at the prompting of nature. But civil Societies are not mere gatherings; they are Alliances, which essentially require good faith and agreement for their making."[133] In the early "Discourse of Rome," meanwhile, Hobbes writes that "no man is born only for himself," such a condition here being associated with the experience of a merely solitary existence.[134] And in his later debate with Bramhall, Hobbes concedes that it is not possible to identify any historical human populations that lived in a state of nature, even if sometimes Hobbes himself does just this for rhetorical purposes, observing that "it is very likely to be true, that since the creation there never was a time in which mankind was totally without society."[135] It is not quite correct to maintain, then, that the most radical Hobbesian break with the Aristotelian tradition centers on the former's rejection of the latter's affirmation of the human as a "naturally social animal."[136] Yves Charles Zarka, by contrast, is perhaps correct to contend that "Hobbes is situated on the terrain opened by Machiavelli," to the degree that it was the latter who first broke with the Aristotelian heritage that located within the political community a principle of being *spontaneously* uniting individuals, each of whom could be subsumed under a shared natural ethic.[137] Human sociality is irreducible to this type of teleological impulse, some articulation of the former naturally emerging in any human context, even if its precise form cannot be specified a priori via reference to a transcendent regulative standard operative in every context.[138]

Hobbes's rejection of the specifically Aristotelian conception of the political animal is no evidence of a radical psychological egoism,[139] nor a latent methodological individualism of a proto-bourgeois type.[140] Readers of Hobbes are increasingly cognizant of the fact that he was centrally concerned with articulating the nature of intersubjectivity and interdependence within a shared material world,[141] human sociality manifesting itself in a variety of modes of association and cooperation even within the hypothetical context of the state of nature.[142] Indeed, as Richard Tuck observes, Hobbes must assume that individuals possess by nature a minimal sociability so as to facilitate mutual aid and assistance independent of sovereignty, to say nothing of the construction of the latter via covenant.[143] What Hobbes would like to specify is just that one cannot delineate in advance some foundational law of laws governing the form of human sociality, which takes a variety of different forms and is achieved through a variety of different modes. The nature of association is structured by the particular motivations of the associating agents, who are always in possession of unique desires, inclinations, interests, and so on. Hobbes thus writes,

> Closer observation of the causes why men seek each other's company and enjoy associating with each other, will easily reach the conclusion that it does not happen because by nature it could not be otherwise, but by chance. For if man naturally loved his fellow man, loved him, I mean, as his fellow man, there is no reason why everyone would not love everyone equally as equally men; or why every man would rather seek the company of men whose society is more prestigious and useful to him than to others. By nature, then, we are not looking for friends but for honour or advantage from them.[144]

Individuals associate for the sake of the advancement of their particular goods, although the diversity of such goods in any particular social-historical context necessarily prohibits their universal satisfaction and delimits the range of potential forms of association facilitating their negotiation. There cannot be, in other words, any political schema that may be generally instituted as a practical model of social institution. Hence Hobbes is generally not interested—in his three major political works at least—in explicating the specific laws or constitutions of historical regimes, but rather only the nature of sovereign power in the abstract.[145]

Hobbes notes the contingent origin of any commonwealth as early as the "Discourse on the Beginning of Tacitus," writing that "the first form of government in any State is accidental."[146] Specifically, and inconsistently with the more theoretically advanced model of originary democratic foundation that would be established in *The Elements of Law*, monarchy is instituted in social conditions in which a single person possesses power, aristocracy where a few do, and democracy where the many do, government being thereby established "according to the condition the Founder happens to be of."[147] Beyond this particular condition, furthermore, Hobbes also notes in the *Horae Subsecivae* that the differing historical conditions inhering in any nation at the point of foundation generates unique customs, and that the specific form of civil law must be attuned to this social-historical particularity should it be functionally stable.[148] Contra the classical tradition, and consistent with his philosophical nominalism, Hobbes's political principles do not have a metaphysical source but are always instituted in unique ways as a result of their leaning on concrete-particular historical inheritances.[149] The accidental origins of the emergence of communal bodies ensures that they cannot be finitely organized on any categorical list, no matter how exhaustive. Speaking of nonsovereign political entities in *Leviathan*, Hobbes thus writes: "The variety of Bodies Politique, is almost infinite: for they are not onely distinguished by the several affairs, for which they are constituted, wherein there is an unspeakable diversity, but also by the times, places, and numbers, subject to many limitations."[150]

What the diversity of forms of social association—including the diversity of forms of commonwealth—reflect is the fact that human beings themselves have sole responsibility for determining the conditions of their communion with one another, independently of any necessary external constraints that would delimit the political potential germinating with the specific social-historical situation.[151] As many readers recognize, the Hobbesian project presupposes a fundamental and unique human capacity for artifice.[152] Victoria Kahn, for example, specifies the relationship between Hobbes's emphasis on artifice, linguistic agreement, and the lack of prepolitical moral principles that would provide a natural ground for human association: "The human capacity for construction is the link between a materialist account of natural law and obligation as the products of linguistic agreements: precisely because humans have no natural inclination to justice and virtue, these must be artificially created by means of human institutions and inventions."[153] In the final instance, the creativity of the human being, reflected in its openness to self-alteration, is the source of social-historical creativity, itself reflected in the variety of modes of collective life that we observe in the world. Ultimately for Hobbes history just is creation, the institution of social form in time.[154] The lucid recognition of this capacity to so institute a world open to human interrogation and intervention is the first condition for democratic life.

Chapter 4

Hobbesian Equality-in-Difference

In chapter 3, I detailed Hobbes's rejection of the idea that the institution of a political community may lean on universally valid exterior standards that guide or regulate the process of foundation. Quentin Skinner has shown that this notion that the commonwealth is founded independently of such prepolitical norms that would structure it was taken to be a general assumption of much parliamentarian thought in seventeenth-century England: "The parliamentarian argument is that what exists in nature is not states and governments but simply free communities endowed with all the necessary means to regulate their own affairs."[1] Such an assumption is given a notable expression, for example, in Henry Parker's 1642 *Observations*, where it is claimed that "If Nations by common consent, can neither set limits, or judge of limits set to sovereignty, but must look upon it as a thing meerly divine, and above al humain consent or comprehension, then all nations are equally slaves."[2] As Skinner notes, to the degree that Parker and other parliamentarian writers see civil societies as simply the products of human will, the latter setting the parameters of the former, then such leads them to democratic conclusions: "If what exists in nature is not government but merely the capacity to institute it, then the whole body of the people must count as the authors of whatever authority is subsequently placed over them."[3] Despite their rhetoric, however, the greater part of parliamentarian writers were no democrats. As we have seen, Hobbes identifies the "democraticall gentlemen" as thoroughly oligarchic in orientation, to the degree that they wished merely to substitute one group of social elites monopolizing decision-making authority for another. Such actors may very well have recognized the openness of the world to autonomous human intervention, but they generally did not recognize the equal capacity of all citizens to so intervene in an equivalently competent mode, this nonrecognition legitimating the exclusion of parts of the citizenry from legislative processes.

If democracy as the autonomous self-institution of the social world by the demos depends upon the first condition, this condition seems insufficient to in itself legitimate this particular form of regime, to the extent that it says nothing about the demos being necessarily endowed with the instituting power. Genuine commitment to democratic life as universal citizen participation in legislative authority must thus, secondly, affirm the fundamental equality of all citizens, none of whom are differentiated from one another on the basis of the possession or nonpossession of any unique skill, knowledge, intelligence, and so on, that would ethically validate the existence of a particular right to rule belonging only to some.[4] Democracy, in other words, refuses all titles to govern. As is well known, it is on this basis that all citizens have a right to participate in major assembly activity, and why the majority of political offices are occupied through the modes of rotation or sortition, election being used only in those instances where the office indeed presumes a particular competency or ability that the average citizen cannot be presumed to possess. It is precisely such a rejection of all qualifications and titles to rule, and the correlative affirmation of a natural human equality, that we find in Hobbes's thought. Needless to say, however, the recognition of natural human equality hardly generates for Hobbes a normative democratic imperative. Equality is notably one of those conditions that renders the natural state one of perpetual anxiety and uncertainty, as "from this equality of ability, ariseth equality of hope in the attaining of our Ends. And therefore if any two men desire the same thing, which nevertheless they cannot both enjoy, they become enemies; and in the way to their End, (which is principally their owne conservation, and sometimes their delectation only,) endeavour to destroy, or subdue one an other."[5]

As I will note in the section below, like so much of Hobbes's intellectual endeavor, the discussion of equality must be situated within the context of the Aristotelian inheritance.[6] On the most obvious level, Hobbes is rejecting Aristotle's affirmation of an inequality of intelligences which becomes politically expressed through differential capacities for rule, the contention that "some things are distinguished right from birth, some suited to rule and others to being ruled."⁷ Hence, most famously, Aristotle contends that natural slaves are fit to be ruled to the extent that they, despite understanding reason, lack the capacity to exercise it themselves and that women, although they possess the deliberative reason lacking in natural slaves, are wanting in authoritative reason and are thus less qualified to rule than men.⁸ Readers of Hobbes have observed the extent to which his rejection of the notion that membership in a supposedly natural group category delimits rational potential produced a variety of conclusions that were, by the standards of the history of Western political thought as developed at the time, quite radical. In the introduction to their important volume on Hobbes and feminist thought, for example, Joanne Wright and Nancy Hirschmann observe that "Hobbes stands with Plato as one of the relatively few thinkers in the canon of Western political philosophy who entertained the idea that women's subordinate position might be the result of convention rather than nature."⁹ Needless to say, however, as Carole Pateman has notably pointed out, Hobbes's recognition of the naturally free and equal status of men and women does not prevent him from thinking a social contract that excludes the latter from participation and ultimately subordinates them to the former in civil society.¹⁰

A distinct operation is at play with respect to Hobbes's treatment of indigenous American persons. On the one hand, Hobbes quite obviously reproduces a particular early modern American imaginary that views indigenous societies as fundamentally deficient in relation to European ones, rhetorically deploying, in an effort to frighten his audience, an image of American life as situated within a historical state of nature, and thus subject to all of the incommodities of the latter. This operation assumes even more significance when we consider that Hobbes, through his involvement in the Virginia Company and Somers Island Company, would almost certainly be familiar with the complex social and political structures of various North American indigenous societies. Noel Malcolm has posed the question as to why precisely Hobbes failed to deploy his unique knowledge, sourced for instance from the descriptions compiled by Virginia Company member Samuel Purchas: "The answer must lie mainly in his distaste for anything that might tie his argument to empirical questions of fact. But it may also be suspected that the data raised more difficulties for Hobbes than they solved . . . he must have been aware, if he had read accounts such as that of Purchas, that some Indian tribes did conform to his model of commonwealth."¹¹ Rather than acknowledge this conformity, Hobbes deliberately suppresses much of his political knowledge, rhetorically treating American societies in a reductive and simplistic way—as manifestations of the natural state—so as to advance his project.[12] At the same time as Hobbes undertakes this vulgarization, however, he seems to clearly affirm, and this time contrary to the dominant intellectual assumptions of his age, that indigenous Americans possessed the same complete range of intellectual capacities and the same potential for reason as Europeans, it being lack of method accounting for allegedly varying levels of technical, cultural, or scientific development.[13] As Hobbes rhetorically asks in *De Corpore* with respect to the "wits" of "the Americans": "Have not all men one kind of soul, and the same faculties of mind? What then makes the difference, except philosophy?"[14]

If the facts detailed in the previous two paragraphs regarding Hobbes's refusal to circumscribe rational potential on the basis of membership in a particular group entity are generally acknowledged, in this chapter I suggest that his thinking extends well beyond them and in fact affirms a radical equality of all individual natural persons. It is this equality that readers of Hobbes have had so much difficulty accepting, often refusing the plausibility of the principle being affirmed sincerely.[15] One of the most strident critics of the attribution to Hobbes of an affirmation of natural equality, for example, is Leon Harold Craig. Indeed, Craig more generally rejects the tendency of readers to accept at face value various of Hobbes's premises regarding human nature, which for him "are philosophically indefensible . . . I can only presume, given such ample evidence of Hobbes's mental acuity, that he understands this at least as well as I do."[16] With respect to the question of equality in particular, Craig writes that it is merely a "bogus argument so flattering to the vast herds of mediocre minds," for Hobbes "could not possibly have supposed [this argument] would convince anyone really intelligent and thoughtful."[17]

As for Hobbes himself, he contends that if certain individuals are scandalized by the thought of human equality, finding it implausible or even inconceivable, such results only from their own erroneous overestimation of their capacities in relation to others. Incredulity at the idea of equality "is but a vain conceit of ones owne wisdome, which almost all men think they have in a greater degree, than the Vulgar."[18] Such an exaggeration of one's faculties, however, is perhaps nevertheless to be expected, it being grounded in an understanding of one's genuine ability. It is not that those who judge themselves to be intellectually superior lack intelligence, but rather that they are only just as intelligent as every other person, the failure to recognize the latter fact being a consequence of their proximity to their own ability. Hobbes writes, "For such is the nature of men, that howsoever they may acknowledge many others to be more witty, or more eloquent, or more learned; Yet they will hardly believe there be many so wise as themselves: For they see their own wit at hand, and other mens at a distance. But this proveth rather that men are in that point equall, than unequall. For there is not ordinarily a greater signe of the equall distribution of any thing, than that every man is contented with his share."[19]

There is, however, a second basis upon which readers of Hobbes reject the notion of a literal equality of natural persons, one that can be evaluated in light of the discussion in chapter 3. In the context of Hobbes's emphasis on the irreducible singularity of every living organism as a natural body, and the consequent diversity of sense and imagination, it might seem strange for him to assert human equality as a natural fact. Perhaps in response to this seeming tension, an additional group of commentators attempts to explain away the affirmation of equality, not in terms of a supposed facetiousness, but rather in terms of pragmatic necessity. Equality from this perspective is not a real fact, but rather a presupposition that all must merely acknowledge as real for peaceable life to be possible. As Hobbes himself writes, for instance, "Individuals *ought to admit* amongst themselves equality."[20] Picking up on the idea of the affirmation of equality as a mere admission, Kinch Hoekstra makes the case that Hobbesian equality is not intended to ultimately be read as physical or ontological, but only political. That is to say, "It is not because we are equal that Hobbes says that we ought to treat each other as equals; rather, it is because we ought to treat each other as equals that Hobbes says that we are equal."[21] It is equal treatment alone—the renunciation of any and all special privileges within civil society on the basis of perceived superiority—that facilitates sovereign rule. As evidence for his position on the mere conventionality of the admittance of equality, Hoekstra notes that Hobbes himself specifies that individuals remain naturally unequal in all four aspects of human nature that he discusses: strength of body, experience, reason, and passion. If such is the case, then the affirmation of equality can only be read in terms of the preconditions for the preservation of civil peace, as a conventional acknowledgment of equal respect and equal status under the rule of the sovereign. Literally, however, the best we can do is assert the "truism that those who have substantially equal natures (being of the same age, education, etc.) are naturally substantially equal."[22]

What I will suggest in this chapter is that the problem with such readings is the extent to which they seem to reduce the idea of natural equality to that of an ideal of a literal equality of characteristics or traits. It is clear that for Hobbes human nature cannot be reduced to the possession of a set of universal properties given the fact of human difference that we already detailed. Differing life histories or experiences, the irregularity of the passions, variance in bodily constitution, and so on, do not constitute inequality, for equality is irreducible to identity, the latter remaining always an ontological impossibility.[23] Hobbes is not theorizing an equality-in-identity, but rather an equality-in-difference. More specifically, each individual is equally capable of practically deploying their natural reason for the sake of the articulation of their highly specific goods and the modes through which these goods are most likely to be actualized. Equality is thus not a conceptual representation of the substantive possession of equivalent traits, abilities, or passions, but rather of the universal formal capacity to reason about objects, the interest in which is structured by necessarily particular traits, abilities, and passions. Ultimately human difference is thus not a refutation of Hobbesian equality, but a reflection of it.

Equality as Natural Law

The theoretical place of the concept of equality within Hobbes's civil science, and in particular within his articulation of the function of the laws of nature, is well known, being reproduced more or less identically in each of the three major variants of Hobbes's system. In *The Elements of Law* the tenth law of nature states "*that every man acknowledge other for his equal.*"[24] In *De Cive* the eighth law of nature states "*everyone should be considered equal to everyone.*"[25] And in *Leviathan* the ninth law of nature states "*that every man acknowledge other for his Equall by Nature,*" the violation of this law constituting pride.[26] Far from being a merely formal acknowledgment designed to facilitate peaceful civic relations, Hobbes is clear that this reflects a real condition, specifically, the nonexistence of any titles to govern grounded in naturally occurring intellectual disparities between persons. That Hobbes's discussion of equality unfolds under the sign of specifically political assumptions regarding legislative competencies is emphasized through each work's contrasting of this natural condition with the false presuppositions underlying Aristotle's defense of natural hierarchy. With specific reference to the Aristotelian conception of differential human being, Hobbes writes in *The Elements:*

> The question, which is the better man, is determinable only in the estate of government and policy, though it be mistaken for a question of nature, not only by ignorant men, that think one man's blood better than another's by nature; but also by him, whose opinions are at this day, and in these parts of greater authority than any other human writings (Aristotle). For he putteth so much difference between the powers of men by nature, that he doubteth not to set down, as the ground of all his politics, that some men are by nature worthy to govern, and others by nature ought to serve.[27]

Although political inequality may be introduced into the civil state to the degree that the institution of the latter requires individuals to give up their right to all things, including legislative right, certain things remain impossible to alienate, as I will examine in more detail in chapter 5.

De Cive reiterates that any inequality that we observe in civil society is the product of the particular organization of civil law, not a reflection of a hierarchy of cognitive ability or capacity, as someone like Aristotle presumes. Indeed, Aristotle founds his defense of social and political inequality on precisely this basis: "I know that in the first book of the *Politics* Aristotle asserts as a foundation of all political knowledge that some men have been made by nature worthy to rule, others to serve, as if Master and slave were distinguished not by agreement among men, but by natural aptitude, i.e., by their knowledge or ignorance."[28] Such a position, in Hobbes's account, is contrary to all reason and experience, "For hardly anyone is so naturally stupid that he does not think it better to rule himself than to let others rule him. Nor in a conflict between the wise and the strong are the wise always or often superior to the strong. If then men are equal by nature, we must recognize their equality."[29] Ultimately all historical expressions of inequality in actually existing societies are unnatural to the extent that they emerge from human artifice. As Hobbes puts it, "All men are equal to each other by nature. Our actual inequality has been introduced by civil law."[30] *Leviathan* similarly emphasizes that any perceivable inequality within civil society is purely conventional. As he puts it, "The inequality that now is, has bin introduced by the Lawes civill."[31] Again it is Aristotle who is largely to blame for the popularization of the false identity between distinctions in social status and distinctions in natural capacity, where the former are interpreted as mere reflections of the latter: "I know that Aristotle in his first booke of his Politiques, for a foundation of his doctrine, maketh men by Nature, some more worthy to Command, meaning the wiser sort (such as he thought himselfe to be for his Philosophy;) others to Serve, (meaning those that had strong bodies, but were not Philosophers by consent of men, but by difference of Wit: which is not only against experience."[32]

From this general precept of natural equality there logically follow several subordinate ones. To begin with, what *De Cive* identifies as the principle of humility requires that whatsoever rights individuals intend to maintain for themselves after the mutual conveyance of right, they must grant the same to all others.[33] Individuals can thus not claim any special privileges or rights for themselves, there no longer existing a ground for such privilege after the rejection of natural hierarchies of an Aristotelian type.[34] In *The Elements of Law* this principle is equated with that of equity itself, although in *De Cive* and *Leviathan* the latter concept is identified as a separate law. The centrality of the concept of equity to Hobbes's thought has been noted by many readers, with some in fact identifying it as the fundamental element structuring his moral philosophy as a whole.[35] Put most simply, equity is "that habit by which we allow equality of nature."[36] Larry May has suggested that Hobbes's discussion implies that unlike all the other laws of nature, equity presupposes civil society, for it specifies that the application of the principle is relevant to the activity of one entrusted to make binding judgments on social relations between persons: "It is that principle of morality which can *only* be applicable in civil society."[37] Crucially, then, it provides an alternative standard of moral evaluation within the commonwealth that is independent of that of justice.[38] Recall that justice refers to the keeping of covenants, and that the sovereign is incapable of doing any injustice to its subjects as a consequence of the fact that it is not a party to the social contract, and thus not bound by any act of promise. In relation to justice, then, equity "has a different normative force,"[39] for as an acknowledgment of natural equality it does not depend exclusively on the conventional establishment of a standard of behavior legislated by an authorized power. On the contrary, it itself is capable of serving as a measure by which that power is evaluated.

Consider, for example, various of Hobbes's reflections on legal right. In a discussion of the scope for interpretation of positive law in *Leviathan*, he notes that neither sovereigns nor duly appointed judges are bound in their interpretation of the law by prior precedent.[40] Any individual may err in their judgment, rendering a judicial decision contrary to equity, such inequity not being thereby legitimated and bound to repeat itself over time. Rather, interpreters of the law must perpetually interrogate and scrutinize established decisions in order to comprehend equity in ever greater detail: "All the Sentences of precedent Judges that have ever been, cannot all together make a Law contrary to naturall Equity: Nor any Examples of former Judges, can warrant an unreasonable Sentence, or discharge the present Judge of the trouble of studying what is Equity (in the case he is to Judge,) from the principles of his own naturall reason."[41] Indeed, the first mark of a good judge is "*a right understanding of that principall Law of Nature called Equity*," this precept not being grasped through the study of existing texts, but rather the reflective deployment of one's own natural reason.[42] Equity is thus the ultimate standard of evaluation, and existing legal norms must be continually probed in light of it.[43]

In *Leviathan* the concept of equity is introduced in a relatively narrow form, the eleventh law of nature stating that "*if a man be trusted to judge between man and man, it is a precept of the Law of Nature, that he deale Equally between them*. For without that, the Controversies of men cannot be determined but by Warre."[44] Otherwise formulated, this law maintains that one must affirm "the equall distribution to each man, of that which in reason belongeth to him."[45] Far from being limited to the application of a principle of impartiality of judgment in civil dispute, however, the precept eventually opens up and extends into a larger domain of equality of distribution, as revealed in the transition to the twelfth law, which states "*that such things as cannot be divided, be enjoyed in Common, if it can be*."[46] As to those things that can be neither divided nor enjoyed in common, they are to be distributed via the democratic mode of lot: "Then, The Law of Nature, which prescribeth Equity, requireth, *That the Entire Right; or else, (making the use alternate,) the First Possession, be determined by Lot*. For equall distribution, is of the Law of Nature; and other means of equall distribution cannot be imagined."[47]

This conceptual movement is consistent with the narrative in the earlier two texts, the equitable division of right logically implying a principle of distributive justice in things more generally.[48] Hobbes is clear that the sphere of equity as distributive justice includes matters relating to the social distribution of resources within society. Hence, for example, an element of equal justice is equal taxation (which should take the form of the equal taxation of consumption as opposed to overall wealth or income), while, as we will see in chapter 5 during our discussion of the true liberty of subjects, any individual who is unable to provide for their own means of subsistence via their labor should be provided for by the commonwealth and not be dependent on private charity.[49] *The Elements of Law* articulates clearly what is at stake: "For when a man alloweth to every man alike, the allowance he maketh will be in the same proportion, in which are the numbers of men to whom they are made. And this is it men mean by distributive justice, and is properly termed EQUITY."[50] Hence the ethical demand that, in situations in which there do not exist prior covenants regulating distribution, "Things that cannot be divided should be used in common, if possible, and (if there is enough of a thing) each should have as much as he wants. But if there is not enough of the thing, then it should be used in fixed shares and proportionately to the number of users."[51] And finally, in cases where the thing in question is incapable of being either divided or used in common, the subsequent law of nature specifies that its use should be apportioned via lot or rotation, the latter techniques of which Hobbes explicitly identifies as affirming the principle of equality.[52] By these means "there is no other way of equality, and equality is the law of nature."[53] In recognizing that these distributive modes affirm a natural human equality, Hobbes thus calls attention to a key characteristic of democracy obscured by those readers who want to reduce Hobbesian democratic potential to aristocratic representative forms. As Hobbes is keenly aware, historically the primary mechanisms for filling offices in democratic societies, precisely to the degree that they reject political stratification grounded in differentiated capacities, are these two modes, and "besides these two ways, there can no other equality be imagined."[54]

Natural Reason and the Equality of Intelligences

Consistent with his treatment of the form of natural law more generally, which will be explicated in chapter 5, Hobbes's discussion of equality within the context of the articulation of the laws of nature says little positive about equality's substance. The revelation of the practical meaning and significance of Hobbesian equality thus depends on supplementary discussions to be found elsewhere. A clue regarding the issue, and in particular with respect to the relation between equality and human difference, is revealed in a discussion in chapter 10 of *The Elements of Law*. As we are familiar with, Hobbes notes first that there exists an ontological human difference that is partially expressed through the identifiable diversity of passion that characterizes the species, for "we see by experience, that joy and grief proceed not in all men from the same causes, and that men differ much in constitution of body, whereby, that which helpeth and furthereth vital constitution in one, and is therefore delightful, hindreth and crosseth it in another, and causeth grief."[55] Now, any apparent distinction between individual intelligences emerges from this natural diversity. Hobbes is clear, however, that such distinctions remain in fact merely apparent. Indeed, shortly after noting the difference in the form of bodily constitution in *The Elements*, he goes on to note that such does not foreclose the possibility of thinking an equality of intelligences.[56] If we identify the latter with the capacity for proper ratiocination, we see that obstacles to the development and practice of reason are not traceable to cognitive deficiency, but rather improper instruction. Hobbes thus writes, "Certainly men are not otherwise so unequal in capacity as the evidence is unequal of what is taught by the mathematicians, and what is commonly discoursed of in other books: and therefore if the minds of men were all of white paper, they would almost equally be disposed to acknowledge whatsoever should be in right method, and right ratiocination delivered unto them."[57] Equality for Hobbes is ultimately expressed primarily through, not the equal capacity to kill, but the equal capacity to reason.

De Cive reiterates the point that the variation of individual desires, and the differing pleasures and displeasures that subsequently result from this variation, does not contradict the principle of equality.[58] This is because for Hobbes natural equality is expressed through the equal potential to practically reason, and in particular, the equal potential to practically reason about difference. That is to say, all individuals are equally capable of deploying natural reason in order to identify their various goods and outline as far as possible, given the contingency of the world as detailed in chapter 3, the form of relation between the desired consequents and the manifold antecedents relevant to these goods' realization. Hobbesian equality in this sense is not a conceptual representation of a substantive identity between natural persons so much as another expression of Hobbes's nominalism. At most, it speaks only to a thin identity considered in terms of a rational potential that affirms difference through its very actualization, human beings separating themselves from one another through the exercise of the universal capacity. Far from positing an homogeneity of being, as represented, for example, in the universal possession of a set of identical traits, characteristics, or tendencies, the concept highlights human nonidentity, or the fundamental fact of equality-in-difference.[59]

A sensorial nonidentity resulting in individuals being more or less close to the truth cannot be the basis for the establishment of an intellectual hierarchy, for one cannot falsely appropriate objects sensuously. It is important to note the distinction between falsity and merely tacit erring. Erring refers to sensuous misperception, as for example when individuals misidentify images as things themselves. Hobbes writes that "errors of this sort are common to all things that have sense; and yet the deception proceeds neither from our senses, nor from the things we perceive; but from ourselves while we feign such things as are but mere images to be something more than images. But neither things, nor imaginations of things, can be said to be false, seeing they are truly what they are."[60] Falsity, however, takes a different form, it being grounded neither in sense nor in the nature of things, but rather the misuse of names: "For names have their constitution, not from the species of things, but from the will and consent of men. And hence it comes to pass, that men pronounce *falsely*, by their own negligence, in departing from such appellations of things as are agreed upon, and are not deceived neither by the things, nor by the sense."[61] Philosophical error is not the result of misperception, but rather of the misapplication of words to conceptions: "Men can never be deceived in the conception of things, though they may be deceived by giving unto them wrong terms or appellations, different from those which are commonly used and constituted to signify their conceptions."[62]

As we recall, standards of truth and falsity adhere only in the realm of speech, and thus depend above all on the establishment and maintenance of a stable order of words: "Seeing then that *truth* consisteth in the right ordering of names in our affirmations, a man that seeketh precise *truth*, had need to remember what every name he uses stands for; and place it accordingly; or else he will find himself entangled in words."[63] Indeed, such an entanglement characterizes what Hobbes identifies as the four abuses of speech, each negatively corresponding to its opposite counterpart, one of the proper uses of speech.[64] It is precisely because truth in speech takes the form that it does that Hobbes is able to posit geometry as a model elucidating the nature of the former: "And therefore in Geometry, (which is the onely Science that it hath pleased God hitherto to bestow on mankind,) men begin at settling the significations of their words; which settling of significations, they call *Definitions*; and place them in the beginning of their reckoning."[65] Again, just as speech must begin with the proper definition of names, so in geometry we start by fixing significations through the construction of a system of definition that orients subsequent reasoning.

Although sensuous perception and memory do constitute knowledge, their immediacy excludes them from the realm of philosophy, which depends on ratiocination, that is to say, computation considered as addition and subtraction, although a computation irreducible to the quantitative calculation of number.[66] In *Leviathan* Hobbes thus defines reason as "nothing but *Reckoning* (that is, Adding and Subtracting) of the Consequences of generall names agreed upon, for the *marking* and *signifying* of our thoughts; I say *marking* them, when we reckon by our selves; and *signifying*, when we demonstrate, or approve our reckonings to other men."[67] All reasoning is reducible to this process of conceiving a sum of elements via addition or a remainder via subtraction. That being said, the nature of the elements being computed are specific to the domain of investigation in question. If in arithmetic we add and subtract numbers, in geometry we add and subtract lines, angles, planes, and so on; in logic we add and subtract names, as in combining two names to produce an affirmation, two affirmations for a syllogism, and multiple syllogisms for a demonstration; in politics we add and subtract compacts and agreements in order to determine duties; and in jurisprudence we add and subtract laws and facts to formulate rules of right and wrong action. Hobbes concludes that "in summe, in what matter soever there is place for *addition* and *subtraction*, there also is place for *Reason*; and where these have no place, there *Reason* has nothing at all to do."[68] Truth refers to nothing other than propositional truth, a true proposition being one in which the predicate contains its subject, a false proposition being one in which it does not.[69] Now, to the extent that truth and falsity are exclusively articulated through speech, among beings that lack speech there can exist no truth or falsity: "For though some brute creatures, looking upon the image of a man in a glass, may be affected with it, as if it were the man himself, and for this reason fear it or fawn upon it in vain; yet they do not apprehend it as true or false, but only like; and in this they are deceived."[70] If only human beings possess the faculties requisite for reasoning, however, there nevertheless remain no distinctions to be made between particular or groups of human beings when it comes to the application of this formal capacity.[71]

That all individuals possess by nature an equal potential for rationality is affirmed at the very beginning of *De Corpore*, where Hobbes writes that "every man brought Philosophy, that is, Natural Reason, into the world with him."[72] The problem, however, is that this germ, which is the capacity for natural reason, has not been properly cultivated, many individuals losing their way in complex reckonings as a result of lack of instruction in proper method. Hobbes concedes that most individuals in his historical environment have been improperly socialized such that they are unable to grasp truth, the specific trajectory of their passions overwhelming the rational faculties that would facilitate the acquisition of the former. He writes that "if we consider the far greatest part of mankind, not as they should be, but as they are, as men whom either the study of acquiring wealth or preterments, or whom the appetite of sensual delights, or the impatience of meditating, or the rash embracing of wrong principles, have made unapt to discuss the truth of things."[73] Under such conditions the relationship between reason and emotion is configured in a counterproductive mode. We can recall that in *De Homine* Hobbes calls emotions *"perturbations* of the mind," to the degree that they have the capacity to interrupt "right reasoning," the imposition of appetite in its immediacy overwhelming rationality so as to short-circuit calculation: "Although the real good must be sought in the long term, which is the job of reason, appetite seizeth upon a present good without foreseeing the greater evils that necessarily attach to it. Therefore appetite perturbs and impedes the operation of reason; whence it is rightly called a *perturbation*."[74] Crucially, however, there is nothing about the particular form of configuration of the relation between reason and passion that may be traced to biological differences in cognitive ability, and to this degree, the potential for correction via exposure to productive pedagogical modes is always latent. Hence this is what Hobbes sees as his educational goal: "My purpose is, as far forth as I am able, to lay open the few and first Elements of Philosophy in general, as so many seeds from which pure and true Philosophy may hereafter spring up little by little."[75]

If the basic principles of moral philosophy upon which peaceful life in common depend, for example, are not generally known, this is not a failure of natural intelligence but rather a failure of pedagogy, a failure of a society to adequately educate and socialize its members. Indeed, Hobbes's entire intellectual project, far from being exclusively targeted at a political or any other class of elites, was intended to function as an exercise in popular education looking toward the rectification of this failure.[76] Reflecting back in "The Prose Life," he highlights the degree to which his civil science was directed to, and thus capable of being comprehended by, the generality of individuals: "He wrote not merely to be read and heard by scholars, but in order that he might be understood by all thinking men of sound judgement, in prose that was simple and direct, not in rhetoric."[77] Such a project of universal socialization is a feasible historical one precisely to the degree that all people everywhere possess the same natural intellectual capacities. To quote Hobbes's relevant question once again, "Have not all men one kind of soul, and the same faculties of mind?"[78] In the final instance, Hobbes's commitment to pedagogy as the primary mode for the securing of the safety of the people via the preservation of sovereignty is itself premised on the recognition that the rational principles upon which the commonwealth is created can be grasped adequately by any person. As Hobbes puts it in *Behemoth*, "The Rules of *Just* and *Vniust* sufficiently demonstrated, and from Principles euident to the meanest capacity, haue not been wanting . . . But they are few in respect of the rest of men, whereof many cannot read, many though they can, haue no leisure, and of them that haue leisure the greatest part haue their minds wholly imployed, and taken vp by their priuate businesses or pleasures. So that it is impossible that the multitude should euer learne their duty but from the Pulpit, and vpon Holy-days. But then and from thence it is, that they learned their disobedience."[79]

It is not true, as is commonly supposed, that only an exclusive class composed of learned intellectual elites is capable of understanding, for understanding is just a matter of will and interest in the correct deployment of natural reason. The commonality of citizens are certainly capable of error and subject to their passions, but such is a liability with respect to all natural persons, no matter their social position, and perhaps even to a greater degree with respect to elites. Hobbes thus writes:

> But they say again, that though the Principles be right, yet Common people are not of capacity enough to be made to understand them. I should be glad, that the Rich, and Potent Subjects of a Kingdome, or those that are accounted the most Learned, were no lesse incapable than they. But all men

know, that the obstructions to this kind of doctrine, proceed not so much from the difficulty of the matter, as from the interest of them that are to learn. Potent men, digest hardly any thing setteth up a Power to bridle their affections; and Learned men, any thing that discovereth their errours, and thereby lesseneth their Authority: the Commonpeoples minds, unlesse they be tainted with dependence on the Potent, or scribbled over with the opinions of their Doctors, are like clean paper, fit to receive whatsoever by Publique Authority shall be imprinted in them.[80]

The so-called learned are just as subject to their narrow passions and interests as anyone else, no human being having the capacity to disembody themselves so as to function as a perfectly rational actor. In short, the generality of citizens is completely fit for education in the principal matters of politics: "I conclude, therefore, that in the instruction of the people in the Essentiall Rights (which are the Naturall, and Fundamentall Lawes) of Soveraignty, there is no difficulty, (whilest a Soveraign has his Power entire,) but what proceeds from his own fault, or the fault of those whom he trusteth in the administration of the Common-wealth; and consequently, it is his Duty, to cause them so to be instructed."[81]

The Plurality of Reasons

It might seem that Hobbes deploys the term *reason* in an ambiguous sense. On the one hand, as we have noted above, he is adamant that all individuals possess an equal capacity for natural reason. On the other hand, he stresses the irreducibility of reason to a singular expression, emphasizing the presence within any social context of a multiplicity of different private reasons. The double use of the terminology is a reflection of the diversity of individual goods, the matter with which private reasons work. Recall that the variety of names arises naturally as a consequence of the variety of the human sensoria, there being "scarce two men agreeing what is to be called good, and what evil; what liberality, what prodigality; what valor, what temerity."[82] There is thus no object that is intrinsically or naturally good, or as Hobbes says, "simply good."[83] Discussion of the formal capacity to reckon from definition in the abstract must thus be distinguished from reference to any concrete-particular process of reckoning in which definitions are configured in a specific mode. Hobbes importantly redefines right reason as the reason of a particular individual, independent of reference to a substantive ethical content.[84] It is precisely the failure to distinguish between expressions of right reasons, thereby taking one's own reason as inherently universal, that characterizes the greater part of traditional philosophical thought.[85]

Indeed, Hobbes traces the origin of the word *heresy* to disputes in ancient Greece over matters of moral and political philosophy, the failure of the philosophers to unequivocally engage one another with a fixed vocabulary in which the proper signification of terms was correctly grasped and affirmed by all parties informing the generation of rival sects grounded in private meaning: "After the study of philosophy began in Greece, and the philosophers, disagreeing amongst themselves, had started many questions, not only about things natural, but also moral and civil; because every man took what opinion he pleased, each several opinion was called a *heresy*; which signified no more than a private opinion, without reference to truth or falsehood."[86] Hobbes thus describes the work of such moral philosophers as nothing "but a description of their own Passions."[87] Hence they disagree among themselves on the fundamental matters of politics and ethics, their particular positions merely reflecting their differing and necessarily private sensibilities: "In so great diversity of taste, there is nothing generally agreed on; but every one doth (as far as he dares) whatsoever seemeth good in his owne eyes, to the subversion of Common-wealth."[88]

Given that the application of different reasons will produce different conclusions on the basis of a nonidentity of signification rooted in the diversity of sensuous perception, the potential for dispute is permanent. The resolution of any dispute between two or more parties can only be definitively reconciled through submitting the dispute to an arbiter, whose judgment will stand in for right reason.[89] The latter, right reason considered not as a private but public reason, cannot be established in any other way "in all debates of what kind so ever," given the "wont of a right Reason constituted by Nature."[90] The rejection of such a principle on the basis of a belief that one's reason is intrinsically right constitutes a type of hubris that ultimately threatens life in common.[91] As is well known, it is thus a primary function of the sovereign authority to terminate such dispute through the definitive construction of a system of definition that decisively fixes the elements of public discourse.[92] Only through such an homogenization of the field of linguistic reference can the potential for social conflict grounded in semantic misunderstanding and competition be neutralized. Consistent with Hobbes's nominalism, however, such a system can only ever be arbitrary. All civil laws are just by virtue of them being civil laws, and although obedience to such laws may be rational, it certainly cannot be the case as a result of their correspondence to some prepolitical standard of rationality which is embodied within them. Such a belief "is an error that hath cost many thousands of men their lives."[93] Given the lack of an objective rational standard for just law, in the final instance all we can do is conventionally take the reason of the sovereign to stand in for right reason itself: "I think rather that the reason of him that hath the sovereign authority, and by whose sword we look to be protected both against war from abroad and injuries at home, whether it be right or erroneous in itself, ought to stand for right to us that have submitted ourselves thereunto by receiving the protection."[94]

There is thus no general application of reason that takes an identical form throughout all historical times and places. Accepted modes of reason vary from society to society, identity adhering only with the recognition of the need for the sovereign to fix the standard of rationality within a united political community. The particular reason of a society, then, is just the particular reason of a particular person, natural or artificial, each of the latter expressing a unique articulation of the former. Hobbes thus writes that "there is not amongst men a universal reason agreed upon in any nation, besides the reason of him that hath the sovereign power. Yet though his reason be but the reason of one man, yet it is set up to supply the place of that universal reason, which is expounded to us by our Saviour in the Gospel."[95] The universality of reason is hence merely conventional, it existing as the particular reason of a particular person only rendered general via authorization. Regardless of the extent of the generalization of the field of signification, however, it remains true that there is no individual in any field capable of mastering reason so as to generate consistently correct affirmations. Hobbes thus writes that "as in Arithmetique, unpracticed men must, and Professors themselves may often erre, and cast up false; so also in any other subject of Reasoning, the ablest, most attentive, and most practiced men, may deceive themselves, and inferre false Conclusions; Not but that Reason it selfe is always Right Reason, as well as Arithmetique is a certain and infallible Art: But no one mans Reason, nor the Reason of any one number of men, makes the certaintie."[96] On this point, however, we must again distinguish between error and absurdity, the latter being defined in terms of the attempt to reckon with common words such that there is produced an internally contradictory and thereby senseless determination. Examples of such senseless determinations include notions such as "A *free Subject*; A *free-Will*, or any *Free*, but free from being hindered by opposition."[97] Although error is something "to which even the most prudent men are subject,"[98] absurdity may be generally avoided through proper application of correct method. If a person avoids the various causes of absurd conclusions,[99] then no matter their particular social position, vocation, or personal experience more generally, they are able to participate in reason. As Hobbes writes, "For all men by nature reason alike, and well, when they have good principles."[100]

Reason is not a biologically differentiated capacity that one possesses or does not possess, or that individuals possess in a stratified mode, but nor is it acquired merely through passive familiarity. On the contrary, it is the result of effort and work: reason is "attayned by Industry; first in apt composing of Names; and secondly by getting a good and orderly Method in proceeding from the Elements, which are Names, to Assertions made by Connexion of one of them to another; and so to Syllogismes, which are the Connexions of one Assertion to another, till we come to a knowledge of all the Consequences of names appertaining to the subject in hand; and that is it, men call SCIENCE."[101] Such work not being undertaken, Hobbes considers the vast majority of what passes for philosophy in his own time to be in fact mere absurdity and senseless speech, the Schoolmen failing to understand science as the knowledge of the consequences derived from the order of words, presuming instead that it inheres in perception of a natural order of things, which they themselves are uniquely qualified to intuit. Hobbes thus writes that "it is most true that *Cicero* sayth of them somewhere; that there can be nothing so absurd, but may be found in the books of Philosophers. And the reason is manifest. For there is not one of them that begins his ratiocination from the Definitions, or Explications of the names they are to use; which is a method that hath been used onely in Geometry; whose Conclusions have thereby been made indisputable."[102]

The question of difference and the equality of intelligences can be approached not just from the standpoint of theoretical reason, but from a practical perspective as well.[103] Here the concept of prudence, which Hobbes initially takes care to differentiate from science, is particularly important. Indeed, Hobbes refers to both types of wisdom in his most well-known passage affirming human equality in chapter 13 of *Leviathan*. Here Hobbes famously writes:

> Nature hath made men so equall, in the faculties of body, and mind; as that though there bee found one man sometimes manifestly stronger in body, or of quicker mind then another; yet when all is reckoned together, the difference between man, and man, is not so considerable, as that one man can thereupon claim to himselfe any benefit, to which another may not pretend, as well as he. For as to the strength of body, the weakest has strength enough to kill the strongest, either by secret machination, or by confederacy with others, that are in the same danger with himself.[104]

Hobbes goes on to specify that this general equality is even greater with respect to intellectual ability than bodily, writing that "and as to the faculties of the mind, (setting aside the arts grounded upon words, and especially that skill of proceeding upon generall, and infallible rules, called Science; which very few have, and but in few things; as being not a native faculty, born with us; nor attained, (as Prudence) while we look after somewhat els,) I find yet a greater equality amongst men, than that of strength."[105] When we look beyond the immediacy of the distribution of capacity, however, just as was the case with ratiocination, we find that all those who equally assert themselves in their various intellectual efforts will over an equal period of time achieve comparable levels of prudence, "For Prudence, is but Experience; which equall time, equally bestowes on all men, in those things they equally apply themselves unto."[106]

Hobbes defines prudence as "a *Praesumption* of the *Future*, contracted from the *Experience* of time *Past*."[107] If remembrance is the movement of the mind from place to place and time to time in the effort to recall a lost conception so as to initiate a new discourse of the mind, then foresight or prudence is the anticipation of the effects of action to follow based on the consideration of past events seen to be similar.[108] Hobbes's recognition that all animate beings endowed with voluntary motion have the capacity for prudence, however, obscures the fact that the linguistic faculty of human beings may be prudentially deployed and that prudence may thereby take on a rational form, as a unique type of practical reason. We recall from chapter 3 Hobbes's account of regulated mental discourse as being constituted by the orderly succession of one thought to another. In general, the regulated discourse of the mind seeks to establish an order of relation between cause and effect. Human beings, however, are able to carry out such regulation with the aid of speech, thereby not just imposing an order on the train of thought, but converting the latter into a train of words that more effectively organizes the elements of the causal chain. As Arash Abizadeh notes, when our mental discourse is converted from a mere train of thoughts into a train of words, "we give our thoughts a propositional form, which in turn enables us to draw inferences from considerations we take to be reasons."[109] To this extent deliberation, for beings endowed with a linguistic capacity, is irreducible to a bare reflection on past experience, the deployment of words facilitating the construction of propositional inferences and thus rational causal analysis.

Hobbes explicitly defines deliberation in terms of consideration of the good and evil consequences of an act, it being an alternation between appetite and aversion culminating in the determination of action or omission: "From whence is to be inferred, that deliberation is nothing but alternate imagination of the good and evil sequels of an action, or (which is the same thing) alternate hope and fear, or alternate appetite to do or acquit the action of which he deliberateth."[110] The will is the last appetite in this alternation of appetite that constitutes deliberation, all other appetites in the deliberative process being intentions or inclinations.[111] As Abizadeh has recently shown, and as the inclusion of the above language of good and evil would suggest, Hobbesian practical deliberation is not a merely passive process excluding reflective normative consideration of one's desires.[112] It is rather a cognitive process which in its linguistic forms depends upon the exercise of reason, as subjects "draw inferences from premises they endorse and thereby take to be reasons for belief or action."[113] Human deliberation, quite unlike nonhuman animal deliberation,[114] is open to rational mediation, cognitive reason playing a productive role in the interrogation of one's appetites and aversions, and the likely good and bad consequences to result from their pursuit or avoidance.[115]

It is thus quite revealing that in *The Questions Concerning Liberty, Necessity, and Chance* Hobbes defines madmen as those who are "in error, concerning what is good and evil for themselves."[116] We have already seen how Hobbes considers madness in terms of the emergence of a surplus of passion that effectively militates against proper ratiocination. Madmen certainly deliberate, but to the extent that they cannot properly apply reason to these deliberations, the former is rendered less effective and their understanding of their practical good is compromised. Hence Hobbes writes in "Of Liberty and Necessity," "*Fools* and *madmen* manifestly *deliberate* no less than the *wisest* men, though they make not so good a *choice*, the images of things being by disease altered."[117]

All human beings, then, minus "fools and madmen" in Hobbes account, are capable of identifying their own good and deploying their reason so as to outline the most plausible mode of actualizing it. And that the incapacity of the former group is traced to a "disease," furthermore, reveals that its members are not by nature cognitively lacking in relation to any of their fellows, but just that their intellectual functioning has been disrupted as a consequence of the abnormal emergence of some particular debilitating condition.

On this subject Hobbes concludes, "Nor do I think that any man is so simple, as not to find that to be good which he loveth; good, I say, so far forth, as it maketh him to love it."[118] As we will have occasion to note again in the next section, it is for this reason that only the individual themselves can be seen as the most qualified interpreter of their own interests, but also of the modes by which the latter may be realized. As Hobbes puts it in an important discussion in *De Cive*, "By natural law *one is oneself the judge* whether the means he is to use and the action he intends to take are necessary to the preservation of his life and limbs or not," the autonomy of this judgment being "a requirement of right reason."[119] Individual competency in this instance is grounded in the recognition of a general equality of capacity considered in terms of an equal potential to practically exercise right reason, the latter a natural faculty embedded in all human beings. Hence Hobbes defines the term in *De Cive*: "By right reason in men's natural state, I mean, not, as many do, an infallible Faculty, but the act of reasoning, that is, a man's own true Reasoning about actions of his which may conduce to his advantage or other men's loss."[120]

Curiosity, Happiness, and the Limits of Practical Wisdom

Hobbes's account of deliberation is useful in contextualizing the unique articulation of the relation between happiness and curiosity in his thought. Human foresight is distinguished from prudence in its nonhuman expressions not only to the degree that humans have a singular capacity for naming, and can thus press reason into the service of the articulation of causal relations, but also to the extent that it is guided by yet another singular human attribute: curiosity.[121] Indeed, Gianni Paganini has noted the relation between curiosity and the rational ordering of words within Hobbes's system, the former passion being the ground of the faculty of scientific thought: "The particular 'passionate thought' or 'train of thoughts' that pushes man to look further and further for possible effects has an exact parallel in Hobbes's theory of scientific method, which warrants our seeing it as a projection of human 'curiosity.'"[122] If curiosity is the desire to know how, to comprehend as far as possible the form of relation between a consequent and its antecedents, the scientific application of rational discourse functions to extend and amplify our knowledge of such. To the extent that curiosity is a uniquely human desire, its expression, whether in a scientific form or not, is considered by Hobbes to be an essential source of species happiness.[123]

Hobbes explicitly triangulates the concepts of curiosity, prudence, and happiness in an important passage at the beginning of chapter 12 of *Leviathan*. Here Hobbes identifies three fundamentally interrelated natural traits that are said to uniquely manifest among members of the human species most generally. The first characteristic is indeed curiosity, the "love of the knowledge of causes":[124] "it is peculiar to the nature of Man, to be inquisitive into the Causes of the Events they see, some more, some lesse; but all men so much, as to be curious in the search of the causes of their own good and evil fortune."[125] Secondly is that trait which motivates them to deploy their foresight so as to discover the causal origins of phenomena already occurred. And thirdly is the specific nature of human happiness, which is irreducible to the satisfaction of any immediate appetite, but rather is actualized through the curious investigation into causality. Ultimately then, "whereas there is no other Felicity of Beasts, but the enjoying of their quotidian Food, Ease, and Lusts; as having little, or no foresight of the time to come, for want of observation, and memory of the order, consequence, and dependence of the things they see; Man observeth how one Event hath been produced by another; and considereth in them Antecedence and Consequence."[126] The consequences that follow for the discussion of human equality can be revealed through further explication of the specificity of Hobbes's conception of human happiness.

Hobbes's most sustained discussion of the nature of human happiness occurs in the *Anti-White*, where he identifies it with "the desire for good that is to come."[127] The limited temporality of the immediate enjoyment that is experienced via the direct appropriation of an object renders human desire fundamentally insatiable: "Now, whatever men do they do with the desire of securing something pleasant; and the 'end' they always take to be that which, through the mind-picture [that it generates], moves or urges them to secure it. Yet as soon as they have obtained what they sought, then what was once their goal is no longer so, but they press forward to other things, because in his lifetime no-one is without the wish to acquire things [*appetitus*]."[128] The motion of the organism is incapable of being terminated through the satisfaction of determinate ends and the subsequent achievement of inertial states of being. The enjoyment that is encountered during the time that the object acts upon our sense organs is extremely brief, but our experience of pleasure may continue after the direct removal of the object. It is this memory of the experience of enjoyment that generates a pleasure that is grounded in the expectation of future happiness. As Hobbes writes, "In the very object we enjoy, enjoyment itself exists only as further yearning that springs from the contemplation of the object's parts. So it remains true that the grounds of good, and hence of happiness, consist in seeking."[129] Such happiness, however, is only possible in circumstances where the object of desire is considered to be within our reach. If we lack the capacities to secure the object, and are thus not able to deliberate over the means to do so, happiness is not possible: "Therefore the yearning for things which there seems no means of attaining is not happiness: it is torment."[130]

In the final instance happiness is ultimately considered as the perpetual movement of desire from goods already obtained to goods that have a reasonable expectation of being obtained in the future: "So happiness is *the joy noticed in a prolonged and serene progress of searching from potential to the next potential*; and that peace of mind the moral philosophers speak of is not rest or inactivity or the deprivation of desire, but a gentle motion from a good that has been acquired to one that must be acquired."[131] The pleasure derived from immediate possession pales in comparison to that derived from expectation, in the thought of advancing from one's present condition to a state of another. There is thus a dialectical relationship between multiple moments of enjoyment, the pleasure emanating from the immediate sensuous appropriation of the object suggesting a prudential anticipation of future enjoyment, which in its uniquely human forms constitutes an intrinsically pleasurable good in-itself, the termination of which—through the actualization of a new sensorial experience—reconstituting the dynamic process.[132] Desire is not terminated in the enjoyment of the object desired at any given point in time, but rather perpetually extends into an indefinite future, such that, as Hobbes puts it in *Leviathan*, "the voluntary actions, and inclinations of all men, tend, not onely to the procuring, but also to the assuring of a contented life."[133] Now, as we already know, although all individuals possess this indeterminate desire, its outward manifestation regarding its objects is uniquely articulated from person to person. This fact "ariseth partly from the diversity of passions, in divers men; and partly from the difference of the knowledge, or opinion each one has of the causes, which produce the effect desired."[134] Hence all individuals notoriously have an interest in maximizing their power in relation to one another so as to most efficiently pursue whatever objects their particular desire is oriented toward.[135]

We recall from chapter 3 that the natural complexity of the world militates against its systematization in thought, the complete mapping of the orders of causality so as to account for the totality of natural motion. Such is just as much the case when we consider the psychic dynamics of the individual natural person. There is no possibility of formalizing knowledge of the direction of individual wills as a consequence of the inherently partial and incomplete knowledge of those elements of the world that would contribute to the shaping of these wills. Hobbes thus writes that "it is a truth manifest to all men, that it is not in a man's power to-day to choose what will he shall have to-morrow, or an hour, or any time after. . . . No man can say what he will do to-morrow, unless he foreknew, which no man can, what shall happen before to-morrow."[136] The being of the world, including the being of individual human desire, is incapable of being thematized, Hobbes bluntly clarifying that "My opinion is no more than this, that a man cannot so determine to-day, the will to which he shall have to the doing of any action to-morrow, as that it may not be changed by some external accident or other, as there shall appear more or less advantage to make him persevere in the will to the same action, or to will it no more."[137] Although all individuals manifest the same general multiplicity of passions, the objects of these passions are unique given the diversity of bodily constitutions and the variety of modes of socialization, this variability ultimately rendering it extremely difficult to outline individual psychological motivation. As

Hobbes observes in the introduction to *Leviathan*: "I say the similitude of *Passions*, which are the same in all men, *desire, feare, hope*, &c; not the similitude of the *objects* of the Passions, which are the things *desired, feared, hoped*, &c: for these the constitution individuall, and particular education do so vary, and they are so easie to be kept from our knowledge."[138]

In the final instance practical reason can never be so refined as to extract from the analysis of relations of succession certain knowledge of the future. For example, "for though a man hath always seen the day and night to follow one another hitherto; yet can he not thence conclude they shall do so, or that they have done so eternally. Experience concludeth nothing universally."[139] Hobbes ultimately claims that there is no ground upon which any individual or group of individuals, regardless of the extent of their personal experience, may claim a special status on the basis of the ability to uniquely reckon according to knowledge of the consequent and antecedent. No such perfect wisdom exists: "There is no man living that seeth all the consequences of an action from the beginning to the end, whereby to weigh the whole sum of the good with the whole sum of the evil consequence. We choose no further than we can weigh. That is good to every man, which is so far good as he can see."[140] Even if there are some marginal degrees of prudence, there is no possibility of establishing a certainty of expectation, even for the seemingly most prudent. Given the universality of the capacity for both foresight and ratiocination, and the unique proximity of any individual to their own specific desires, all we can do is conclude that it is most reasonable to assume that any one particular individual is most competent to articulate the potential means for the actualization of their good. In chapter 5 we will have occasion to note the radically democratic implications that might emerge from this dimension of the Hobbesian conception of equality.

The Practice of Equality

The capacity of common people to actualize their rational potentials and thereby express the equality of intelligences is not for Hobbes a merely theoretical presupposition, but a concrete fact proven through historical practice. Indeed, Hobbes asserts that the universal capacity to reason from definition is the basis for the achievement of the excellence that we can observe in a wide variety of spheres of human activity. Such an achievement would be impossible if, as Bramhall suggests, the generality of people were incapable of grasping words such as "*empty* and *body*," Hobbes noting that "yes, but they do, just as well as learned men."[141] All individuals are capable of mastering such definitions and from them participating in reason, an ability that is only further augmented through exposure to productive educating forces: "A man is born with a capacity after due time and experience to reason truly; to which capacity of nature, if there be added no discipline at all, yet as far as he reasoneth he will reason truly; though by a right discipline he may reason truly in *more numerous and various matters*."[142] Indeed, if anyone is predisposed toward failing to acquire knowledge through the proper deployment of established definitions in propositional relationships, it is the Schoolmen, who merely acquire their definitions from their past masters without reflection on their appropriateness.[143] In general the establishment of a relation of dependence of some on others in matters of interpretation does not reflect, as Aristotle or the Schoolmen might assume, qualitative distinctions in cognitive ability, but at most a lack of method in reason. As Hobbes puts it, "Want of Science, that is, Ignorance of causes, disposeth, or rather constraineth a man to rely on the advise, and authority of others. For all men whom the truth concernes, if they rely not on their own, must rely on the opinion of some other, whom they think wiser than themselves, and see not why he should deceive them."[144] The institution of such a trust generalizes error, for the latter cannot be perceived without independent knowledge of causes: "Ignorance of the signification of words; which is, want of understanding, disposeth men to take on truth, not onely the truth they know not; but also the errors; and which is more, the non-sense of them they trust; For neither Error, nor non-sense, can without a perfect understanding of words, be detected."[145]

The identification of universal natural reason as the ground for the achievement of proficiency in a plurality of social roles or functions is further elaborated on in *A Dialogue between a Philosopher and a Student of the Common Law of England*. Hobbes again contends that not only do individuals not enter the world with but rather acquire reason, but also that every individual has the potential to acquire as efficient a use of reason as any other. As he puts it in his rejection of the lawyers' idea of a privileged rationality or skill bestowing legal right, "Though it be true, that no man is born with, yet all men grow up to it as well as lawyers;

and when they have applied their reason to the laws, (which were laws before they studied them, or else it was not law they studied), may be as fit for and capable of judicature, as Sir Edward Coke himself, who whether he had more or less use of reason, was not thereby a judge, but because the King made him so."[146] One becomes an expert in law not because one has uniquely perfected or applied some exceptional mode of natural reason, but rather because one has been appointed as one by the sovereign. But once more, the universal capacity for reason upon which the performance of expertise depends is only actualized through the deployment of a concrete-particular reason, each of which is distinct from every other. Within the *Dialogue* the particularity of reasons is expressed in the diversity of judgments that we see with respect to judicial decisions, each conclusion of the courts reflecting the unique applied reason of the subjects of the legal determination. There is again no purely rational basis for fixing such judgment, which must be as inevitably diverse as any other form. Hobbes hence observes how "divers men in divers ages, upon the same case give divers judgments."[147]

Ultimately there exists no set of particular intelligences internal to distinct natural persons that would predispose them toward excellence in technical fields such as law or government, or which would legitimate exclusive occupation of elite social positions or roles.[148] Hobbes attempts to demystify the various forms of aristocratic privilege that masquerade as mere reflections of an internally differentiated human nature. Hence, for example, Hobbes is adamant that no individual possesses an intrinsic worth or value in themselves. He writes that "the *Value*, or WORTH of a man, is as of all other things, his Price; that is to say, so much as would be given for the use of his Power: and therefore is no absolute; but a thing dependant on the need and judgement of another."[149] Worth is thus a social relationship, reflecting not a substantial content within the person of value, but merely contingent bonds derived from the perception of the external party. Such is especially the case with respect to those civil honors characteristic of human association within a commonwealth, which are derived only from the judgment of the sovereign, who "can make whatsoever they please, to stand for signes of Honour."[150] The various signs and titles of aristocratic privilege are established by an arbitrary exercise of sovereign will, not a necessary perception of the intrinsic faculties of the individuals thus endowed: "Titles of *Honour*, such as are Duke, Count, Marquis, and Baron, are Honourable; as signifying the value set upon them by the Soveraigne

Power of the Common-wealth."¹⁵¹ Such a right to bestow titles of nobility, the latter having no intrinsic basis in the natural form of the person, is thus identified as one of the fundamental marks of sovereignty: "To the sovereign therefore it belongeth also to give titles of Honour; and to appoint what Order of place, and dignity, each man shall hold; and what signes of respect, in public or private meetings, they shall give to one another."¹⁵² Hobbes's ultimate contempt for those who fail to understand this, those who would judge themselves exceptional with respect to their natural capacities and subsequently misinterpret their social situation as grounded in this uniqueness, is perhaps revealed most acutely in *Leviathan*'s discussion of the sources of crime, where he notes that one of the most passionate sources of the latter is vainglory: "Of the Passions that most frequently are the causes of Crime, one, is Vain-glory, or a foolish over-rating of their own worth; as if the difference of worth, were an effect of their wit, or riches, or blood, or some other naturall quality, not depending on the Will of those that have Soveraign Authority."¹⁵³ It is this "foolish" belief in a natural superiority that generates the sense within social elites that they somehow remain immune to civil law or should not be subject to the same penalties as those common people lacking their unique traits and characteristics.¹⁵⁴

Regardless of the rejection of the idea of an intrinsic aristocratic being, it remains nonetheless true that one can be worthy of a position or office in the sense of being fit or able to perform the range of tasks associated with it, a fact that grounds the conceptual distinction between worth and worthiness. There is still, however, no movement from this recognition of worthiness to an affirmation of entitlement based upon it: "WORTHINESSE, is a thing different from the worth, or value of a man; and also from his merit, or desert; and consisteth in a particular power, or ability for that, whereof he is said to be worthy: which particular ability, is usually named FITNESSE, or *Aptitude*."¹⁵⁵ Worthiness to perform a task is thus irreducible to individual worth, the lack of an intrinsic measure of the latter precluding the establishment of an entitlement of merit. One merits a thing only where one has a right to it, and this right always presupposes a social relationship whereby access is granted via promise: "A man may be Worthy of Riches, Office, and Employment, that nevertheless, can plead no right to have it before another; and therefore cannot be said to merit or deserve it. For Merit, praesupposeth a right, and that the thing deserved is due by promise."¹⁵⁶ The principle applies to the activity of governing as much as any other, there existing no natural inequality between individuals sufficient to sanction a unique title to govern via application of a principle of merit or desert.[157] Hence, as we have already observed, Hobbes contends that no individual is by nature "worthy to govern."[158] There is simply no substantive qualification for holding sovereign office, beyond the title to govern generated through the act of institution, and hence Hobbes's nonconcern about any particular characteristics or traits—be they technical, moral, or otherwise—that an occupier of sovereign office should possess.[159]

The general capacity of all individuals to deploy reason in order to participate in affairs of government is specifically affirmed by Hobbes in an important passage in chapter 8 of *Leviathan*, in which he simultaneously dissociates the question of equality from the substantive variability that might emerge as a consequence of the differing trajectories of human desire. Here Hobbes is concerned with specifying the nature of intellectual virtues, those "abilityes of the mind, as men praise, value, and desire should be in themselves; and go commonly under the name of a *good wit*."[160] These intellectual virtues are subdivided into natural and acquired categories. Contrary to what we might think, however, even differences in natural intellectual virtues are irreducible to any biological stratification of individual intelligences. No such inequality of intelligences exists in this sense: "By Naturall, I mean not, that which a man hath from his Birth: that is nothing else but Sense; wherein men differ so little one from another, and from brute Beasts, as it is not to be reckoned amongst Vertues."[161] This particular manifestation of good wit, on the contrary, refers to a capacity gained through practice, although "without Method, Culture, or Instruction"—these latter constituting the means by which we come into possession of acquired wit, of which reason is the only form—natural wit being revealed through "*Celerity of Imagining*, (that is, swift succession of one thought to another; and *steddy direction* to some approved end."[162] The quickness of imagination that structures distinctions in natural wit thus "is caused by the difference of mens passions," where certain individuals "love and dislike, some one thing, some another: and therefore some mens thoughts run one way, some another; and are held to, and observe differently the things that pass through their imagination."[163] Differences in wit are thus manifestations of differences in passion, which as we know are themselves derived from differences in bodily constitution and education. As Hobbes writes, "The causes of this difference of Witts, are in the Passions: and the difference of Passions, proceedeth partly from the different Constitution of the body, and partly from different Education. For if the difference proceeded from the temper of the brain, and the organs of Sense, either exterior or interior, there would be no lesse difference of men in their Sight, Hearing, or other Senses, than in their Fancies, and Discretions. It proceeds therefore from the Passions; which are different, not onely from the difference of mens complexions; but also from their difference of customes and education."[164]

In any case, however, when we are interrogating the question of equality with respect to political competency, it is not wit that is most relevant, but rather that which must moderate it so as to provide it with a stable order: judgment. Hobbes says that those who excel in the perception of similitudes between the various sensuous impressions of things have good wit, while those who excel in the perception of dissimilitudes have good judgment.[165] The one activity identifies and relates, and the other distinguishes and discerns. The actualization of each, however, differs with respect to the question of the necessity of the other. Specifically, whereas good wit or fancy is not a virtue without the correspondent application of judgment, judgment is without fancy, the latter manifesting itself as a form of madness without the virtue of discretion that judgment allows for: "Without Steddinesse, and Direction to some End, a great Fancy is one kind of Madnesse; such as they have, that entering into any discourse, are snatched from their purpose, by every thing that comes in their thought, into so many, and so long digressions, and Parentheses, that they utterly lose themselves: Which kind of folly, I know of no particular name for."[166] Although properly moderated fancy has a role to play in various types of its expression, when it comes to science proper, Hobbes maintains that judgment is singularly essential: "In Demonstration, in Councell, and all rigorous search of Truth, Judgement does all; except sometimes the understanding have need to be opened by some apt similitude; and then there is so much use of Fancy."[167] Crucially, Hobbes is explicit in maintaining that unlike in cases of wit and fancy, we do not observe great degrees of difference with respect to the individual capacity for judgment. It is this general equality of judgment that provides the foundation for the expression of that already noted human aptitude facilitating achievement in a wide variety of spheres of activity, spheres of activity which demand not their own specific and exclusive faculties or techniques, and of which governing is one. Hobbes thus writes that "to govern well a family, and a kingdome, are not different degrees of Prudence; but different sorts of businesse; no more than to draw a picture in little, or as great, or greater then the life, are different degrees of Art. A plain husband-man is more Prudent in affaires of his own house, then a Privy Counseller in the affaires of another man."[168]

In specifying the concrete domains of activity within which it is manifested, Hobbes asserts again that equality is not merely a formal philosophical principle, but a lived reality that has been historically proven in action. Indeed, this can be seen as one of the important lessons of *Behemoth*, where the common people emerge in Hobbes's narration of events as critical actors in possession of a reflective judgment facilitating their entry onto the political scene.[169] Needless to say, however, such is not to suggest that these or any other individuals are perfectly rational and self-aware actors who are not prone to error in their assessment of their interest and the means to its actualization.[170] If chronic errors are observed among the greater part of citizens, such results not from a deficiency of reason, but rather from the ambitious few actively misleading them. Any apparent criticism Hobbes makes of the ignorance of the common people is grounded not in an understanding of them as cognitively inferior, but rather takes as its object the form of society that stultifies them through inadequate education. As Don Herzog writes, "Hobbes's dour comments on human ignorance needn't be read as claims about abstract human nature; we can read them instead as observations about contemporary England. We should remember that this was a society drenched in superstition: fascinated with monsters, committed to magic, believing in witches, fond of astrologers . . . However confused they are, however full of nonsense their heads and their lives, these believers are still worthy of regard; they have the potential to improve."[171] This potential to improve is always latent precisely to the extent that, as Hobbes asserts in *De Homine*, "few are those who cannot be taught."[172]

An important passage in *Behemoth* is useful in contextualizing Hobbes's sporadic, yet merely apparent critique of the intellectual competencies of the generality of the people. In his discussion of the use and abuse of the scriptures as a political tool, Hobbes notes the extent to which the translation of these texts facilitated the multiplication of erroneous private interpretation: "For after the Bible was translated into English, euery man, nay euery boy and wench that could read English, thought they spoke with God Almighty and vnderstood what he said, when by a certain numbers of chapters a day, they had read the Scriptures once or twice over . . . euery man became a Judge of Religion, and Interpreter of the Scriptures to himselfe."[173] Contrary to what one predisposed to thinking human inequality might immediately intuit, Hobbes is here very much not thereby suggesting that scriptural interpretation should be left to established experts within the church, or professors of religion, or any such group at all. Indeed, in the preceding pages Hobbes critiques precisely such individuals for claiming rights of interpretative authority. Hobbes begins by noting again that the original signification of the word *heresy* was merely private opinion.[174] The Christian church, however, appropriated the term in order to signify a sinful opposition to those possessing doctrinal authority, heresy thus becoming a form of rebellion against spiritual power. Needless to say, however, the possession of such authority was not and is not grounded in unique knowledge of or access to a specific realm of truth, which even in the case that it were, would not be sufficient to generate assent among others who lack the means of validating the specific privilege. The fundamental problem is that different individuals will necessarily interpret scripture in different ways, the number of heretics being multiplied in relation to the number of people claiming spiritual authority, which anyone may do in situations lacking a sovereign determination of a particular right to do so. Hobbes asks, "Who can tell what is declared by the Scripture which euery man is allowed to read and interpret to himselfe? Nay more, what Protestant either of the Layity or Clergy (if euery generall Councell be a competent Judge of Hæresy) is not already condemned? For diuers Councells haue declared a great many of our Doctrins to be Hæresy, and that, as they pretend, vpon the Authority of the Scriptures."[175] The Roman Church ultimately succeeded in its attempt to gain favor and authority through the particular form of their obfuscation of scripture and rite, convincing believers that spiritual matters were so complicated so as to necessitate expert authority: "Striuing to make good many points of Faith incomprehensible, and calling in the Philosophy of *Aristotle* to their assistance, wrote great bookes of Schoole Diuinity, which no man else, nor they themselues are able to vnderstand."[176] The Church multiplied its sermons and lobbied for the institution of universities, all in an effort to enlarge its sphere of influence. The success of the latter project, however, far from reflecting a proximity to divine reality, merely intensified confusion and mystification regarding the actual source of doctrinal right.

Ultimately no one can be sure that their own or any other's interpretation of scripture is true, each particular reading being mediated by the specificities of that person's perception. It hence falls upon the sovereign once again to substitute their own reason for every other, it possessing an exclusive right to interpret scripture and overcome the diversity of private reading: "Because men do for the most part rather draw the Scripture to their owne sense, then follow the true sense of the Scripture, there is no other way to know certainly and in all cases what God commands or forbids vs to doe, but by the Sentence of him or them that are constituted by the King to determine the sense of the Scripture vpon hearing of the particular case of Conscience which is in question."[177] Such is part of the reason why, as Hobbes consistently emphasizes, religion is not philosophy or art, but law.[178] Nevertheless, despite the problematic issues raised by the practice of private interpretation, it still remains the case that it is clearly more beneficial to civil society as a whole to have the scriptural texts translated into English, thus breaking the interpretative monopoly of the priestly elites: "There are so many places of Scripture easy to be vnderstood, that teach both true Faith and good Morality, and that as fully as is necessary to saluation (of which no seducer is able to dispossesse the mind of any ordinary readers) that the reading of them is so profitable as not to be forbidden without great dammage to them and the Common wealth."[179] The fundamental principles and lessons of the texts, in other words, are capable of being extracted and comprehended through the exercise of the critical and reflective hermeneutic faculties of the generality of the people.

This particular example is perfectly consistent with the message of *Behemoth* more generally.[180] Hence in part 4, Hobbes has interlocuter B interpret the parliamentary oligarchs' seduction of the people as evidence of the latter's political naivety, B proclaiming "What silly things are the common sort of people, to be cousen'd, as they were so grossly!"[181] A, however, adamantly resists such a reading of events, going on to defend the people on the basis of their nonaccess to modes of socialization capable of educating them to their civic responsibility. A claims that the acquisition of knowledge of the duty of obedience is not a matter of "naturall wit," but rather of pedagogy and proper instruction: "For it is a Science, and built vpon sure and clear principles, and to be learned by deep and carefull study, or from Masters that haue deeply studyed it."[182] The people before and during the civil war did not have access to this instruction, while their only leisure resulted in them being misinformed by "the Presbyterian Ministers, . . . Independent and other Fanatick Ministers."[183] In the final instance, A asserts that "your calling the People silly things obliged me by this digression to shew you, that it is not want of wit, but want of the Science of Justice, that brought them into these troubles . . . They wanted not Wit, but the knowledge of the Causes and Grounds vpon which one person has a Right to Gouerne, and the rest an Obligation to Obey."[184] Contrary to B's claim of popular simplicity, A goes on to argue that the people, through the functional performance of their social roles and activities in a variety of diverse fields, demonstrate that they do in fact possess a natural wit, even if in this case they were deceived by elites who wished to appropriate authority for themselves. As Hobbes writes, "Persuade if you can that man that has made his fortune, or made it greater, or an Eloquent Orator, or a rauishing Poet, or a subtile Lawyer, or but a good Hunter, or a cunning Gamester, that he has not a good Wit."[185] As Hobbes perpetually stresses, and as I have tried to detail in this section, the equality of intelligences is revealed in manifold modes. This equality is not evidence of an identical capacity of all to simultaneously do everything, nor of the substantive possession of uniform traits or characteristics, but rather of the faculty to deploy human rationality for the sake of the actualization of whatever particular ends the individual is disposed toward.

PART III
DEMOCRATIC ETHICS

Chapter 5

Democracy and Natural Law

In chapters 3 and 4 I attempted to demonstrate that various of Hobbes's reflections on the being of the world and the being of the human reveal his understanding of the ontological conditions that render democratic life possible. Recall that if all politics is characterized in terms of the institution of a social world independently of a transcendent source that would orient the direction of such institution, democracy specifically is that mode of political being in which this fact is reflectively affirmed, as Hobbes notes in his discussion of the hubris of the ancient Athenians. It is worth emphasizing again that it was the Athenian experiment that was Hobbes's primary source for thinking democratic life and that this conception is, of course, very distinct from that which is predominant in our modern political imaginary. What we see emerge in ancient Greece, recognized by Hobbes, is an example of a community that takes its law to be an object of permanent interrogation and deliberation. Law is something that can be changed through the self-activity of the demos, who know no external constraints on their action. The establishment of such a relation with the law is facilitated by the Greek metaphysical conception, the idea of chaos being fundamental here. As Cornelius Castoriadis observes, "In the proper, initial sense 'chaos' in Greek means void, nothingness. It is out of the total void that the world emerges. But already in Hesiod, the world is also chaos in the sense that there is no complete order in it, that it is not subject to meaningful laws."[1] The democratic questioning of the validity of the law is an explicit recognition of the chaotic form of being, no possibility of self-alteration being possible if the law is given once and for all, that is, if there exists some extrasocial order that regulates human life.

What Hobbes picks up on is the fact that Athenian politics was, in the words of Josiah Ober, simultaneously "strongly democratic and nonfoundationalist."[2] The metaphysical openness of the world takes on a special significance in democratic society. At the same time that political institution proceeds without being attributed to an external source, democracy singularly affirms an equivalent capacity on the part of all citizens to competently participate in the instituting process. In the case of Athens, political equality as the equal sharing of public power was achieved through a variety of mechanisms: for example, the sovereign status of the *ecclesia*, public participation in judicial procedure, the selection of magistrates through sortition and rotation, the absolute subjection of magistrates to popular recall, and so on.[3] Such institutional mechanisms, though, although crucial to the mediation of the collective power of the people, do not determine the democratic form. Hence Ober distinguishes between the modern political imaginary, in which the power of democracy tends to be reduced to a conception of legitimate authority expressed through decisions reached via a particular instituted voting mechanism, and the ancient Greek one, where power is considered in terms of a "capacity to do things."[4] Unlike terms that contain an *-arche* root (*monarchia, oligarchia*), which designate the number of people occupying political office within a constitutionally specified political order, terms with a *-kratos* root refer to power as ability or capacity. On this understanding democracy as the power of the people designates not a particular constitutional order or institutional configuration monopolized by a part of the citizenry (the many), but rather the effective capacity of the people to do things: "It is the regime in which the *demos* gains a collective capacity to effect change in the public realm. And so it is not just a matter of *control* of a public realm but the collective *strength* and *ability* to act within that realm and, indeed, to reconstitute the public realm through action."[5]

I have suggested that Hobbes understands perfectly well the nature and conditions of what Castoriadis calls the capacity to autonomously interrogate the law, or Ober that to reconstitute the public realm through action. Indeed, for the reasons laid out such a capacity worries Hobbes deeply. He thus does not attempt to theoretically move from his perception of the democratic recognition of metaphysical openness and the democratic affirmation of natural human equality to any normative defense of democracy as a preferred sovereign form. In this final chapter, however, I will switch methodological modes in an effort to think precisely this possibility. My aim is not, to be clear, to textually reveal a democratic logic intentionally operating within Hobbes's work. As I have shown through earlier analysis in chapter 2—the textual context of the critique of the democracy—Hobbes's intention was always to prevent the emergence of such logics. Instead, through critically redeploying specific Hobbesian categories in relation to one another in new ways, I attempt to participate in an alternative mode of practicing the history of political thought, in which the development of new conceptual constellations is capable of generating a normative content that would otherwise remain obscured. Specifically, I focus on the unique Hobbesian articulations of natural law—a manifestation of the nonfoundational structure of the world that was the subject of chapter 3—and the true liberty of subjects—a manifestation of the equality-in-difference that was the subject of chapter 4.

The place of the deployment of classical natural law terminology within Hobbes's work, and in particular its relation to established natural law traditions within seventeenth-century European philosophy, has been one of the most discussed issues within recent Hobbes studies.[6] Rather than entering these debates, in the first part of the chapter I will focus only on one of the fundamental distinctions that Hobbes himself makes regarding the singularity of his approach. If classical natural law philosophy assumes that juridical norms can be derived from consideration of perpetual moral principles emanating from an extrasocial source, Hobbes emphasizes the basis of all social institutionalization in the immanent self-activity of individuals themselves. Hence the laws of nature are simply rational theorems directing individuals to institute civil society for the sake of the advancement of their only universally shared good—the preservation of life—independently of reference to exterior norms that would delimit the range of such institution. Hobbesian natural law ultimately speaks to the human capacity for autonomous politics, that is, the capacity to generate collective rules of behavior lacking a transcendent foundation.[7] This political capacity, however, persists simultaneously with an antipolitical impulse. That is to say, for Hobbes the goal of the institution of the commonwealth should look toward the termination of politics through the establishment of a sovereign monopoly on signification, thus homogenizing the social field and eliminating that conflict which in most cases characterizes politics as an activity, to the extent that the latter is marked by contestation between distinct individuals with distinct normative conceptions. What Hobbes understands is that, as a result of the ontological diversity of beings, politics—after the foundation of the commonwealth, which all have an interest in—is fundamentally ant/agonistic, and hence his belief that social peace depends upon its neutralization.[8]

In the subsequent part of the chapter I analyze the significance of Hobbes's concept of liberty to the articulation of natural law's minimal substantive content, a relationship that commentators on Hobbes have not sufficiently explored. For Hobbes the consideration of the liberty of an entity entails a correlative consideration of that entity's particular capacities, an entity being free to the extent that it is externally unimpeded in its ability to do that which it is capable of doing. If all human beings are radically singular, they nevertheless share, as noted, a universal desire for the extension and affirmation of life, the general precondition for the actualization of whatever their particular goods or interests happen to be. Hobbesian natural law looks to facilitate the preservation of a sphere of right that is able to reproduce that general motion represented by the concept of life, for the sake of the pursuit of the particular motion of individual natural persons. When Hobbes speaks of the so-called true liberty of the subjects, he speaks to those truly universal human powers whose expression is ethically demanded by natural law as a basic prerequisite for the preservation of commodious life. The perpetuation of this sphere of true liberty preserves within the commonwealth, contrary to Hobbes's own desire, a minimal political substance that resists Hobbesian antipolitics.

In the final part of the chapter I suggest that there is embedded within Hobbes's political thought a rudiment for considering the generalization of public participation in political affairs as a freedom of the subject demanded by natural law. Hobbes himself does not pursue such a line of thought in any way, but a germinal ground for the argument can be located in an innovation found within *Leviathan*. Here Hobbes notes in multiple places that, contrary to his earlier suggestion in *De Cive*, the human desire for political participation is a natural one that manifests in each individual, despite the otherwise considerable variation in their passions and appetites. This would be to the extent that individuals recognize that, firstly, they themselves remain the most competent judges of their particular goods and the potential modes to these goods' actualization, and secondly, the political, in which interest is negotiated for the sake of the formulation of collective trajectories of action, is that sphere of human association that most effectively affirms particular goods at the expense of others. However, whereas a specifically democratic politics would institutionalize spaces of participation so as to allow all citizens to partake in deliberative activities that look to advance their ends through sovereign legislation, Hobbes wants to restrict collective negotiation to bodies politic within the realm of what today we might call civil society. As we have seen in chapter 1, Hobbes's critique of democratic sovereign organization is grounded in his perception of the nature of the mechanics of deliberation in assembly fora, in which the need for persuasion elevates eloquence as a rhetorical instrument, overwhelming reason and thereby frustrating the end to which natural law is directed. If we reject Hobbes's critique of democracy, however, allowing that popular assemblies may be structured so as to facilitate the prudential deployment of judgment grounded in reasoned knowledge acquisition, then there emerges a new ethical preference for the democratic sovereign form relative to those that do not provide opportunities for popular political self-expression. Democracy would in this case singularly allow for the actualization of an essential human power.

Hobbes's Critique and Reconstruction of the Idea of Natural Law

In *The Elements of Law* and *De Cive* Hobbes explicitly specifies that fundamental component differentiating his political project from those that remain grounded in traditional natural law theory. As we have already seen, traditional practitioners of moral and political philosophy, those whom in the former work Hobbes labels the *dogmatici*, and of which the classical natural law writers are exemplary, proceed dogmatically. Their political conclusions are arrived at through contemplation of abstract norms emanating from an extrasocial source perceived to be universally applicable to all human self-organization. Natural law is just one manifestation of that tendency to affirm a transcendent structure that is seen to function as a ground for the establishment of an empirical order of things.[9] For Hobbes, simple reflection on the concrete facts of lived political experience invalidates such a conception. For example, he notes how there is virtually no agreement among those who write on natural law regarding the fundamental principles of this law of laws, nor the mode of their positive actualization.[10] The clear equivocation regarding the content of natural law among the philosophers—to say nothing yet of the instauration of this content in positive law—are manifestations of the impossibility of such an articulation. Far from discovering a definite ground capable of structuring the determination of civil life, the writers simply attempt to legitimate their own particular good through positing it as a universal one.[11] Any overlapping of consensus among societies regarding ethical criteria must thus be taken as merely conventional: "For the most part, such writers as have occasion to affirm, that anything is against the law of nature, do allege no more than this, that it is against the consent of all nations, or the wisest and most civil nations."[12] The very fact that collections of individuals persist externally to the latter nations reveals the nonuniversalizability of natural law, the allowance of the possibility of disobedience of such law rendering it neither universal nor natural. If the law of nature were that to which all individuals would consent, then nobody could violate it, "for the nature of every man is contained under the nature of mankind."[13] The anthropological and historical recognition of the diversity of modes of social being renders any of the totalizing ethical assumptions of natural law theory invalid.[14]

Even if we can identify some circumstances in which different societies affirm shared principles of so-called natural law, this coalescence of moral sentiment is incapable of functioning as a normative standard for any community outside of the sphere of articulation of this law, given that there exists no definitive standard by which we are able to make determinations regarding questions of degrees of wisdom and civility: there are no "wisest and most civil nations." In the final instance, Hobbes rejects any conceptual effort to transmute a necessarily particular moral conception into a universally valid principle applicable in all human contexts, an impossible operation that must of necessity be violently exclusive toward that exterior to said particular conception.[15] And indeed, in *Leviathan* he identifies as one of the three defects of reasoning that may be the source of crime the elevation of particular private doctrines to such shared normative principles of natural law, referring to those "false Teachers, that either mis-interpret the Law of Nature, making it thereby repugnant to the Law Civill; or by teaching for Lawes, such Doctrines of their own, or traditions of former times, as are inconsistent with the duty of a Subject."[16] What Hobbes rejects is the classical tradition's ideological tendency to affirm particular images of modes of living as somehow natural and thus as the source of a unique normativity.[17]

In the end, the positing of such natural law conceptions is highly conditioned by various historical circumstances, this circumscription precluding any movement of generalization culminating in the establishment of a universal legitimacy. Hobbes is explicit regarding his belief that all moral philosophy takes form only within political contexts, its articulation being not independent of, but necessarily leaning on, social determinations.[18] Here it is important to refer back to an earlier discussion I undertook in chapter 3. Recall that human beings most definitely lack that natural homogeneity of inclination that characterizes various forms of animal association, such that particular interest coalesces in group interest. However, as I noted, Hobbes's rejection of the Aristotelian assumption that human sociality is grounded in the universal possession of certain necessary traits or characteristics—an assumption that reappears in the Thomist tradition of natural law prevalent during his time, which saw the exercise of reason as capable of intuiting a positive and substantive essence to morality that could orient human behavior[19]—is not equivalent to the rejection of all principles of natural sociality. Hobbes does not deny that human beings lack an intrinsic tendency to associate with one another, but only that there is a specific principle of sociality that determines in advance of their association the precise form that it will take.[20] Even if nature does compel us to commune with one another, the specifically political mode of communion is one that lacks a foundational ground structuring the institution of the civil relation. Human beings themselves have sole responsibility for determining the parameters of their social life, the latter taking a wide range of different forms, being conditioned as they are by the particular motivations, interests, and desires of the associating agents. As Hobbes writes, "Closer observation of the causes why men seek each other's company and enjoy associating with each other, will easily reach the conclusion that it *does not happen because by nature it could not be otherwise, but by chance.*"[21] It is precisely here that we can begin to specify the singularity of the Hobbesian concept of natural law.

It is not the case, as is sometimes suggested, that this specificity is one that Hobbes himself fails to recognize.[22] If such were the case it would be difficult to fully explain the direction and force of Hobbes's critique of the natural law writers as glossed above, to say nothing of the latter's own antipathy toward Hobbes.[23] In line with his deployment of certain parliamentarian terminology in the formulation of the theory of authorization and representation, in rejecting the major theoretical assumptions of traditional natural law theory, Hobbes utilizes the tradition's language in order to radically subvert its fundamental presuppositions.[24] Such a methodological strategy is thus one with precedent in Hobbes's work.[25] Needless to say, the particular application of this technique was not always appreciated by Hobbes's interlocuters, as in, for example, John Wallis's well-known complaint: "For Mr. Hobs is very dexterous in confuting others by putting a new sense on their words rehearsed by himself: different from what the words signifie with other Men. And therefore if you [Boyle] shall have occasion to speak of Chalk, He'll tell you that by Chalk he means Cheese: and then if he can prove that what you say of Chalk is not true of Cheese, he reckons himself to have gotten a great victory."[26]

The particular signification of the term *natural law* for Hobbes must first of all be reconcilable with the critique of that set of natural law philosophies noted above. Once we abstract from the shared form of all substantive prepolitical moral conceptions, emanating from whatever transcendent source, to consider only the immanent tendencies of the natural form of the human organism, we find simply the latter's desire to pursue its own good. Given the radical nonidentity of such goods, a genuinely universal natural law can only be oriented toward the establishment of that social peace that is a prerequisite for the facilitation of this pursuit of the good.[27] Thus the only logically noncontradictory conception of the law of nature is that which defines the latter in terms of the exercise of right reason for the sake of outlining those necessities required for self-preservation.[28] As we have already seen in chapter 4, such reason may be properly called natural to the degree that its potential exercise is embedded in human nature itself, it being one of the few nontedious universal characteristics specified by Hobbes's philosophical anthropology. Hence Hobbes's definition of a law of nature in *Leviathan* emphasizes not any particular positive modes of being, but is instead a negative injunction to preserve, via action or omission, whatever mode of being characterizes any specific life in its singularity: "A LAW OF NATURE, *(Lex Naturalis,)* is a Precept, or generall Rule, found out by Reason, by which a man is forbidden to do, that, which is destructive of his life, or taketh away the means of preserving the same; and to omit, that, by which he thinketh it may be best preserved."[29]

If we are justified in properly characterizing natural law as natural, however, it remains true that natural law may not be properly characterized as law. The status of Hobbesian laws of nature as rational theorems as opposed to properly juridical commands is well known. Hobbes writes that "these dictates of Reason, men use to call by the name of Lawes; but improperly: for they are but Conclusions, or Theoremes concerning what conduceth to the conservation and defence of themselves; whereas Law, properly is the word of him, that by right hath command over others."[30] When Hobbes says that "the whole of the natural law is contained within the civil,"[31] he means not that civil law reproduces a substantive prepolitical content, but that the end to which natural law is directed—self-preservation—is realized only through the institution of a system of civil law, largely but not entirely irrespective of the latter's precise form of articulation. Specifying not a universal moral substance that would ground and organize the specific form of social relation through placing limits on political potential, Hobbesian natural law speaks simply to the uniquely human capacity to develop such social relationships—independently of particular models—through the translation of right that reason and speech make possible. Hence again the obvious fact that the form of appearance of civil law varies from commonwealth to commonwealth, there existing no essential content to civil law manifesting itself in every particular time and place, even if the general function of civil law in all commonwealths can be specified. Hobbes provides an instructive example of such variation in *A Dialogue between a Philosopher and a Student of the Common Law*, noting that "he that should have said in Queen Mary's time, that the Pope had authority in England, should have been burnt at a stake; but for saying the same in the time of Queen Elizabeth, should have been commended. You see by this, that many things are made crimes, and no crime, which are not so in their own nature, but by diversity of law, made upon diversity of opinion or of interest by them which have authority."[32]

Ultimately, then, civil law contains the natural law in every commonwealth irrespective of the particular content of the former, and this because the latter demands only the restriction of natural liberty via the institution of this former for the sake of peace. The positive realization of natural law through the form of civil law is also that which explains how the laws of nature may be always binding internally yet not always externally. Hobbes writes that "the Lawes of Nature oblige *in foro interno*, that is to say, they bind to a desire they should take place: but *in foro externo*; that is, to the putting them in act, not alwayes. For he that should be modest, and tractable, and performe all he promises, in such time, and place, where no man els should do so, should but make himself a prey to others, and procure his own certain ruine, contrary to the ground of all Lawes of Nature, which tend to Natures preservation."[33] The *in foro externo* content of the laws of nature are thus creatively generated out of the concrete and practical self-activity of individuals, who in instituting positive laws externalize the *in foro interno* form of human nature as the orientation toward self-preservation.[34]

We see ultimately that there exists no transcendent rational standard for civil law. Positive laws are equally fundamental and equally demanding of obligation, they being expressions of the fundamental natural law that rationally requires obedience to the particular sovereign that we have bound ourselves to. As Hobbes puts it in *Behemoth*: "I vnterstand not how one Law can be more fundamentall then another, except onely that Law of Nature that binds vs all to obey him, whosoeuer he be, whom lawfully and for our own safety we haue promised to obey."[35] In one of his replies to Bramhall, Hobbes is explicit that even if particular systems of positive law contradict one another, they may not contradict the law of God, for what the latter requires is simply rational submission to civil law, regardless of this law's specific content.[36] If reason is unhinged from law then the former is capable of serving as an arbiter judging the legitimacy of the latter, thus frustrating the very end to which law was created in the first place. One cannot refuse law on the basis of its nonidentity with reason, for reason itself demands obedience to law.

Hobbes formulates this principle in the seemingly most extreme terms, famously writing in *De Cive* that "*Theft, Murder, Adultery* and all *wrongs* are forbidden by the laws of nature, but what is to count as a *theft* on the part of a citizen or as *murder* or *adultery* or a *wrongful act* is to be determined by the *civil*, not the *natural*, *law*."[37] The concrete expression of the natural law, to the degree that it lacks a positive or substantive content in itself, is achieved only through the instauration of civil law, which gives matter to the empty form.[38] The natural law may forbid theft, murder, adultery, and so on, but it is incapable, independently of civil law, of even defining what these things are: "Thus one learns what *Theft* is, what *Murder* is and *Adultery*, and generally what a *wrong* is, from the *civil law*, that is from the commands of the holder in that commonwealth of *sovereign power*."[39] And indeed, anthropological and historical analysis of the specification of these crimes clearly reveals the extent of the variation of their content, again disclosing the error of those who would posit the existence of substantive natural laws, thereby affirming that many or most societies are somehow unnatural. For Hobbes this determination is one that no philosopher can presume they have the right to make, his opposition to such projects being further revealed in the following passage from *The Elements of Law*: "The civil laws are to all subjects the measures of their actions, whereby to determine, whether they be right or wrong, profitable or unprofitable, virtuous or vicious; and by them the use and definition of all names not agreed upon, and tending to controversy, shall be established. As for example, upon the occasion of some strange and deformed birth, it shall not be decided by Aristotle, or the philosophers, whether the same be a man or not, but by the laws."[40] Hobbes is here rejecting the European tradition derived from Aristotle regarding so-called monstrous births as deviations from the form of the human and the relevance of the consequent disputes over what constituted this form that inevitably followed.[41] The rejection of the theoretical presumption of being capable of making such judgment is just one manifestation of Hobbes's larger critique of the totalizing pretensions of the mainstream of moral and political philosophy, including classical natural law theory.

Politics and Antipolitics

We have seen that the laws of nature oblige only in the civil state to the degree that different communities articulate the precise demands of these laws in unique ways, there being no basis to operationalize natural law independently of a shared community of meaning achieved via institutionalization.[42] In their diversity particular systems of positive law each tend toward the same end, the preservation of peace, actualizing the rational principles of natural law through rendering them effective in the civil condition. The innovation here with respect to those conceptions characteristic of classical natural law philosophy is thus clear.[43] In the final instance, what Hobbes's laws of nature speak to is the human potential for political artifice, to create ex nihilo a moral universe.[44] I have already suggested that when Hobbes criticizes Aristotle for theorizing a natural sociality among human beings, he denies not the uniquely human capacity for politics, but rather the suggestion that sociality is a direct expression of a homogeneous common interest that naturally unites individual wills.⁴⁵ Human beings are definitely political beings, although in a different sense, politics referring to the acts of covenanting—leaning always on the singular human capacities of curiosity and naming—that bring into existence an always artificial order of things.⁴⁶ It is precisely this generation that the laws of nature look toward. That natural law for Hobbes specifies a uniquely human capacity for artifice is notably revealed in *Leviathan*'s third law of nature, where justice and injustice are identified with the transfer of right characteristic of the creation of covenants, whose validity cannot be seen as derived from any natural moral properties independent of the coercive power endowed with the capacity to enforce them.⁴⁷ Human beings are those who are capable of themselves formulating the rules that govern their lives in common (although not as a necessarily collective entity, it being exclusively those who act as the sovereign representative who legislate these rules), independently of exterior models or schemata that would structure the precise form of the their association. The laws of nature are those rational theorems that reveal to them this potentiality.⁴⁸

As we have already detailed, acknowledgment of the human capacity to institute in a world lacking transcendent standards of action does not logically imply a normative preference for the democratic generalization of this capacity beyond the original instituting moment. Indeed, as I will note in this section, it may even generate a radically antipolitical imperative. In asserting the nonfoundation of human social institution in a law of laws exterior to the instituting community, as well as a fundamental equality-in-difference considered in terms of the equal potential to apply natural reason for the sake of the articulation of one's goods and the modes for the latter's realization, Hobbes recognizes the ontological conditions that render democracy a practicable form of regime. It is interesting to note that Hobbes's contribution here, his assertion of both the equality of rationalities and the contingency of the social order, has been recognized by one of the most prominent of contemporary radical democratic political theorists, Jacques Rancière.⁴⁹ In Rancière's account, if a social order introduces an inequality that takes the form of a distinction between those who command and those who obey, this inequality is only possible as a consequence of a prior presumption of an equality of intelligences, for "in order to obey an order at least two things are required: you must understand the order and you must understand that you must obey it. And to do that, you must already be the equal of the person who is obeying you."⁵⁰ Within Rancière's political thought, the social order is governed by a logic—that of the police—which is oriented toward a determinate distribution of the elements or parts of the community within a particular sensible field, defining that which can be seen and heard through the assignation of fixed places and functions.[51] Politics, however, in his own idiosyncratic account, is that activity which interrupts the existing configuration through the presentation of an alternative order of appearances in which previously un- or miscounted parts declare and demonstrate their equal ability to think, speak, and understand, thus revealing the absolute contingency of the distribution of the sensible order through the reconfiguration of the organization of places and functions.[52] Now, intuiting the extent to which politics as such is a demonstration of equality requires the staging of a conflict between two heterogenous orders, and worrying so much about the threat that disagreement poses to self-preservation, Hobbes not only demands the construction of a sovereign order in which the possibility of dispute is neutralized, but that such construction be authorized by supposedly independent contractors, thus denying the very existence of social parts that might endeavor to act politically. In this account, "there is no part of those who have no part. There are only individuals and the power of the state. Any party putting right and wrong at stake contradicts the very concept of a community."[53]

Although, as will be clear from the discussion below, I do not in this study adopt Rancière's conception of politics, his analysis nevertheless implicitly highlights a significant intellectual operation at play within the civil science of Hobbes. On some level Hobbes's political thought is a thought of the possibility of effacing politics, or a thought of antipolitics. As I have already suggested, it his recognition of the conditions for democratic practice—the equality of intelligences and the nonfoundational structure of the world—that renders the critique of democracy especially urgent. As observed in chapter 1, democracy is a regime of internal chaos, a reintroduction into the civil sphere of the mad logic of multitude. This chaotic condition is indeed a reflection of the metaphysical chaos that defines an empirical world lacking teleological direction. But the institution of the commonwealth was intended precisely to overcome this condition through the construction of a conventional unity, reintegrating the diversity of beings into a figure of the One,[54] represented by a sovereign from which emanates all right.[55] In a sense, Hobbes seems to have Plato's desire for the instauration of a rational and stable order of things, despite rejecting the Platonic view that this order can be derived from a source exterior to the empirical world.[56] Hobbesian sovereignty is thus an artificial transcendence intended to function as a response to the lack of a natural one.[57] For the reasons we have seen, democracy is counterproductive to the stable maintenance of this transcendence, and hence the need to privilege the monarchical sovereign form.

It is in light of this operation that many critics of Hobbes have interpreted him as a fundamentally antipolitical thinker.[58] Yves Charles Zarka, for example, explains how the institution of the commonwealth, itself a seemingly political act, paradoxically functions to neutralize the political function (in its nondemocratic variants at least), through the exclusive designation of legislative power to one or a minority of sovereign office holders: "By instituting the sovereign as the only actor, subjects deprive themselves of all status as political subject-actors. Recognition by subjects of the sovereign's action as their own is the counterpart of this deprivation. Or rather, we ought to say that if the individual is an actor-subject, it is by virtue of a single act: that of the social covenant. Now this act is precisely the one by which he gives up the status of actor in order to recognize the sovereign henceforth as the only actor."[59] The political self-expression of the people, if we concede that institution is a fundamentally political act (that is, despite Hobbes's contention that authorization remains a singularly individual process simultaneously undertaken by members of the multitude), has as its end the definitive termination of the capacity for such self-expression. Whereas the first political moment—the institution of the commonwealth—proceeds unproblematically given its stimulation by rational agreement regarding the only good that is shared by all, self-preservation, subsequent moments—whose deliberative matter is composed of always variegated individual goods and moral conceptions—are perpetual threats to social stability.

The problem of politics is essentially the problem of the good, or rather, of the intrinsic nonidentity of the good that results from the radical singularity of individual human psyches. Let us consider politics here in a most general sense as that mode of activity that seeks to negotiate this nonidentity for the sake of formulating collective trajectories of action. Hobbes's antipolitics thus wants to neutralize political life through, not the literal homogenization of the good, but rather the substitution as public of one conception of the good for the manifold of private conceptions.[60] As we know, it is ultimately impossible to construct a shared realm of mutual understanding grounded in the accurate perception of the trajectory of the desire of others.[61] Indeed, it is this diversity of modes of life and the latter's reciprocal incommensurability that renders the creation of civil society a necessity.[62] Hobbes's pluralism, however, is a genuine one. That is to say, there is no objective basis for preferring particular modes of being over others and subjecting these others to the former. The concern of civil science is the articulation of an authoritative right to "judge in cases of disagreement," cases of disagreement which are incapable of being negotiated via appeal to some standard of natural right reason.[63] The neutralization of conflict and the natural diversity of being that generates it cannot proceed via reference to any objective standards of right living, desire being incapable of being subjected or subordinated to an ultimate principle of any sort. The substitution of the reason of the sovereign agent for the particular reasons of each natural person, and the identification of the former with right reason itself, is the political response to the ontological condition of disagreement, the politics that institutes antipolitics.

Despite the fact that Hobbes emphasizes repeatedly the structural equivalencies of distinct forms of commonwealth, the antipolitical condition articulated above is one that manifests in societies represented by monarchical sovereigns alone: it is only the monarchical commonwealth that terminates disputation and deliberation between individuals regarding the trajectory of social institution. The conceptual reduction of monarchical sovereignty to sovereignty as such, as revealed through the emphasis on the establishment of conditions that only this specific form can establish, is an indication of Hobbes's normative preference. To the extent that both aristocracies and democracies must utilize assembly modes of organization to facilitate negotiation between distinct natural persons, they are intrinsically political. Needless to say, however, the major assembly composition of democracies—despite the fact that, as we noted earlier, many administrative responsibilities may be delegated to magistrates who take responsibility for certain quotidian tasks of governing—exponentially increases the number of sovereign office holders, rendering for Hobbes unbearable the inconveniences that result from political deliberation. But is the rejection of shared legislative responsibility truly adequate to the task of repressing the conflict that characterizes political life? Many readers find Hobbes's solution ultimately implausible, doubting that a sovereign can ever succeed in imposing unity on society, no matter how artful or extensive are the socializing techniques deployed to this end. As Richard Flathman writes, for example, the entire project seems in some sense internally contradictory: "In historical and social fact, there is a good deal of disagreement about and fluctuation concerning what is good, wise, noble, etc., and that more than a little of the conflict in human affairs results from disputation concerning the content to be given these and related notions. Thus to look to authority to diminish and control conflict and disorder, and at the same time to base it or make it depend on agreement concerning these notions, is to seek the cure in one of the main causes of the disease."[64] Flathman thus suggests that the Hobbesian project must be reinterpreted in order to be rendered useful in the face of fundamental pluralism. Given human particularity, all we can take Hobbes as plausibly attempting to do is encourage individual motion and activity, allowing distinct natural persons to energetically pursue their own goods as conceived by themselves to the greatest possible extent.[65]

Rather than successfully construct an impermeable artificial unity, more likely is that in the face of the state's incapacity to neutralize difference, political contestation will simply reemerge exterior to the governing organ. In light of Hobbes's abstractly utopian desire to overcome politics, it is thus worth reconsidering the unique political potentialities of the democratic commonwealth. A democratic reconceptualization of the sovereign as an institutional form capable of productively sublimating difference allows us to repoliticize Hobbes's civil science, the democratic affirmation of the political principle being in fact more faithful to Hobbes's pluralism than the mere emphasis on the private pursuit of good within those spheres of activity unregulated by civil law. Indeed, my suggestion is that Hobbes's own philosophy provides the conceptual ground for the identification of a normative preference for democracy. Specifically, considering what we have said thus far regarding the function of natural law within Hobbes's system in relation to the concepts of liberty and power provides a potential basis for the ethical privileging of this specific type of sovereign office.

Liberty and Natural Power

We have seen that Hobbes maintains that obedience to civil law is commanded by natural law regardless of the particular form of configuration of sovereign authority. The relationship between civil law and natural law as presented thus far may therefore appear to turn Hobbes into a forerunner of legal positivism,[66] even if only in a *de jure* sense.[67] As Arash Abizadeh points out, however, it is difficult to read Hobbes in such terms to the degree that the latter contends that natural law does minimally constrain what civil laws the sovereign may institute. The "self-effacing" readings of Hobbesian natural law associated with scholars such as Norberto Bobbio and Sharon Lloyd—which maintain that natural law abolishes itself through its embodiment in a positive system of civil law—"ignore Hobbes's characterization of the persistent role played, even after the commonwealth's establishment, by *specific* laws of nature whose point is to regulate the functioning of the legal system and the role of judges in it. These include natural laws concerning cruelty in punishment (seventh law), equity in judicial interpretation (eleventh), and the character of judges and judicial testimony (sixteenth through eighteenth)."[68] Here, however, I will focus only on what I take to be the fundamental manifestation of the extent to which the laws of nature function to impose ethical constraints on civil law within the commonwealth. This manifestation is irreducible to the form of constraint characteristic of traditional natural law theory, for whereas the latter ethically privileges particular modes of life at the expense of others, Hobbesian natural law takes as its object only that general human motion that makes any particular motion possible. Now, Hobbes is clear that subjects owe obedience to all effective government, independent of its specific configuration. He is just as clear, however, that government is effective only to the extent to which it guarantees the security of its subjects. This important fact has been picked up by many readers of Hobbes in order to construct various theories of legitimate sovereign resistance.[69] My suggestion, however, is that reflection on the content of the concept of security allows us to think, beyond such already existing resistance models, a potential democratic imperative.

Hobbes's laws of nature must be interpreted within the context of his concept of liberty and the latter's specifically human application within a precise philosophical anthropology. In *Leviathan* Hobbes writes that "LIBERTY, or FREEDOM, signifieth (properly) the absence of Opposition; (by Opposition I mean externall Impediments to motion;) and may be applied no lesse to Irrationall, and Inanimate creatures, than to Rationall. For whatsoever is tyed, or environed, as it cannot move, but within a certain space, which space is determined by the opposition of some externall body, we say that it hath not Liberty to go further."[70] As is often pointed out, however, it is misleading to interpret Hobbes's definition of liberty as the "the absence of externall Impediments"[71] as an affirmation of some form of " 'pure' negative freedom."[72] In his discussion of liberty in chapter 18, Hobbes continues that these impediments "may oft take away part of a mans power to do what hee would; but cannot hinder him from using the power left him, according as his judgement, and reason shall dictate to him."[73] The consideration of the freedom of any entity thus entails a correlative consideration of the natural power of that entity to do that which it is able to do.[74] The range of possible action is structured by both liberty and power components, one being free to act in a certain way only if one does not lack the internal impediments to said action, that is to say, only if one has the power to act. Hence the definition of a free person—which is not at all identical to "A *free Subject*," an example of absurd and senseless speech[75]—is one having both liberty and power to do what they would will to do: "A FREE-MAN, *is he, that in those things, which by his strength and wit he is able to do, is not hindred to doe what he has a will to do.*"[76] If freedom refers to the ability to do or not to do that which one has the capacity to do, the variation in such capacities is perhaps often obscured by Hobbes's tendency to explicate the concept of natural liberty in terms of the physical motions of inanimate entities, whose movement may be just as much impeded by external obstructions, but which lack the specific deliberative capacities of animate entities.

Hobbes's discussion in the *Anti-White* is particularly revealing on this point. Here Hobbes differentiates the quality of freedom on the basis of the animate or inanimate nature of the subject of action, the former's freedom lying in the possession of the ability to choose to do or not to do that which it is capable of doing: "Among animals, the one is properly said to be free which, though possessing the remaining power [*cetera potestas*] to carry out every action, does not yet possess the wish [to act]. Among inanimates, that is called free which is in no degree hindered from doing whatever, from its own nature, it can do."[77] The fact that animates can elect to act or not to act, needless to say, does not imply that said action or nonaction is uncaused, the necessary causes determining the choice of the action being either coercion or inducement.[78] Freedom ultimately lies in the alternating consideration of the advantages or disadvantages that result from the action or nonaction: "The freedom of animals is, then, merely the exchange or reciprocation of appetite and aversion; and the reason for this is that appetite and revulsion, and the will of all animals, have their causes. The said alternation is correctly called freedom, because the impediment [to action] works not through external factors but through internal, i.e., through the intellect and through the mind-picture of things to be chosen; for if the will lacked a cause, [the will itself] would be freedom."[79] A natural person, as an animate being, is thus free if they have the capacity to choose to do or not to do that which is in their power to do: "For he is *free* to do a thing, that may do it if he has the will to do it, and may forebear if he have the will to forbear."[80] And needless to say, as Hobbes is persistently at pains to emphasize, the fact that the actor lacks the freedom to determine the desire that structures elective deliberation regarding this doing or not-doing does not render the freedom to do or not-do illusory.[81]

Liberty is to be located not in the choice of appetite, but rather in the choice of action, in light of consideration of always necessary appetite. The mistake of Bramhall and others is to assume that the affirmation of the fact that every action is necessitated, having a necessary cause which would otherwise not stimulate the emergence of the effect, somehow or other implies that deliberation over the action is irrelevant to the latter's realization: "If there be a necessity that an action shall be done, or that any effect shall be brought to pass, it does not therefore follow that there is nothing necessarily required as a means to bring it to pass. And therefore, when it is determined that one thing shall be chosen before another, it is determined also for what cause it shall be chosen; which cause, for the most part, is deliberation or consultation. And therefore consultation is not in vain."[82] All actions that result from deliberation are indeed voluntary actions, a voluntary agent—that is, a free agent—being one who has not yet willed, that is, one for whom deliberation is not yet complete. The consistency of freedom and necessity is located in the simultaneous facts that, although one may be free to act, one may not be free to desire, that is to say, to voluntarily determine the content of the appetite. That the will is necessitated means simply that it is determined by some combination of causes external to it, it being impossible for any appetite to be the cause of itself. Hobbes thus writes that "I conceive nothing taketh beginning from itself, but from the action of some other immediate agent without itself: and that therefore when first a man had an appetite or will to something, to which immediately before he had no appetite nor will, the cause of his will is not the will itself, but something else not in his own disposing."[83] If the necessity of all causes is not apparent to us, such is no indication of a metaphysical nondetermination of being, but only the limits of our understanding. But "in him that could see the connexion of those causes, the *necessity* of all mens voluntary actions, would appear manifest."[84] It matters little that we are generally incapable of mapping the totality of causes, many of which must remain invisible to us, that necessitate appetite. Just as in the case of the motion of natural bodies within the universe, our inability to identify every efficient and material cause of a determination is not evidence of a natural spontaneity, by which we mean the emergence of a willed phenomenon lacking causal necessitation.

To summarize, the being of a thing is considered in terms of the actual capacity of that thing to do that which it is capable of doing: "The nature of any body is its potential to work or to act—a nature essential to it—i.e., included in, or to be inferred from, its definition."[85] Juhani Pietarinen has situated Hobbes's characterization here within a larger tradition of theorizing "active power" in seventeenth-century European philosophy: "The idea is as follows: if not prevented, bodies necessarily do certain things in virtue of their power."[86] As we have already noted in a previous discussion, power in *De Corpore* is considered as the immanent capacity of a body to move or generate effects within another body. In Pietarinen's account, this formulation "led Hobbes to consider active power as the nature or essence of things."[87] There exists an "*inherent power* of things" grounded in the latter's initial motions, the self-identity of things consisting in the perpetuation of their essence considered in this sense.[88] For Hobbes an object's natural activity refers to the actualization of its inherent potential to realize its innate tendencies via its movement, all natural bodies being distinguished from one another in terms of their internal motions.[89] As we have seen, however, for Hobbes all natural bodies are singular, nothing in the world being universal except for names, each thing existing naturally only as that particular thing that it is. Such applies to human beings just as much as any other. Consideration of the complex of particular motions of particular human bodies is thus no ground on which to theorize the institution of political life, given the radical differentiation of human interest and desire, the latter being generative of a plurality of noncommensurate goods incapable of being immediately reconciled. Indeed, this tendency to attempt to draw universal political conclusions from observation of the mode of being of particular human entities is precisely the error characteristic of natural law philosophy in its traditional Aristotelian-Thomist variants.

Hobbes's concept of natural law must thus be grounded in a minimal naturalism affirming a shared identity of the thinnest type. According to Hobbes, once we abstract from all particular determinations regarding individual human inclinations or dispositions toward particular objects, we are left with the only truly universal human desire: that for the extension and affirmation of life itself, the basic precondition for the pursuit of the particular good of every particular natural person, regardless of the specific trajectory of their appetite.[90] Even though the good is relationally defined—the form of its articulation being "relative to person, place, and time"—because all individuals naturally desire their particular good, it must be the case that all individuals share in a minimal identity, a common good that seeks after particular self-preservation: "The greatest of goods for each is his own preservation. For nature is so arranged that all desire good for themselves. Insofar as it is within their capacities, it is necessary to desire life, health, and further, insofar as it can be done, security of future time."[91] Life itself—considered in terms of the movement of the organism, the expulsion of its energy for the sake of its actualization of an always variable good—is thus one of the few nontedious elements of human nature. Recognition of this natural being generates a normative imperative, an ethical commitment to the facilitation of the expression of the intrinsic natural tendencies of the organism that the idea of the extension of life suggests.[92]

Natural Law and the True Liberty of the Subject

That Hobbes's analysis of natural being—his effort to discover "the empirical form of human nature in its immanence, excluding in principle all exterior finality grounded in some transcendent beyond"[93]—structures his ethics is suggested as early as *The Elements of Law*, where Hobbes identifies the primary sovereign duty as "the good government of the people."[94] Notably, this good government includes "not the mere preservation of their lives, but generally their benefit and good. So that this is the general law for sovereigns: that they procure, to the utmost of their endeavor, the good of the people."[95] Here Hobbes isolates four objects that collectively compose this latter good: multitude, commodity of living, peace, and defense. Of particular interest is how Hobbes articulates commodity of living, which he says "consisteth in liberty and wealth," with liberty here specifying a capacity for movement restricted only by what is necessary for the good of the commonwealth.[96] Hobbes thus constructs an ethical obligation grounded in consideration of the particular motion of subjects, the sovereign existing largely to facilitate the expression of the intrinsic tendencies and dispositions of the former. It is through this expression that the subjects are capable of actualizing their "well and delightful being," here associated with the enjoyment of those material resources required for the pursuit of individual good.[97] Indeed, the wealth of the people in *The Elements* is seen as requiring three conditions: "the well ordering of trade, procuring of labor, and forbidding the superfluous consuming of food and apparel."[98] Readers of Hobbes are increasingly aware of the extent to which he recognized that an equitable allocation of property within a commonwealth is essential to the realization of the security of the people, and hence the maintenance of civil peace.[99] All citizens must have access to those contentments of life that in any given social-historical context are seen as required to live well, the sovereign possessing the right to redistribute resources as changing circumstances require in order to maintain this situation.[100]

In subsequent work the basic Hobbesian principle regarding the end of government is captured by the concept of the safety of the people, which in *Leviathan* Hobbes identifies as the state's very business.[101] As is often noted, and as was already suggested in the passage from the *Elements* cited above, the safety of the people extends far beyond mere physical self-preservation.[102] As Hobbes puts it in *De Cive*, "By *safety* one should understand not mere survival in any condition, but a happy life so far as that is possible. For men willingly entered commonwealths *which they had formed by design* in order to be able to live as pleasantly as the human condition allows."[103] For the government to fail to promote and advance this happiness of the people, by not affording them the means to indulge their delights, is "contrary to the law of nature."[104] The centrality of the notion of public safety is reiterated in *Leviathan*, the good of the people being identified as the ultimate goal of sovereign rule: "The OFFICE of the Soveraign, (be it a Monarch, or an Assembly,) consisteth in the end, for which he was trusted with the Soveraign Power, namely the procuration of the *Safety of the people*; to which he is obliged by the Law of Nature, and to render an account thereof to God, the Author of that Law, and to none but him."[105] And also again, Hobbes explicitly confirms that the word *safety* signifies an extended concept of preservation as prosperity and human flourishing: "But by Safety here, is not meant a bare Preservation, but also all other Contentments of life, which every man by lawfull Industry, without danger, or hurt to the Common-wealth, shall acquire to himself."[106] Ultimately, then, the duty of the sovereign to ensure the maintenance of this condition of delightful being obliges "by the Law of Nature"[107] and is the "highest law"[108] or the "fundamentall Law to a King."[109]

In each of his three major political works Hobbes maintains that the preservation of this expansive security of the people is mediated by the maintenance of a sphere of right whose transgression can only violate the rational principles that motivate the institution of civil society in the first place. Any voluntary alienation of right is undertaken for the sake of the advancement of the individual's good, it thus following that certain rights, to the extent that they are necessary to any potential actualization of this good, cannot be renounced or transferred. Specifically, the individual cannot divest themselves of right where that divestment would threaten death, the integrity of the physical body, or the procurement of those things necessary to maintain a delighted life. In *The Elements of Law*, it is within the context of his discussion of that law of nature demanding that each acknowledge one another as equals that Hobbes brings up those rights which cannot be alienated. Although the right to everything needs to be given up to establish civil peace, the individual must retain their rights to certain things: "to his own body (for example) the right of defending, whereof he could not transfer; to the use of fire, water, free air, and place to live in, and to all things necessary for life."[110] The law of nature ultimately commands giving up only those rights that "cannot be retained without loss of peace."[111] *De Cive*, within the discussion of humility, the ninth dictate of natural law, repeats this partial list of those rights that demand to be maintained after the general conveyance of right: "Just as it was necessary for each man's preservation that he should relinquish certain of his *rights*, so it is no less necessary to his preservation that he retain certain *rights*, namely the *Right* of protecting his person, the right of enjoying the open air, water, and all other things necessary for life."[112] It is within *Leviathan*, however, that Hobbes expresses the general principle in its most-well known form, through the concept of the true liberty of subjects.[113]

In explicating the content of the true liberty of the subject, Hobbes redeploys a familiar language. As distinct from both natural liberty, as well as the basic liberties of the subject that exist where law within a commonwealth does not regulate specific spheres of action, the so-called "true liberty of the subject" refers to "the things, which though commanded by the Sovereign, he may nevertheless, without Injustice, refuse to do."[114] They outline a specific set of concrete conditions that we can understand as being essential to the realization of the sovereign imperative to ensure the safety of the citizens. Hobbes specifies here that subjects always have a right, for example, to defend themselves against assaults on their physical bodies, to not implicate or accuse themselves, to refuse dangerous and dishonorable orders, and to not interfere in the punishment of another citizen.[115] Under circumstances in which sovereign command works to hinder the subject's self-preservation, this subject has a legitimate right to resist. For example, "If the Soveraign command a man (though justly condemned,) to kill, wound, or mayme himselfe; or not to resist those that assault him; or to abstain from the use of food, ayre, medicine, or any other thing, without which he cannot live; yet hath that man the Liberty to disobey."[116] In short, what true liberty aims at is the prevention of the frustration of that primary end to which sovereignty was instituted, the affirmation and extension of human life.

Susanne Sreedhar has noted that "much commentary on Hobbes's political philosophy simply ignores his discussion of the true liberties of subjects. When it is addressed in detail, it is often denigrated."[117] Indeed, Hobbes's contention that subjects living under sovereign authority must retain a set of rights to certain things certainly seems to raise difficult problems for his political theory.[118] Yet at the same time, through its complication of the established scholarly image of the Hobbesian civil science, true liberty opens the latter up to new political possibilities, possibilities that Hobbes himself would seem to want to occult.[119] The existence of the true liberties can be read, counter to the Hobbesian impulse to antipolitics, as preserving a space within the commonwealth, no matter how limited, for the political. Such requires logically extending the principle of the right of legitimate sovereign disobedience that Hobbes says adheres in particular circumstances. It certainly seems possible for the individual right to resist in the face of the sovereign threat to one's self-preservation to be translated into a political right to resist on the basis of an overlapping perception of identical such threats. If subjects retain the right to do that which they deem necessary to preserve their lives, then that must include the possibility of combining with others for the sake of mutual preservation. And indeed, Hobbes himself suggests as much in the following passage, where he qualifies the claim that one cannot justly interfere in the punishment of another citizen by the sovereign: "But in case a great many men together, have already resisted the Soveraign Power unjustly, or committed some Capitall crime, for which every one of them expecteth death, whether have they not the Liberty then to joyn together, and assist, and defend one another?

Certainly they have: For they but defend their lives, which the Guilty man may as well do, as the Innocent."[120] Hobbes seems here to take the doctrine of the individual right to self-defense to its logical conclusion, positing the legitimacy of political resistance on the part of a corporate body that is united with respect to the nature of its collective end.[121] As Sreedhar sums up the logical movement: "Hobbes himself claims that if one lacks the basic necessities of life (e.g., food, water, medicine), one is permitted to disobey the sovereign in order to procure them. Presumably, if such things are denied to a group, then the members of that group are justified in joining forces if such collective action is what they judge necessary to the same."[122]

Given that the appearance of the sovereign is always constituted through the judgment of the subjects, as revealed in the implication that sovereign legitimacy is grounded in the preservation of a safety of the people of which the latter are the evaluators, there is always the possibility for the emergence of a legitimation crisis, should the direction of public judgment shift in light of sovereign endeavor.[123] No matter the particular form of configuration of sovereign authority, then, within the commonwealth sovereignty remains perpetually precarious to the extent that citizens retain the liberty to collectively resist or disobey authority in those instances in which they individually perceive their lives to be in danger.[124] It is certainly the case that for Hobbes the safety of the people depends on, not just the legislation and execution of "good Lawes," but also "publique Instruction" on the basic principles of civil science, so as to facilitate the maximal internalization of the content of this science.[125] Such internalization, however, can never be so extensive so as to produce an assured acceptance of and identification with sovereign imperative, not only as a result of the limitation of pedagogical technique in the face of the critical-rational capacities of human beings, but also because the science itself, through the recognition of the inalienability of certain rights, forecloses such an operation. Despite what Hobbes may desire, and contra the criticism of certain radical democratic readers,[126] the Hobbesian project is incapable of completely eliminating politics through the inclusive integration of all elements within the social field into a permanently fixed distribution that forecloses the emergence of collective projects in a potentially oppositional mode.[127] The perpetuation of the sphere of true liberty resists the instauration of complete social closure.

Hobbes's deployment of the term *liberty* within this context is especially important and refers us back to our previous discussion regarding the relationship between liberty and power. True liberties of subjects are unique, for they speak to and aim to protect those truly universal conditions needed for the perpetuation of human life, considered in terms of the facilitation of necessary internal motion. They aim at the preservation of that sphere of activity whose maintenance constitutes the condition for the expression of essential human power, regardless of the specific direction of individual desire. For Hobbes natural right is not derived from some transcendent source exterior to human experience, but is rather logically derived from consideration of the immanent being of the organism. Hobbes's laws of nature specify that minimal content that can be said to constitute the essential internal tendencies of the natural human being and the means to institute a political order capable of facilitating these tendencies' expression. The true liberties of subjects, meanwhile, whose maintenance is demanded by natural law, are those necessary to ensure the continued and ongoing actualization of these tendencies within a commonwealth. That they reflect this universal content is revealed particularly acutely through the central significance of the concept of equity, the fundamental principle of natural law. As we have already had occasion to note in chapter 4, for Hobbes "equality is the law of nature,"[128] equity being defined as "that habit by which we allow equality of nature."[129] Equity is thus prudentially suggested by natural law to the extent that it reflects a natural equality or universality of being. What I will go on to suggest in the next section of this chapter is that Hobbes provides a theoretical basis for conceptually extending the concept of equity so as to include an equality of legislative activity, political participation being interpreted as an expression of an essential human power. On this basis it becomes possible to generate an ethical preference for democracy as a sovereign form.

The Reappearance of Participatory Desire in *Leviathan*

Through the conceptual juxtaposition of the Hobbesian concepts of natural law and liberty I have thus far attempted to reveal several key facts. First, the safety of the people can only be thought in terms of an expansive concept of human life as well-being and flourishing. Second, the preservation of this safety is concretely achieved through the establishment of certain definite conditions of existence, such "as right to governe their owne bodies; enjoy aire, water, motion, waies to go from place to place; and all things else, without which a man cannot live, or not live well."¹³⁰ Third, it is toward the procurement of these necessities that the sphere of true liberty looks, such being an imperative demanded by natural law. And fourth, the concepts of natural law and life refer us to the essential motion or power of all human beings, those few universal intrinsic tendencies and forces that, as a result of this universality, ethically warrant having their expression facilitated. Overall, there is no tension between Hobbes's affirmation of the radical singularity of human beings and their desires and his contention that there exist such universal powers. This is because, regardless of the particular motions of particular organisms, the unique goods to which this motion tends are capable of being realized only through the preservation of a general motion that is captured by the concept of life itself.

If it were the case that one could identify among those minimally general human inclinations a natural desire for political participation, to act collectively with others for the sake of the competitive advancement of a perceived to be shared good in relation to contending goods, then one could posit an ethical imperative that demands preference for democratic sovereign forms, to the degree that such forms are those that universally facilitate for citizens the expression of this internal tendency of the natural being. The articulation of this new essential human power, mediated by the uniquely human capacities for reason and speech, would subsequently problematize Hobbes's effort, after *The Elements of Law*, to theorize an identity of freedom in all forms of commonwealth. Hobbes's critique of the classical writers for falsely identifying freedom with popular regimes would be rendered invalid, for it would in fact be the case that the citizens of Lucca possess a liberty that is denied in Constantinople, not to the degree that in the former citizens are not bound by civil law, but rather to the degree that they possess a means to express an essential power whose affirmation conforms to natural law. And indeed, one of the innovations found within *Leviathan*, which has thus far not been adequately noticed, is precisely the positing on Hobbes's part of a fundamental participatory desire.

There are at least four passages within *Leviathan* that suggest this characteristic of the natural orientation of the human being. Firstly, in his discussion of the biological principle of sociality characteristic of animals whose private and common interests immediately coalesce with one another by nature, Hobbes maintains, contrary to the argument in *De Cive*, that "very many" people desire to participate in public affairs.¹³¹

Secondly, in the context of the ninth law of nature's affirmation of natural equality and the repudiation of the Aristotelian notion that distinctions in civil status may be grounded in cognitive differences of capacity, Hobbes contends that we can perceive among the majority of people a preference for self-government, "For there are very few so foolish, that had not rather govern than be governed by others."[132] Thirdly, in chapter 36, within the context of a discussion of prophecy and the need to remain suspicious of those who would claim direct access to the will of God, Hobbes asserts a natural desire on the part of individuals to rule: "For he that pretends to teach men the way of so great felicity, pretends to govern them; that is to say, to rule, and reign over them; which is a thing, that *all men naturally desire*, and is therefore worthy to be suspected of Ambition and Imposture."[133] By far the most significant evidence on this point, however, should be drawn from, fourthly, chapter 22's discussion of bodies politic. If Hobbes generally excludes citizens from participatory political processes, this chapter of *Leviathan* presents several seeds from which there might emerge a more robust theory of Hobbesian political participation.[134]

Hobbes begins by providing a basic definition of a system: "By SYSTEMES; I understand any numbers of men joined in one Interest, or one Businesse."[135] They are thus collective entities, composed of a multiplicity of individual natural persons who voluntarily unite with one another for the sake of the advancement of what is perceived to be a shared interest or end. Hobbes outlines a typology of systems, beginning by distinguishing between regular and irregular forms, the former being those in which one person or assembly acts as a representative for all participants, and the latter being all others.[136] Of regular systems there are both independent or absolute and dependent variants. Absolute systems, such as commonwealths, are subject to no authority but that of their representative, whereas dependent systems are subject always to a sovereign authority. Of subordinate systems, some are political and some are private. Political systems are those made by the authority of the sovereign, while private are those constituted by subjects themselves or via a foreign authority. Of private systems, finally, some are lawful and some are unlawful, the former those legally permitted within the commonwealth, the latter all others. Irregular systems, meanwhile, also lawful by the authority of the sovereign, are those lacking a representative, and thus "consist only in concourse of People."[137]

In chapter 22 Hobbes's main concern is the political system, or body politic. It is important to emphasize here that Hobbes deploys this latter term in a revised way in *Leviathan*, it no longer referring to the independent political society or commonwealth itself.[138] The power of bodies politic is thus always limited, the sovereign determining the scope of their permission: "For Power Unlimited, is absolute Soveraignty. And the Soveraign, in every Commonwealth, is the absolute Representative of al the subjects; and therefore no other, can be Representative of any part of them, but so far forth, as he shall give leave."[139] The object of Hobbes's analysis here is thus not democracy, inasmuch as he understands the latter to be characterized by popular deliberative activity by a unified people in possession of a sovereign right. His discussion, rather, focusing as it does on the mode of operation of subordinate organizations that allow individuals to collectively pursue their interests in a manner that is consistent with the requirements of civil law, speaks to what today we might identify as the realm of civil society. The political significance of the discussion of bodies politic, however, is not compromised by the fact that these systems remain limited and nonlegislative: their importance is not to be located in a reproduction of the structural form of the democratic regime. The relevant issue, on the contrary, is what they reveal to us about the extent of the human desire for collective deliberation in group fora. Hobbes's exhaustive detailing of the extent of the typology of systems suggests that the commonwealth is always traversed through by a widespread participatory desire to act with others. Indeed, the extent of the range of such associations, itself a reflection of the breadth and diversity of human desire, is so great so as to belie comprehensive categorization. As Hobbes writes, "The variety of Bodies Politique, is almost infinite: for they are not onely distinguished by the several affaires, for which they are constituted, wherein there is an unspeakable diversitie; but also by the times, places, and numbers, subject to many limitations."[140] In light of this "unspeakable diversitie," it is thus not a surprise when Hobbes ultimately concludes, again contra *De Cive*, that individuals do have a natural desire for political participation: "For though every man, where he can be present, *by Nature* desires to participate of government."[141]

Indeed, now in *Leviathan*, just as was the case in *The Elements of Law*, this desire for participation, far from being intrinsically restricted to the vainglorious, is a general one that is only lost through the failure to preserve institutional spaces that function to express or mediate it. It is thus just where citizens lack the opportunity for direct participation in common affairs that they prefer monarchical forms: "Yet where they cannot be present, they are by Nature also enclined, to commit the Government of their common Interest rather to a Monarchicall, then a Popular form of government: which is also evident in those men that have great private estates; who when they are unwilling to take the paines of administering the businesse that belongs to them, choose rather to trust one Servant, then an Assembly either of their friends or servants."[142] It is significant that this discussion, furthermore, takes place within the context of Hobbes's claim that in fact there are very few historical examples of provinces being represented by an assembly, as for example when citizens who are not physically present in a province commit authority to select individuals as opposed to councils: "The Romans who had the Soveraignty of many Provinces; yet governed them alwaies by Presidents, and Praetors; and not by Assemblies, as they governed the City of *Rome*, and Territories adjacent. In like manner, when there were Colonies sent from *England*, to plant *Virginia*, and *Sommer-Ilands*; though the government of them here, were committed to Assemblies in *London*, yet did those Assemblies never commit the Government under them to any Assembly there; but did to each Plantation send one Governour."[143] The lack of assembly organization is thus not a manifestation of a lack of participatory desire per se, but rather of concrete institutional impediments to the setting up of such arrangements within specific social-historical contexts.

It is notable that in chapter 22, after maintaining that individuals possess a natural desire to participate in deliberative political bodies for the sake of the advancement of their good, Hobbes then goes on to reassert his belief that no one is more competent to articulate the nature of their good and the modes for its realization than individuals themselves. Such is revealed through his discussion of the ordering of a body politic for trade, members of said entity being identified as those most knowledgeable of their affairs, and thus best suited to the administration of the latter: "In a Bodie Politique, for the well ordering of forraigne Traffique, the most commodious Representative is an assembly of all the members; that is to say, such a one, as every one that adventureth his mony, may be present at all the Deliberations, and Resolutions of the Body, if they will themselves. For proof whereof, we are to consider the end, for which men that are Merchants, and may buy and sell, export and import their Merchandise, according to their own discretions, doe nevertheless bind themselves up in one Corporation."[144] Hobbes is here discussing private or corporate affairs as opposed to specifically public ones, but as we have already seen, there is no qualitative difference in the rational capacities that are exercised in the diversity of human endeavors, individuals deploying in each of the latter the same prudential reason. To requote a passage referenced in chapter 4, "To govern well a family, and a kingdome, are not different degrees of Prudence; but different sorts of businesse."[145] Whatever the sphere of activity, Hobbes rejected the notion that any single individual or group of individuals has access to a special knowledge or technique that would provide them with a superior ability to determine the nature of goods and outline the structure of the relation between consequent and antecedent so as to more consistently determine the path to these goods' realization.

Hobbes's seemingly marginal concession in *Leviathan* of a natural participatory desire takes on a special significance in light of two important facts. To begin with, we must here recall the discussion in chapter 2, where I attempted to show that Hobbes's effort to prevent the emergence of any source of democratic normativity motivated him to significantly revise various elements of his political philosophy. In *De Cive* we saw that this effort was composed of multiple moments. Firstly, Hobbes repudiated his earlier conception of civic liberty, emphasizing the fact that subjects remain bound by civil law in every form of commonwealth, freedom and sovereignty referring to distinct conditions: the lack of limits to movement and the authorship of limits to movement. True liberty, however, is irreducible to this schema. Now, if a preference for democracy is incapable of being grounded in the latter's actualization of a unique form of civil liberty that evades obligation, there still remains the possibility, as I have suggested, that it can be grounded in an understanding of participation in government as an expression of a fundamental intrinsic tendency of the organism, and thus one that is deserving of being included under that list of modes of being whose preservation is essential for the procurement of the safety of the people. Hobbes is aware of this possible line of argument, and hence the second element of *De Cive*'s anti-democratic strategy: the rejection of the idea of such a universal political desire. To quote the relevant passage again:

> I will tell you. To see the proposal of a man whom we despise preferred to our own; to see our wisdom ignored before our eyes; to incur certain enmity in an uncertain struggle for empty glory; to hate and be hated because of differences of opinion

(which cannot be avoided, whether we win or lose); to reveal our plans and wishes when there is no need to and to get nothing by it; to neglect our private affairs. These, I say, are disadvantages. But to lose the opportunity to pit your wits against another man, however enjoyable such contests may be to clever debaters, is not such a disadvantage for them.[146]

In Hobbes's account, people only wish to participate in government for the sake of vainglorious self-aggrandizement: "There is no reason why anyone would not prefer to spend his time on his *private business* rather than on *public affairs*, except that he sees scope for his eloquence, to acquire a reputation for intelligence and good sense."[147]

If such is Hobbes's stated position in *De Cive*, in *Leviathan* the ground of the critique of democracy shifts substantially and in such a way that should cause us to question the sincerity of Hobbes's positing of a general political apathy. As we have seen, whereas in *De Cive* the institution of the commonwealth was still thought in terms of a necessarily originary democratic moment, in *Leviathan* Hobbes thought he had jettisoned this necessity with the introduction of the schema of authorization, in which collective political participation on the part of a people united prior to sovereign institution was unnecessary for the foundation of the state. Given this situation, in which the self-activity of the people—the generalized participation of all in collective political processes—is not required for political institution, the critique of democratic sovereign preference became far less urgent. Hobbes simply lays out his case as to why democracy is the inferior sovereign form, but there is no basis to presume that it is somehow the most natural, reflecting a fundamental popular sovereignty preexisting representation. Hence the paradoxical situation in which the disappearance of the language of original democracy is simultaneously accompanied by a reappearance of the language of participatory desire, which contrary to *De Cive*, Hobbes now says that all individuals do in fact possess.

The second important fact to take note of here was discussed extensively in chapter 3 and that is the Hobbesian recognition of the radical diversity of human appetite and sensory experience. It is important to remember this diversity in light of what might be formulated as a potential objection to my argument: Is it not the case, for example, that human beings naturally desire many things, such as glory and preeminence, whose pursuit is clearly antithetical to the maintenance of peace? From my perspective such an argument is not valid, for it universalizes particular psychic orientations that Hobbes was clear to maintain are not in fact species characteristics. Contrary to various vulgarizations of Hobbes, there is very little that is essential about the trajectory of human desire, Hobbes being extremely skeptical about the possibility of identifying a set of natural human appetites shared by all. This fact is revealed with special clarity in Gabriella Slomp's important work on Hobbes and the problem of glory, the latter being most often identified as that essential human passion in need of, if not absolute renunciation, at least complex regulation. As Slomp convincingly shows, however, even if in his earlier work glory appears to function as the "*genus* of all passions," it becomes evident in *Leviathan* and *De Homine* that it is in fact "just a *species*, or instance of human emotions."[148] Although all individuals may very well desire power as the means to acquire those objects which our appetites direct us toward, not only the objects but the motivating psychological forces are quite varied from person to person. As Hobbes observes in *De Homine*, there exist "an almost infinite number of passions," this uncategorizable multiplicity reflecting the lack of a shared human psychology that would unite all individual natural persons.[149] As Slomp observes, "In *De Homine*, as in *Leviathan*, Hobbes seems keener to show the link between passions and observable behaviour than to offer a universal psychological interpretation of man."[150] Human behavior, as we have already noted, is far more influenced by social and institutional factors than by natural ones, human nature being so individually diverse as to have little explanatory power. In light of these already observed facts, then, it thus seems highly significant that in *Leviathan* Hobbes does identify the desire for political participation as a genuinely natural one that adheres in "all men." There thus seems to be an implicit recognition on the part of Hobbes of politics as a fundamental modality of human experience.

Chapter 22's conjunction of the two particular issues that I have highlighted—that of an ontological orientation toward involvement in participatory modes and that of an immanent capacity to articulate the form of particular goods—raises an immediate issue. If all individuals desire participation in political organs to the extent that the latter are identified as effective modes for the advancement of one's interest, and if the proximity of particular individuals to their own desire renders them the most effective evaluators of said interest, then why is democracy not identified as the most preferable form of political regime, to the extent that it institutionally generalizes spaces for such collective self-activity?

This is a question, however, to which we already know the answer. As we saw in chapter 1, the problem with democratic political organization, according to Hobbes, is that the formal mechanics of deliberative assembly activity inherently tend to upset the order of relation between reason and passion so as to render impossible proper ratiocination. Within assembly fora the instrument of rhetoric is deployed in the effort to win partisans to one's positions through the inflammation of the passions, opinions circulating "independently of reasoned consideration."[151] Hence Hobbes interprets democracy in terms of the concept of madness, the latter defined precisely as a surplus of passion that militates against reasoned moderation and self-limitation. If reason and madness are potentialities that all individuals carry within themselves to the degree that they are each subject to the vicissitudes of their affects and passions, democracy as a sovereign configuration tends to multiply the potential for the appearance of the latter at the level of society, to the extent that it increases the number of inherently passionate individuals occupying sovereign office and, more significantly, further stimulates passion via the confrontation of individual opinions expressed through eloquence. The public expression of a multiplicity of opinion grounded in immediate consideration of the trajectory of passion can only result in the emergence of faction—given the radical singularity of individual desire—as particular individuals self-organize themselves on the basis of contingent shared conceptions, clearing the way for eventual civil discord and social breakdown. If such mechanics do not characterize the internal functioning of subordinate bodies politic within the commonwealth, this apparently results from the fact that the individual members of such organizations share an already established minimal identity of interest—this interest itself being the foundation of the existence of the body—that neutralizes normative competition. Conflict is abated to the extent that deliberative negotiation between individuals in such fora aims at the articulation of particular modes of action for the sake of the realization of shared values, as opposed to the election of a single specific value to be pursued from a set of fundamentally opposed ones. In short, for Hobbes political participation may be rational when realized through involvement in deliberative bodies politic under a monarchical sovereign form, but remain irrational in different political contexts. Hence in a democracy sovereignty itself is destabilized as a result of the generalization of participation, the political internalization of the latter within the sovereign assembly organ. From this perspective human sociability is much more carefully and safely cultivated within monarchies than democracies. But how compelling is such an argument for us today?

Toward a Hobbesian Democracy

In chapter 30 of *Leviathan* Hobbes famously distinguishes between a good law and a just law. Whereas all genuine law is just, "A good Law is that, which is Needfull, for the *Good of the People*, and withal *Perspicuous*."[152] The question arises: Can sovereign forms be differentiated on the basis of their capacity to generate laws needful of this good of the people? Hobbes is explicit that even if there exist no essential differences in the structure of power in unique sovereign configurations (such as, for example, in the marks, rights, or consequences of sovereignty), these configurations do differ with respect to the "Convenience, or Aptitude to produce the Peace, and Security of the people."[153] Hence he prefers a monarch over an assembly, and in particular a democratic assembly. If, however, we do not accept Hobbes's critique of what he sees as the internal tendencies of assembly rule, then the ground for monarchical prejudice dissolves, and the question may be approached from a new perspective. Here contemporary political theory intersects with the history of political thought, the former demonstrating the extent to which it is able to enrich the productivity of the latter through revealing latent political potentialities closed off by the work's historical context. Although discussion of the issue is outside of the scope of the present work, we are aware of the extent to which contemporary political theorists and philosophers attempt to demonstrate how democracy may exceed merely passionate factional conflict that short-circuits reason and prevents the prudential deployment of judgment. It is possible to think deliberative spaces in which actors, accepting the legitimacy of the instituted decision-procedure, agonistically confront one another for the sake of the mutual negotiation and adjustment of opinion, in light of rational consideration of established knowledge.

The possibility of instituting such modes of political interaction, meanwhile, is empirically supported by many recent experiments in sortition-based deliberative mini-publics, such as citizens' assemblies, deliberative polling, participatory budgeting, and so on.[154] As was the case with the earlier discussion of Hobbesian bodies politic—where the democratic significance of the phenomenon is irreducible to the structural production of the democratic institutional form, but is located rather in the revelation of that political desire that would stimulate positive civic investment in that form—these institutions are clearly not themselves experiments in democratic sovereignty as Hobbes understands it. They likewise, however, suggest something important about the nature of political desire, specifically about its negotiation. The lottocratic structure of the institutional innovations, drawing in participants who lack that preestablished identity of interest that Hobbes seems to think bodies politic require, demonstrates the extent to which participatory organs may be deployed beyond the realm of what today we call civil society. What deliberative micro-publics speak to is the possibility of opening up administrative and legislative institutions to occupation by random citizens from a diversity of backgrounds and with a diversity of normative conceptions, and that this openness can produce—certainly not consensus—but reasonably accepted decisions whose legitimacy is affirmed by each participant.

Hobbes on this point, however, might further push back on the issue of the scalability of such deliberative organs. If unlike in bodies politic participants do not necessarily have an already identical orientation toward the object of the institution—such providing a common ground that works against the emergence of fundamental conflict—it might nevertheless be the case that mini-publics still operate on the basis of a continuity of conscious or unconscious assumptions derived from shared experience in a communal context not exhausting the being of society as a whole. In large and complex societies, for example, such organs may function adequately at a municipal or provincial level, but perhaps not a national one. Relatively commodious coordination at the level of the subunit might thus very well give way to antagonistic dispute at a higher level within a federally structured democratic polity. As interesting and important as this and other related questions are, they do not admit of solution through the modes of political theory or philosophy, but can be clarified only through political testing and experimentation. Indeed, recall that Hobbes himself is perfectly aware of the limitations of his own civil science with respect to the issue of regime efficacy, and hence his acknowledgment of the inability to definitively prove democracy's inferiority relative to other sovereign forms. Hobbes, rather, only believes that there are strong reasons to prefer monarchy on the basis of the limited facts of historical experience. Such is similarly the case with respect to my suggestion here. The goal of my reading in this chapter is to open up the Hobbesian texts in order to reveal within them political potentialities that have thus far not been recognized. Contemporary innovations in democratic practice, furthermore, merely lend some support to the productivity of such an endeavor, a productivity that was concealed to Hobbes as a consequence of a certain obtuseness on the question of human co-relation.

My suggestion is that Hobbes fails to recognize the extent to which individuals in democracies are capable of living up to *Leviathan*'s fifth law of nature, "compleasance," which states *"that every man strive to accommodate himself to the rest."*[155] Again, such mutual accommodation is a necessity given the nonidentity of individual subjects, a nonidentity which is not simply effaced as a result of the commonwealth's fixing of the terms of justice and injustice. As Hobbes puts it, "For the understanding whereof, we may consider, that there is in mens aptnesse to Society, a diversity of Nature, rising from their diversity of Affections."[156] Hobbes never allowed, however, for the possibility of the generalization of this principle of accommodation so as to produce a relative democratic stability, sociability—which every individual is capable of recognizing and affirming via the exercise of their reason—manifesting itself in the mutual recognition of the legitimacy of democratic procedure, however such procedure is specified in the concrete case.[157] We have already seen the extent to which Hobbes's concept of equity—the central category structuring his moral philosophy—has a wide range of practical application extending well beyond the adjudication of disputes. This range is only further broadened once we make the effort to move beyond Hobbes's context in order to deploy the principle in light of contemporary political knowledge. Affirmation of the precept of complaisance in a mode so as to acknowledge democratic amiability, for example, allows for a further extension of equity's possible scope of application. What is simply essential to remember—and indeed this is one of Hobbes's most important lessons—is that amiability must be cultivated and maintained through careful institutional design, there existing no natural ground that guarantees shared popular commitment to political equality. As we saw, in Hobbes's account in *The Elements of Law* it is precisely the failure to refine the political form so as to reproduce democratic commitment that ultimately stimulates the movement to aristocracy.

Recognizing that democracy singularly allows for the equal participation of all citizens in the formulation of law permits us to see it as the form of regime most adequately affirming, not just abstract equality, but the specifically Hobbesian notion of equality-in-difference. That Hobbes himself recognizes this on some level can be gleaned through a revealing passage in *De Cive*. The topic of the section in question is the argument of "those who object to a Government of *one* man precisely because it is by one man."[158] Here Hobbes maintains that one cannot consistently criticize monarchy on the basis of its disproportionate distribution of political authority without at the same criticizing aristocracy. Critics of rule by one, Hobbes maintains, would generally be perfectly contented with rule by a few, if those critics were one of these few. It is not a concern with equality that motivates their critique, but rather private ambition. As Hobbes puts it, "It is envy that suggests this objection to *one*; they see that one man has what all men want. The same people would think it unfair on the same grounds if a *few* ruled, unless they either were or expected to be in the number; for it is unfair that there is not an equal right for all, then the regime of the optimates is also unfair."[159] What is notable is that within this discussion democracy is not mentioned at all, the critique of monarchy being rejected on the basis of its application to aristocracy: both forms of regime establish political inequality considered as the monopolization of legislative authority by a minor part of the community. There is thus no interrogation of whether the critique would be ethically legitimated from the standpoint of a sovereignty that affirms political equality through institutionally facilitating shared rule on the part of all citizens. Indeed, within this paragraph the "state of equality" is associated only with the "state of war," monarchy and aristocracy being contrasted not with democracy, but rather anarchy: "But it has been shown that the state of equality is a state of war, and therefore inequality has been introduced with everyone's agreement. So one should no longer regard inequality as an unfair condition, when the one who has more is the one to whom we have voluntarily given more. Thus the disadvantages consequent on the rule of *one man*, are a consequence not of the rule of *one* but of the rule of *a man*. The question therefore is whether the rule of one *man* or of several *men* causes more disadvantages to the citizens."[160] The issue of conventional political equality, and its potential relationship to that ethics derived from consideration of natural equality, is not raised.

The necessity of this movement from lived equality to inequality via the institution of the commonwealth is one that is taken as a given by the majority of readers of Hobbes, who de facto exclude democratic sovereignty from the Hobbesian scheme. The tension is articulated, for example, by Christopher Brooke, who notes that "while in the civil condition the citizens may stand in a certain kind of relationship of equality vis-à-vis one another, that civil society itself is constructed around, even constituted by an awesome inequality between the subjects and the sovereign."[161] Extending the scope of sovereign potentiality, however, allows us to address what appears to be this inadequacy in Hobbes's civil science. Recall that although all individuals are competent to articulate the form of their good, the radical human difference that characterizes the members of the human species necessarily precludes the simultaneous realization of these goods, and hence the need to institute a civil society as an artificial mechanism to overcome this diversity. If all individuals are equally capable of deploying right reason to articulate with relative competency the trajectory tending toward the actualization of their particular good, in the commonwealth the singular reason of the sovereign is substituted for each particular reason, it being deployed to realize a now public good determined by the sovereign exclusively. This public good, however, as a manifestation of one or more particular reasons, is distinguished from that general good that the concept of the safety of the people is intended to capture, and which the true liberties of the subject are meant to safeguard. For Hobbes the insufficiency of democracy as a sovereign form emerges from the fact that within democratic assemblies deliberative procedures, largely characterized by the deployment of eloquence as a persuasive technique, tend to distort individual perception of the good through the recalibration of the relation between passion and reason. Individual desire overwhelms concern with the safety of the people, such that the sovereign form is no longer capable of preserving that end for which sovereignty was instituted in the first place.

If democratic institutional design is capable of constructing fora that elude such dynamics, however—and recall, as I note above, that such may remain an open question awaiting verification—then not only is it the case that there remains no basis to discriminate against democratic sovereignty, but there may be a strong reason to prefer it. As we know, for Hobbes self-preservation, the only truly universal and thus highest good, is identified with the active desire for the body's movement and the expulsion of its essential energy. If the true liberties of the subject speak to the necessity of preserving a sphere of right that facilitates the reproduction of this good, my suggestion in this chapter has been that political participation in a democratic context can be interpreted as a foundational freedom that maximally actualizes the human power to socially coordinate communal behavior for the sake of the pursuit of particular ends. That the latter is indeed an essential power is suggested by Hobbes in *Leviathan*, where he asserts a seemingly ontological desire for involvement in participatory modes. Human beings are specific types of beings, who despite their difference possess a minimal set of universally shared powers and tendencies. Through the mediation of a uniquely human reason and speech, individuals are capable of self-organizing themselves on the basis of what are perceived to be their overlapping interests, developing collective practices aimed at the latter's realization. This effort is a manifestation of a uniquely human curiosity, that intrinsic impulse to investigate and interrogate causal relations generating a uniquely human happiness, realized through the anticipation of future enjoyment.

Whereas within the Hobbesian commonwealth as typically imagined such participatory activity is restricted to the realm of civil liberty, a specifically democratic commonwealth would extend the opportunity for the pursuit of the good beyond that characteristic of the freedom to act with respect to that which civil laws do not speak, whether within subordinate bodies politic or not. Democracy in this sense can be rethought in Hobbesian terms as the sovereign form that most completely institutes the general conditions of self-preservation, producing spaces of action that allow always distinct individuals to interact with one another for the sake of the pursuit of their always distinct goods, which they themselves remain always the most competent interpreters of. Note, then, that democracy is not being advocated to the extent that it is seen as being more likely to accurately represent the diversity of opinion and interest found within a commonwealth. The singularity of desire prevents any subsumption of interest—beyond those essentials that true liberty looks toward preserving—under a representative will, whether that will is seen as spontaneously embodying a collective interest in its immediacy, or whether that will is seen as being constructed via a deliberative process of collective interest formation. Hobbesian democracy, if it is to remain faithful to Hobbes's nominalism, is thus irreducible to representative government as traditionally conceived. The ethical preference for democracy in relation to monarchy and aristocracy derives from the fact that it maximally affirms Hobbesian equality-in-difference, the equal right of all to actively participate in legislative processes facilitating the extended expression of and pursuit of individual citizens' desires. Needless to say, however, this abstract preference grounded in consideration of Hobbes's conception of natural law and natural human power suggests to us nothing concrete about issues of constitutional arrangement, or the institutional configuration of political offices capable of mediating democratic participation within actually existing large and complex societies. Hobbes's philosophy implies merely the extent to which such a project remains a potentially important one.

Summation

Operating at the intersection of the history of political thought and democratic theory, this book argued that the work of Thomas Hobbes—one of the tradition's most notorious enemies of democracy—has something profound to teach us about the problems, stakes, and ethics of democratic life. The contribution unfolded along three axes, utilizing distinct methodological modes in the effort to reveal this democratic Hobbesian content. To begin with, in chapter 1 I reconstructed the essential elements of Hobbes's critique of democracy, which readers have thus far not been properly attentive to. Contrary to those interpreters who attempt to assimilate Hobbes's model of democracy to contemporary representative forms in which the people are primarily passive observers of the political process—who at most awaken merely periodically in order to display their sovereign status—I attempted to demonstrate that the main elements of Hobbes's critique are only fully comprehensible to the degree that we recognize the radically direct and participatory characteristics of the object of analysis. Particularly important here is Hobbes's concept of madness, which is defined in terms of a surplus or excess of passion in which the latter, externalizing itself without regulation, militates against the exercise of reason. In identifying democracy as a regime of madness, Hobbes directs us to the central issue. Whereas the will of the sovereign representative in monarchies is already unified in the natural form of the monarch, in cases where the sovereign office is an assembly such a will can only be generated through a deliberative process in which a plurality of distinct natural persons negotiate with one another for the sake of its determination. Such a process is bound to be conflictual given the radical nonidentity of such persons, who each are in possession of a unique set of desires, values, normative conceptions, and so on. This general problem of assembly, however, is exponentially exacerbated in the democratic regime, in which participation in the deliberative process is generalized, thus extending the ground for disagreement and conflict. Such quarrel is further intensified, meanwhile, as a consequence of the fact that democratic assembly members typically utilize techniques of eloquence in order to attract others to their position, communication tending to enflame passion to such a degree that reason—which would be necessary to moderate the natural conflict traversing the assembly, placing limits on the action of its members—is overwhelmed. Democracy, then, precisely because it radically generalizes participation, is intrinsically antagonistic: it is immanently oriented toward conflict and instability as a result of its popular and direct institutional form.

After detailing the nature of Hobbes's critique of democracy in chapter 1, in chapter 2 I set out to reveal how central the rejection of democracy is to the overall elaboration of the Hobbesian civil science. The contribution here can be appreciated through considering the well-known conceptual innovation that occurs with respect to the account of political foundation in *Leviathan*. Specifically, in this text Hobbes introduces the language of representation and authorization, an introduction that historical contextualist readers have explained in terms of the opposition to parliamentarian philosophies of political representation that emerged during the English Civil War, after the production of *The Elements of Law* and *De Cive*. Seemingly moving away from his earlier accounts, in which the institution of the body politic necessitated an originary democratic moment—the definitive selection of a sovereign form first necessitating a prior unity of the people, who assemble in order to choose said form via a democratic decision-procedure—in *Leviathan* Hobbes attempts to think institution in terms of the multitude of subjects, as individuals as opposed to a corporate body, simultaneously authorizing the representative relations necessary to produce both the state and the sovereign. Utilizing their own language, Hobbes attempts to refute the parliamentarians' suggestion that any political form leans upon an original sovereign subject predating the foundation of the state, a subject that might thus retain a natural right against the sovereign. While in broad agreement regarding this conceptual operation, in this chapter I attempted to further contextualize the historical contextualist account through demonstrating it to be just one manifestation of a larger dynamic that centers around Hobbes's uninterrupted opposition to democratic rule. I argue that key changes within each expression of

Hobbes's political philosophy, from the *Elements of Law* to *Leviathan*, can only be comprehended in light of his effort to deny any possible normative ground upon which individuals might prefer democracy relative to other sovereign forms. In *The Elements of Law* such a ground could be located in the assertion that democratic commonwealths facilitate the actualization of a unique type of liberty found only in these regimes, to the extent that they alone are capable of allowing all citizens to directly participate in the formulation of legal norms. Recognizing the extent to which such might generate a democratic preference, in *De Cive* Hobbes looks to foreclose this possibility through making two substantial theoretical innovations: first, the concept of liberty is reconceptualized in terms of simply the absence of impediments to motion, the effort to distinguish commonwealths on the basis of a freedom to formulate law being now identified as a manifestation of the confusion between liberty and sovereignty; and second, a strong denial of any intrinsic desire on the part of most citizens to participate in political activity, desire now being seen as oriented toward merely private affairs. As noted, however, the experience of the English Civil War revealed to Hobbes *De Cive's* leftover democratic problem: the fact that political foundation continues to be thought in terms of an originary democratic moment allowed for the possibility of democracy being ethically privileged as a consequence of it being the temporally earliest, and hence the most natural of political forms. Putting aside the question as to whether Hobbes was ultimately successful on this front or not, what seems clear is that *Leviathan* attempted to neutralize this normative threat through reconceptualizing political institution in terms of a process of authorization that did not depend upon prior collective action on the part of an already unified people.

Part 1 of the study both reconstructed Hobbes's critique of democratic sovereignty and uncovered the centrality of this critique to the elaboration of his political philosophy as a whole. While still operating through close textual analysis of the Hobbesian oeuvre, part 2 turned to the issue of democratic theory, and in particular to that which Hobbes's natural philosophy and philosophical anthropology have to contribute to thinking the possibility of democratic life. In particular, in chapters 3 and 4 I located in Hobbes's thought the recognition of what I call the two ontological conditions for democracy: the lack of a transcendent ground that would structure or delimit political institution and a particular form of human equality that renders conceivable shared legislative capacity and responsibility. Hobbes's materialism considers objects in their absolute singularity, there existing no shared purpose or essence intrinsic to things that would direct their motion in identical and predictable ways. With respect to human beings particularly, such is revealed through the detailed account of human perception, which highlights the impossibility of natural persons sensuously appropriating objects in a collective mode that results in the generation of universally recognized images and conceptions. Hobbes explains the diversity of forms of human association in light of the impossibility of constructing systems of value and meaning on the basis of natural first principles that would spontaneously unite individuals in a common way. What the fact of social-historical alterity reveals is that individuals themselves are responsible for the institution of their collective world, independently of any standards or norms external to their association. What is unique about democracy is that it is the form of regime in which this responsibility is reflectively affirmed, the law becoming as a consequence a perpetual object of interrogation. And indeed, Hobbes himself recognizes this fact, as revealed in his critique of the ancient Athenian people for failing to limit themselves in the face of their correct perception of their absolute legislative power. Such self-limitation is precisely a necessity in a democracy given the understanding of the lack of any exterior norms that could intervene so as to regulate popular self-activity.

In chapter 4 I turned to the second ontological condition of democratic life that Hobbes's philosophy affirms: a natural human equality that renders every individual a potentially competent participator in political life as an active member of the sovereign body. Importantly, Hobbes's positing of human equality does not contradict his positing of human difference. Unlike those theorists of democracy who interpret the realization of the latter as depending upon the maximal coalescence of human desire or interest, attempting to think the conditions for the homogenization of individual wills, Hobbes understands the futility of such an endeavor. Hobbesian equality does not speak to a thick identity of positive traits, tendencies, or characteristics, but rather a formal rational capacity. I labeled this conception of equality an equality-in-difference, for it is a conception that acknowledges the radical nonidentity of individual natural persons. Despite the massive variation in human goods, what all individuals share is an equal capacity to deploy natural reason in order to articulate the nature of these goods and in order to discover the potential modes for their actualization. Hence my suggestion that Hobbesian equality not only does not deny human difference, but actually reflects it. In any case, Hobbes further recognizes the most significant social and political consequences that result from the fact of natural equality. Hence, for example, his repeated efforts to refute all aristocratic logics, consistently emphasizing the popular proficiencies of common individuals, who in performing their various social roles utilize that same intelligence deployed in all other human endeavors, no matter how exalted. Hence also his persistent emphasis on the fact that there is no intellectual qualification for sovereign office. Hobbes understands that the essence of democracy lies in the rejection of all such titles to govern, no individual or minor group of individuals possessing a right to rule on the basis of their possession of some supposedly unique skill, competency, or intelligence.

In part 3 of the study I turned to the question of the ethics of democracy and in particular to the question of whether Hobbes's thought was capable of providing us with any conceptual resources for normatively preferring democratic sovereignty to alternative forms. This undertaking necessitated a variation in my methodological mode up to this point, given Hobbes's persistent effort to refute or cover up any elements of his thought that might potentially produce just such a normative preference. My implicit assumption here was that the history of political thought is capable of being legitimately practiced in a way that is not entirely reducible to the effort to recuperate a definite textual meaning or authorial intention. Taking inspiration from early Critical Theory, I characterized my method in this chapter as a type of thinking in constellations. The starting point was the dialectical recognition of the impossibility of thought generating concepts that adequately exhaust the being of their objects. As Hobbes's own analysis of human perception reveals, the process of conceptualization is conditioned by the specific form of subjective mediation that organizes it, with the consequence that the alteration of the latter may work to break up the perceived identity of the thing and multiply its meaning, generating a representational content that was previously obscured. To think in constellations is to produce such a multiplication of meaning through the rearrangement of concepts in new forms. The representation of the object is thus structured by a critical assembly of concepts in a specific mode, the reorganization of conceptual elements generating unique interpretative orders. Through critically arranging certain Hobbesian concepts in a novel way, I attempted to unlock a previously obscured content—specifically a democratic ethic—that would otherwise not be apparent.

At the center of my analysis in chapter 6 is the juxtaposition of Hobbes's reconstruction of the idea of natural law with his concept of the true liberty of subjects. The ideological character of traditional natural law philosophies lay in their effort to posit their own singular moral conceptions as universally binding, regardless of the particularity of the historical context, as a consequence of their supposed derivation from a transcendent or extrasocial source. Rejecting what he considers to be the dogmatism at the heart of such operations, Hobbes's own concept of natural law abstracts from all thick assumptions regarding the nature of human being. Once such an abstraction is carried out, we are left simply with the human organism's need for self-preservation, a requirement for the satisfaction of desire regardless of its particular orientation. Self-preservation, in other words, looks to maintain that general human motion upon which all specific and diverse motions depend. It is precisely with this self-preservation that true liberty is concerned, the latter being realized through the establishment of a sphere of right which guarantees individuals access to those objects that, regardless of the specificity of desire, are necessary means for the realization of not just bare life, but good life. Going beyond his own catalog of such objects—which included things such as physical security, adequate material resources, safe shelter, and more—I argued that one of Hobbes's innovations within *Leviathan* is of high potential import here. Specifically, and contrary to his earlier analysis in *De Cive*, Hobbes now makes a point of emphasizing that the desire for active participation in political processes is a fundamental one that naturally adheres in all human beings, it being an expression of an essential impulse for self-determination. Hobbes, of course, wants to restrict such participation to subordinate bodies politic within the commonwealth, as a consequence of what he sees as the destructive tendencies of democratic sovereign decision-making. My suggestion, however, was that if we reject Hobbes's critique of democratic deliberation—and much contemporary evidence suggests that we should—then we can approach the question of sovereign preference from a new perspective. In the final analysis, I argued that it was possible to favor democracy as a consequence of its capacity to maximally generalize popular political participation, which can be plausibly considered as one of the very few truly universal of human desires. This universality would be precisely that which warrants such an extension of the commonwealth's participatory apparatus. Hobbes's political thought, read in this particular way, was thus ultimately seen as capable of providing an idiosyncratic natural law defense of democratic rule.

Notes

Introduction

1. For one account of several such ways in which democracy in the present moment has become "disfigured," see Nadia Urbinati, *Democracy Disfigured: Opinion, Truth, and the People* (Cambridge, MA: Harvard University Press, 2014).

2. For an account of some of the ways in which the de la Courts and Spinoza adapted Hobbes's political philosophy see, for example, Noel Malcolm, "Hobbes and Spinoza," in *Aspects of Hobbes* (Oxford: Oxford University Press, 2002), 27–52. On the immediate reception of Hobbes's political thought more generally, see Quentin Skinner, "The Context of Hobbes's Theory of Political Obligation," in *Visions of Politics, Volume 3: Hobbes and Civil Science* (Cambridge: Cambridge University Press, 2002), 265–86; Quentin Skinner, "Hobbes and His Disciples in France and England," in *Visions of Politics, Volume 3: Hobbes and Civil Science* (Cambridge: Cambridge University Press, 2002), 308–23; Mark Goldie, "The Reception of Hobbes," in *The Cambridge History of Political Thought, 1450–1700*, ed. J. H. Burns and Mark Goldie (Cambridge: Cambridge University Press, 1991), 589–615; Noel Malcolm, "Hobbes and the European Republic of Letters," in *Aspects of Hobbes* (Oxford: Oxford University Press, 2002), 457–545; G. A. J. Rogers, "Hobbes and His Contemporaries," in *The Cambridge Companion to Hobbes's Leviathan*, ed. Patricia Springborg (Cambridge: Cambridge University Press, 2007), 413–40; Jon Parkin, "The Reception of Hobbes's Leviathan," in *The Cambridge Companion to Hobbes's Leviathan*, ed. Patricia Springborg (Cambridge: Cambridge University Press, 2007), 441–59.

3. Some readers trace back the liberal appreciation of Hobbes much further. Although it is questionable to what extent each may be unproblematically situated within the political liberal tradition, Mark Goldie maintains with reference to the use made of Hobbes by Spinoza, Pufendorf, and Tyrell, that "the liberal minimalist state was discovered in Hobbes at an early stage." Goldie, "The Reception of Hobbes," 605.

4. For readings that locate various liberal in ideas in Hobbes, some of which interpret him as the founder of modern political liberalism, see Richard Ashcraft, "Hobbes's Natural Man: A Study in Ideology Formation," *Journal of Politics* 33, no. 4 (1971): 1111–17; Theodore Waldman, "Hobbes on the Generation of a Public Person," in *Thomas Hobbes in His Time*, ed. Ralph Ross, Herbert W. Schneider, and Theodore Waldman (Minneapolis: University of Minnesota Press, 1974), 61–83; Frank M. Coleman, *Hobbes and America: Exploring the Constitutional Foundations* (Toronto: University of Toronto Press, 1977); George Mace, *Locke, Hobbes, and the Federalist Papers* (Carbondale: Southern Illinois University Press, 1979); Robert P. Kraynak, "Hobbes's *Behemoth* and the Argument for Absolutism," *American Political Science Review* 76, no. 4 (1982): 847; Gregory S. Kavka, *Hobbesian Moral and Political Theory* (Princeton, NJ: Princeton University Press, 1986); David van Mill, *Liberty, Rationality, and Agency in Hobbes* (Albany: State University of New York Press, 2001), 154–56; Gregory S. Kavka, "Some Neglected Liberal Aspects of Hobbes's Philosophy," *Hobbes Studies* 1, no. 1 (1988): 89–018; Pierre Manent, *An Intellectual History of Liberalism*, trans. Rebecca Balinski (Princeton, NJ: Princeton University Press, 1995), 20–38; Vickie B. Sullivan, *Machiavelli, Hobbes, and the Formation of a Liberal Republicanism in England* (Cambridge: Cambridge University Press, 2004), 105; Lucien Jaume, "Hobbes and the Philosophical Sources of Liberalism," in *The Cambridge Companion to Hobbes's* Leviathan, ed. Patricia Springborg (Cambridge: Cambridge University Press, 2007), 181–98; Quentin Taylor, "Leviathan Bound; or the Re-Education of Thomas Hobbes," *Hobbes Studies* 22, no. 2 (2009): 123–42; Yves Charles Zarka, ed., *Hobbes et le libéralisme* (Paris: Éditions Mimésis, 2016); Noel Malcolm, "Thomas Hobbes: Liberal Illiberal," *Journal of the British Academy*, no. 4 (2016): 113–36; Kody W. Cooper, *Thomas Hobbes and the Natural Law* (Notre Dame: Notre Dame University Press, 2018), 26.

5. See, for example, Howard Warrender, *The Political Philosophy of Hobbes: His Theory of Obligation* (Oxford: Oxford University Press, 1957), 111; J. W. N. Watkins, *Hobbes's System of Ideas* (London: Hutchinson & Co., 1965), 43; Julien Freund, "Le Dieu mortel," in *Hobbes-Forschungen*, ed. Reinhart Koselleck and Roman Schnur (Berlin: Duncker & Humbolt, 1969), 46; Michel Villey, "Le droit de l'individu chez Hobbes," in *Hobbes-Forschungen*, ed. Reinhart Koselleck and Roman Schnur (Berlin: Duncker & Humbolt, 1969), 188; Simone Goyard-Fabre, *Le droit et la loi dans la philosophie de Thomas Hobbes* (Paris: Librarie C. Klincksieck, 1975), 117; Anthony K. Kronman, "The Concept of an Author and the Unity of the Commonwealth in Hobbes's *Leviathan*," *Journal of the History of Philosophy* 18, no. 2 (1980): 71; Manent, *An Intellectual History of Liberalism*, 32; Giuseppe Sorgi, "Hobbes on 'Bodies Politic,'" *Hobbes Studies* 9, no. 1 (1996): 82; Peter Vanderschraaf, "Instituting the Hobbesian Commonwealth," *Pacific Philosophical Quarterly* 82, no. 3–4 (2001): 383–405; A. P. Martinich, "Hobbes's Reply to Republicanism," *Rivista di Storia della Filosofia* 59, no. 1 (2004): 228; Pierre Manent, *Naissances de la politique moderne* (Paris: Gallimard, 2007), 130;

Peter J. Steinberger, "Hobbes, Rousseau, and the Modern Conception of the State," *Journal of Politics* 70, no. 3 (2008): 603; Devin Stauffer, *Hobbes's Kingdom of Light: A Study of the Foundations of Modern Political Philosophy* (Chicago: University of Chicago Press, 2018), 246.

    6. Although not one of the democratic readers of Hobbes, Kinch Hoekstra highlights the revolutionary character of this element of Hobbes's thought, noting how for Hobbes within any type of regime "political obligation and authority depend on popular consent, the traditional requirement of the revolutionary." Kinch Hoekstra, "The *de facto* Turn in Hobbes's Political Philosophy," in Leviathan *After 350 Years*, ed. Tom Sorell and Luc Foisneau (Oxford: Oxford University Press, 2004), 64. For a reading that, leaning on a renewed appreciation of the Erastian dimension of his thought, interprets Hobbes as a historical revolutionary in a strong sense, and indeed an eventual Cromwellian, see Jeffrey R. Collins, *The Allegiance of Thomas Hobbes* (Oxford: Oxford University Press, 2005). Contra Collins, however, most readers strongly dispute the notion that Hobbes was ever particularly sympathetic to the aims of the revolution, let alone those of Cromwell. As Johann Sommerville observes, "When Hobbes was accused of writing *Leviathan* to please Cromwell's regime, he angrily denied the charge, claiming that there was scarcely a page in the book that did not upbraid him with 'abominable hypocrisie and villainy.'" Johan P. Sommerville, "Hobbes and Independency," *Rivista di Storia della Filosofia* 59, no. 1 (2004): 170.

    7. Kinch Hoekstra, "A Lion in the House: Hobbes and Democracy," in *Rethinking the Foundations of Modern Political Thought*, ed. Annabel Brett, James Tully, and Holly Hamilton-Bleakley (Cambridge: Cambridge University Press, 2006), 192.

    8. Gianfranco Borrelli, "Hobbes e la teoria moderna della democrazia rappresentanza assoluta e scambio politico," *Trimestre* 24, no. 3-4 (1991): 262. On Hobbes as fleshing out the theoretical foundation for representative government, see also Harvey C. Mansfield, "Hobbes and the Science of Indirect Government," *American Political Science Review* 65, no. 1 (1971): 97–110; Coleman, *Hobbes and America*, 97–98; David Runciman, "The Sovereign," in *The Oxford Handbook of Hobbes*, ed. A. P. Martinich and Kinch Hoekstra (Oxford: Oxford University Press, 2016), 359–77. For the claim that Hobbes, were he to live in our own historical moment, might prefer a type of representative or liberal constitutional government as his ideal sovereign form, see Alan Ryan, "Hobbes's Political Philosophy," in *The Cambridge Companion to Hobbes*, ed. Tom Sorell (Cambridge: Cambridge University Press, 1996), 232; David Braybrooke, "A Note on Hobbesian Lessons on Bipartisanship," in *Hobbes Today: Insights for the 21st Century*, ed. S. A. Lloyd (Cambridge: Cambridge University Press, 2013), 20–24.

    9. David Runciman, "Hobbes's Theory of Representation: Anti-Democratic or Proto-Democratic?," in *Political Representation*, ed. Ian Shapiro et al. (Cambridge: Cambridge University Press, 2010), 32.

10. Richard Tuck, *The Sleeping Sovereign: The Invention of Modern Democracy* (Cambridge: Cambridge University Press, 2015), ix.

11. Richard E. Flathman, *Thomas Hobbes: Skepticism, Individuality, and Chastened Politics* (Lanham, MD: Rowman & Littlefield, 2002), 170.

12. See also Alan Ryan, "Hobbes and Individualism," in *Perspectives on Thomas Hobbes*, ed. G. A. J. Rogers and Alan Ryan (Oxford: Clarendon Press, 1988), 105; Peter Hays, "Hobbes's Bourgeois Moderation," *Polity* 31, no. 1 (1998): 53–74; van Mill, *Liberty, Rationality, and Agency in Hobbes*, 154–56; Philippe Crignon, "Diversité humaine et pluralisme: La reprise d'un thème hobbesien dans le libéralisme contemporain," in *Hobbes et le libéralisme*, ed. Yves Charles Zarka (Paris: Éditions Mimésis, 2016), 75–102.

13. Paul Downes, *Hobbes, Sovereignty, and Early American Literature* (Cambridge: Cambridge University Press, 2015).

14. Downes, 16.

15. James Martel, *Subverting the Leviathan: Reading Thomas Hobbes as a Radical Democrat* (New York: Columbia University Press, 2007), 2.

16. See also James Martel, "The Radical Promise of Thomas Hobbes: The Road Not Taken in Liberal Theory," *Theory & Event* 4, no. 2 (2000); Patrick Craig, "Jacques Rancière, Thomas Hobbes, and a Politics of the Part That Has No Part," *Theory & Event* 18, no. 1 (2015); Patrick T. Giamario, "The Laughing Body Politic: The Counter-Sovereign Politics of Hobbes's Theory of Laughter," *Political Research Quarterly* 69, no. 2 (2016): 309–19.

17. Thomas Hobbes, "Elements of Philosophy. The First Section, Concerning Body," in *The English Works of Thomas Hobbes of Malmesbury, Volume One*, ed. Sir William Molesworth (London: John Bohn, 1839), 3.7.

18. e.g., Martel, *Subverting the Leviathan*.

19. e.g., Paul Patton, "Nietzsche and Hobbes," *International Studies in Philosophy* 33, no. 3 (2001): 99–116.

20. e.g., Tuck, *The Sleeping Sovereign*.

21. Thomas Hobbes, *Leviathan, Volume Two: The English and Latin Texts (i)*, ed. Noel Malcolm (Oxford: Clarendon Press, 2012), 5, 68.

22. Hobbes, 5, 68.

23. Hobbes, "Elements of Philosophy. The First Section, Concerning Body," 5.1. To take Hobbes's example, it is "as if from seeing the sun first by reflection in water, and afterwards again directly in the firmament, we should to both those appearances give the name of sun, and say there are two suns: which none but men can do, for no other living creatures have the use of names." Hobbes, 5.1.

24. Hobbes, *Leviathan, Volume Two*, 5, 70.

25. Hobbes, 5, 68.

26. Hobbes, 4, 56.

27. For an explication of Hobbes's account of democracy in terms of tragedy see Christopher Holman, "Hobbes and the Tragedy of Democracy," *History of Political Thought* 40, no. 4 (2019): 649–75.

28. Cornelius Castoriadis, "The Greek Polis and the Creation of Democracy," in *Philosophy, Politics, Autonomy: Essays in Political Philosophy*, ed. and trans. David Ames Curtis (New York: Oxford University Press, 1991), 114.

29. Cornelius Castoriadis, "La démocratie athénienne: fausses et vraies questions," in *La montée de l'insignifiance: les carrefours du labyrinthe, 4* (Paris: Éditions du Seuil, 1996), 225.

30. Cornelius Castoriadis, *La cité et les lois: ce qui fait la Grèce, 2*, ed. Enrique Escobar, Myrto Gondicas, and Pascal Vernay (Paris: Éditions du Seuil, 2008), 127.

31. Castoriadis, "The Greek Polis and the Creation of Democracy," 115.

32. This normative dimension of the Hobbesian project is often obscured as a result of Hobbes's own framing of the latter in terms of a science modeled on geometric method. It is always important to remember, though, that his civil science is a practical one driven by prescriptive goals. As Tom Sorell puts it, "Civil science is the normative science *par excellence*." Tom Sorell, "The Normative and the Explanatory in Hobbes's Political Philosophy," *Rivista di Storia della Filosofia* 59, no. 1 (2004): 216. On how Hobbes's conception of philosophy is irreducible to certain contemporary conceptions, to the degree that its proper end is always considered in terms of the achievement of practical benefit for humanity, see Kinch Hoekstra, "The End of Philosophy (The Case of Hobbes)," *Proceedings of the Aristotelian Society* 106, no. 1 (2006): 25–62.

33. And as Quentin Skinner observes, "Faced with this sore point in his argument, Hobbes takes considerable pains to cover it up. He does so in part by calling attention to his lack of proof as little as possible." Quentin Skinner, *From Humanism to Hobbes: Studies in Politics and Rhetoric* (Cambridge: Cambridge University Press, 2018), 317.

34. Thomas Hobbes, *On the Citizen*, ed. and trans. Richard Tuck and Michael Silverthorne (Cambridge: Cambridge University Press, 1998), Preface, 22.

Chapter 1

1. Larry May calls attention to this undertheorization, writing that "Hobbes is generally so focused on monarchy that he fails to heed his own remarks about how this is only one of three main forms of government." Larry May, *Limiting Leviathan: Hobbes on Law and International Affairs* (Oxford: Oxford University Press, 2013), 165.

2. One of the few readers to grasp this profundity is Mikko Jakonen, who writes that "despite his negative feelings against democracy as a mode of government, Hobbes in fact constructed one of the most prominent theories of democracy in the early modern period." Mikko Jakonen, "Needed but Unwanted: Thomas Hobbes's Warnings on the Dangers of Multitude, Populism and Democracy," *Las Torres de Lucca*, no. 9 (2016): 91.

3. I thus disagree with David Runciman, for whom Hobbes's utilization of the term *democracy* is an element of a more general project through which Hobbes redeploys the meaning of specific concepts in a way contrary to popular understanding, so as to reveal the arbitrariness of all definition. Runciman argues that in treating democracy as little more than arbitrary rule, Hobbes highlights the extent to which its mode of functioning is equivalent to that of monarchy or aristocracy, all regimes being characterized by absolute sovereign power: "It is a mistake to overvalue such labels as 'democracy,' since the essential character of the regimes they describe is unaffected by the terms being used." David Runciman, *Political Hypocrisy; The Mask of Power from Hobbes to Orwell and Beyond* (Princeton, NJ: Princeton University Press, 2008), 33.

4. For a reading of Hobbes that reminds us of the importance of remembering that the sovereign is not a natural person or any group of natural persons, but rather an office, sovereignty inhering in the position of government as opposed to the occupier(s) of this office, see Christine Chwaszcza, "The Seat of Sovereignty: Hobbes on the Artificial Person of the Commonwealth or State," *Hobbes Studies* 25, no. 2 (2012): 123–42.

5. It should be noted, however, that despite only three general types of regime existing, there is in fact much potential for variation within each with respect to the specific mode of articulation of the particular form. This is pointed out by Leon Craig, who notes with respect to democracy that "the actual quality of life in a Democracy could vary from puritanical to libertarian according to differing institutional arrangements: what offices are established (e.g., whether there are public censors); how they are distributed (e.g., by election, or by lot); the length of their terms; and how legislation is proposed, debated, and approved." Leon Howard Craig, *The Platonian* Leviathan (Toronto: University of Toronto Press, 2010), 293.

6. Thomas Hobbes, *Leviathan, Volume Two: The English and Latin Texts (i)*, ed. Noel Malcolm (Oxford: Clarendon Press, 2012), 19, 284.

7. Hobbes, *Leviathan, Volume Two*, 19, 284.

8. Thomas Hobbes, *On the Citizen*, ed. and trans. Richard Tuck and Michael Silverthorne (Cambridge: Cambridge University Press, 1998), 7.2.

9. Hobbes, 7.2.

10. Hobbes, *Leviathan, Volume Two*, 19, 284. Emphasis added.

11. Janine Chanteur notes that in Hobbes's thought the multitude is defined negatively, in terms of all that which it lacks: order, singularity, will, unity, and so on. Janine Chanteur, "Note sur les notions de 'peuple' et de 'multitude' chez Hobbes," in *Hobbes-Forschungen*, ed. Reinhart Koselleck and Roman Schnur (Berlin: Duncker & Humbolt, 1969), 227.

12. Indeed, Richard Tuck interprets the distinction between concord and union, which the contrast of the multitude with the people speaks to, to be at the very heart of Hobbes's political theory. Richard Tuck, "Hobbes and Democ-

racy," in *Rethinking the Foundations of Modern Political Thought*, ed. Annabel Brett, James Tully, and Holly Hamilton-Bleakley (Cambridge: Cambridge University Press, 2006), 172.

13. As Paolo Virno writes, "The person who grasps all the implications and nuances of a concept is precisely the one who wishes to expunge it from the theoretical and practical horizon." Paolo Virno, *A Grammar of the Multitude: For an Analysis of Contemporary Forms of Life*, trans. Isabella Bertoletti, James Cascaito, and Andrea Casson (Los Angeles: Semiotext(e), 2004), 22. For the suggestion that Hobbes was not in fact opposed to multitude at all, but merely faction—a multitude that incorrectly considers itself to be a people—see Malcolm Bull, "The Limits of Multitude," *New Left Review*, no. 35 (2005): 24.

14. Thomas Hobbes, *The Elements of Law, Natural and Politic*, ed. Ferdinand Tönnies (London: Simpkin, Marshall, and Co., 1889), 1.19.5.

15. Hobbes, *The Elements of Law, Natural and Politic* 1.19.6.

16. Hobbes, *On the Citizen*, 6.1.

17. Hobbes, *The Elements of Law, Natural and Politic*, 2.1.2.

18. In Janine Chanteur's words, "we cannot speak of a unity of the multitude, because naturally, each is enclosed within its own movement: the multitude is magma, confusion, incoherence, anarchy." Chanteur, "Note sur les notions de 'peuple' et de 'multitude' chez Hobbes," 226. See also Jakonen, "Needed but Unwanted," 95. Jakonen has written what is perhaps the most comprehensive overview of the place of the concept of the multitude within Hobbes's project. Mikko Jakonen, "Multitude in Motion: Re-Readings of the Political Philosophy of Thomas Hobbes." PhD diss. University of Jyväskylä, 2013.

19. On why Hobbes thinks confusing the people with the multitude generates sedition, see Omar Astorga, "Hobbes's Concept of Multitude," *Hobbes Studies* 24, no. 1 (2011): 5–14.

20. Hobbes, *The Elements of Law, Natural and Politic*, 2.4.12.

21. Hobbes, 2.1.3.

22. Hobbes, 2.1.3.

23. Hobbes, *On the Citizen*, 5.7.

24. Hobbes, 6.1.

25. Several readers of Hobbes accuse him of failing to recognize this, and thus of downplaying the political potential of the multitude. For various suggestions that the multitude possesses a range of specifically political capacities revealed either theoretically or historically, see David Copp, "Hobbes on Artificial Persons and Collective Actions," *Philosophical Review* 89, no. 4 (1980): 603–6; Mikko Jakonen, "Thomas Hobbes on Revolution," *La Révolution Française*, no. 5 (2011): para. 33; May, *Limiting Leviathan*, 168–72; Craig, "Jacques Rancière, Thomas Hobbes, and a Politics of the Part That Has No Part"; Diego A. Fernández Peychaux, "The Multitude in the Mirror: Hobbes on Power, Rhetoric, and Materialism," *Theory & Event* 21, no. 3 (2018): 666. Peter Steinberger,

meanwhile, interprets Hobbes not as suggesting that a multitude is incapable of ever acting as a corporate entity, but only that it is incapable of acting as such consistently. Peter Steinberger, "Hobbes, Rousseau, and the Modern Conception of the State," *Journal of Politics* 70, no. 3 (2008): 600.

26. Hobbes, *On the Citizen*, 6.1. Translation altered. For reasons explained in their edition, Tuck and Silverthorne generally translate the term *multitudo* as "crowd," despite Hobbes himself using the term "multitude" in his other English political works. See Hobbes, xl–xli.

27. Hobbes, *On the Citizen*, 6.2. Translation altered.

28. Hobbes, *The Elements of Law, Natural and Politic*, 2.3.1.

29. Hobbes, 2.2.1.

30. Hobbes, *On the Citizen*, 7.5.

31. Hobbes, 7.7.

32. Hobbes, 7.5.

33. Hobbes, 7.6.

34. Hobbes, 5.6.

35. David van Mill is thus correct to note that a democratic sovereign would be a "fully participatory democratic assembly." David van Mill, *Liberty, Rationality, and Agency in Hobbes* (Albany: State University of New York Press, 2001), 178. As David Braybrooke observes, Hobbes always "assumes that he is dealing with a direct democracy of the ancient Greek sort or the late medieval instances in Italy." David Braybrooke, "A Note on Hobbesian Lessons on Bipartisanship," in *Hobbes Today: Insights for the 21st Century*, ed. S. A. Lloyd (Cambridge: Cambridge University Press, 2013), 22. For the suggestion that Hobbes's reflections on democracy are not inspired solely by Aristotle's "extreme democracy," but also other democratic forms detailed by Aristotle and expanded on by early modern commentators, see Sophie Smith, "Democracy and the Body Politic from Aristotle to Hobbes," *Political Theory* 46, no. 2 (2018): 8.

36. Tuck, "Hobbes and Democracy," 186–87. In earlier work Tuck rejects the idea that Hobbesian democracy could function as a practical political form, writing that "the only serious candidates for sovereignty were monarchies and aristocratic republics." Richard Tuck, *Philosophy and Government, 1572–1651* (Cambridge: Cambridge University Press, 1993), 311.

37. Richard Tuck, *The Sleeping Sovereign: The Invention of Modern Democracy* (Cambridge: Cambridge University Press, 2015), 91–94. For Tuck's account of the distinction between sovereignty and government, and its relevance to the modern, nondeliberative democracies characteristic of contemporary commercial societies, see Richard Tuck, "Democratic Sovereignty and Democratic Government: The Sleeping Sovereign," in *Popular Sovereignty in Historical Perspective*, ed. Richard Bourke and Quentin Skinner (Cambridge: Cambridge University Press, 2016), 115–41.

38. Hobbes, *On the Citizen*, 7.16.

39. Hobbes, 7.16.
40. Tuck, "Hobbes and Democracy," 187, 189. Emphasis added.
41. Tuck, *The Sleeping Sovereign*, ix.
42. Hobbes, *On the Citizen*, Preface, 8. Translation altered.
43. Hobbes, 12.8. Translation altered.
44. Hobbes, 6.20.
45. Hobbes, 10.16. In deploying the language of capacity and act here, we should note the recent contribution of Sandra Leonie Field, who argues that Hobbes's early work is still produced in a scholastic mode that allows for a conception of power in terms of an intrinsic potential that either may or may not be actively deployed. The fact that Hobbes's later work precludes the separation of power and act invalidates the interpretation of a reader like Tuck, whose distinction between sovereignty and government implicitly relies on the earlier framework. Sandra Leonie Field, *Potentia: Hobbes and Spinoza on Power and Popular Politics* (Oxford: Oxford University Press, 2020), 95–98. Here my critique of Tuck proceeds along a different track, emphasizing the extent to which Hobbes never suggested such an absolute separation of sovereign power from self-activity.
46. Hobbes, *On the Citizen*, 10.16.
47. Hobbes, *The Elements of Law, Natural and Politic*, 2.1.17.
48. Hobbes, 2.1.17.
49. Luc Foisneau, *Hobbes: La vie inquiète* (Paris: Gallimard, 2016), 34.
50. Hobbes, *On the Citizen*, 10.9. Emphasis added.
51. Hobbes, *The Elements of Law, Natural and Politic*, 2.2.9.
52. Hobbes, 2.2.9.
53. Hobbes, 2.2.10.
54. Hobbes, 2.2.10.
55. Hobbes, *On the Citizen*, 9.11.
56. Hobbes, 7.16.
57. Hobbes, 7.16.
58. On what Hobbes sees as the conditions of "absolute democracy" see Francis Edward Devine, "Absolute Democracy or Indefeasible Right: Hobbes Versus Locke," *Journal of Politics* 37, no. 3 (1975): 736–68.
59. Hobbes, *On the Citizen*, 6.17.
60. Hobbes, *Leviathan, Volume Two*, 29, 500.
61. Hobbes, *On the Citizen*, 6.17.
62. Craig, *The Platonian* Leviathan, 478. Jean Hampton also notes that contemporary liberal democratic regimes "do not fit the classical definition of democracy; that is, they are not regimes in which *all* the people are literally members of the legislative." Jean Hampton, *Hobbes and the Social Contract Tradition* (Cambridge: Cambridge University Press, 1986), 284.
63. See Aristotle, *Politics*, trans. C. D. C. Reeve (Indianapolis: Hackett, 1998), 1294b7–10. On the aristocratic dimensions of election and the extent

to which the latter inherently affirms a "principle of distinction," see Bernard Manin, *The Principles of Representative Government* (Cambridge: Cambridge University Press, 1997).

64. Hobbes, *On the Citizen*, 7.8.

65. Hobbes, *Leviathan, Volume Two*, 18, 282. See also Hobbes, 20, 320.

66. Hobbes, 19, 288.

67. For some treatments of Hobbes's critique of democracy see Leo Strauss, *The Political Philosophy of Hobbes: Its Basis and Genesis* (Chicago: Chicago University Press, 1952), 59–60; Alan Apperley, "Hobbes on Democracy," *Politics* 19, no. 3 (1999): 165–71; Richard Flathman, *Thomas Hobbes: Skepticism, Individuality, and Chastened Politics* (Lanham, MD: Rowman & Littlefield, 2002), 135–42; Kinch Hoekstra, "A Lion in the House: Hobbes and Democracy," in *Rethinking the Foundations of Modern Political Thought*, ed. Annabel Brett, James Tully, and Holly Hamilton-Bleakley, 191–218 (Cambridge: Cambridge University Press, 2006); William Lund, "Neither 'Behemoth' nor 'Leviathan': Explaining Hobbes's Illiberal Politics," in *Hobbes and Behemoth: Religion and Democracy*, ed. Tomaž Mastnak (Exeter: Imprint Academic, 2009), 288–91; Tomaž Mastnak, "Godly Democracy," in *Hobbes's Behemoth: Religion and Democracy*, ed. Tomaž Mastnak (Exeter: Imprint Academic, 2009), 210–40; Daniel J. Kapust, "The Problem of Flattery and Hobbes's Institutional Defense of Monarchy," *Journal of Politics* 73, no. 3 (2011): 680–91; Jakonen, "Needed but Unwanted"; Foisneau, *Hobbes: La vie inquiète*, 27–47; Bruce J. Smith, *The Sense of Injustice and the Origin of Modern Democracy* (Rochester, NY: University of Rochester Press, 2018), 70–89; Christopher Holman, "Hobbes and the Tragedy of Democracy," *History of Political Thought* 40, no. 4 (2019): 649–75; Christopher Holman, "'That Democratic Ink Must Be Wiped Away': Hobbes and the Normativity of Democracy," *Review of Politics* 83, no. 3 (2021): 305–28.

68. See, for example, Strauss, *The Political Philosophy of Hobbes*, 59–60; Hampton, *Hobbes and the Social Contract Tradition*, 105; Yves Charles Zarka, *Hobbes and Modern Political Thought*, trans. James Griffith (Edinburgh: Edinburgh University Press, 1995), 136; Deborah Baumgold, "Hobbes's and Locke's Contract Theories: Political Not Metaphysical," in *Contract Theory in Historical Context: Essays on Grotius, Hobbes, and Locke* (Leiden: Brill, 2010), 9; Michael Hardt and Antonio Negri, *Empire* (Cambridge, MA: Harvard University Press, 2000), 85; Hoekstra, "A Lion in the House: Hobbes and Democracy," 201.

69. Thomas Hobbes, "The Prose Life," in *The Elements of Law, Natural and Politic*, ed. J. C. A. Gaskin (Oxford: Oxford University Press, 1994), 247.

70. Thomas Hobbes, "The Verse Life," in *The Elements of Law, Natural and Politic*, ed. J. C. A. Gaskin (Oxford: Oxford University Press, 1994), 256.

71. For an account of Hobbes's translations as political interventions see Alicia Steinmetz, "Hobbes and the Politics of Translation," *Political Theory* 49, no. 1 (2021): 83–108. A. P. Martinich interprets Hobbes's translation of Thu-

cydides as a political rebuke of the normative preference for democracy as a form of regime. A. P. Martinich, *Hobbes: A Biography* (Cambridge: Cambridge University Press, 1999), 77. Kinch Hoekstra, by contrast, suggests that in his introduction to Thucydides Hobbes is not so much providing a critique of democratic decision-making as he is outlining the potentially destructive consequences of elite competition. Kinch Hoekstra, "Hobbes's Thucydides," in *The Oxford Handbook of Hobbes*, ed. A. P. Martinich and Kinch Hoekstra (Oxford: Oxford University Press, 2016), 551. Much commentary has been produced on the topic of Hobbes's relation to Thucydides more generally. For a sample of some of the more well-known interpretations that emphasize the latter's influence on the former, see Richard Schlatter, "Thomas Hobbes and Thucydides," *Journal of the History of Ideas* 6, no. 3 (1945): 350–62; George Klosko and Daryl Rice, "Thucydides and Hobbes's State of Nature," *History of Political Thought* 6, no. 3 (1985): 405–9; Clifford W. Brown Jr., "Thucydides, Hobbes, and the Derivation of Anarchy," *History of Political Thought* 8, no. 1 (1987): 33–62; Clifford W. Brown Jr., "Thucydides, Hobbes and the Linear Causal Perspective," *History of Political Thought* 10, no. 2 (1989): 215–56; Gabriella Slomp, "Hobbes, Thucydides and the Three Greatest Things," *History of Political Thought* 11, no. 4 (1990): 565–86; Gabriella Slomp, *Thomas Hobbes and the Political Philosophy of Glory* (Basingstoke: Macmillan Press, 2000), 51–83; Ted Butler, "Image, Rhetoric, and Politics in the Early Thomas Hobbes," *Journal of the History of Ideas* 67, no. 3 (2006): 465–87; James J. Hamilton, "The Origins of Hobbes's State of Nature," *Hobbes Studies* 26, no. 2 (2013): 152–70. For some examples of fundamental differences between Hobbes and Thucydides that readers often overlook, see Peter J. Ahrensdorf, "The Fear of Death and the Longing for Immortality: Hobbes and Thucydides on Human Nature and the Problem of Anarchy," *American Political Science Review* 94, no. 3 (2000): 579–93.

72. Thomas Hobbes, "Of the Life and History of Thucydides," in *The History of Thucydides, The English Works of Thomas Hobbes of Malmesbury, Volume Eight*, ed. Sir William Molesworth (London: John Bohn, 1839), xvi–xvii.

73. Hobbes, "Of the Life and History of Thucydides," xvi.

74. Hobbes, xvi.

75. Hobbes, xvi.

76. In his argument that Hobbes's political thought was largely motivated by the threats posed by Puritan radicalism, George Shulman contends that it was precisely the Puritans' inability to comprehend the finitude of collective life and the need to place limits on human action that was what so troubled Hobbes. George Shulman, "Hobbes, Puritans, and Promethean Politics," *Political Theory* 16, no. 3 (1988): 434. See also Andrzej Rapaczynski, *Nature and Politics: Liberalism in the Philosophies of Hobbes, Locke and Rousseau* (Ithaca, NY: Cornell University Press, 1987), 25; Corey Robin, *Fear: The History of a Political Idea* (Oxford: Oxford University Press, 2004), 33. That is to say, Puritan excess

demonstrates what democracy may become without self-limitation. On Hobbes's concern with the human capacity for self-limitation see also Tuck, *Philosophy and Government*, 307.

77. Thomas Hobbes, "A Discourse on the Beginning of Tacitus," in *Three Discourses*, ed. Noel B. Reynolds and Arlene W. Saxonhouse (Chicago: University of Chicago Press, 1995), 57. Martin Bertman calls attention to the fact that even monarchs may be subject to hubris and fail to practice self-limitation: "The mortal God can be maddened by *hubris* and he may desire what for a mortal person is impossible." Martin A. Bertman, "God and Man: Action and Reference in Hobbes," *Hobbes Studies* 3, no. 1 (1990): 29.

78. Hobbes, "A Discourse on the Beginning of Tacitus," 57.

79. Hobbes, *On the Citizen*, 10.7.

80. Hobbes, 10.7.

81. Hobbes, 10.6.

82. Hobbes, *Leviathan, Volume Two*, 19, 290.

83. Kapust, "The Problem of Flattery and Hobbes's Institutional Defense of Monarchy."

84. Kapust, 681. Jeffrey Barnouw notes how this principle applies to Hobbes's own project. If persuasion in assemblies has the effect of inflaming passion as a result of the confrontation of particular citizens, Hobbes's own use of rhetorical modes in *Leviathan* avoids this consequence to the degree that it operates on individual readers alone, it being persuasion of a fundamentally different type. Jeffrey Barnouw, "Persuasion in Hobbes's *Leviathan*," *Hobbes Studies* 1, no. 1 (1988): 11.

85. Hobbes, *Leviathan, Volume Two*, 19, 288.

86. Hobbes, *On the Citizen*, 5.7.

87. As Ned O'Gorman notes, what distinguishes democracy from monarchy "is the form and internal dynamics" of the representative person, democracy being characterized by a plurality of actors who express differing and contradictory political desires, each one looking to advance their own particular interest relative to others. Ned O'Gorman, "Hobbes, Desire, and the Democratization of Rhetoric," *Advances in the History of Rhetoric* 16, no. 1 (2013): 20.

88. Mónica Brito Vieira, *The Elements of Representation in Hobbes: Aesthetics, Theatre, Law, and Theology in the Construction of Hobbes's Theory of the State* (Leiden: Brill, 2009), 183.

89. In Kapust's words once more, "The interests of the king *qua* king and *qua* man are united, which is not the case in assemblies. The king's reason is the only reason that counts, and a king reasoning in isolation—and with the assistance of isolated counsellors—reasons better than groups." Kapust, "The Problem of Flattery and Hobbes's Institutional Defense of Monarchy," 690.

90. Hence Paul Rahe identifies Hobbes's preference for monarchy to be a consequence of his general distrust of the mechanics of political deliberation:

"The English philosopher was acutely aware that assemblies deliberate where monarchs command: the former provide a middle ground where rivals can compete in displaying their capacity for *lógos* and their putative dedication to the common good; they presuppose, even when they do not explicitly assert, man's capacity to distinguish by natural reason the advantages, the just, and the good." Paul A. Rahe, *Republics Ancient & Modern, Volume II: New Modes and Orders in Early Modern Political Thought* (Chapel Hill: University of North Carolina Press, 1994), 158.

91. I will further discuss this issue in chapter 3.

92. The connection between rhetoric and democratic instability has been recently highlighted by Luc Foisneau, who locates Hobbes's distaste for democracy specifically in the mode of interaction that characterizes decision-making processes within it, processes that render it an inherently "fragile regime." Foisneau, *Hobbes: La vie inquiète*, 35. Foisneau concludes that "Hobbes's argument against democracy is thus also an argument against the function of rhetoric and, more generally, of communication in such a regime." Foisneau, 37.

93. Thomas Hobbes, *Behemoth, or the Long Parliament*, ed. Paul Seaward (Oxford: Clarendon Press, 2010), 196.

94. For an account of the place of the distinction between what Hobbes identifies as the productive and destructive modes of eloquence within his rhetorical theory more generally, see Jeremy Rayner, "Hobbes and the Rhetoricians," *Hobbes Studies* 4, no. 1 (1991): 76–95.

95. Hobbes, *On the Citizen*, 12.12.

96. Hobbes, 12.12.

97. For readings that emphasize this negative relation between assembly deliberation and rational analysis of public issues see, for example, Frederick G. Whelan, "Language and Its Abuses in Hobbes's Political Philosophy," *American Political Science Review* 75, no. 1 (1981): 63; Jakonen, "Needed but Unwanted, 109; Timothy Raylor, *Philosophy, Rhetoric, and Thomas Hobbes* (Oxford: Oxford University Press, 2018), 73.

98. Hobbes, *On the Citizen*, 10.11.

99. Hobbes, *Leviathan, Volume Two*, 25, 400.

100. Hobbes, 25, 398.

101. Hobbes, 25, 402.

102. Hobbes, 25, 406.

103. Hobbes, 19, 288.

104. Hobbes, 25, 408–10.

105. Hobbes, 25, 412.

106. Hobbes, *The Elements of Law, Natural and Politic*, 1.10.9. For Bernard Gert this characterization of madness as an excessive surplus of passion is a clear manifestation of the irreducibility of Hobbes's account of rationality to that dominant interpretation which identifies reason exclusively with the maximization

of the satisfaction of desire. Bernard Gert, "Hobbes's Account of Reason and the Passions," in *Thomas Hobbes: De la métaphysique à la politique*, ed. Martin Bertman and Michel Malherbe (Paris: Librairie Philosophique J. Vrin, 1989), 84.

107. Hobbes, *Leviathan, Volume Two*, 8, 110.

108. Hobbes, 8, 114.

109. Hobbes, 8, 114.

110. Hobbes, 8, 114.

111. Hobbes, 8, 112.

112. Hobbes, 8, 112.

113. Hobbes, "On Man," in *Man and Citizen (De Homine and De Cive)*, trans. Charles T. Wood, T. S. K. Scott-Craig, and Bernard Gert (Indianapolis: Hackett, 1991), 55.

114. Brito Vieira, *The Elements of Representation in Hobbes*, 79.

115. Hobbes, *The Elements of Law, Natural and Politic*, 2.5.4.

116. When a reader such as Bernard Gert, for example, maintains that the occupiers of monarchical sovereign office are just as subject to the vicissitudes of human nature as citizens are, and that on this basis democracy might become Hobbes's preferred sovereign form, he seems to overlook precisely the extent to which the democratic flux of passion is not grounded in a differentiation of human nature, but rather the dynamics of assembly mechanics. See Bernard Gert, *Hobbes: Prince of Peace* (Cambridge: Polity, 2010), 142.

117. Such is noted by Mikko Jakonen, who writes that "Hobbes saw that the democratic mode of government strengthens populist leaders who rhetorically mislead both common and educated people to the point where demagogy turns into chaos and the logic of the multitude gets to reign." Jakonen, "Needed but Unwanted, 92. Loralea Michaelis makes a similar observation, writing that "government by assembly does not bring an end to the state of nature so much as it transforms it into a public spectacle in which the uncertainty of the future is magnified by the precariousness of its members' policy commitments." Loralea Michaelis, "Hobbes's Modern Prometheus: A Political Philosophy for an Uncertain Future," *Canadian Journal of Political Science* 40, no. 1 (2007): 120. See also Joshua Mitchell, "Hobbes and the Equality of All," *Political Theory* 21, no. 1 (1993): 85.

118. Jakonen, "Multitude in Motion," 33. This is further noted by Patrick Craig, who, citing the multiple places in which Hobbes continues to refer to the their existence within commonwealths, identifies the error of those readers who associate the creation of the people with the abolition of the multitude. Craig, "Jacques Rancière, Thomas Hobbes, and a Politics of the Part That Has No Part." One may contrast this recognition with the reading of Paolo Virno, who interprets the very existence of multitude and people as mutually incompatible: "If there are a people, there is no multitude; if there is a multitude, there are no people." Virno, *A Grammar of the Multitude*, 23. The multitude

is here interpreted as being both anti-state and anti-people, thus rendering it difficult to make sense of Hobbes's suggestion that the democratic assembly—whose existence clearly implies both a state and a people—is a reemergence of multitude within the instituted commonwealth.

119. As Christopher Scott McClure notes, "One of the requirements of peaceful politics, for Hobbes, is that citizens have more or less disquiet minds." Christopher Scott McClure, *Hobbes and the Artifice of Eternity* (Cambridge: Cambridge University Press, 2016), 5.

120. Hobbes, *Leviathan, Volume Two*, 19, 290.

121. Hobbes, 26, 420.

122. Hobbes, *The Elements of Law, Natural and Politic*, 2.5.7. It is thus not insignificant that, as Melissa Schwartzberg has noted, a conspicuous feature of Leveller political thought was the emphasis on the need to affirm the human capacity to regularly amend and remake law. Melissa Schwartzberg, *Democracy and Legal Change* (Cambridge: Cambridge University Press, 2007), 84–91. As Richard Overton argues, for example, the capacity of the people to reflect upon and debate law "ought to be the form and life of every government." Richard Overton, "A Remonstrance of Many Thousand Citizens and Other Freeborn People of England to Their Own House of Commons . . . ," in *The English Levellers*, ed. Andrew Sharp (Cambridge: Cambridge University Press, 1998), 46.

123. Hobbes, *On the Citizen*, 10.13.

124. Hobbes, *The Elements of Law, Natural and Politic*, 2.5.8.

125. Very much unlike Machiavelli, however, Hobbes denies that such conflict has any socially productive value. On this point see Rahe, *Republics Ancient & Modern, Volume II*, 137; Sullivan, *Machiavelli, Hobbes, & the Formation of a Liberal Republicanism in England* (Cambridge: Cambridge University Press, 2004), 81; Daniela Coli, "Hobbes's Revolution," in *Politics and the Passions: 1500–1850*, ed. Victoria Kahn, Neil Saccamano, and Daniela Coli (Princeton, NJ: Princeton University Press, 2006), 92; Paul A. Rahe, *Against Throne and Altar: Machiavelli and Political Theory under the English Republic* (Cambridge: Cambridge University Press, 2008), 273.

126. Hobbes, *Leviathan, Volume Two*, 11, 354. Moshe Berent finds it strange that Hobbes accuses Aristotle of being a democrat, which he clearly was not. Moshe Berent, "Hobbes and the 'Greek Tongues,'" *History of Political Thought* 17, no. 1 (1996): 36. As Robert Kraynak notes, however, Hobbes would certainly have been aware that Aristotle was not a partisan of democracy, but he could nevertheless still identify the fact that the latter's political philosophy exerted a real historical influence on democratic theory. Robert P. Kraynak, *History and Modernity in the Thought of Thomas Hobbes* (Ithaca, NY: Cornell University Press, 1990), 52. Hence the identification of "the democraticall principles of Aristotle and Cicero." Hobbes, *Behemoth, or the Long Parliament*, 164.

127. See, for example, Thomas Hobbes, *Leviathan, Volume Three: The English and Latin Texts (ii)*, ed. Noel Malcolm (Oxford: Clarendon Press, 2012), 47, 1129–31; Thomas Hobbes, "Six Lessons to the Professors of the Mathematics," in *The English Works of Thomas Hobbes of Malmesbury, Volume Seven*, ed. Sir William Molesworth (London: Longman, Brown, Green, and Longmans, 1845), 335. Hobbes would continue to reiterate this need for the universities to teach absolute obedience to the established laws of the sovereign later in *Behemoth*, where the existing schools are identified as the "coar of Rebellion," and in need of being "disciplin'd." Hobbes, *Behemoth, or the Long Parliament*, 182.

Chapter 2

1. Yves Charles Zarka is representative of the majority of readers who view Hobbes's account of authorization in *Leviathan* as constituting a radically and fundamentally new way of thinking the social compact. Most notably, "Authorization is not alienation: in instituting the State, the individuals, becoming citizens, do not lose all rights over themselves and their action. This theory allows for a complete reworking of the political doctrine." Yves Charles Zarka, "Droit de resistance et droit penal chez Hobbes," in *Hobbes oggi*, ed. Andrea Napoli and Guido Canziani (Milano: Franco Angeli, 1990), 187.

2. On the extent to which in *De Cive* individuals are characterized in terms of a "radical passivity," to the degree that they mutually renounce their natural rights without this renunciation establishing any form of ownership, see Annabel Herzog, "Hobbes and Corneille on Political Representation," *European Legacy* 14, no. 4 (2009): 380.

3. To the extent that the new account in *Leviathan* still supposes a renunciation, some readers have posited what Michael J. Green labels the "inconsistency objection": authorization necessitates the subjects' extension of their rights to the sovereign, thus enabling the latter to act on these rights, yet subjects can only so extend rights if they possess them, which they no longer do given the fact of alienation. Alienation and authorization are thus incompatible. Michael J. Green, "Authorization and Political Authority in Hobbes," *Journal of the History of Philosophy* 53, no. 1 (2015): 29. In Green's account, however, the mistake of the inconsistency objection lay in the exclusive identification of authorization with the extension of rights, an identification that ignores the possibility of thinking authorization in terms of an ownership that establishes responsibility: "Authorization is not used to extend the subjects' rights to the sovereign. Rather, it is used to establish the subjects' ownership of the sovereign's actions. The social contract is internally consistent because it is possible to authorize someone else's actions by taking ownership of them while alienating one's own rights." Green, 36. For a particularly articulate and concise expression of the

inconsistency position, see A. P. Martinich, "Authorization and Representation in Hobbes's *Leviathan*," in *The Oxford Handbook of Hobbes*, ed. A. P. Martinich and Kinch Hoekstra (Oxford: Oxford University Press, 2016), 315–38.

4. On the distinction between true representation and fictitious representation, and the well-known identification of the state as a person by fiction, see David Runciman, "What Kind of Person Is Hobbes's State? A Reply to Skinner," *Journal of Political Philosophy* 8, no. 2 (2000): 268–78.

5. It is important to note, however, that the introduction of the language of authorization and representation has important implications for Hobbes's thought that go well beyond those that I will call attention to in this chapter. Perhaps most significantly is the role that the idea of personation comes to play in Hobbes's theology. Bryan Garsten, for example, argues that such language "can be best understood as part of his effort to use Christian concepts against the political influence of the Christian clergy." Bryan Garsten, "Religion and Representation in Hobbes," in *Leviathan*, by Thomas Hobbes, ed. Ian Shapiro (New Haven, CT: Yale University Press, 2010), 522. We know that Hobbes was especially concerned with repudiating those individuals who would claim some unique authority on the basis of the ability to speak directly with God. God, however, enters into no relations, and hence the fact that "the true God may be personated." Thomas Hobbes, *Leviathan, Volume Two: The English and Latin Texts (i)*, ed. Noel Malcolm (Oxford: Clarendon Press, 2012), 16, 248. For a further attempt to link the political and religious functions of *Leviathan*'s linguistic innovation, see Arash Abizadeh, "The Representation of Hobbesian Sovereignty: Leviathan as Mythology," in *Hobbes Today: Insights for the 21st Century*, ed. S. A. Lloyd (Cambridge University Press, 2013), 113–52. Like the state, God is a natural nonperson who only exists artificially through the act of personation. For Abizadeh the sovereign right to represent the state necessarily implies the sovereign right to represent God, and hence "the capacity to personate God is one of the ideological *bases* of sovereign power." Abizadeh, 142.

6. Quentin Skinner, *From Humanism to Hobbes: Studies in Politics and Rhetoric* (Cambridge: Cambridge University Press, 2018), 190–221. For Pitkin's famous account of Hobbesian representation see Hanna Pitkin, "Hobbes's Concept of Representation—I," *American Political Science Review* 58, no. 2 (1964): 328–40; Hanna Pitkin, "Hobbes's Concept of Representation—II," *American Political Science Review* 58, no. 4 (1964): 902–18; Hanna Pitkin, *The Concept of Representation* (Berkeley: University of California Press, 1967), 14–37.

7. Quentin Skinner, "Hobbes on Persons, Authors and Representatives," in *The Cambridge Companion to Hobbes's* Leviathan (Cambridge: Cambridge University Press, 2007), 159–61. See also, for example, Deborah Baumgold, *Hobbes's Political Theory* (Cambridge: Cambridge University Press, 1988), 43–45; Glenn Burgess, "Contexts for the Writing and Publication of Hobbes's *Leviathan*," *History of Political Thought* 11, no. 4 (1990): 675–702; Alison McQueen, "Mosaic

Leviathan: Religion and Rhetoric in Hobbes's Political Thought," in *Hobbes on Politics and Religion*, ed. Laurens van Apeldoorn and Robin Douglass (Oxford: Oxford University Press, 2018), 128–32.

8. Skinner, *From Humanism to Hobbes*, 208.

9. Skinner, 211. Operating within a strongly contextual methodological paradigm, although one very different from Skinner—not deemphasizing socio-economic conditions for narrowly intellectual ones—Ellen Wood also notes Hobbes's conceptual deployment of various of his opponents' notions: "While his conclusions were anything but democratic, Hobbes reached them by appropriating some of the most radically democratic ideas of his day." Ellen Meiksins Wood, *Liberty and Property: A Social History of Western Political Thought from Renaissance to Enlightenment* (London: Verso, 2012), 255. For a programmatic account of the main principles of Wood's social history of political thought and how the latter differs from Cambridge school approaches, see Ellen Meiksins Wood, *Citizens to Lords: A Social History of Western Political Thought from Antiquity to the Late Middle Ages* (London: Verso, 2008), 1–27.

10. Adrian Blau has recently highlighted the importance of both historical-contextual and philosophical-textual analysis to research in the history of political thought. Just as interpretative misunderstanding of a text's meaning may result from ignoring the particular historical circumstances structuring authorial intention, so too might misunderstanding emerge from focusing exclusively on isolated textual elements at the expense of others. Interpretation must thus include not only historical analysis, but philosophical analysis as well, the latter looking to reconstruct a potentially definite theoretical logic through placing passages in their textual contexts. See especially Adrian Blau, "Textual Context in the History of Political Thought," *History of European Ideas* 45, no. 8 (2019): 1191–1210, but also Adrian Blau, "History of Political Thought as Detective Work," *History of European Ideas* 41, no. 8 (2015): 1178–94; Adrian Blau, "Extended Meaning and Understanding in the History of Ideas," *History and Theory* 58, no. 3 (2019): 342–59. For an elaboration of these methodological principles in relation to Hobbes scholarship specifically, see Adrian Blau, "Methodologies of Interpreting Hobbes: Historical and Philosophical," in *Interpreting Hobbes's Political Philosophy*, ed. S. A. Lloyd (Cambridge: Cambridge University Press, 2019), 10–28. Note, however, that Blau believes that although it is obscured by his programmatic methodological writings, it remains true that Skinner's interpretations are exemplary in their combination of historical and philosophical analysis. Especially significant here, for example, is Skinner's reading of Hobbes on liberty. Blau, "History of Political Thought as Detective Work," 1189.

11. Deborah Baumgold, "The Difficulties of Hobbes Interpretation," *Political Theory* 36, no. 6 (2008): 829.

12. Baumgold, 846.

13. I do not here consider the Latin *Leviathan* to constitute a substantial new moment in Hobbes's political philosophical development, at least with respect to the issues I deal with in this chapter, the major conceptual formulations I highlight from the English *Leviathan* being re-presented in the Latin version. For a recent and highly useful summary of the differences in the two *Leviathans*, see Mónica Brito Vieira, "'Leviathan' Contra 'Leviathan,'" *Journal of the History of Ideas* 76, no. 2 (2015): 271–88. See also Noel Malcolm, "General Introduction," in *Leviathan, Volume One: Editorial Introduction*, by Thomas Hobbes, ed. Noel Malcolm (Oxford: Clarendon Press, 2012), 175–95. In any case, however, it should be noted that Hobbes himself declares that he wished for *Leviathan* to appear in Latin as part of the pedagogical effort to counter the "seditious principles" of the democrats. Thomas Hobbes, *Leviathan, Volume Three: The English and Latin Texts (ii)*, ed. Noel Malcolm (Oxford: Clarendon Press, 2012), 47, 1129. Ed. translation.

14. Thomas Hobbes, "A Discourse on the Beginning of Tacitus," in *Three Discourses*, ed. Noel B. Reynolds and Arlene W. Saxonhouse (Chicago: University of Chicago Press, 1995), 34.

15. Hobbes, "A Discourse on the Beginning of Tacitus," 34.

16. Hobbes, 35.

17. Hence, for example, after Caesar's appropriation of authority, "Rome utterly lost her liberty." Hobbes, 36.

18. For a systematic effort to trace out Hobbes's changing conception of liberty from *The Elements of Law* to *Leviathan*, particularly in relation to republicanism, see Quentin Skinner, *Hobbes and Republican Liberty* (Cambridge: Cambridge University Press, 2008). For a recent challenge to Skinner's account, which does not see the conceptual mutation as being motivated by an engagement with republican thought, see Robin Douglass, "Thomas Hobbes's Changing Account of Liberty and Challenge to Republicanism," *History of Political Thought* 36, no. 2 (2015): 281–309. For arguments that there is in fact a proximity between Hobbes's political thought and the philosophical presuppositions of republicanism see Barry Hindess, *Discourses of Power: From Hobbes to Foucault* (Oxford: Blackwell Publishers, 1996), 39–43; Lars Vinx, "Hobbes on Civic Liberty and the Rule of Law," in *Hobbes and the Law*, ed. David Dyzenhaus and Thomas Poole (Cambridge: Cambridge University Press, 2012), 145–64. Contra Skinner and many others, for the claim that the most important elements of Hobbes's concept of liberty are consistent from the *Elements* to *Leviathan*, see Daniel J. Kapust and Brandon P. Turner, "Democratical Gentlemen and the Lust for Mastery: Status, Ambition, and the Language of Liberty in Hobbes's Political Thought," *Political Theory* 41, no. 4 (2013): 648–75; Philip Pettit, "Liberty and Leviathan," *Politics, Philosophy and Economics* 4, no. 1 (2005): 131–51.

19. Thomas Hobbes, *The Elements of Law, Natural and Politic*, ed. Ferdinand Tönnies (London: Simpkin, Marshall, and Co., 1889), 2.8.3.

20. Hobbes, *The Elements of Law, Natural and Politic*, 2.2.1.
21. Hobbes, 2.2.3.
22. Hobbes, 2.2.5.
23. Hobbes, 2.2.5.
24. See, for example, Quentin Skinner, "Hobbes and the *studia humanitatis*," in *Visions of Politics, Volume 3: Hobbes and Civil Science* (Cambridge: Cambridge University Press, 2002), 55; Mikko Jakonen, "Needed But Unwanted: Thomas Hobbes's Warnings on the Dangers of Multitude, Populism and Democracy," *Las Torres de Lucca*, no. 9 (2016): 105.
25. Tomaž Mastnak sees *Behemoth* as illustrating how so-called democratic rule tends to be democratic in name only: "In effect, it was a reign of orators and 'Neros,' of ambitious men seeking 'absolute power' for themselves." Tomaž Mastnak, "Godly Democracy," in *Hobbes's* Behemoth: *Religion and Democracy*, ed. Tomaž Mastnak (Exeter: Imprint Academic, 2009), 225. Daniel Kapust and Brandon Turner likewise interpret the "democratical gentlemen" of *Behemoth* as ambitious elites looking to advance their private interests, in this case through the exploitation and misuse of the language of liberty. Kapust and Turner, "Democratical Gentlemen and the Lust for Mastery" See also Robert P. Kraynak, *History and Modernity in the Thought of Thomas Hobbes* (Ithaca, NY: Cornell University Press, 1990), 38.
26. Thomas Hobbes, *Behemoth, or the Long Parliament* ed. Paul Seaward (Oxford: Clarendon Press, 2010), 110.
27. Hobbes, *Behemoth*, 110.
28. Hobbes, 136–37.
29. Hobbes, 137.
30. Hobbes, 205.
31. A very large number of readers have devoted significant attention to the question of Hobbes's relationship to the rhetorical tradition, outlining not only his critique of various rhetorical modes, but also his strategic utilization of them. For some such notable contributions see David Johnston, *The Rhetoric of Leviathan: Thomas Hobbes and the Politics of Cultural Transformation* (Princeton, NJ: Princeton University Press, 1986); Conal Condren, "On the Rhetorical Foundations of *Leviathan*," *History of Political Thought* 11, no. 4 (1990): 703–20; Raia Prokhovnik, *Rhetoric and Philosophy in Hobbes's* Leviathan (New York: Garland Publishing, 1991); Charles Cantalupo, *A Literary* Leviathan: *Thomas Hobbes's Masterpiece of Language* (Lewisburg, PA: Bucknell University Press, 1991); Quentin Skinner, *Reason and Rhetoric in the Philosophy of Hobbes* (Cambridge: Cambridge University Press, 1996); Quentin Skinner, "Hobbes on Rhetoric and the Construction of Morality," in *Visions of Politics, Volume 3: Hobbes and Civil Science* (Cambridge: Cambridge University Press, 2002), 87–141; Ted H. Miller, "The Uniqueness of *Leviathan*: Authorizing Poets, Philosophers, and Sovereigns," in Leviathan *After 350 Years*, ed. Tom Sorell and Luc Foisneau

(Oxford: Oxford University Press, 2004), 75–104; Karen S. Feldman, *Binding Words: Conscience and Rhetoric in Hobbes, Hegel, and Heidegger* (Evanston, IL: Northwestern University Press, 2006); James Martel, *Subverting the Leviathan: Reading Thomas Hobbes as a Radical Democrat* (New York: Columbia University Press, 2007), 21–38; Ioannis Evrigenis, *Images of Anarchy: The Rhetoric and Science in Hobbes's State of Nature* (Cambridge: Cambridge University Press, 2014); Timothy Raylor, *Philosophy, Rhetoric, and Thomas Hobbes* (Oxford: Oxford University Press, 2018).

32. Skinner, *Reason and Rhetoric in the Philosophy of Hobbes*, 431–35.

33. Hobbes, *Behemoth, or the Long Parliament*, 319. Hence I do not think that Mastnak is correct to see in *Behemoth* a departure from the earlier analysis of democracy as a positive form of government. For Mastnak democracy in this text is no longer analyzed as a particular type of regime, but is rather interpreted negatively as a process of deconstitution, as a as "a set of opinions and actions bent on unmaking government. . . . Democracy here means designing a process of change and implementing that design more than it refers to an outcome—a particular form of government." Mastnak, "Godly Democracy," 211, 216. Such a negative logic inheres, in fact, in all of Hobbes's accounts of democratic institutionalization, the positive form of which is still affirmed in *Behemoth*, as the quoted text suggests.

34. Sandra Field has criticized my interpretation here, suggesting that for Hobbes the nondemocratic character of the Rump was not to be found in the inherently exclusive form of the parliamentary body, but rather "the much more specific fact that this parliament had permanently and formally excluded some people on the basis of their political views." Sandra Leonie Field, "Response to Critics," *European Hobbes Society Online Colloquium*, June 9, 2021, http://www.europeanhobbessociety.org/general/online-colloquium-5-reply-to-critics-by-sandra-leonie-field. Consider, though, the following passage from *Leviathan*, where Hobbes, in the context of his interrogation of the nature of sovereign rule in Judea under Roman governance, repeats the definition of democracy in terms of universal access to assembly space. Judea was not "a Democracy; because they were not governed by any Assembly, into the which, *any of them, had right to enter*; nor by an Aristocracy; because they were not governed by any Assembly into which, *any man could enter by their Election.*" Hobbes, *Leviathan, Volume Two*, 19, 298. Emphases added.

35. Hobbes, *The Elements of Law, Natural and Politic*, 2.2.9.

36. David P. Gauthier, *The Logic of Leviathan: The Moral and Political Theory of Thomas Hobbes* (Oxford: Oxford University Press, 1969), 146.

37. As Don Herzog writes, "Some of our historically minded theorists have complained that Hobbes's account of liberty seems too stifling and have called on us to resurrect notions of ancient liberty. They shouldn't be surprised that Hobbes's concept confines our political discourse. That's precisely what it

was designed to do." Don Herzog, *Happy Slaves: A Critique of Consent Theory* (Chicago: University of Chicago Press, 1989), 104.

38. Thomas Hobbes, *On the Citizen*, ed. and trans. Richard Tuck and Michael Silverthorne (Cambridge: Cambridge University Press, 1998), 9.9.

39. Hobbes, *On the Citizen*, 9.9.

40. Hobbes, 9.9.

41. Hobbes, 10.1.

42. Hobbes, 13.15.

43. Hobbes, 13.15. Along these lines, Bernard Willms, who reads Hobbes as a dialectical thinker, considers the institution of the commonwealth not in terms of the one-sided abolition of liberty, but rather in terms of the sublation of liberty: the state "does not suspend the state of nature, i.e., liberty, but rather turns it into a liveable condition, realizing it in a precise sense." Bernard Willms, "Liberty as *conditio humana*," in *Thomas Hobbes: His View of Man*, ed. J. G. van der Bend (Amsterdam: Rodopi, 1982), 111. On Hobbes as a dialectical thinker see also Gary B. Herbert, "Thomas Hobbes's Dialectic of Desire," *New Scholasticism* 50, no. 2 (1976): 137–63; Paul J. Johnson, "Deduction and Dialectic in Hobbes's Theory of Civility," *Hobbes Studies* 4, no. 1 (1991): 96–114; Gary Browning, "The Politics of Recognition: Life and Death Struggles in Hobbes and Hegel," *Hobbes Studies* 28, no. 1 (2015): 9; Michael Byron, "Hobbes's Confounding Foole," in *Interpreting Hobbes's Political Philosophy*, ed. S. A. Lloyd (Cambridge: Cambridge University Press, 2019), 210.

44. Hobbes, *On the Citizen*, 10.8.

45. Skinner, *Hobbes and Republican Liberty*, 107; Corey Robin, *Fear: The History of a Political Idea* (Oxford: Oxford University Press, 2004), 102; Douglass, "Thomas Hobbes's Changing Account of Liberty and Challenge to Republicanism," 291.

46. Skinner, *Hobbes and Republican Liberty*, 128–30. It should also be noted that not all commentators take this alteration in the definition to be particularly slight. For a reading that sees this shift in meaning as the most important change in the whole of Hobbes's philosophy, see F. C. Hood, "The Change in Hobbes's Definition of Liberty," *Philosophical Quarterly* 17, no. 67 (1967): 150–63.

47. Hobbes, *Leviathan, Volume Two*, 14, 198. For examples of different ways in which individuals may be free, depending on the different absences of external impediments to motion, see Lena Halldenius, "Liberty, Law and Leviathan," *Theoria*, no. 131 (2012): 1–20.

48. Hobbes, *Leviathan, Volume Two*, 21, 328.

49. Hobbes, 21, 328.

50. Hobbes, 21, 332.

51. Hobbes, 21, 332. Although we will not deal with the question specifically here, Perez Zagorin (among others) has argued that "Hobbes's claim that individuals possessed an identical freedom in every type of polity is one of

the worst defended in his work." Perez Zagorin, *Hobbes and the Law of Nature* (Princeton, NJ: Princeton University Press, 2009), 81.

52. In Philip Pettit's words, "When we obey laws, according to Hobbes's way of thinking, we do not do so freely, and this whether we live in a democracy, an aristocracy, or a monarchy. But that is only because we are obligated by our covenants (to one another when the commonwealth is instituted and to the sovereign when it is acquired) to accept and live by the laws that the sovereign makes in pursuit of the commonwealth's ends. Whatever form the political covenant may have taken, it means that we are subjected to the sovereign." Pettit, "Liberty and Leviathan," 147.

53. Hobbes, *Leviathan, Volume Three*, 46, 1095. Ed. translation.

54. Hobbes, *On the Citizen*, 10.9.

55. Hobbes, 10.9.

56. Hobbes, 7.5. Some readers, however, question the robustness of the characterization of originary democracy in *De Cive*. Deborah Baumgold and Ryan Harding, for example, focus on the use of the term *almost* here: "The qualifier 'almost democracy' is explained via a new distinction between the constitutional assembly in which the state is created and democracy as a form of government. The assembly's agreement on majority rule qualifies it as democracy only in a rudimentary sense." Deborah Baumgold and Ryan Harding, "Excavating *On the Citizen*," in *Hobbes's* On the Citizen, ed. Robin Douglass and Johan Olsthoorn (Cambridge: Cambridge University Press, 2020), 20.

57. Recognizing that by Hobbes's standards "England's revolutionary regimes" were thoroughly aristocratic, Jeffrey Collins observes that "Only the Levellers envisioned anything like a democratic assembly." Jeffrey Collins, "Malcolm's *Leviathan*: Hobbes's 'Thing,'" *Modern Intellectual History* 12, no. 1 (2015): 111, n. 57.

58. Anonymous, "England's Miserie and Remedie in a Judicious Letter from an Utter-Barrister to His Speciall Friend, Concerning Leiutenant Col. Lilburn's Imprisonment in Newgate, Sept. 14 1645," in *Divine Right and Democracy: An Anthology of Political Writing in Stuart England*, ed. David Wootton (Harmondsworth: Penguin Books, 1986), 277.

59. Richard Overton, "An Arrow Against All Tyrants and Tyranny . . .," in *The English Levellers*, ed. Andrew Sharp (Cambridge: Cambridge University Press, 1998), 62–63.

60. Anonymous, "To the Right Honorable and Supreme Authority of This Nation, The Commons in Parliament Assembled," in *The English Levellers*, ed. Andrew Sharp (Cambridge: Cambridge University Press, 1998), 77.

61. Baumgold, *Hobbes's Political Theory*, 54.

62. See, for example, M. M. Goldsmith, *Hobbes's Science of Politics* (New York: Columbia University Press, 1966), 157–60; Alexandre Matheron, "The Theoretical Function of Democracy in Spinoza and Hobbes," in *The New Spinoza*,

ed. Warren Montag and Ted Stoltze (Minneapolis: University of Minnesota Press, 1997), 207–17; Noel Malcolm, "Hobbes and Spinoza," in *Aspects of Hobbes* (Oxford: Oxford University Press, 2002), 38; Karlfriedrich Herbe, "Au-delà de la citoyenneté: Hobbes et le problème de l'autorité," *Rivista di Storia della Filosofia* 59, no. 1 (2004): 220–21; Paul Sagar, "Of Mushrooms and Method: History and the Family in Hobbes's Science of Politics," *European Journal of Political Theory* 14, no. 1 (2015): 109. There are, however, some dissenting opinions on this matter. For example, James Hamilton finds it problematic to suggest that the change in the language of political institution toward that of authorization is in any way related to Hobbes's concern over the necessity of originary democracy: "There is no special reason why Hobbes's appeal to original democracy, or original government by the whole people, should be taken in itself to imply democratic sympathies." James J. Hamilton, "Hobbes the Royalist, Hobbes the Republican," *History of Political Thought* 30, no. 3 (2009): 440.

63. In Karlfriedrich Herbe's words, "The new logic of *Leviathan* puts the traditional forms of political regimes on the same plane. Monarchy, aristocracy, and democracy have the same contractual origin, the same absolute character, and can guarantee the same degree of civil liberties." Herbe, "Au-delà de la citoyenneté," 221.

64. Hobbes, *On the Citizen*, 5.8.

65. Hobbes, 5.9.

66. Hobbes, 6.13.

67. Hobbes, 6.14.

68. For a recent attempt to outline the various types of personhood and representation that can be identified within *Leviathan*, many of which have not been generally noticed by readers, see Sean Fleming, "The Two Faces of Personhood: Hobbes, Corporate Agency and the Personality of the State," *European Journal of Political Theory* 20, no. 1 (2021): 5–26.

69. Hobbes, *Leviathan, Volume Two*, 16, 244. In the most detailed study of the place of representation in Hobbes's thought yet produced, Mónica Brito Vieira emphasizes the extent to which theatricality functions to designate an essential characteristic of almost all modes of human activity, the latter involving a presentation characterized in terms of the revelation of personae: "Sociability is not natural to the Hobbesian man. It requires art, a kind of theatricality, sustained by the social conventions of play, which helps us hide behind a mask of sustained decorousness, while moulding the externals of our conduct to the specific requirements of our roles as citizens and subjects." Brito Vieira, *The Elements of Representation in Hobbes: Aesthetics, Theatre, Law, and Theology in the Construction of Hobbes's Theory of the State* (Leiden: Brill, 2009), 85. In short, the human person is an actor, playing many roles and performing many identities.

70. Thomas Hobbes, "On Man," in *Man and Citizen (De Homine and De Cive)*, trans. Charles T. Wood, T. S. K. Scott-Craig, and Bernard Gert (Indianapolis: Hackett, 1991), 72.

71. Hobbes, *Leviathan, Volume Two*, 16, 244.

72. Hobbes, 16, 246.

73. In Mónica Brito Vieira's words, "In handing over authority to procure the thing's maintenance, the owner or governor makes manifest his intention to treat the thing as something enjoying an existence and interests of its own, which deserve special protection, in so far as they may stand over and above the transient interests of its several owners or governors." Brito Vieira, *The Elements of Representation in Hobbes*, 154. On the differing number of subjects of personality characterizing the different forms of personation, see David Runciman, *Pluralism and the Personality of the State* (Cambridge: Cambridge University Press, 2009), 9.

74. Paul Weithman shows that Hobbes is basically following Edward Coke's distinction in *The Institutes of the Laws of England* between two types of person, natural and incorporate. Paul Weithman, "Hobbes on Persons and Authorization," in *Interpreting Hobbes's Political Philosophy*, ed. S. A. Lloyd (Cambridge: Cambridge University Press, 2019), 173–90.

75. Hobbes, *Leviathan, Volume Two*, 16, 244.

76. Hobbes, "On Man," 84.

77. Hobbes, *Leviathan, Volume Two*, 16, 246.

78. Hobbes, "On Man," 84.

79. Hobbes, *Leviathan, Volume Two*, 16, 246.

80. Hobbes, 17, 256.

81. Hobbes, 17, 256.

82. Specifically, the social animals lack competition for honor among themselves; have private interests that immediately coalesce with common interest; lacking reason, cannot dispute the order of public affairs; lack the capacity for dissimulation; cannot distinguish between injury and damage; and do not require an external guarantee for the perpetuation of agreement. Hobbes, 17, 258–60.

83. The fact that such reduction is necessary is extremely important for Hobbes and indicates what he takes to be one of the many errors of the parliamentarian writers. For somebody like Henry Parker, for example, Parliament is the natural representation of the diversity of constituents constituting the population. Henry Parker, *Some Few Observations Upon His Majesties Late Answer to the Declaration or Remonstance Sic of the Lords and Commons of the 19 of May, 1642*. London: s.n., 1642. Hobbes rejects this line of thinking, arguing that the function of the state is not to express the diversity of the multitude but to overcome it via the artificial production of social unity.

84. Hobbes, *Leviathan, Volume Two*, 16, 248.

85. As David Runciman points out, without this representation, authorization would reduce politics to a set of fragmented interpersonal relations, the multitude of individuals remaining a mere conglomeration of distinct natural persons as opposed to a collective body. David Runciman, "Hobbes's Theory of Representation: Anti-Democratic or Proto-Democratic?," in *Political Representation*,

ed. Shapiro, Susan C. Stokes, Elisabeth Jean Wood, and Alexander S. Kirshner (Cambridge: Cambridge University Press, 2010), 21.

86. Hobbes, *Leviathan, Volume Two*, 16, 248.

87. Hobbes, 17, 260.

88. Hobbes, 17, 260.

89. Hobbes, 26, 416.

90. Hobbes, 17, 260.

91. Runciman, "Hobbes's Theory of Representation," 19.

92. Regarding the former, Arash Abizadeh highlights that the sovereign bears not only the person of the state, but in addition that of each individual who authorizes the representative relation: "The state is an artificial person that a sovereign represents by fiction. It is not the state itself but the individuals who covenant to establish it, who authorize the sovereign to represent the state. . . . The sovereign bears not only the person of the state, but also the person of each individual covenanter: each authorizes the sovereign to act in the name of both the commonwealth as a whole and in his own name as subject." Arash Abizadeh, *Hobbes and the Two Faces of Ethics* (Cambridge: Cambridge University Press, 2018), 257.

93. Paul Sagar perceives a problem in this conception of a sovereign that represents the commonwealth by fiction. As Sagar notes, "The role of fiction enters when we pretend that inanimate objects or other things incapable of authorizing others (because they are immature, or mad, or imaginary, or whatever) have in fact done so, and treat the resulting artificial person as the legitimate representative of what is being personated." Paul Sagar, "What Is the Leviathan?," *Hobbes Studies* 31, no. 1 (2018): 82–83. Fictional authorization is thus only possible in a commonwealth, that is, when its legitimacy is ensured through its legal recognition. If a person by fiction necessitates the existence of the state, the state cannot be a person by fiction, for there is no prior sovereign to bestow the recognition. For Johan Olsthoorn, though, it is a mistake to presume that the commonwealth only comes into existence by being represented by a sovereign, and this because there are two levels of personation in Hobbes: a first, in which the sovereign represents each individual citizen, thus uniting the multitude into one corporate body, and a second, in which the sovereign bears the commonwealth. Only the second of these is fictional, this explaining how the creation of the commonwealth can be conceived of independently of being fictionally personated by the sovereign. Johan Olsthoorn, "Leviathan, Inc.: Hobbes on the Nature and Person of the State," *History of European Ideas* 47, no. 1 (2021): 17–32.

94. Skinner here sees Hobbes as appreciating that which is overlooked by much contemporary Anglophone political theory, which has a reductive view that narrowly identifies the state with government, the former being thereby reduced to a mere apparatus of rule. Skinner, *From Humanism to Hobbes: Studies*

in Politics and Rhetoric (Cambridge: Cambridge University Press, 2018), 377. On the importance of maintaining this distinction see also Brian Trainor, "Hobbes, Skinner, and the Person of the State," *Hobbes Studies* 14, no. 1 (2001): 59–70.

95. Hobbes, *Leviathan, Volume Three*, 47, 1129–31. Ed. translation.

96. J. Matthew Hoye has argued that in *The Elements of Law* the image of the democratic city is essential to the account of sovereign institution, whereas what marks *Leviathan* is the effort to purge the city from the account of political foundation. The elimination of the language of democracy, in Hoye's account, must be considered in terms of Hobbes's engagement with urban borough politics. J. Matthew Hoye, "*Leviathan* against the City," *History of Political Thought* 41, no. 3 (2020): 419–49.

97. In M. M. Goldsmith's words, "Because the creation of the community and the creation of the sovereign are accomplished by the same act, the community only exists by virtue of the existence of the sovereign, and the community can only act through its representative, the sovereign." Goldsmith, *Hobbes's Science of Politics*, 160.

98. And if we can provide examples of people participating in the two-stage process, Noel Malcolm notes, such is only because individuals already live in a commonwealth that makes such activity possible. Noel Malcolm, "The Title Page of *Leviathan*, Seen in a Curious Perspective," in *Aspects of Hobbes* (Oxford: Oxford University Press, 2002), 223.

99. Here we might note the minority view of Murray Forsyth, who, while accepting that *Leviathan* overcomes the model of originary democratic institution in a real and substantial way (contrary to the authors who will be cited below), nevertheless interprets the theory of representation as providing a germinal account of the constituent power of the people. Murray Forsyth, "Thomas Hobbes and the Constituent Power of the People," *Political Studies* 29, no. 2 (1981): 191–203. Forsyth's reading requires interpreting authorization as a process carried out by a necessarily pre-state collective entity, as opposed to one carried out by every single natural person as a distinct individual. It thus imposes onto the multitude a unity that Hobbes, whether successful or not, intends to oppose, inverting the order of relation between the commonwealth and the people by interpreting the generation of the former in terms of the activity of the latter. For an alternative account of constituent power in Hobbes, not as a material force but as an imaginative fiction capable of being deployed so as to generate the collective framework necessary for the maintenance of sovereign obedience, see Adam Lindsay, "'Pretenders of a Vile and Unmanly Disposition': Thomas Hobbes and the Fiction of Constituent Power," *Political Theory* 47, no. 4 (2019): 475–99.

100. Andrew Arato contrasts Hobbes with Locke on this point. Unlike for Hobbes, Locke does recognize the existence of the people as a corporate body unified in a significant way prior to the institution of the commonwealth:

"In Locke, unlike in Hobbes, unanimity, the horizontal and mutual agreement of all does 'constitute' a body, variously referred to as the community, society, political society and the people." Andrew Arato, *The Adventures of Constituent Power: Beyond Revolutions* (Cambridge: Cambridge University Press, 2017), 67.

101. Philip Pettit, *Made with Words: Hobbes on Language, Mind, and Politics* (Princeton, NJ: Princeton University Press, 2008), 80. Arash Abizadeh goes into further detail on the specificity of democratic representation, it being the most complicated form of representation by fiction. Here the representative is obviously not a natural person, but an entity that must be constituted as an artificial person through the establishment of a decision procedure whose outputs can be taken as those of a single unified will. Significantly, though, "the assembly *qua* representer represents four sets of artificial persons: it represents itself *qua* represented body; it represents each individual assembly member; it represents the commonwealth; and it represents each individual subject." Abizadeh, *Hobbes and the Two Faces of Ethics*, 257.

102. Pettit, *Made with Words*, 80.

103. This reemergence appears to be even more pronounced through the introduction of a new passage in the Latin *Leviathan*. This fact, combined with the comparison to the Latin variant's chapter 16, has been taken by some commentators to constitute evidence of a reversion to the earlier model of political institution, or indeed in the case of a few—most notably François Tricaud in his highly regarded French translation (Thomas Hobbes, *Léviathan*, trans. François Tricaud [Paris: Sirey, 1971])—as evidence that some parts of the Latin version of the work predate the English. For my part I agree with the interpretation of Mónica Brito Vieira in her recent comparative analysis of the two *Leviathans*, who contra a reader such as Tricaud, does not see a major change in the general structure of the conceptual apparatus: "In the Latin *Leviathan* the conceptions of representation and authorization, and the correlated language of authors and actors, are fully present. We seem, therefore, to have a case of mistaking word for concept: Tricaud sees Hobbes's occasional struggle to replace a verb of impossible direct translation into Latin, the verb 'to authorize,' as the non-possession of the corresponding concept. This is unwarranted, and prevents him from seeing in the Latin *Leviathan* what is in effect but a marginally edited version of the English *Leviathan*'s theory of authorization." Brito Vieira, "'Leviathan' Contra 'Leviathan,'" 283.

104. On the extent to which chapter 18 continues to affirm a democratic basis for sovereign institution see Janine Chanteur, "Note sur les notions de 'peuple' et de 'multitude' chez Hobbes," in *Hobbes-Forschungen*, ed. Reinhart Koselleck and Roman Schnur (Berlin: Duncker & Humbolt, 1969), 233; Glenn Burgess, "Contexts for the Writing and Publication of Hobbes's *Leviathan*," 690; R. E. Ewin, *Virtues and Rights: The Moral Philosophy of Thomas Hobbes*

(Boulder, CO: Westview Press, 1991), 165–66; Richard Tuck, *Philosophy and Government, 1572–1651* (Cambridge: Cambridge University Press, 1993), 328; Kinch Hoekstra, "A Lion in the House: Hobbes and Democracy," in *Rethinking the Foundations of Modern Political Thought*, ed. Annabel Brett, James Tully, and Holly Hamilton-Bleakley (Cambridge: Cambridge University Press, 2006), 212; Arash Abizadeh, "Sovereign Jurisdiction, Territorial Rights, and Membership in Hobbes," in *The Oxford Handbook of Hobbes*, ed. A. P. Martinich and Kinch Hoekstra (Oxford: Oxford University Press, 2016), 414–15.

105. Hobbes, *Leviathan, Volume Two*, 17, 260.

106. In Robin Douglass's words, "If the people confer sovereignty to another individual or an assembly, this presupposes that the people is already capable of acting in its own name, or assuming its own personality. If that is the case, the people is thus already sovereign and already represents itself, until it confers its sovereignty to another individual or assembly." Robin Douglass, "Hobbes sur la représentation et la souveraineté," in *Les défis de la représentation: Langages, pratiques et figuration du gouvernement*, ed. Manuela Albertone and Dario Castiglione (Paris: Classiques Garnier, 2018), 104.

107. Abizadeh, "Sovereign Jurisdiction, Territorial Rights, and Membership in Hobbes," 415.

108. Hobbes, *Leviathan, Volume Two*, 18, 264.

109. Hobbes, 18, 268.

110. Hobbes, 16, 248.

111. For example, Robin Douglass argues that the account in *Leviathan* simply fills in the gaps of the alienation model, the earlier texts also including something like a process of authorization. Robin Douglass, "Authorization and Representation before *Leviathan*," *Hobbes Studies* 31, no. 1 (2018): 30–47. Katrin Flikshuh claims that the *Leviathan* does not abandon the logic of relinquishment, but rather integrates it into the more mature account. Katrin Flikshuh, "Elusive Unity: The General Will in Hobbes and Kant," *Hobbes Studies* 25, no. 1 (2012): 24. Clifford Orwin does not consider the authorization model to constitute a significant theoretical advance over the earlier formulations, but rather simply a "rhetorical advance." Clifford Orwin, "On the Sovereign Authorization," *Political Theory* 3, no. 1 (1976): 31. Yves Charles Zarka argues that, although in *Leviathan* the originary democratic moment is not characterized as a historical phase of institution, it remains a necessary analytical moment that is still required for the generation of sovereignty, the latter logically presupposing two distinct temporal acts. Yves Charles Zarka, *La décision métaphysique de Hobbes: Conditions de la politique* (Paris: Librairie Philosophique J. Vrin, 1987), 330–31. And M. M. Goldsmith, while recognizing the reappearance of the earlier account in chapter 18, calls it simply an "inconsistent passage" and "an oversight." Goldsmith, *Hobbes's Science of Politics*, 161. Some readers, meanwhile, do not accept that there exists

a tension here at all. Deborah Baumgold, for example, maintains that the earlier idea of democracy as the original form of government is an "odd claim" that was hastily assembled prior to being definitively discarded. Deborah Baumgold, "The Composition of Hobbes's *Elements of Law*," in *Contract Theory in Historical Context: Essays on Grotius, Hobbes, and Locke* (Leiden: Brill, 2010), 106.

112. Let me briefly note here, however, a couple of alternative possibilities. Recall that in *The Elements of Law* Hobbes clarifies that the necessity of originary democratic foundation adheres in a "commonwealth institutive," as opposed to "a body politic by acquisition." Hobbes, *The Elements of Law, Natural and Politic*, 2.3.1. *Leviathan*, by contrast, adds in chapter 17 an account of the general principles of the generation of the commonwealth, whereas the logic of democratic institution apparently reappears only in chapter 18, and commonwealth by acquisition is treated in chapter 20. It might be argued that this new presentation is intended to knowingly reproduce the original logic, originary democracy being still essential only with respect to the commonwealth by institution. Ultimately, however, I don't think such an interpretation would be plausible, given both the innovation of the generic treatment in the seventeenth chapter, that is to say, the addition of the language of authorization, and the complete subtraction of the language of democracy in the eighteenth chapter, a language we would expect to reoccur if Hobbes was straightforwardly reproducing his original schema. Another possibility could be that that the conceptual slippage is simply a consequence of the fact that the account of commonwealth by institution is intended to be largely hypothetical, Hobbes assuming that the actual historical generation of new political authority is achieved primarily through the mode of acquisition. The precise details of the mechanics of institution would thus not be Hobbes's primary concern, and hence chapter 18's reversion to the original language is simply a manifestation of a general noninterest in this type of political foundation. Regardless of whether Hobbes is more concerned with commonwealth by institution or acquisition, what seems clear is that post-Hobbesian revolutionary experience, and its association with the idea of the constituent power of the people, demonstrates the extent to which issues of institutive political foundation remain historically and politically concrete.

113. It may be noted that for some readers of Hobbes, and contrary to their claim regarding the essential similarity of commonwealths by acquisition and institution, the account of the first suggests that it is in fact a unique form. Notably, as A. P. Martinich suggests, Hobbes seems to suggest that in a commonwealth by acquisition the sovereign is a party to the covenant. For Martinich's attempt to reconstruct the notion of sovereignty by acquisition in order to render it consistent with sovereignty by institution, see A. P. Martinich, *Hobbes's Political Philosophy: Interpretation and Interpretations* (Oxford: Oxford University Press, 2021), 176–92.

Chapter 3

1. Christopher Holman, "Hobbes and the Tragedy of Democracy," *History of Political Thought* 40, no. 4 (2019): 649–75.

2. Thomas Hobbes, "Elements of Philosophy. The First Section, Concerning Body," in *The English Works of Thomas Hobbes of Malmesbury, Volume One*, ed. Sir William Molesworth (London: John Bohn, 1839), 1.2.

3. Thomas Hobbes, *Thomas White's De mundo Examined*, trans. Harold Whitmore Jones (London: Bradford University Press, 1976), 1.1.

4. Hobbes, "Elements of Philosophy. The First Section, Concerning Body," 1.9.

5. Thomas Hobbes, "Decameron physiologicum; or, Ten Dialogues of Natural Philosophy," in *The English Works of Thomas Hobbes of Malmesbury, Volume Seven*, ed. Sir William Molesworth (London: Longman, Brown, Green, and Longmans, 1845), 81.

6. As noted in the Introduction, I here largely deploy the terminology of Cornelius Castoriadis, the contemporary political theorist who has most systematically detailed this democratic condition.

7. Thomas Hobbes, "Of the Life and History of Thucydides," in *The History of Thucydides, The English Works of Thomas Hobbes of Malmesbury, Volume Eight*, ed. Sir William Molesworth (London: John Bohn, 1839), xvi.

8. Hobbes, "Elements of Philosophy. The First Section, Concerning Body," 8.1, 8.2.

9. Hobbes, 8.23.

10. For a detailed account of the significance and novelty of Hobbes's concept of accident, and its "non-metaphysical definition," see Michel Malherbe, "Hobbes et la doctrine de l'accident," *Hobbes Studies* 1, no. 1 (1988): 45–62.

11. Hence Jeffrey Barnouw observes how "Hobbes resists [the accident's] reification." Jeffrey Barnouw, "Hobbes's Causal Account of Sensation," *Journal of the History of Philosophy* 18, no. 2 (1980): 125.

12. Hobbes, "Elements of Philosophy. The First Section, Concerning Body," 9.3. In the *Anti-White* Hobbes defines the efficient cause as those collective causes in the agent necessary for the production of the event, the material cause as those collective causes in the patient necessary for the event, and the integral causes as the efficient and material causes considered together. Hobbes, *Thomas White's De mundo Examined*, 27.2.

13. Hobbes, "Elements of Philosophy. The First Section, Concerning Body," 10.1. As Douglas Jesseph notes, this encounter is the only basis upon which, from the standpoint of Hobbes's natural philosophy, we can account for worldly alteration: "The world consists of bodies endowed only with magnitude (extension) and motion (or rest). All else is to be accounted for in terms of

magnitude and motion, and the only way that anything can be brought about is by the collision of one body with another." Douglas M. Jesseph, "Hobbes on the Foundations of Natural Philosophy," in *The Oxford Handbook of Hobbes*, ed. A. P. Martinich and Thomas Poole (Oxford: Oxford University Press, 2016), 139.

14. On this point see Emilia Giancotti, "The Birth of Modern Materialism in Hobbes and Spinoza," in *The New Spinoza*, ed. Warren Montag and Ted Stoltze (Minneapolis: University of Minnesota Press, 1997), 49–63. Giancotti writes, for example, that "it is only through the reality of the body, observed and experienced through sense, that reason is in a position to exercise its characteristic functions of calculation, whose practical goal is that of acting on the body in order to adapt it to our usefulness." Giancotti, 52.

15. As Iain Hampsher-Monk notes, and as we will see shortly, to this degree the imposition of names on matter "cannot be that of isolating and correctly defining a natural kind." Iain Hampsher-Monk, *A History of Modern Political Thought: Major Political Thinkers from Hobbes to Marx* (Oxford: Blackwell Publishers, 1992), 18. To the extent that names cannot correspond to such kinds, they must be purely conventional.

16. On Hobbes's rejection of teleological thinking see Guido Parietti, "Hobbes on Teleology and Reason," *European Journal of Philosophy* 25, no. 4 (2017): 1107–31.

17. Thomas A. Spragens, *The Politics of Motion: The World of Thomas Hobbes* (Lexington: University Press of Kentucky, 1973), 63.

18. Paul J. Johnson, "Deduction and Dialectic in Hobbes's Theory of Civility," *Hobbes Studies* 4, no. 1 (1991): 104.

19. Joshua Mitchell, "Hobbes and the Equality of All," *Political Theory* 21, no. 1 (1993): 81.

20. Richard E. Flathman, *Thomas Hobbes: Skepticism, Individuality, and Chastened Politics* (Lanham, MD: Rowman & Littlefield, 2002), 1, 5.

21. It is not quite true, as Gabriella Slomp suggests, that "Hobbes had a plan: to offer a philosophical system that explained everything from cosmology and natural science to morality and politics." Gabriella Slomp, "The Politics of Motion and the Motion of Politics," in *International Political Theory after Hobbes: Analysis, Interpretation and Orientation*, ed. Raia Prokhovnik and Gabriella Slomp (Basingstoke: Palgrave Macmillan, 2000), 21. See also Machiel Karskens, "Hobbes's Mechanistic Theory of Science, and Its Role in His Anthropology," in *Thomas Hobbes: His View of Man*, ed. J. G. van der Bend (Amsterdam: Rodopi, 1982), 45–56; Yves Charles Zarka, "Liberté, nécessité, hasard: la théorie fénérale de l'événement chez Hobbes," *Rivista di Storia della Filosofia* 59, no. 1 (2004): 249–61. For a reading articulating the tension between Hobbes's supposed desire to neutralize uncertainty via the application of scientific method to politics and the perpetual manifestation of contingency in political life, see Emily C. Nacol, *An Age of Risk: Politics and Economy in Early Modern Britain* (Princeton, NJ: Princeton University Press, 2016), 9–40.

22. Martin Bertman goes so far as to write that "nature is as mysterious as God." Martin A. Bertman, "*Conatus* in Hobbes' *De Corpore*," *Hobbes Studies* 14, no. 1 (2001): 25. Human knowledge is always finite to the degree that the motion of objects eludes human sense-perception, and hence why, as we will see below, truth can only adhere in an order of words, not an actual order of things. Martin A. Bertman, "Hobbes on Miracles (and God)," *Hobbes Studies* 20, no. 1 (2007): 62.

23. For a consideration of some of the issues for political theory raised by Hobbes's modelling of his civil science on geometric demonstration see John W. Danford, "The Problem of Language in Hobbes's Political Science," *Journal of Politics* 42, no. 1 (1980): 102–34.

24. Thomas Hobbes, "Seven Philosophical Problems and Two Propositions of Geometry," in *The English Works of Thomas Hobbes of Malmesbury, Volume Seven*, ed. Sir William Molesworth (London: Longman, Brown, Green, and Longmans, 1845), 28.

25. Hobbes, 59–60.

26. Hobbes, *Thomas White's De mundo Examined*, 14.1. Hereafter referred to as the *Anti-White*.

27. Hobbes, 26.2.

28. Hobbes, 23.1.

29. On how such provides a basis for thinking a methodological continuity between Hobbes's civil and natural sciences, see Alan Carter, "The Method in Hobbes' Madness," *Hobbes Studies* 12, no. 1 (1999): 72–89.

30. Thomas Hobbes, "On Man," in *Man and Citizen (De Homine and De Cive)*, trans. Charles T. Wood, T. S. K. Scott-Craig, and Bernard Gert (Indianapolis: Hackett, 1991), 41.

31. Hobbes, 42.

32. As Yves Charles Zarka puts it, "The first principles of all demonstration have lost their ontological content; they no longer bear the essence of things, but consist only of nominal definitions that simply explicate the signification of the term employed." Zarka, *La décision métaphysique de Hobbes: Conditions de la politique* (Paris: Librairie Philosophique J. Vrin, 1987), 170.

33. Hobbes, "Elements of Philosophy. The First Section, Concerning Body," 2.16.

34. Hobbes, *Thomas White's De mundo Examined*, 36.8.

35. Hobbes, 36.8. For a reading of Hobbes emphasizing uncertainty as a natural human condition inevitably resulting from the limits of natural knowledge, see Loralea Michaelis, "Hobbes's Modern Prometheus: A Political Philosophy for an Uncertain Future," *Canadian Journal of Political Science* 40, no. 1 (2007): 101–27.

36. As Victoria Kahn observes, "Hobbes had a strong sense of the realm of contingency and the impossibility of certain knowledge of the external world." Victoria Kahn, *Rhetoric, Prudence, and Skepticism in The Renaissance* (Ithaca, NY: Cornell University Press, 1985), 154.

37. Hobbes, *Thomas White's* De mundo *Examined*, 38.1.
38. Hobbes, 38.1.
39. Hobbes, "Elements of Philosophy. The First Section, Concerning Body," 10.5.
40. Thomas Hobbes, *Leviathan, Volume Three: The English and Latin Texts (ii)*, ed. Noel Malcolm (Oxford: Clarendon Press, 2012), 37, 682. As Michael Bray has observed, it was largely Hobbes's understanding of the impossibility of grasping the future via the perception of fixed chains of natural causality that grounds his opposition to those who claim status as prophets: "This is why the threat of a determinate religiosity or prophecy is so great in Hobbes's mind: it purports to name a cause that can determine the future in an absolute manner to which no (natural) science could aspire." Michael Bray, "The Hedges That Are Set: Hobbes and the Future of Politics," *Epoché: A Journal for the History of Philosophy* 11, no. 1 (2006): 183. For an account of the trajectory of Hobbes's increasing concern with prophecy in his political works, and his effort to refute prophetic claims of independent authority grounded in self-belief, see Kinch Hoekstra, "Disarming the Prophets: Thomas Hobbes and Predictive Power," *Rivista di Storia della Filosofia* 59, no. 1 (2004): 97–153.
41. Thomas Hobbes, "The Questions Concerning Liberty, Necessity, and Chance," in *The English Works of Thomas Hobbes of Malmesbury, Volume Five*, ed. Sir William Molesworth (London: John Bohn, 1841), 189. For a comprehensive overview of the main contours of the Hobbes-Bramhall debate, see Nicholas D. Jackson, *Hobbes, Bramhall and the Politics of Liberty and Necessity: A Quarrel of the Civil Wars and Interregnum* (Cambridge: Cambridge University Press, 2007).
42. Hobbes, "The Questions Concerning Liberty, Necessity, and Chance," 47.
43. Hobbes, *Leviathan, Volume Three*, 46, 1088.
44. Thomas Hobbes, "Of Liberty and Necessity: A Treatise, Wherein All Controversy Concerning Predestination, Election, Free-Will, Grace, Merits, Reprobation, &c Is Fully Decided and Cleared," in *The English Works of Thomas Hobbes of Malmesbury, Volume Four*, ed. Sir William Molesworth (London: John Bohn, 1840), 246.
45. Michael Byron observes that "Hobbes has a methodological predisposition in favour of overdetermination." Michael Byron, *Submission and Subjection in Leviathan: Good Subjects in the Hobbesian Commonwealth* (Basingstoke: Palgrave Macmillan, 2015), 29.
46. As Richard Flathman observes, "His metaphysics may warrant the claim that there will be constant contact among the moving particles of which the universe consists but it provides no support for the claim that these contacts will form an integrated system of relationships." Flathman, *Thomas Hobbes: Skepticism, Individuality, and Chastened Politics*, 14. See also Paul A. Rahe, *Republics Ancient & Modern, Volume II: New Modes and Orders in Early Modern Political Thought* (Chapel Hill: University of North Carolina Press, 1994), 311.

47. Hobbes, "Of Liberty and Necessity," 246–47.

48. Hobbes, "Decameron physiologicum; or, Ten Dialogues of Natural Philosophy," 78.

49. See, for example, Alan Ryan, *The Philosophy of the Social Sciences* (London: The Macmillan Press, 1970), 102–3.

50. Samantha Frost, *Lessons from a Materialist Thinker: Hobbesian Reflections on Ethics and Politics* (Stanford, CA: Stanford University Press, 2008), 84. For a reading that attempts to draw democratic conclusions from Hobbes's account of the complexity and interdependence of causal orders, see Diego A. Fernández Peychaux, "The Multitude in the Mirror: Hobbes on Power, Rhetoric, and Materialism," *Theory & Event* 21, no. 3 (2018): 652–72.

51. As Raymond Geuss observes, "Hobbes was rather clear that his political philosophy presupposed a kind of philosophical anthropology, which he describes explicitly and at length." Raymond Geuss, *Changing the Subject: Philosophy from Socrates to Adorno* (Cambridge, MA: Harvard University Press, 2017), 143. For a critique of the effort to divorce the study of Hobbes's moral and political philosophy from his conception of human nature or psychology, see Kinch Hoekstra, "Hobbes on Law, Nature, and Reason," *Journal of the History of Philosophy* 41, no. 1 (2003): 111–20.

52. Hobbes, *Thomas White's* De mundo *Examined*, 6.6.

53. Hobbes, 2.6.

54. Hobbes, 6.6.

55. Indeed, as Alice Ristroph notes, Hobbes was uniquely attuned to the human being "as a sentient, embodied and mortal being." Alice Ristroph, "Criminal Law for Humans," in *Hobbes and the Law*, ed. David Dyzenhaus and Thomas Poole (Cambridge: Cambridge University Press, 2012), 98.

56. Thomas Hobbes, *The Elements of Law, Natural and Politic*, ed. Ferdinand Tönnies (London: Simpkin, Marshall, and Co., 1889), 1.1.8. Cees Leijenhorst sees Hobbes's account of sense as a further manifestation of his quarrel with Aristotelianism, rejecting as it does two key elements of Aristotelian theories of sense-perception: that of the latter as a non-mechanic process oriented toward actualizing inner potentialities of the soul, and as appropriating the actual properties of physical objects in the world. Cees Leijenhorst, "Sense and Nonsense about Sense: Hobbes and Aristotle on Sense Perception and Imagination," in *The Cambridge Companion to Hobbes's* Leviathan, ed. Patricia Springborg (Cambridge: Cambridge University Press, 2007), 84.

57. Thomas Hobbes, *Leviathan, Volume Two: The English and Latin Texts (i)*, ed. Noel Malcolm (Oxford: Clarendon Press, 2012), 1, 22.

58. William Sacksteder highlights the fact that all sensation involves an active component on the part of the organism, the latter being not a merely passive receptacle in the process of perception. Hobbes postulates "in all sensing an unavoidable *reaction*, from heart or whatever. This is an endeavor outward inherent in all motions of imagination. It is this which leads the sensor to impute

an external and causal object with which he interacts. By a counter-endeavor in this peculiar sense, inevitable in all animate nature, any organic thing adds its own stamp, so to speak, to each engagement with whatsoever object else. The product combines whatsoever outside motions occur with what the sensor *is*—with his or its own nature, generic (and peculiar as well)." William Sacksteder, "Hobbes's Science of Human Nature," *Hobbes Studies* 3, no. 1 (1990): 45.

59. Hobbes, *Leviathan, Volume Two*, 1, 24.
60. Hobbes, *The Elements of Law, Natural and Politic*, 1.2.7.
61. Hobbes, 1.2.10. The consequences of such deception can take many forms. For example, in his identification of Hobbes's critique of demonology in Part 4 of *Leviathan* with Benjamin and Debord's diagnosis of the image's distortion of reality in contemporary society, James Martel notes that what demonology shares with metaphysics is the confusion of the representation of being with being itself, with actually existing objects: "For Hobbes metaphysics does not discover being, it produces it. It does this chiefly by treating the symbols and representations of beings as if they had an existence of their own, as if the term 'being' were itself not simply a figure (of speech) but was in fact 'being' itself." James Martel, "The Spectacle of the Leviathan: Thomas Hobbes, Guy Debord, and Walter Benjamin," *Law, Culture, and the Humanities* 2, no. 1 (2006): 80.
62. Hobbes, *Leviathan, Volume Two*, 1, 24.
63. As Emilia Giancotti observes, "The *phantasma*, that is, the knowledge to which sensation gives a content, is always particular. The diversity of *phantasmata* corresponded to the diversity of the organs on which is exerted the action of the external body, an accident that prompts another type of motion inside the human body." Giancotti, "The Birth of Modern Materialism in Hobbes and Spinoza," 51.
64. Hobbes, *The Elements of Law, Natural and Politic*, 1.2.9.
65. Hobbes, *Leviathan, Volume Two*, 15, 242.
66. Hobbes, *Thomas White's* De mundo *Examined*, 7.4.
67. Hobbes, *Leviathan, Volume Two*, 2, 26. Robin Douglass has made the case that the notion of imagination is central to Hobbes's thought, although most scholars tend to devalue it through exclusively focusing on words and language independently of it. As Douglass writes, "Imagination is necessary for people to understand the world and their relationship with it. This is due to the crucial role it plays in human understanding as, in a sense, it is all encompassing and cannot be distinguished from reasoning or deliberation." Robin Douglass, "The Body Politic 'Is a Fictitious Body': Hobbes on Imagination and Fiction," *Hobbes Studies* 27, no. 2 (2014): 132. Hobbes's political theory is ultimately attempting to effect a change in the imaginations of people through the generation of the image of the body politic, which can be deployed in the service of a productive civil project countering the destructive images of "the schoolmen and ecclesiastics." Douglass, 133.

68. Hobbes, *Leviathan, Volume Two*, 4, 48. As Yves Charles Zarka observes, for Hobbes language thus has an "absolutely essential role in the institution of a specifically ethico-political world." Yves Charles Zarka, "Aspects sémantiques, syntaxiques et pragmatiques de le théorie du langage chez Hobbes," in *Thomas Hobbes: De la métaphysique à la politique*, ed. Martin Bertman and Michel Malherbe (Paris: Librairie Philosophique J. Vrin, 1989), 46. This centrality has led Terence Ball to identify Hobbes as the first political theorist to take a linguistic turn, the latter being constituted in the recognition that language does not merely reflect the structure of the world, but at least partially constitutes it. Terence Ball, "Hobbes's Linguistic Turn," *Polity* 17, no. 4 (1985): 740–41.

69. As David Johnston writes, "The imagination is naturally lively and uncontrolled." Johnston, *The Rhetoric of Leviathan: Thomas Hobbes and the Politics of Cultural Transformation* (Princeton, NJ: Princeton University Press, 1986), 125.

70. Hobbes, *Leviathan, Volume Two*, 3, 38.

71. As Samantha Frost very importantly notes, however, if ratiocination is an attempt to order the inconstant and plural generation of phantasms and representations, it remains nevertheless ultimately impossible to completely neutralize the flux of sense: "Because phantasms are multiply constituted, because desire can shape the direction of our thoughts, and because language itself is liable to metonymic and metaphoric slippage, we may sometimes unknowingly drift off the course of ratiocination and arrive at a conclusion that we believe to be true but is not." Frost, *Lessons from a Materialist Thinker*, 62.

72. Hobbes, *Leviathan, Volume Two*, 3, 38.

73. Hobbes, 3, 40.

74. Hobbes, 3, 44–46.

75. Hobbes, "Elements of Philosophy. The First Section, Concerning Body," 2.2; Hobbes, *Leviathan, Volume Two*, 4, 50.

76. Arash Abizadeh has recently cautioned against interpreting the process of naming in referential terms. Rejecting both original—which see names as referring to subjects' mental states—and contemporary—which perceive a referential relation between names and objects in the world—interpretations of Hobbes's philosophy of language, he argues that for Hobbes names do not refer to any things, be they mental states or worldly objects: "When Hobbes insisted that words signify conceptions and not things, his point was that when one uses words to signify, one provides evidence to others that one has such-and-such internal thoughts or passions, but not necessarily evidence for the presence of any external objects." Arash Abizadeh, "The Absence of Reference in Hobbes's Philosophy of Language," *Philosopher's Imprint* 15, no. 22 (2015): 4. Names merely mark and signify conceptions of things, as opposed to refer to things or conceptions of things. Rather than being directly referential, the relation between names and things is ultimately mediated by conceptions, the latter being that with a representational content referring to things in the world. Abizadeh, 14.

For a brief overview of the debate as to whether for Hobbes names signify things (the object view) or concepts (the idea view), see Stewart Duncan, "Hobbes, Signification and Insignificant Names," *Hobbes Studies* 24, no. 2 (2011): 158–78.

77. Hobbes, "Elements of Philosophy. The First Section, Concerning Body," 2.5.

78. Hobbes, 2.4.

79. Gottfried Wilhelm Leibniz, *Philosophical Papers and Letters*, ed. and trans. Leroy E. Loemker (Dordrecht: Kluwer Academic Publishers, 1989), 128.

80. Kerry H. Whiteside, "Hobbes's Ultranominalist Critique of Natural Right," *Polity* 20, no. 3 (1988): 457–78. Whiteside identifies three elements of Hobbes's ultranominalism that extend it beyond nominalism as traditionally conceived: "(1) classification of objects under a universal does not require resemblance relations; (2) mental processes are merely sequences of fluctuating particulars; (3) truth itself is a relationship between words which represent overlapping sets of particulars." Whiteside, 466.

81. J. W. N. Watkins, *Hobbes's System of Ideas* (London: Hutchinson & Co., 1965), 103; Gordon Hull, "Hobbes's Radical Nominalism," *Epoché: A Journal for the History of Philosophy* 11, no. 1 (2006): 201–23. Not all readers accept the radical nominalist reading of Hobbes, emphasizing instead the commonality of perception in the face of real, common qualities and accidents. See, for example, F. S. McNeilly, *The Anatomy of Leviathan* (London: Macmillan & Co., 1968), 89; Donald W. Hanson, "Reconsidering Hobbes's Conventionalism," *Review of Politics* 53, no. 4 (1991): 627–51; Donald W. Hanson, "Thomas Hobbes on 'Discourse' in Politics," *Polity* 24, no. 2 (1991): 199–226; Gary Remer, "Hobbes, the Rhetorical Tradition, and Toleration," *Review of Politics* 54, no. 1 (1992): 18–19; Deborah Hansen Soles, *Strong Wits and Spider Webs: A Study in Hobbes's Philosophy of Language* (Aldeishot: Avebury, 1996), 14; Bernard Gert, "Hobbes on Language, Metaphysics, and Epistemology," *Hobbes Studies* 14, no. 1 (2001): 40–58; Noel Malcolm, "Hobbes's Science of Politics and His Theory of Science," in *Aspects of Hobbes* (Oxford: Oxford University Press, 2002), 152; Philip Pettit, *Made with Words: Hobbes on Language, Mind, and Politics* (Princeton, NJ: Princeton University Press, 2008), 40; Jeffrey Barnouw, "Reason as Reckoning: Hobbes's Natural Law as Right Reason," *Hobbes Studies* 21, no. 1 (2008): 48.

82. Hobbes, *Leviathan, Volume Two*, 4, 52.

83. Hobbes, *Thomas White's De mundo Examined*, 30.16.

84. Hobbes, "Elements of Philosophy. The First Section, Concerning Body," 2.9.

85. Michael Krom has articulated the main elements of what Hobbes takes to constitute vain as opposed to true philosophy, the former being grounded in ill-defined names that are subsequently compounded with one another so as to multiply absurdity. Michael P. Krom, "Vain Philosophy, the Schools and Civil Philosophy," *Hobbes Studies* 20, no. 1 (2007): 93–119. It is worth quoting

Krom at length with respect to how vain philosophers specifically misattribute an essential nature to human beings through their failure to understand the function of naming:

> Vain philosophers think that they know the essence of man, saying that his nature is to be a "rational, social, political animal": Since they fail to recognize that the nature of something is only a word used to signify the accidents of an external body as perceived by the mind through the sense organs, they wrongly attribute this word "man" to the actual body. They proceed to claim that the nature is some external body's definition, when in actuality the word "man" is only a word used to represent the physical object that appears to men through the influence of an external body upon the sense organs. Since they think that a definition is a statement of the nature of a body that they have knowledge of, through reason, the vain philosophers join the name "man" to the name "rational, social, and political animal," claiming that the definition of man is his nature. (Krom, 104)

86. Hobbes, *Leviathan, Volume Two*, 4, 62.
87. Hobbes, 4, 62.
88. Deborah Baumgold argues that Hobbes was aware that it was possible to affirm democracy on nominalist grounds. Baumgold, *Hobbes's Political Theory* (Cambridge: Cambridge University Press, 1988), 42. Hence his attempt to politically deploy nominalism in order to foreclose the possibility of affirming ethical principles typically associated with democratic notions of popular accountability and resistance: "The principles of non-accountability and non-resistance can be derived simply from the nominalist idea that groups lack natural social agency. A 'multitude' gains agency only through institution of the sovereign and therefore there is literally no human body to whom the sovereign could be accountable." Deborah Baumgold, "When Hobbes Needed History," in *Contract Theory in Historical Context: Essays on Grotius, Hobbes, and Locke* (Leiden: Brill, 2010), 60. With respect to democratic potential, James Martel's radical democratic rereading of Hobbes's thought as potentially countersovereign is largely grounded in the latter's nominalism, which suggests an alternative form of reading that decenters the principle of textual authority so as to facilitate the creative redeployment of the work. Martel, *Subverting the Leviathan: Reading Thomas Hobbes as a Radical Democrat* (New York: Columbia University Press, 2007), 2. Contrary to my own reading, which interprets Hobbes's political absolutism as a potential answer to the problems posed by the fact of nominalism, see Stephen Finn, who suggests in fact that Hobbes's nominalism, in addition to other elements of his natural philosophy, is adopted to the degree that it confirms his political absolutism: "In

relation to Hobbes's political philosophy, nominalism provides theoretical support because it implies that goodness, justice or other moral notions are created by the wielder of absolute power." Stephen J. Finn, *Thomas Hobbes and the Politics of Natural Philosophy* (London: Continuum, 2006), 164. Overall, Finn argues that "Hobbes has strong *political* reasons to *accept* certain 'strictly philosophical' views, even though he has strong *philosophical* reasons to *reject* these views," this fact producing notable aporias in his natural philosophy. Finn, 24.

89. Hobbes, *The Elements of Law, Natural and Politic*, 1.14.3. For just some of the many studies on the centrality of passion within Hobbes's philosophical anthropology and political thought, see Norman Jacobson, *Pride and Solace: The Functions and Limits of Political Theory* (Berkeley: University of California Press, 1978); Arrigo Pacchi, "Hobbes and the Passions," *Topoi* 6, no. 2 (1987): 111–19; Victoria Kahn, *Wayward Contracts: The Crisis of Political Obligation in England, 1640–1674* (Princeton, NJ: Princeton University Press, 2004); Daniela Coli, "Hobbes's Revolution," in *Politics and the Passions: 1500–1850*, ed. Victoria Kahn, Neil Saccamano, and Daniela Coli, 75–92 (Princeton, NJ: Princeton University Press, 2006); Robin Douglass, *Rousseau and Hobbes: Nature, Free Will, and the Passions* (Oxford: Oxford University Press, 2015).

90. Hobbes, *Thomas White's De mundo Examined*, 4.1.

91. On this point see Andrew Lister, "Skepticism and Pluralism in Thomas Hobbes's Political Thought," *History of Political Thought* 29, no. 1 (1998): 35–60. For a study of Hobbes's relation to the skeptical tradition see also Gianni Paganini, "Hobbes e lo scetticismo continentale," *Rivista di Storia della Filosofia* 59, no. 1 (2004): 303–28.

92. Hobbes, *Leviathan, Volume Two*, 6, 78.

93. Hobbes, 6, 78.

94. Hobbes, 6, 78.

95. Hobbes, 6, 80.

96. Hobbes, *Thomas White's De mundo Examined*, 30.22.

97. Hobbes, "On Man," 47.

98. Thomas Hobbes, *On the Citizen*, ed. and trans. Richard Tuck and Michael Silverthorne (Cambridge: Cambridge University Press, 1998), 3.31. Rejecting J. W. N. Watkins's contention that for Hobbes human beings have an identical structure, operating only at differing speeds, M. M. Goldsmith correctly observes this fundamental nonidentity of natural persons, who are essentially differentiated from one another on the basis of their "fundamental passions, opinions, and experience." Goldsmith, *Hobbes's Science of Politics* (New York: Columbia University Press, 1966), 77. Compare with Watkins, *Hobbes's System of Ideas*, 72.

99. Hobbes, *Leviathan, Volume Two*, 11, 158.

100. For an example of a contrary interpretation of Hobbes's account of the passions, in terms of mathematical analysis aiming at systematization, see

Timo Airaksinen, "Hobbes on the Passions and Powerlessness," *Hobbes Studies* 6, no. 1 (1993): 80–104.

101. Hobbes, *Leviathan, Volume Two*, 6, 80. As Gabriella Slomp observes, "Hobbes is as keen to stress that there are considerable variations across people as he is to point out that the same individual is different at different times, with different values, desires, thoughts." Gabriella Slomp, *Thomas Hobbes and the Political Philosophy of Glory* (Basingstoke: Macmillan Press, 2000), 16.

102. Hobbes, "On Man," 47.

103. Hobbes, 47.

104. Hobbes, *Leviathan, Volume Two*, 6, 80–82.

105. Tom Sorell, *Hobbes* (London: Routledge & Kegan Paul, 1986), 92.

106. Alissa MacMillan has recently highlighted how an individual's social context structures their desires and beliefs in manifold ways. Alissa MacMillan, "Conditioned to Believe: Hobbes on Religion, Education, and Social Context," *Hobbes Studies* 30, no. 2 (2017): 156–77. For example, "What is desired and valued, the material world one encounters, what one is taught to think, the opinions expressed, the customs of a place, its traditions, and the language used, form a complex social world that serves to shape individuals and provides the background conditions for believing certain claims." MacMillan, 174.

107. Hobbes, "On Man," 38. For an account of Hobbes's doctrine of private marking as necessarily presupposing an implicit sociality, the process reproducing the structure of intersubjective communication, see Gayne Nerney, "*Homo notans*: Marks, Signs, and Imagination," *Hobbes Studies* 4, no. 1 (1991): 53–75.

108. Hobbes, *Thomas White's* De mundo *Examined*, 30.20.

109. Hobbes, "Of Liberty and Necessity," 303–4. And thus as might be expected, Bramhall accuses Hobbes of not displaying a proper respect for established intellectual authority, writing that "'it is strange to see with what confidence now-a-days particular men slight all the School-men, and philosophers, and classical authors of former ages.'" Quoted in Hobbes, "The Questions Concerning Liberty, Necessity, and Chance," 62.

110. Thomas Hobbes, "An Answer to a Book Published by Dr. Bramhall, Late Bishop of Derry; Called the 'Catching of the Leviathan,'" in *The English Works of Thomas Hobbes of Malmesbury, Volume Four*, ed. Sir William Molesworth (London: John Bohn, 1840), 381.

111. Steven Lukes famously, although in my view incorrectly, identifies Hobbes as the first systematic theorist of methodological individualism. Steven Lukes, "Methodological Individualism Reconsidered," *British Journal of Sociology* 19, no. 2 (1968): 119–29.

112. Hobbes, "On Man," 63.

113. Hobbes, 63.

114. Gabriella Slomp helpfully calls attention to the historicity of sources of human behavior, although it is perhaps not even the case, as she suggests,

that even one—the constitution of the body—is absolutely immune to social intervention. Slomp writes that "the other five sources (namely, experience, habit, fortune, one's opinion, authorities) take place in the interaction between the individual and the world in which he happens to live." Slomp, *Thomas Hobbes and the Political Philosophy of Glory*, 115.

115. Hobbes, "On Man," 65.

116. Hobbes, 65–66. As will be examined in the next chapter, Hobbes thus suggests that elites, as a result of their privileged social status, tend toward insolence, and thereby threaten social stability.

117. Hobbes, 66.

118. Hobbes, 68.

119. In the words of Ross Rudolph, "Individual deliberations do not take place in isolation, but against a background that is compounded of the kind of person one is, and the kinds of experience he has had." Ross Rudolph, "The Micro-Foundations of Hobbes's Political Theory," *Hobbes Studies* 4, no. 1 (1991): 79.

120. As Paul Johnson observes, "man has very few innate appetites or desires for particular sorts of things; Hobbes mentions only appetites for food and excretion plus a few more he finds too negligible to mention." Paul J. Johnson, "Hobbes and the Wolf-Man," in *Thomas Hobbes: His View of Man*, ed. J. G. van der Bend (Amsterdam: Rodopi, 1982), 40. See also Rudolph, "The Micro-Foundations of Hobbes's Political Theory," 40; Roger Paden, "Hobbesian Deliberators," *Hobbes Studies* 7, no. 1 (1994): 30.

121. See, for example, J. W. N. Watkins, "Philosophy and Politics in Hobbes," in *Hobbes Studies*, ed. K. C. Brown (Oxford: Basil Blackwell, 1965), 254–55; Fred Dallmayr, "Hobbes and Existentialism: Some Affinities," *Journal of Politics* 31, no. 3 (1969): 619; Johnson, "Hobbes and the Wolf-Man," 44; Andrzej Rapaczynski, *Nature and Politics: Liberalism in the Philosophies of Hobbes, Locke and Rousseau* (Ithaca, NY: Cornell University Press, 1987), 49; Rudolph, "The Micro-Foundations of Hobbes's Political Theory," 40; Bernard Gert, "Hobbes's Psychology," in *The Cambridge Companion to Hobbes*, ed. Tom Sorell (Cambridge: Cambridge University Press, 1996), 164; María L. Lukac de Stier, "The Notion of Good in Hobbes's System," *Hobbes Studies* 15, no. 1 (2002): 97; Raia Prokhovnik, "Hobbes's Artifice as Social Construction," *Hobbes Studies* 18, no. 1 (2005): 85.

122. See, for example, Bernard Gert, "Hobbes and Psychological Egoism," *Journal of the History of Ideas* 28, no. 4 (1967): 519; Gary B. Herbert, "Thomas Hobbes's Dialectic of Desire," *New Scholasticism* 50, no. 2 (1976): 137–63; Bernard Willms, "Liberty as *conditio humana*," in *Thomas Hobbes: His View of Man*, ed. J. G. van der Bend (Amsterdam: Rodopi, 1982), 103; Slomp, *Thomas Hobbes and the Political Philosophy of Glory*, 115; James Martel, "The Radical Promise of Thomas Hobbes: The Road Not Taken in Liberal Theory," *Theory & Event* 4, no. 2 (2000).; Richard Tuck, "The Utopianism of *Leviathan*," in Leviathan

After 350 Years, ed. Tom Sorell and Luc Foisneau (Oxford: Oxford University Press, 2004), 125–38; S. A. Lloyd, *Morality in the Philosophy of Thomas Hobbes: Cases in the Law of Nature* (Cambridge: Cambridge University Press, 2009), 86; Gordon Hull, *Hobbes and the Making of Modern Political Thought* (London: Continuum, 2009), 24; Gordon Hull, "Building Better Citizens: Hobbes Against the Ontological Illusion," *Epoché: A Journal for the History of Philosophy* 20, no. 1 (2015): 105. Didier Deleule, however, makes the point that Hobbes's affirmation of the openness of human beings to alteration is not assimilable to the totalitarian effort to remake humanity: "It is not a question of changing human nature, of creating a 'new man,' but of making do with what we have, of 'composing' with human nature." Didier Deleule, "La fuite en avant : Une approche du chapitre 11 du *Léviathan*," in *Hobbes et le libéralisme*, ed. Yves Charles Zarka (Paris: Éditions Mimésis, 2016), 23.

123. In the words of María Lukac de Stier, "Human nature itself is reduced by Hobbes to a sum of faculties and powers that do not express an essence but rather a set of forces. There is no norm. One has only a living system in perpetual movement." Lukac de Stier, "The Notion of Good in Hobbes's System," 97.

124. Hobbes, *On the Citizen*, 3.9.

125. Hobbes, 5.5.

126. Hobbes, 5.5. See also Hobbes, *Leviathan, Volume Two*, 17, 258–60.

127. Hobbes, *On the Citizen*, 5.6.

128. Hobbes, *The Elements of Law, Natural and Politic*, 1.13.4.

129. Hobbes, 1.13.3.

130. Hobbes, 1.13.2.

131. This issue will be returned to in the final chapter, with respect to the question of the specificity of the Hobbesian concept of natural law.

132. Hobbes, *Leviathan, Volume Two*, 15, 242. A comprehensive discussion of the place of Hobbes's theology within the context of this critique of absolute morality is outside the scope of our discussion. Jeffrey Epstein, however, perceives a contradiction between Hobbes's notion of sovereignty as purely artificial and thus independent of transcendent sources, and the modeling of the commonwealth on the image of God: "From the very first sentence of a work dedicated to justifying the legitimacy of the sovereign *qua* artificial, the legitimacy of Leviathan rests upon the claim that it comes into existence through mimesis or imitation of the divine." Jeffrey H. Epstein, *Democracy and Its Others* (New York: Bloomsbury, 2016), 132. The problem here, however, is the presumption that Hobbes's is a positive as opposed to negative theology, one in which it is possible to come to minimally understand the form of being of God through acquisition of knowledge of the divine essence. Hobbes, on the contrary, perpetually stresses the impossibility of establishing such a proximity, humans being utterly incapable of perceiving divine attributes that could then subsequently be deployed so as to serve as a foundation for civil science. As Gilbert Boss observes, Hobbes used

the concept of God as a signification of the infinite, whose determinations we are unable to grasp: "How can we philosophically comprehend the idea of God? Hobbes's response is very radical and absolutely destructive of all theology: we cannot in any way understand it, because we do not have this idea and are incapable of forming or conceiving it." Gilbert Boss, "La doctrine libertine de Hobbes," *Hobbes Studies* 16, no. 1 (2003): 19. On Hobbes's "negative theology" see also, for example, Martel, *Subverting the Leviathan*, 68; Julien Freund, "Le dieu mortel," in *Hobbes-Forschungen*, ed. Reinhart Koselleck and Roman Schnur (Berlin: Duncker & Humbolt, 1969), 34.

133. Hobbes, *On the Citizen*, 1.2.

134. Thomas Hobbes, "A Discourse of Rome," in *Three Discourses*, ed. Noel B. Reynolds and Arlene W. Saxonhouse (Chicago: University of Chicago Press, 1995), 74.

135. Hobbes, "The Questions Concerning Liberty, Necessity, and Chance," 183. As Theodore Waldman observes, for instance, Hobbes "recognizes the truth of the Greek view of man as a political animal although he explores it in his own way." Theodore Waldman, "Hobbes on the Generation of a Public Person," in *Thomas Hobbes in His Time*, ed. Ralph Ross, Herbert W. Schneider, and Theodore Waldman (Minneapolis: University of Minnesota Press, 1974), 70.

136. Raymond Polin, *Politique et philosophie chez Thomas Hobbes* (Paris: Presses Universitaires de France, 1953), xvii. It is probably not even enough to qualify, as Martin Bertman does, that Hobbesian subjects are naturally "gregarious" as opposed to naturally social or political. Martin A. Bertman, "The Natural Body and the Body Politic," *Philosophy & Social Criticism* 5, no. 1 (1978): 21.

137. Zarka, *La décision métaphysique de Hobbes*, 244.

138. On the lack of a transcendent natural order that is capable of regulating human affairs through serving as a source for the construction of some universal ethical standard, see Simone Goyard-Fabre, *Le droit et la loi dans la philosophie de Thomas Hobbes* (Paris: Librarie C. Klincksieck, 1975), 175; Angelo Campodonico, "Secularization in Thomas Hobbes's Anthropology," in *Thomas Hobbes: His View of Man*, ed. J. G. van der Bend (Amsterdam: Rodopi, 1982), 113; Zarka, *La décision métaphysique de Hobbes*, 230; Whiteside, "Hobbes's Ultranominalist Critique of Natural Right," 468; Simone Goyard-Fabre, "La léglisation civile dans l'état-Léviathan," in *Thomas Hobbes: De la métaphysique à la politique*, ed. Martin Bertman and Michel Malherbe (Paris: Librairie Philosophique J. Vrin, 1989), 191; Remer, "Hobbes, the Rhetorical Tradition, and Toleration," 18; Gary K. Browning and Raia Prokhovnik, "Hobbes, Hegel and Modernity," *Hobbes Studies* 8, no. 1 (1995): 88; Arlene W. Saxonhouse, "Hobbes and the Beginnings of Modern Political Thought," in *Three Discourses*, by Thomas Hobbes, ed. Noel B. Reynolds and Arlene W. Saxonhouse (Chicago: University of Chicago Press, 1995), 123–54; Martin A. Bertman, "Justice and Contra-Natural Dissolution," *Hobbes Studies* 10, no. 1 (1997): 23; John R. Visintainer, "Hobbes on Goodness

and Pressure on the Sovereign," *Hobbes Studies* 12, no. 1 (1999): 26; Samantha Frost, "Faking It: Hobbes's Thinking Bodies and the Ethics of Dissimulation," *Political Theory* 29, no. 1 (2001): 32; Flathman, *Thomas Hobbes: Skepticism, Individuality, and Chastened Politics*; Giuseppe Duso, "Hobbes et l'invention moderne du pouvoir," *Hobbes Studies* 27, no. 1 (2005): 35; Bray, "The Hedges That Are Set," 174; Timothy Stanton, "Hobbes and Locke on Natural Law and Jesus Christ," *History of Political Thought* 29, no. 1 (2008): 71.

139. For a demonstration that Hobbes's deployment of the proverb *Homo homini lupus* is not an indication of radical egoism, but rather just a recognition of the potentially antagonistic form of group relations in a state of nature lacking a spontaneous species harmony, see Cécile Voisset-Veysseyre, "The Wolf Motif in the Hobbesian Text," *Hobbes Studies* 23, no. 2 (2010): 124–38.

140. For C. B. Macpherson's well-known reading of Hobbes's conception of human being as giving an expression to the emerging imperatives of bourgeois society and morality, the individual being a self-contained subject lacking a natural social orientation, see C. B. Macpherson, *The Political Theory of Possessive Individualism* (Oxford: Oxford University Press, 1962); C. B. Macpherson, "Hobbes's Bourgeois Man," in *Hobbes Studies*, ed. K. C. Brown (Oxford: Basil Blackwell, 1965), 169–83. On Hobbes as a theorist of the bourgeoisie see also Leo Strauss, *The Political Philosophy of Hobbes: Its Basis and Genesis* (Chicago: Chicago University Press, 1952), 120–26; Hannah Arendt, *The Origins of Totalitarianism* (San Diego: Harcourt, 1968), 139; Gauthier, *The Logic of Leviathan: The Moral and Political Theory of Thomas Hobbes* (Oxford: Oxford University Press, 1969), 90; Antonio Negri, *The Savage Anomaly: The Power of Spinoza's Metaphysics and Politics*, trans. Michael Hardt (Minneapolis: University of Minnesota Press, 1991), 70. For attempts to defend or reinvigorate certain elements of the Macpherson thesis, which for some time has been dismissed within Hobbes scholarship, see James M. Glass, "Hobbes and Narcissism: Pathology in the State of Nature," *Political Theory* 8, no. 3 (1980): 335–63; Jules Townshend, "Hobbes as Possessive Individualist: Interrogating the C. B. Macpherson Thesis," *Hobbes Studies* 12, no. 1 (1999): 52–71; Richard Hillyer, "Keith Thomas's 'Definitive Refutation' of C. B. Macpherson: Revisiting 'The Social Origins of Hobbes's Political Thought,'" *Hobbes Studies* 15, no. 1 (2002): 32–44; Michael Bray, "Macpherson Restored? Hobbes and the Question of Social Origins," *History of Political Thought* 28, no. 1 (2007): 56–90.

141. Especially important here is the work of Samantha Frost. See Frost, *Lessons from a Materialist Thinker*; Samantha Frost, "Hobbes, Life, and the Politics of Self-Preservation," in *Interpreting Hobbes's Political Philosophy*, ed. S. A. Lloyd (Cambridge: Cambridge University Press, 2019), 70–92. More recently, Sandra Leonie Field has explored this issue within the context of Hobbes's concept of power, perceiving a shift between his early and late works. Whereas the conception within the early works seems to be exclusively grounded in a

consideration of individual faculties, within the later works it is understood as socially constituted within a complex web of human relations, there thus emerging a newfound notion of human sociality: "Where the discussion of power in *The Elements of Law* stressed the tendency of humans to isolation and fragmentation unless they are brought together in a formal union, now *Leviathan*'s discussion of power brings to the fore an opposite phenomenon. Humans have a constant tendency to form associations, some of which are politically significant even though they are not bound into a union." Sandra Field, "Hobbes and the Question of Power," *Journal of the History of Philosophy* 52, no. 1 (2014): 75. For more detailed discussion of this theme, in relation to the question of the need to reconstruct the notion of popular power in terms of the durable establishment of equality, see Sandra Field, *Potentia: Hobbes and Spinoza on Power and Popular Politics* (Oxford: Oxford University Press, 2020).

142. On the variety of substantive social relations observable within the state of nature see Richard Ashcraft, "Political Theory and Practical Action: A Reconsideration of Hobbes's State of Nature," *Hobbes Studies* 1, no. 1 (1988): 68; Nancy A. Stanlick, "Hobbesian Friendship: Valuing Others for Oneself," *Journal of Social Philosophy* 33, no. 3 (2002): 345–59; Peter J. Steinberger, "Hobbes, Rousseau, and the Modern Conception of the State," *The Journal of Politics* 70, no. 3 (2008): 597.

143. Richard Tuck, *The Rights of War and Peace: Political Thought and the International Order from Grotius to Kant* (Oxford: Oxford University Press, 1991), 132–35. It should be noted, however, that some readers suggest that the conditions of psychic life set out in Hobbes's materialist anthropology militate against the establishment of that minimal agreement necessary to institute a sovereign form. Nicholas Dungey argues that "the generative process of Hobbes's materialism creates a situation in which the senses, imagination, and passions lead to a diffusion of meaning and perceptions that frustrate the development of common accounts of things. Hobbes's materialism leads toward greater anarchy, and away from political agreement, because at each stage of the argument the potential diversity of images, perceptions, and ideas multiply exponentially, resulting in deeply subjective interpretations of the physical and shared environments." Nicholas Dungey, "Thomas Hobbes's Materialism, Language, and the Possibility of Politics," *The Review of Politics* 70, no. 2 (2008): 200. Gary Herbert, meanwhile, does not consider it plausible to suggest that Hobbesian actors could be capable of mutually agreeing to create a commonwealth given their fundamental distrust of one another: "The idea that people in the natural condition, in conditions of extreme distrust and alienation, could sit down together, in mutual trust, to institute a civil association, is incomprehensible." Gary B. Herbert, "The Non-Normative Nature of Hobbesian Natural Law," *Hobbes Studies* 22, no. 1 (2009): 26. See also Matthew M. Kramer, *Hobbes and the Paradoxes of Political Origins* (Basingstoke: Macmillan Press, 1997), 61–125;

Daniel Skinner, "Political Theory beyond the Rhetoric-Reason Divide: Hobbes, Semantic Indeterminacy, and Political Order," *The Review of Politics* 73, no. 4 (2011): 561–80.

144. Hobbes, *On the Citizen*, 1.2.

145. Goyard-Fabre, *Le droit et la loi dans la philosophie de Thomas Hobbes*, 23.

146. Hobbes, "A Discourse on the Beginning of Tacitus," 31.

147. Hobbes, 31.

148. Thomas Hobbes, "A Discourse of Laws," ed. Noel B. Reynolds and Arlene W. Saxonhouse (Chicago: University of Chicago Press, 1995), 115.

149. For an account of Hobbes's recognition of the wide variation of ethical standards among societies in light of his nominalism see Visintainer, "Hobbes on Goodness and Pressure on the Sovereign."

150. Hobbes, *Leviathan, Volume Two*, 22, 358.

151. As Gilbert Boss observes, the human being is "neither creature of God, nor production of nature," but is itself "the creator of society," the latter being an artifact that is not the product of reflection on some eternal order beyond or before it. Gilbert Boss, "Raison et convention, ou la raison politique chez Hobbes," *Hobbes Studies* 9, no. 1 (1996): 70.

152. On the significance of artifice and the human capacity for making in Hobbes's thought see Waldman, "Hobbes on the Generation of a Public Person"; Michael Oakeshott, "Introduction to *Leviathan*," in *Hobbes on Civil Association* (Oxford: Basil Blackwell, 1975), 56–57; Richard Ashcraft, "Ideology and Class in Hobbes's Political Theory," *Political Theory* 6, no. 1 (1978): 34; Anthony K. Kronman, "The Concept of an Author and the Unity of the Commonwealth in Hobbes's *Leviathan*," *Journal of the History of Philosophy* 18, no. 2 (1980): 159–75; William Sacksteder, "Hobbes: Man the Maker," in *Thomas Hobbes: His View of Man*, ed. J. G. van der Bend (Amsterdam: Rodopi, 1982), 77–88; William Sacksteder, "Man the Artificer: Notes on Animals, Humans and Machines in Hobbes," *Southern Journal of Philosophy* 22, no. 1 (1984): 105–21; Amos Funkenstein, *Theology and the Scientific Imagination: From the Middle Ages to the Seventeenth Century* (Princeton: Princeton University Press, 1986), 334–35; Martin A. Bertman, "Semantics and Political Theory in Hobbes," *Hobbes Studies* 1, no. 1 (1988): 134–43; Browning and Prokhovnik, "Hobbes, Hegel and Modernity"; Anat Biletzki, *Talking Wolves: Thomas Hobbes on the Language of Politics and the Politics of Language* (Dordrecht: Kluwer Academic Publishers, 1997), 88; Zarka, "Liberté, nécessité, dasard," 260–61; Prokhovnik, "Hobbes's Artifice as Social Construction"; Polin, *Politique et philosophie chez Thomas Hobbes*, 7–10.

153. Kahn, *Wayward Contracts*, 137.

154. As Raymond Polin puts it, "There is no creation without history, nor history without creation." Polin, *Politique et philosophie chez Thomas Hobbes*, 101. On creativity as being for Hobbes a key element of human nature, see also, for example, Craig Walton, "The *philosophia prima* of Thomas Hobbes," in

Thomas Hobbes in His Time, ed. Ralph Ross, Herbert W. Schneider, and Theodore Waldman (Minneapolis: University of Minnesota Press, 1974), 31–41; Sacksteder, "Man the Artificer," 105; Funkenstein, *Theology and the Scientific Imagination*, 289; Biletzki, *Talking Wolves*, 117.

Chapter 4

1. Quentin Skinner, *From Humanism to Hobbes: Studies in Politics and Rhetoric* (Cambridge: Cambridge University Press, 2018), 198.

2. Henry Parker, *Some Few Observations Upon His Majesties Late Answer to the Declaration or Remonstance Sic of the Lords and Commons of the 19 of May, 1642* (London: s.n., 1642), 15.

3. Skinner, *From Humanism to Hobbes*, 199.

4. Gordon Hull, for example, has observed that Hobbes's affirmation of a substantive human equality has obviously democratic implications: "The move to natural equality allows the question of democracy to be posed quite radically, since it is no longer the case that the *demos'* being unfit to rule can be attributed to nature." Gordon Hull, *Hobbes and the Making of Modern Political Thought* (London: Continuum, 2009), 31. Leo Strauss also recognizes, albeit regretfully, just how radical Hobbes's position here is, in fact upsetting the mainstream of the entire philosophical tradition that Strauss so esteems: "Because all men are equal, i.e., because there is no natural order in general, and therefore no natural gradation of mankind, the difference between the wise minority and the unwise majority loses the fundamental importance it had for traditional political philosophy." Leo Strauss, *The Political Philosophy of Hobbes: Its Basis and Genesis* Chicago: Chicago University Press, 1952), 101–102.

5. Thomas Hobbes, *Leviathan, Volume Two: The English and Latin Texts (i)*, ed. Noel Malcolm (Oxford: Clarendon Press, 2012), 13, 190.

6. Karl Schumann, for example, reminds us that Hobbes's entire philosophical project is largely formed in opposition to Aristotelianism, which the seventeenth century European scholastic tradition thoroughly embodied. Karl Schuhmann, "Skinner's Hobbes," *British Journal for the History of Philosophy* 6, no. 1 (1998): 117.

7. Aristotle, *Politics*, 1254a20–22.

8. Aristotle, 1254b20–24, 1260a11–13. Some readers of Aristotle, it should be noted, question the legitimacy of attributing to him the belief in the existence of absolute boundaries between categories of people on the basis of supposedly natural and necessary characteristics. For Jill Frank, for instance, politics shapes human nature in various ways, the latter not absolutely delimiting the former. If nature is changeable, then, so too are the hierarchical forms and relations that

it appears to construct. Jill Frank, "Citizens, Slaves, and Foreigners," *American Political Science Review* 98, no. 1 (2004): 91–104.

9. Joanne H. Wright and Nancy J. Hirschmann, "Introduction: The Many Faces of 'Mr. Hobs,'" in *Feminist Interpretations of Thomas Hobbes*, ed. Nancy J. Hirschmann and Joanne H. Wright (University Park: Pennsylvania State University Press, 2012), 1–17. For a brief summary of some of the most prominent feminist interpretations and debates within Hobbes studies see Eva Odzuck, "'Not a Woman-Hater,' 'No Rapist,' or Even Inventor of 'the Sensitive Male'? Feminist Interpretations of Hobbes's Political Theory and Their Relevance for Hobbes Studies," in *Interpreting Hobbes's Political Philosophy*, ed. S. A. Lloyd (Cambridge: Cambridge University Press, 2019), 223–41.

10. Carole Pateman, *The Sexual Contract* (Stanford, CA: Stanford University Press, 1988), 48–49. For further discussion on the problem of the movement from a natural state of equality between men and women to a civil society characterized by women's subordination see S. A. Lloyd, "By Force or Wiles: Women in the Hobbesian Hunt for Allies and Authority," *Hobbes Studies* 33, no. 1 (2020): 5–28; Gianni Paganini, "How Far Can a 'Radical' Philosopher Go? Thomas Hobbes's Paradox of Gender Relations and One Possible Solution," *Hobbes Studies* 33, no. 1 (2020): 29–53.

11. Noel Malcolm, "Hobbes, Sandys, and the Virginia Company," in *Aspects of Hobbes* (Oxford: Oxford University Press, 2002), 75.

12. On this point see Srinivas Aravamudan, "Hobbes and America," in *The Postcolonial Enlightenment: Eighteenth-Century Colonialism and Postcolonial Theory*, ed. Daniel Carey and Lynn Festa (Oxford: Oxford University Press, 2009), 44–47. For a critical account of the extent to which social contract theory more generally was developed through the negative production of a certain image of indigenous peoples see Robert Lee Nichols, "Realizing the Social Contract: The Case of Colonialism and Indigenous Peoples," *Contemporary Political Theory* 4, no. 1 (2005): 42–62.

13. It is not the case, as John F. Moffitt and Santiago Sebastián claim, that Hobbes "consign[s] the Native Americans en masse to the lowest ranks of subhumanity." John F. Moffitt and Santiago Sebastián, *O Brave New People: The European Invention of the American Indian* (Albuquerque: University of New Mexico Press, 1998), 284. For a more nuanced critical account of Hobbes on this point, recognizing the extent to which Hobbes considers the Americans to possess the full range of human faculties, see Stephanie B. Martens, *The Americas in Early Modern Political Theory* (New York: Palgrave Macmillan, 2016), 69–93.

14. Thomas Hobbes, "Elements of Philosophy. The First Section, Concerning Body," in *The English Works of Thomas Hobbes of Malmesbury, Volume One*, ed. Sir William Molesworth (London: John Bohn, 1839), 1.7. For further discussion on this topic see Pat Moloney, "Hobbes, Savagery, and International

Anarchy," *American Journal of Political Science* 105, no. 1 (2011): 189–204. Charles Mills offers a competing view, asserting that despite Hobbes's explicit claims regarding the equality of reason, his treatment of the state of nature implicitly affirms a division between rational Europeans—for whom the state of nature is indeed hypothetical—and the less rational "nonwhites," for whom it is on the contrary literal: "But really we know that whites are too rational to allow this to happen to *them*. So the most notorious state of nature in the contractarian literature—the bestial war of all against all—is really a *nonwhite* figure, a racial object lesson for the more rational whites, whose superior grasp of natural law (here in its prudential rather than altruistic version) will enable them to take the necessary steps to avoid it and not behave as 'savages.'" Charles W. Mills, *The Racial Contract* (Ithaca, NY: Cornell University Press, 1997), 66.

15. A. P. Martinich, *Hobbes* (New York: Routledge, 2005), 241, n5. Martinich himself writes that "One might well think that Hobbes is joking. Surely, he knew that there are great differences in intelligence." Martinich, 65. For additional statements maintaining the insincerity of Hobbes's positing of equality see Gary B. Herbert, "Thomas Hobbes's Counterfeit Equality," *Southern Journal of Philosophy* 14, no. 3 (1973): 269–83; Paul A. Rahe, *Republics Ancient & Modern, Volume II: New Modes and Orders in Early Modern Political Thought* (Chapel Hill: University of North Carolina Press, 1994), 150–51; A. P. Martinich, *Hobbes: A Biography* (Cambridge: Cambridge University Press, 1999), 144–45; Art Vanden Houten, "Prudence in Hobbes's Political Philosophy," *History of Political Thought* 33, no. 2 (2002): 276–79; Travis D. Smith, "On the Fourth Law of Nature," *Hobbes Studies* 16, no. 1 (2003): 84–94; Jeffrey R. Collins, *The Allegiance of Thomas Hobbes* (Oxford: Oxford University Press, 2005), 34; Pierre Manent, *Naissances de la politique moderne* (Paris: Gallimard, 2007), 100–101; George MacDonald Ross, *Starting with Hobbes* (New York: Continuum, 2009), 102; Leon Howard Craig, *The Platonian Leviathan* (Toronto: University of Toronto Press, 2010), 418–27; Ioannis Evrigenis, *Images of Anarchy: The Rhetoric and Science in Hobbes's State of Nature* (Cambridge: Cambridge University Press, 2014), 234; Elad Carmel, "'Philosophy, Therefore Is within Yourself': The Rational Potential in Hobbes's Theory," *Hobbes Studies* 31, no. 2 (2018): 166–87.

16. Craig, *The Platonian* Leviathan, 480.

17. Craig, 421, 426.

18. Hobbes, *Leviathan, Volume Two*, 13, 188.

19. Hobbes, 13, 188.

20. Thomas Hobbes, *The Elements of Law, Natural and Politic*, ed. Ferdinand Tönnies (London: Simpkin, Marshall, and Co., 1889), 1.14.2. Emphasis added.

21. Kinch Hoekstra, "Hobbesian Equality," in *Hobbes Today: Insights for the 21st Century*, ed. S. A. Lloyd (Cambridge: Cambridge University Press, 2013), 112. While recognizing the centrality of the affirmation of social equality to the Hobbesian project, Chou Chia-Yu similarly gives expression to the

latent assumption behind this position: "What Hobbes is saying is that only by acknowledging equality, *which might never have actually existed among men*, can men establish a society in cooperation with others." Chia-Yu Chou, *Rethinking Hobbes and Kant: The Role and Consequences of Assumption in Political Theory* (London: Routledge, 2017), 64. Emphasis added.

22. Hoekstra, "Hobbesian Equality," 89.

23. For an example of a reading that conflates Hobbes's account of the heterogeneity of being with a necessarily stratified range of specifically intellectual competencies, see Eva Helene Odzuck, "'I Professed to Write Not All to All': Diversified Communication in Thomas Hobbes's Political Philosophy," *Hobbes Studies* 30 (2017): 123–55.

24. Hobbes, *The Elements of Law, Natural and Politic*, 1.17.2.

25. Thomas Hobbes, *On the Citizen*, ed. and trans. Richard Tuck and Michael Silverthorne (Cambridge: Cambridge University Press, 1998), 3.13.

26. Hobbes, *Leviathan, Volume Two*, 15, 234. For an interpretation of the Hobbesian concept of vainglory as failure to acknowledge the fact of natural equality, the recognition of the latter constituting modesty, see Julie E. Cooper, "Vainglory, Modesty, and Political Agency in the Political Theory of Thomas Hobbes," *Review of Politics* 72, no. 2 (2010): 241–69. For an account of Hobbes's personal modesty and how this trait should inform political theory see Julie E. Cooper, "Thomas Hobbes on the Political Theorist's Vocation," *Historical Journal* 50, no. 3 (2007): 519–47.

27. Hobbes, *The Elements of Law, Natural and Politic*, 1.17.1.

28. Hobbes, *On the Citizen*, 3.13.

29. Hobbes, 3.13.

30. Hobbes, 1.3.

31. Hobbes, *Leviathan, Volume Two*, 15, 234.

32. Hobbes, 15, 234.

33. Hobbes, *On the Citizen*, 3.14.

34. Hobbes, *Leviathan, Volume Two*, 15, 234.

35. See, for example, Larry May, "Hobbes on Equity and Justice," in *Hobbes's "Science of Natural Justice,"* ed. Craig Walton and Paul J. Johnson (Dordrecht: Kluwer, 1987), 241–52; David van Mill, *Liberty, Rationality, and Agency in Hobbes* (Albany: State University of New York Press, 2001), 161; Perez Zagorin, *Hobbes and the Law of Nature* (Princeton, NJ: Princeton University Press, 2009), 92; Lee Ward, "Equity and Political Economy in Thomas Hobbes," *American Journal of Political Science* 64, no. 4 (2020): 823–35. For a rejection of the view that equity is the fundamental moral category structuring Hobbes's ethics see Tom Sorell, "Law and Equity in Hobbes," *Critical Review of International Social and Political Philosophy* 19, no. 1 (2016): 29–46.

36. Hobbes, *The Elements of Law, Natural and Politic*, 1.17.14.

37. May, "Hobbes on Equity and Justice," 245.

38. It should be noted that not all readers of Hobbes accept this conceptual separation of equity and justice. See, for example, William Mathie, "Commentary on Professor May's 'Hobbes on Equality and Justice,'" in *Hobbes's "Science of Natural Justice,"* ed. Craig Walton and Paul J. Johnson (Dordrecht: Kluwer, 1987), 253–56; William Mathie, "Justice and Equity: An Inquiry into the Meaning and Role of Equity in the Hobbesian Account of Justice and Politics," in *Hobbes's "Science of Natural Justice,"* ed. Craig Walton and Paul J. Johnson (Dordrecht: Kluwer, 1987), 257–76.

39. Ward, "Equity and Political Economy in Thomas Hobbes," 4.

40. Hobbes, *Leviathan, Volume Two*, 26, 432.

41. Hobbes, 26, 432.

42. Hobbes, 26, 438.

43. For an account of the diversity of roles that the concept of equity plays in Hobbes's legal theory—specifically, equity as a law of nature, as a criterion of legality, and as the basis of the jurisdiction of the institution of Chancery—see Dennis Klimchuk, "Hobbes on Equity," in *Hobbes and the Law*, ed. David Dyzenhaus and Thomas Poole (Cambridge: Cambridge University Press, 2012), 165–85. For a contemporary example of how the scope of application of Hobbes's concept of equity can be even further extended so as to productively intervene in contemporary political debates, see Eleanor Curran, "Hobbes Comes Out for Equal Marriage," in *Hobbesian Applied Ethics and Public Policy*, ed. Shane D. Courtland (London: Routledge, 2017), 161–78.

44. Hobbes, *Leviathan, Volume Two*, 15, 236.

45. Hobbes, 15, 236.

46. Hobbes, 15, 236.

47. Hobbes, 15, 236.

48. According to Johan Olsthoorn, "Hobbes is the first thinker, as far as I know, to subsume distributive justice under equity." Johan Olsthoorn, "Hobbes's Account of Distributive Justice as Equity," *British Journal for the History of Philosophy* 21, no. 1 (2013): 14. Importantly for Olsthoorn, though, the violation of distributive justice does not constitute injustice proper, but just iniquity, and hence does not violate the rights of citizens.

49. Hobbes, *Leviathan, Volume Two*, 30, 536–38. For an account of the increasingly important normative role played by the concept of equity within Hobbes's thought, and how it influenced his political economy, see Ward, "Equity and Political Economy in Thomas Hobbes."

50. Hobbes, *The Elements of Law, Natural and Politic*, 1.17.2.

51. Hobbes, *On the Citizen*, 3.16. Johan Olsthoorn has characterized Hobbes's conception of distributive justice as one of "pure procedural justice," the justice of the distribution not being realized in the specific outcome, but rather the process that generated it. Olsthoorn, "Hobbes's Account of Distributive Justice as Equity," 29. Hence the examples here, where equity ethically

conditions the modes by which common goods are distributed. The realization of the principle of fairness lay in the equal treatment of citizens who are all subject to the procedural process.

52. Hobbes, *On the Citizen*, 3.17.
53. Hobbes, *The Elements of Law, Natural and Politic*, 1.17.4.
54. Hobbes, 1.17.4. As Johan Olsthoorn observes in his discussion of Hobbes's innovations with respect to property right, "Lot is the morally sound procedure for allocating indivisible goods which cannot be held in common because this procedure alone acknowledges *natural equality*." Johan Olsthoorn, "Hobbes on Justice, Property Rights and Self-Ownership," *History of Political Thought* 36, no. 3 (2015): 479–80. Emphasis added.
55. Hobbes, *The Elements of Law, Natural and Politic*, 1.10.2.
56. For an example of a reader who recognizes that Hobbes posits "the equality of intelligence," see Frank M. Coleman, *Hobbes and America: Exploring the Constitutional Foundations* (Toronto: University of Toronto Press, 1977), 76. For further interpreters who take seriously Hobbes's affirmation of equality, see also Martin A. Bertman, "Equality in Hobbes, with Reference to Aristotle," *Review of Politics* 38, no. 4 (1976): 534–44; George Mace, *Locke, Hobbes, and the Federalist Papers* (Carbondale: Southern Illinois University Press, 1979), 33; Joel Kidder, "Acknowledgements of Equals: Hobbes's Ninth Law of Nature," *Philosophical Quarterly* 33, no. 131 (1983): 133–46; Gayne Nerney, "The Hobbesian Argument for Human Equality," *Southern Journal of Philosophy* 24, no. 4 (1986): 561–76; Bernard Baumrin, "Hobbes's Egalitarianism," in *Thomas Hobbes: De la métaphysique à la politique*, ed. Martin Bertman and Michel Malherbe (Paris: Librairie Philosophique J. Vrin, 1989), 119–27; Richard E. Flathman, *Thomas Hobbes: Skepticism, Individuality, and Chastened Politics* (Lanham, MD: Rowman & Littlefield, 2002), 80; Vickie B. Sullivan, *Machiavelli, Hobbes, and the Formation of a Liberal Republicanism in England* (Cambridge: Cambridge University Press, 2004), 90–91; Eleanor Curran, "Hobbes on Equality: Context, Rhetoric, Argument," *Hobbes Studies* 25, no. 2 (2012): 166–87.
57. Hobbes, *The Elements of Law, Natural and Politic*, 1.10.8.
58. Hobbes, *On the Citizen*, 1.7.
59. A few readers recognize in some way this feature of Hobbesian equality. Andrzej Rapaczynski writes that "Far from being the unifying bond among men, equality is, for Hobbes, the most important dividing principle." Andrzej Rapaczynski, *Nature and Politics: Liberalism in the Philosophies of Hobbes, Locke and Rousseau* (Ithaca, NY: Cornell University Press, 1987), 51. Bernard Baumrin, meanwhile, observes that "Hobbes is not arguing for rough equality . . . but real metaphysical equality; i.e., some kind of identity in the context of difference." Baumrin, "Hobbes's Egalitarianism," 119. See also Yves Charles Zarka, *La décision métaphysique de Hobbes: Conditions de la politique* (Paris: Librairie Philosophique J. Vrin, 1987), 303.

60. Hobbes, "Elements of Philosophy. The First Section, Concerning Body," 5.1.

61. Hobbes, 5.1.

62. Thomas Hobbes, "The Questions Concerning Liberty, Necessity, and Chance," in *The English Works of Thomas Hobbes of Malmesbury, Volume Five*, ed. Sir William Molesworth (London: John Bohn, 1841), 299–300.

63. Hobbes, *Leviathan, Volume Two*, 4, 56.

64. Hobbes, 4, 50.

65. Hobbes, 4, 56.

66. Hence "*magnitude, body, motion, time, degrees of quality, action, conception, proportion, speech, and names* (in which all kinds of philosophy consist) are capable of addition and subtraction." Hobbes, "Elements of Philosophy. The First Section, Concerning Body," 1.3.

67. Hobbes, *Leviathan, Volume Two*, 5, 64.

68. Hobbes, 5, 64.

69. Hobbes, "Elements of Philosophy. The First Section, Concerning Body," 3.5.

70. Hobbes, 3.8.

71. As David Johnston notes, for Hobbes logic and reason are "essential attributes of human nature." David Johnston, *The Rhetoric of Leviathan: Thomas Hobbes and the Politics of Cultural Transformation* (Princeton, NJ: Princeton University Press, 1986), 64.

72. Hobbes, "Elements of Philosophy. The First Section, Concerning Body," 1.1. Although recognizing Hobbes's contention that all humans possess a basic capacity for natural reason, Elad Carmel sees philosophy as depending upon a surplus development of this potential, not all individuals being capable of such a refinement in light of what Carmel sees as the stratification of particular rationalities. Carmel, "'Philosophy, Therefore Is within Yourself': The Rational Potential in Hobbes's Theory." See also Sorell, *Hobbes*, 7–8. Such readings do not, to me, seem to be supported by the textual evidence, as I will document throughout this chapter.

73. Hobbes, "The Questions Concerning Liberty, Necessity, and Chance," 199.

74. Hobbes, "On Man," 55.

75. Hobbes, "Elements of Philosophy. The First Section, Concerning Body," 1.1.

76. Despite Hobbes's own claims on this issue, several scholars dispute the notion that Hobbes's writings were directed toward a popular audience. Paul Johnson, for example, argues that *Leviathan* was written firstly for sovereigns and then for students in universities, with the hope that sovereigns would direct those future teachers among them to instruct Hobbesian principles. Paul J. Johnson, "*Leviathan*'s Audience," in *Thomas Hobbes: De la métaphysique à la politique* (Paris:

Librairie Philosophique J. Vrin, 1989), 232. Teresa Bejan meanwhile, recognizes that Hobbes was concerned with developing a model for a "truly universal civic education." Teresa M. Bejan, "Teaching the *Leviathan*: Thomas Hobbes on Education," *Oxford Review of Education* 36, no. 5 (2010): 609. For Bejan, however, with respect to the common people, this project is concerned not with the development or refinement of individual capacities, but rather, given their intellectual limitations, the unreflective imprinting of sovereign reason upon their minds. In a subsequent section I suggest that Hobbes is much more optimistic about the critical-rational capacities of the so-called vulgar.

77. Thomas Hobbes, "The Prose Life," in *The Elements of Law, Natural and Politic*, ed. J. C. A. Gaskin (Oxford: Oxford University Press, 1994), 250.

78. Hobbes, "Elements of Philosophy. The First Section, Concerning Body," 1.7.

79. Thomas Hobbes, *Behemoth, or the Long Parliament*, ed. Paul Seaward (Oxford: Clarendon Press, 2010), 158–59. Indeed, Geoffrey Vaughan reads *Behemoth* as above all a pedagogical intervention, an effort to educate the people through conversation. Geoffrey M. Vaughan, "The Audiences of 'Behemoth' and the Politics of Conversation," in *Hobbes's* Behemoth: *Religion and Democracy*, ed. Tomaž Mastnak (Exeter: Imprint Academic, 2009), 170–85.

80. Hobbes, *Leviathan, Volume Two*, 30, 524.

81. Hobbes, 30, 524.

82. Hobbes, *The Elements of Law, Natural and Politic*, 1.5.14.

83. Hobbes, 1.7.3.

84. As Johan Olsthoorn observes, "Reasoning about how to conduct oneself among others just is prudential reasoning—in the sense of thinking through what conduces to the agent's ongoing felicity." Johan Olsthoorn, "On the Absence of Moral Goodness in Hobbes's Ethics," *Journal of Ethics*, 24, no. 2 (2020): 241–66.

85. Michael LeBuffe argues, however, that *De Cive* constitutes an exception here, it positing a shared standard of morality emerging from the equivalent deployment of a singular right reason: "*On the Citizen* differs from the other texts in its clear emphasis on right reason as a source of right action, knowledge of the good and virtue." Michael LeBuffe, "Motivation, Reason, and the Good in *On the Citizen*," in *Hobbes's* On the Citizen, ed. Robin Douglass and Johan Olsthoorn (Cambridge: Cambridge University Press, 2020), 105.

86. Thomas Hobbes, "An Historical Narration Concerning Heresy, and the Punishment Thereof," in *The English Works of Thomas Hobbes of Malmesbury, Volume Four*, ed. Sir William Molesworth (London: John Bohn, 1840), 387.

87. Thomas Hobbes, *Leviathan, Volume Three: The English and Latin Texts (ii)*, ed. Noel Malcolm (Oxford: Clarendon Press, 2012), 46, 1058.

88. Hobbes, 46, 1060.

89. As David Gauthier notes, the willingness to voluntarily take the reason of an arbiter as right reason becomes itself a marker of rationality. David Gauthier,

"Public Reason," *Social Philosophy and Policy* 12, no. 1 (1995): 26. Gauthier ultimately attempts to revise Hobbes's account of public reason in such a way as to place limits on it, thus reining in the scope of sovereign authority. For a critique of this operation for violating the principle of Hobbesian absolutism see Shane D. Courtland, "Public Reason and the Hobbesian Dilemma," *Hobbes Studies* 20, no. 1 (2007): 63–92. See also Michael Ridge, who argues, contra Gauthier, that rather than theorize a constrained sovereign whose judgment stands in for public reason in limited ways, we should prioritize public principles over a public person (i.e., sovereign). Michael Ridge, "Hobbesian Public Reason," *Ethics* 108, no. 3 (1998): 538–68.

90. Hobbes, *Leviathan, Volume Two*, 5, 66.

91. Hobbes, 5, 66.

92. On the central task of the sovereign as the creation of a shared political language through the fixing of definitions, thus establishing a common system of meaning that functions as an objective moral standard of evaluation, see Dorothea Krook, "Thomas Hobbes's Doctrine of Meaning and Truth," *Philosophy* 31, no. 116 (1956): 20; Martin A. Bertman, "Hobbes and Performatives," *Critica: Revista Hispanoamericana de Filosofía* 10, no. 30 (1978): 45; Frederick G. Whelan, "Language and Its Abuses in Hobbes's Political Philosophy," *American Political Science Review* 75, no. 1 (1981): 59–75; Terence Ball, "Hobbes's Linguistic Turn," *Polity* 17, no. 4 (1985): 754; Kenneth Minogue, "From Precision to Peace: Hobbes and Political Language," *Hobbes Studies* 3, no. 1 (1990): 75–88; Anat Biletzki, *Talking Wolves: Thomas Hobbes on the Language of Politics and the Politics of Language* (Dordrecht: Kluwer Academic Publishers, 1997), 86–87; Pat Moloney, "Leaving the Garden of Eden: Linguistic and Political Authority in Thomas Hobbes," *History of Political Thought* 18, no. 2 (1997): 242–66; Sheldon Wolin, *Politics and Vision: Continuity and Innovation in Western Political Thought* (Princeton, NJ: Princeton University Press, 2004), 232; Kirk Wetters, *The Opinion System: Impasses of the Public Sphere from Hobbes to Habermas* (New York: Fordham University Press, 2008), 130–31; Philip Pettit, *Made with Words: Hobbes on Language, Mind, and Politics* (Princeton, NJ: Princeton University Press, 2008), 115; Thomas Poole, "Hobbes on Law and Prerogative," in *Hobbes and the Law*, ed. David Dyzenhaus and Thomas Poole (Cambridge: Cambridge University Press, 2012), 68–96; Gordon Hull, "Building Better Citizens: Hobbes Against the Ontological Illusion," *Epoché: A Journal for the History of Philosophy* 20, no. 1 (2015): 114. For a contrary argument, suggesting that scholars tend to overemphasize the extent to which Hobbes is concerned with the need to fix or stabilize the semantic order, see Daniel Skinner, "Political Theory beyond the Rhetoric-Reason Divide: Hobbes, Semantic Indeterminacy, and Political Order," *Review of Politics* 73, no. 4 (2011): 561–80.

93. Hobbes, "The Questions Concerning Liberty, Necessity, and Chance," 176.

94. Hobbes, 176.

95. Thomas Hobbes, "A Dialogue between a Philosopher and a Student of the Common Laws of England," in *The English Works of Thomas Hobbes of Malmesbury, Volume Six*, ed. Sir William Molesworth (London: John Bohn, 1840), 22.

96. Hobbes, *Leviathan, Volume Two*, 5, 66.

97. Hobbes, 5, 68.

98. Hobbes, 5, 68. As Kinch Hoekstra comments, all humankind is "highly prone" to error. Kinch Hoekstra, "Hobbes and the Foole," *Political Theory* 25, no. 5 (1997): 630.

99. For Hobbes's account of the causes of absurd conclusions see Hobbes, *Leviathan, Volume Two*, 5, 70.

100. Hobbes, 5, 72.

101. Hobbes, 5, 72.

102. Hobbes, 5, 68.

103. For as Michael LeBuffe observes, "Reason is the same faculty whether we apply it to theoretical or to practical questions." LeBuffe, "Motivation, Reason, and the Good in On the Citizen," 89.

104. Hobbes, *Leviathan, Volume Two*, 13, 188.

105. Hobbes, 13, 188.

106. Hobbes, 13, 188. Art Vanden Houten produces a dissenting opinion here, arguing that contrary to Hobbes's own statements, there are significant differences with respect to the individual capacity to deploy prudence. Vanden Houten, "Prudence in Hobbes's Political Philosophy."

107. Hobbes, *Leviathan, Volume Two*, 3, 44.

108. Hobbes, 3, 40.

109. Arash Abizadeh, "Hobbes on Mind: Practical Deliberation, Reasoning, and Language," *Journal of the History of Philosophy* 55, no. 1 (2017): 31.

110. Hobbes, "The Questions Concerning Liberty, Necessity, and Chance," 358.

111. Hobbes, 360.

112. Abizadeh, "Hobbes on Mind." See also Laurens van Apeldoorn, "Reconsidering Hobbes's Account of Practical Deliberation," *Hobbes Studies* 25, no. 2 (2012): 143–65; Adrian Blau, "Reason, Deliberation, and the Passions," in *The Oxford Handbook of Hobbes*, ed. A. P. Martinich and Kinch Hoekstra (Oxford: Oxford University Press, 2016), 195–220.

113. Abizadeh, "Hobbes on Mind," 3.

114. On the extent to which practical deliberation is clearly distinguished from the deliberation of animals see van Apeldoorn, "Reconsidering Hobbes's Account of Practical Deliberation."

115. Hence Roger Paden identifies reason as a psychological capacity that allows individuals to locate and satisfy the diversity of their interests: "It performs

this function by determining the probable future consequences of actions or the necessary antecedents of desired effects. Practical reasoning, therefore, is nothing more than reasoning about causes and effects: Given a particular interest, reason can determine its likely consequences." Roger Paden, "Hobbesian Deliberators," *Hobbes Studies* 7, no. 1 (1994): 33.

116. Hobbes, "The Questions Concerning Liberty, Necessity, and Chance," 191.

117. Thomas Hobbes, "Of Liberty and Necessity: A Treatise, Wherein All Controversy Concerning Predestination, Election, Free-Will, Grace, Merits, Reprobation, &c Is Fully Decided and Cleared," in *The English Works of Thomas Hobbes of Malmesbury, Volume Four*, ed. Sir William Molesworth (London: John Bohn, 1840), 244. As Robert Lawton and Helen Pringle write, "Perturbations of mind lead us to misjudge what is *to ourselves* an evil, given that others are worked into our very grain, our conceptions of ourselves, *in the moment of making* of our projects. Defective self-knowledge is not ignorance of some purposive inner principle shared by all men, but simply of the common structure of our passions." Rob Lawton and Helen Pringle, "A Life Well Lost? Hobbes and Self-Preservation," *Hobbes Studies* 6, no. 1 (1993): 69.

118. Hobbes, "The Questions Concerning Liberty, Necessity, and Chance," 399.

119. Hobbes, *On the Citizen*, 1.9.

120. Hobbes, 2.1.

121. Jeffrey Barnouw goes so far as to write that "no thinker has granted greater importance to curiosity as an inherent human drive, man's distinguishing characteristic for Hobbes." Jeffrey Barnouw, "Hobbes's Causal Account of Sensation," *Journal of the History of Philosophy* 18, no. 2 (1980): 129–30. For further statements of curiosity as a uniquely human trait see Zarka, *La décision métaphysique de Hobbes*, 283; Jeffrey Barnouw, "Hobbes's Psychology of Thought: Endeavours, Purpose and Curiosity," *History of European Ideas* 10, no. 5 (1989): 519–45; Luc Foisneau, "Les savants dans la cité," in *Thomas Hobbes: Philosophie première, théorie de la science politique*, ed. Yves Charles Zarka (Paris: Presses Universitaires de France, 1990), 181–92; William R. Lund, "Hobbes on Opinion, Private Judgment and Civil War," *History of Political Thought* 13, no. 1 (1992): 61; Rahe, *Republics Ancient & Modern, Volume II*, 144; Pettit, *Made with Words*, 27; van Apeldoorn, "Reconsidering Hobbes's Account of Practical Deliberation," 159; Kathryn Tabb, "The Fate of Nebuchadnezzar: Curiosity and Human Nature in Hobbes," *Hobbes Studies* 27, no. 1 (2014): 13–34; Joanne Boucher, "The Erotic Political Philosophy of Thomas Hobbes," *Canadian Journal of Political Science* 49, no. 1 (2016): 96–97; Tracy B. Strong, "Glory and the Law in Hobbes," *European Journal of Political Theory* 16, no. 1 (2017): 69; David Wootton, *Power, Pleasure, and Profit: Insatiable Appetites from Machiavelli to Madison* (Cambridge: Belknap Press, 2018), 90; Gianni Paganini, "Hobbes's Philosophical Method and the

Passion of Curiosity," in *Interpreting Hobbes's Political Philosophy*, ed. S. A. Lloyd (Cambridge: Cambridge University Press, 2019), 59–60.

122. Paganini, "Hobbes's Philosophical Method and the Passion of Curiosity," 60.

123. Hence Jeffrey Barnouw has identified the active manifestation of curiosity as an intrinsically pleasurable good in itself. Barnouw, "Hobbes's Psychology of Thought: Endeavours, Purpose and Curiosity," 538.

124. Hobbes, *Leviathan, Volume Two*, 11, 160.

125. Hobbes, 12, 164.

126. Hobbes, 12, 164.

127. Hobbes, *Thomas White's* De mundo *Examined*, 38.5.

128. Hobbes, 32.1.

129. Hobbes, 38.5.

130. Hobbes, 38.6.

131. Hobbes, 38.6. Referring to the well-known passage in chapter 11 of *Leviathan*, it is common for readers to consequently note Hobbes's rejection of any specifically human *summum bonum*. This majority presumption has been recently challenged by Arash Abizadeh, who interprets the perpetual anticipation of future pleasure as an ultimate human good, just not one realized in the actualization of a static or terminal state: "Hobbes was committed to the intrinsic value of pleasure and, in line with his eudaimonism about the good, to felicity as the overarching and ultimate value of a human life." Arash Abizadeh, *Hobbes and the Two Faces of Ethics* (Cambridge: Cambridge University Press, 2018), 141.

132. Indeed, Severin Kitanov interprets Hobbes's concept of happiness, to the extent that it refers not to a static state of attainment that would terminate desire, but rather a perpetually dynamic process of movement and rest, as fundamentally dialectical in form. Severin V. Kitanov, "Happiness in a Mechanistic Universe: Thomas Hobbes on the Nature and Attainability of Happiness," *Hobbes Studies* 24, no. 2 (2011): 117–18. On the extent to which such dialectical movement perpetually transforms both external nature as well as the nature of human need and being, see Gary B. Herbert, "Thomas Hobbes's Dialectic of Desire," *New Scholasticism* 50, no. 2 (1976): 160.

133. Hobbes, *Leviathan, Volume Two*, 11, 150.

134. Hobbes, 11, 150.

135. Hobbes famously writes, "So that in the first place, I put for a generall inclination of all mankind, a perpetuall and restlesse desire of Power after power, that ceaseth onely in Death. And the cause of this, is not always that that a man hopes for a more intensive delight." Hobbes, 11, 150.

136. Hobbes, "The Questions Concerning Liberty, Necessity, and Chance," 174–75.

137. Hobbes, 209.

138. Hobbes, *Leviathan, Volume Two*, Introduction, 18.

139. Hobbes, *The Elements of Law, Natural and Politic*, 1.4.10.
140. Hobbes, "The Questions Concerning Liberty, Necessity, and Chance," 194.
141. Hobbes, 398.
142. Hobbes, 398–99. Emphasis added.
143. Hobbes, 399.
144. Hobbes, *Leviathan, Volume Two*, 11, 156.
145. Hobbes, 11, 158.
146. Hobbes, "A Dialogue between a Philosopher and a Student of the Common Laws of England," 14. As Paulette Carrive notes, Hobbes's opposition to various common law jurists was largely grounded in his contention that, as a result of the fact of natural equality, the generality of people was capable of rationally understanding law independent of extensive study and habituation available only to a few. Paulette Carrive, "Hobbes et les juristes de la common law," in *Thomas Hobbes: De la métaphysique à la politique*, ed. Martin Bertman and Michel Malherbe (Paris: Librairie Philosophique J. Vrin, 1989), 158.
147. Hobbes, "A Dialogue between a Philosopher and a Student of the Common Laws of England," 53.
148. Indeed, as Richard Tuck has observed, much of Hobbes's hostility to the Royal Society is grounded in this opposition to the location of exclusive knowledge in presumed-to-be-expert groups: "He mistrusted any privileged body of intellectuals who might come to have some kind of independent ideological authority over their fellow citizens." Richard Tuck, *Hobbes* (Oxford: Oxford University Press, 1989), 59. Despite this, in Noel Malcolm's account, Hobbes's mechanistic philosophy of nature was in many respects consistent with the scientific positions held by members of the Royal Society. Noel Malcolm, "Hobbes and the Royal Society," in *Aspects of Hobbes* (Oxford: Oxford University Press, 2002), 317–35.
149. Hobbes, *Leviathan, Volume Two*, 10, 34.
150. Hobbes, 10, 138.
151. Hobbes, 10, 146.
152. Hobbes, 18, 276.
153. Hobbes, 27, 460.
154. On Hobbes's political rejection of the aristocratic virtues, interests, or modes of elites, see Strauss, *The Political Philosophy of Hobbes*, 45; Richard Ashcraft, "Ideology and Class in Hobbes's Political Theory," *Political Theory* 6, no. 1 (1978): 51–52; Jean Hampton, *Hobbes and the Social Contract Tradition* (Cambridge: Cambridge University Press, 1986), 27; Don Herzog, *Happy Slaves: A Critique of Consent Theory* (Chicago: University of Chicago Press, 1989), 87–88; Deborah Baumgold, "Hobbes's Political Sensibility: The Menace of Political Ambition," in *Thomas Hobbes and Political Theory*, ed. Mary Dietz (Lawrence: University Press of Kansas, 1990), 74–90; Alan Ryan, "Hobbes's Political Phi-

losophy," in *The Cambridge Companion to Hobbes*, ed. Tom Sorell (Cambridge: Cambridge University Press, 1996), 217; Gabriella Slomp, *Thomas Hobbes and the Political Philosophy of Glory* (Basingstoke: Macmillan Press, 2000), 38; Sullivan, *Machiavelli, Hobbes, and the Formation of a Liberal Republicanism in England*, 93; Gabriella Slomp, "On Ambition, Greed, and Fear," in *Hobbes's* Behemoth: *Religion and Democracy*, ed. Tomaž Mastnak (Exeter: Imprint Academic, 2009), 137; Devin Stauffer, *Hobbes's Kingdom of Light: A Study of the Foundations of Modern Political Philosophy* (Chicago: University of Chicago Press, 2018), 258. For the contrary suggestion that his thought contains many aristocratic features and that Hobbes "was most decidedly a proponent of reform and revitalization of an aristocracy in disarray," see Neal Wood, "Thomas Hobbes and the Crisis of the English Aristocracy," *History of Political Thought* 1, no. 3 (1980): 437. For the classic study, against C. B. Macpherson, of Hobbes as a supporter of aristocratic virtue, see Keith Thomas, "The Social Origins of Hobbes's Political Thought," in *Hobbes Studies*, ed. K. C. Brown (Oxford: Basil Blackwell, 1965), 185–236.

155. Hobbes, *Leviathan, Volume Two*, 10, 148.

156. Hobbes, 10, 148.

157. On Hobbes's rejection of the notion that a right to rule can be grounded in any substantive qualification, such as a superior reason or intelligence, see Strauss, *The Political Philosophy of Hobbes*, 158–59; M. M. Goldsmith, *Hobbes's Science of Politics* (New York: Columbia University Press, 1966), 148; Harvey C. Mansfield, "Hobbes and the Science of Indirect Government," *American Political Science Review* 65, no. 1 (1971): 100; Coleman, *Hobbes and America*, 60; Mace, *Locke, Hobbes, and the Federalist Papers*, 33–34; Nerney, "The Hobbesian Argument for Human Equality," 564; Hampton, *Hobbes and the Social Contract Tradition*, 26; Fritz Levy, "The Background of Hobbes's *Behemoth*," in *The Historical Imagination in Early Modern Britain: History, Rhetoric, and Fiction, 1500–1800*, ed. Donald R. Kelley and David Harris Sacks (Cambridge: Cambridge University Press, 1997), 246; Richard E. Flathman, "Hobbes: Premier Theorist of Authority," *Hobbes Studies* 10, no. 1 (1997): 3–22; Moloney, "Leaving the Garden of Eden," 261; Geoffrey M. Vaughan, Behemoth *Teaches* Leviathan: *Thomas Hobbes on Political Education* (Lanham, MD: Lexington Books, 2002), 34; Sullivan, *Machiavelli, Hobbes, & the Formation of a Liberal Republicanism in England*, 87; Paul Downes, *Hobbes, Sovereignty, and Early American Literature* (Cambridge: Cambridge University Press, 2015), 33; David Runciman, "The Sovereign," in *The Oxford Handbook of Hobbes*, edited by A. P. Martinich and Kinch Hoekstra (Oxford: Oxford University Press, 2016), 359.

158. Hobbes, *The Elements of Law, Natural and Politic*, 1.17.1. Joanne Paul has shown how this principle was also deployed in his struggle against parliamentarianism. Joanne Paul, "Council, Command and Crisis," *Hobbes Studies* 28, no. 2 (2015): 107–31. Specifically, Hobbes rejects Henry Parker's argument that Parliament, to the degree that it most adequately captures the

contours of popular interest through a proportional composition of a variety of elements mirroring that of the populace, has a unique insight into fundamental political things, thereby meriting a right to counsel. As Skinner reconstructs this parliamentarian conception, "when the people originally authorised Parliament to speak and act in their name, they brought into existence an assembly that remains a lifelike and exactly proportionate representation of their real body as a whole." Quentin Skinner, "Hobbes on Representation," *European Journal of Philosophy* 13, no. 2 (2005): 164. Thus the voice of Parliament can be taken as identical with the voice of the people. Hobbes, on the contrary, "denies any political body a right to give advice, completely subjecting counsel to the will of the sovereign." Paul, "Council, Command and Crisis," 130.

159. Such a position has been criticized not only by readers of an aristocratic orientation, but democratic ones as well. Sheldon Wolin is a prominent example of the latter type, as he criticizes the fact that within Hobbes's oeuvre "no extended discussion is to be found concerning the education or moral qualities necessary to the exercise of sovereignty." Sheldon Wolin, "Hobbes and the Epic Tradition," in *Fugitive Democracy and Other Essays*, by Sheldon Wolin, ed. Nicholas Xenos (Princeton, NJ: Princeton University Press, 2016), 133. We should note, however, that not all readers share this interpretation. J. Matthew Hoye, for example, has recently argued that Hobbes's thought manifests a certain type of virtue ethic, as represented in his recognition that sovereigns who lack particular virtues of ruling, in particular magnanimity, often meet their demise. J. Matthew Hoye, "Obligation and Sovereign Virtue in Hobbes's *Leviathan*," *Review of Politics* 79, no. 1 (2017): 23–47. See also Ross Rudolph, "Hobbes et la psychologie morale: l'obligation et la vertu," in *Thomas Hobbes: Philosophie première, théorie de la science et politique*, ed. Yves Charles Zarka (Paris: Presses Universitaires de France, 1990), 247–63.

160. Hobbes, *Leviathan, Volume Two*, 8, 104.
161. Hobbes, 8, 104.
162. Hobbes, 8, 104.
163. Hobbes, 8, 104.
164. Hobbes, 8, 110.
165. Hobbes, 8, 104.
166. Hobbes, 8, 106.
167. Hobbes, 8, 104.
168. Hobbes, 8, 108.

169. As Ingrid Crepell has noted, in *Behemoth* "Hobbes consistently credits the people with the capacity to reason about politics to the extent necessary for the stability and development of a regime." Ingrid Crepell, "The Democratic Element in Hobbes's 'Behemoth,'" in *Hobbes's* Behemoth: *Religion and Democracy*, ed. Tomaž Mastnak (Exeter: Imprint Academic, 2009), 258. See also Mary G.

Dietz, "Hobbes's Subject as Citizen," in *Thomas Hobbes and Political Theory*, ed. Mary G. Dietz (Lawrence: University Press of Kansas, 1990), 99.

170. On this point see Stephen Holmes, "Political Psychology in Hobbes's *Behemoth*," in *Thomas Hobbes and Political Theory*, ed. Mary G. Dietz (Lawrence: University Press of Kansas, 1990), 120–52. For a critique of Hobbes for failing to fully render his defense of political absolutism compatible with his account of the limits of human rationality, see Sandra Leonie Field, "Hobbes and Human Irrationality," *Global Discourse* 5, no. 2 (2015): 207–20. For Field, Hobbes's political science is ultimately composed of two key elements that exist in uneasy tension with one another: "humans as complex material bodies in a network of mechanical forces, prone to passions and irrationality; and humans as subjects of right and obligation, morally exhortable by appeal to the standards of reason." Field, 207.

171. Herzog, *Happy Slaves*, 89. As Bernard Willms notes furthermore, "The ignorance of the people is not the result of the latter's stupidity, but is due to the influence of ignorant ecclesiastical Presbyterians, ambitious pseudo-politicians, who spread false definitions." Bernard Willms, "La politique comme philosophie première: Hobbes penseur radical de la politique," in *Thomas Hobbes: Philosophie première, théorie de la science et politique*, ed. Yves Charles Zarka (Paris: Presses Universitaires de France, 1990), 98. Speaking to the commonality of people being actively misled by the ambitious few, Donald Hansen opines that "there are few, if any, themes in Hobbes's work more prominent than this one." Donald W. Hanson, "Science, Prudence, and Folly in Hobbes's Political Theory," *Political Theory* 21, no. 4 (1993): 655.

172. Hobbes, "On Man," 52.

173. Hobbes, *Behemoth, or the Long Parliament*, 135.

174. Hobbes, 116.

175. Hobbes, 118.

176. Hobbes, 129.

177. Hobbes, 174–75.

178. See, for example, Hobbes, "On Man," 72.

179. Hobbes, *Behemoth, or the Long Parliament*, 177. Tracy Strong has suggested that Hobbes's political thought was an effort to apply to civil affairs the logic underlying Luther's reconceptualization of interpretation and authority: "The key lay in finding an equivalent in politics for Scripture, that is, a written document that, when taught, allowed each person severally access to the same authority without ever being able to claim that she or he knew what the author intended." Tracy B. Strong, "How to Write Scripture: Words, Authority, and Politics in Thomas Hobbes," *Critical Inquiry* 20, no. 1 (1993): 131.

180. It is important to remember that *Behemoth* is not intended to function as a literal narration or re-presentation of a trajectory of factual events.

Like all of Hobbes's histories, it is a political intervention intended to persuade and instruct. See, for example, Royce MacGillivray, "Thomas Hobbes's History of the English Civil War: A Study of *Behemoth*," *Journal of the History of Ideas* 31, no. 2 (1970): 182–84; Patricia Springborg, "*Leviathan*, Mythic History, and National Historiography," in *The Historical Imagination in Early Modern Britain: History, Rhetoric, and Fiction, 1500–1800*, ed. Donald R. Kelley and David Harris Sacks (Cambridge: Cambridge University Press), 292–93.

181. Hobbes, *Behemoth, or the Long Parliament*, 322.
182. Hobbes, 322.
183. Hobbes, 323.
184. Hobbes, 323–24.
185. Hobbes, 323.

Chapter 5

1. Cornelius Castoriadis, "The Greek Polis and the Creation of Democracy," in *Philosophy, Politics, Autonomy: Essays in Political Philosophy*, ed. and trans. by David Ames Curtis (New York: Oxford University Press, 1991), 103. For Castoriadis's account of the main metaphysical principles of ancient Greek thought relevant to the invention of democracy and expressed in the work of figures such as Homer, Hesiod, Anaximander, and Heraclitus, see Cornelius Castoriadis, *Ce qui fait la Grèce, 1: D'Homère à Héraclite*, ed. Enrique Escobar, Myrto Gondicas, and Pascal Vernay (Paris: Seuil, 2004).

2. Josiah Ober, *The Athenian Revolution: Essays on Ancient Greek Democracy and Political Theory* (Princeton, NJ: Princeton University Press, 1996), 11.

3. Castoriadis, "The Greek Polis and the Creation of Democracy," 106–10. For Castoriadis's most sustained discussion of the nature of ancient Athenian democracy, see Cornelius Castoriadis, *La cité et les lois: Ce qui fait la Grèce, 2.*, ed. Enrique Escobar, Myrto Gondicas, and Pascal Vernay (Paris: Éditions du Seuil, 2008).

4. Josiah Ober, "The Original Meaning of 'Democracy': Capacity to Do Things, Not Majority Rule," *Constellations* 15, no. 1 (2008): 3.

5. Ober, 7.

6. For a summary of some of the most dominant contemporary approaches to interpreting Hobbes's laws of nature, see S. A. Lloyd, *Morality in the Philosophy of Thomas Hobbes: Cases in the Law of Nature* (Cambridge: Cambridge University Press, 2009), 151–210.

7. David van Mill has pointed out the extent to which Hobbes was ethically committed to an idea of autonomy, despite his belief that the realization of autonomy was impossible within assembly contexts: "To be fully autonomous, individuals have to formulate a rational-life plan in terms of finding the best means to ends, and choosing the best ends dictated to us by reason." David van Mill,

Liberty, Rationality, and Agency in Hobbes (Albany: State University of New York Press, 2001), 74. In van Mill's account, however, not all individuals are capable of living up to this ideal, to the extent that he sees practical rationality, which all individuals have the capacity for, as insufficient for autonomy's realization. From the standpoint of autonomy, ends must be rationally reconciled with a general normative orientation that takes priority over instrumental consideration of immediate interest, the latter being the object of practical reason. van Mill, 90. As noted in chapter 4, however, I don't take there to be evidence that Hobbes divorces practical rationality from such a normative project in the way suggested by van Mill.

    8. As Francis Edward Devine rightfully notes, for Hobbes "the fundamental fact of politics is conflict." Francis Edward Devine, "Hobbes: The Theoretical Basis of Political Compromise," *Polity* 5, no. 1 (1972): 69. Hobbes, however, refuses to conceptually distinguish between agonistic and antagonistic manifestations of this conflict, entirely reducing the former to the latter. This is recognized in Raia Prokhovnik, "Hobbes, Sovereignty, and Politics: Rethinking International Political Space," in *International Political Theory after Hobbes: Analysis, Interpretation and Orientation*, ed. Raia Prokhovnik and Gabriella Slomp (Basingstoke: Palgrave Macmillan, 2010), 205.

    9. On Hobbes's rejection of such a conception of natural law see, for example, Leo Strauss, *The Political Philosophy of Hobbes: Its Basis and Genesis* (Chicago: Chicago University Press, 1952), viii; Kerry H. Whiteside, "Hobbes's Ultranominalist Critique of Natural Right," *Polity* 20, no. 3 (1988): 468; Richard Tuck, *Hobbes* (Oxford: Oxford University Press, 1989), 67; Gary K. Browning and Raia Prokhovnik, "Hobbes, Hegel and Modernity," *Hobbes Studies* 8, no. 1 (1995): 88; Arlene W. Saxonhouse, "Hobbes and the Beginnings of Modern Political Thought," in *Three Discourses*, by Thomas Hobbes, ed. Noel B. Reynolds and Arlene W. Saxonhouse (Chicago: University of Chicago Press, 1995), 150–51; Martin A. Bertman, "Justice and Contra-Natural Dissolution," *Hobbes Studies* 10, no. 1 (1997): 23; Andrew Lister, "Skepticism and Pluralism in Thomas Hobbes's Political Thought," *History of Political Thought* 29, no. 1 (1998): 35–60; Karlfriedrich Herbe, "Au-delà de la citoyenneté: Hobbes et le problème de l'autorité," *Rivista di Storia della Filosofia* 59, no. 1 (2004): 219–25; Timothy Stanton, "Hobbes and Locke on Natural Law and Jesus Christ," *History of Political Thought* 29, no. 1 (2008): 71; Jeffrey Barnouw, "Reason as Reckoning: Hobbes's Natural Law as Right Reason," *Hobbes Studies* 21, no. 1 (2008): 51; Perez Zagorin, *Hobbes and the Law of Nature* (Princeton, NJ: Princeton University Press, 2009), 114; Martin Loughlin, "The Political Jurisprudence of Thomas Hobbes," in *Hobbes and the Law*, ed. David Dyzenhaus and Thomas Poole (Cambridge: Cambridge University Press, 2012), 19.

    10. Thomas Hobbes, *The Elements of Law, Natural and Politic*, ed. Ferdinand Tönnies (London: Simpkin, Marshall, and Co., 1889), 1.15.1.

11. Thomas Hobbes, *On the Citizen*, ed. and trans. Richard Tuck and Michael Silverthorne (Cambridge: Cambridge University Press, 1998), 2.1.

12. Hobbes, *The Elements of Law, Natural and Politic*, 1.15.1.

13. Hobbes, 1.15.1.

14. As Iain Hampsher-Monk observes, "In *The Elements of Law* Hobbes had asserted that previous thinkers were mistaken in attempting to redefine natural law in terms of the common customs of men, for there could be no agreement about which customs are to count, and if all are to count, then to derive uniform, general prescriptions is impossible because of the diversity of customs deriving from men's various passions. The pursuit of a universal human *good* proved an illusory basis for human sociality." Iain Hampsher-Monk, *A History of Modern Political Thought: Major Political Thinkers from Hobbes to Marx* (Oxford: Blackwell Publishers, 1992), 29–30.

15. For a reading that counterposes Hobbes with those liberal projects that attempt to transcendently ground themselves in universal sacred ideals that are dangerously exclusive of that exterior to them, see Christopher Trigg, "Drones, Hobbes, and Liberal Enchantment," *Political Theology* 19, no. 7 (2018): 553–71. See also Michael Jackson, "Mushrooms, Like Men?," *Hobbes Studies* 13, no. 1 (2000): 57. For examples of the claim that Hobbes's laws of nature are consistent with various philosophical presuppositions of liberalism, see Theodore Waldman, "Hobbes on the Generation of a Public Person," in *Thomas Hobbes in His Time*, ed. Ralph Ross, Herbert W. Schneider, and Theodore Waldman (Minneapolis: University of Minnesota Press, 1974), 77–79; Malcolm, "Thomas Hobbes: Liberal Illiberal," *Journal of the British Academy*, no. 4 (2016): 121.

16. Thomas Hobbes, *Leviathan, Volume Two: The English and Latin Texts (i)*, ed. Noel Malcolm (Oxford: Clarendon Press, 2012), 27, 460.

17. In Kenneth Minogue's words, "The elitism of the philosophers was always to be seen as supporting one or other specific form of life (commended as 'natural') and Hobbes took the view that the inevitable obsolescence of any such particular way of life (a *summum bonum*) would endanger civil order itself." Kenneth Minogue, "From Precision to Peace: Hobbes and Political Language," *Hobbes Studies* 3, no. 1 (1990): 76.

18. Hobbes, *Leviathan, Volume Two*, 15, 242.

19. Michael Lobban, "Thomas Hobbes and the Common Law," in *Hobbes and the Law*, ed. David Dyzenhaus and Thomas Poole (Cambridge: Cambridge University Press, 2012), 39. A minority of readers assert that Hobbes should in fact be situated within the classical Aristotelian-Thomist tradition of natural law philosophy. Kody Cooper, for example, argues that Hobbes shares the two fundamental assumptions of the latter: an idea of an ultimate human good grounded in the perception of a fixed human nature that guides our activity, and the existence of positive norms corresponding to this fact which have a legal character. Kody

Cooper, *Thomas Hobbes and the Natural Law* (Notre Dame, IN: Notre Dame University Press, 2018), 3. For the suggestion that Hobbes's interpretation of the relation between civil and natural law specifically is in fact perfectly consistent with the natural law theory of civil life held by Aquinas, see also Mark C. Murphy, "Was Hobbes a Legal Positivist?," *Ethics* 105, no. 4 (1995): 846–73.

20. See Hobbes, *On the Citizen*, 1.2.

21. Hobbes, 1.2. Emphasis added.

22. For a reader such as David Gauthier, for example, Hobbes has not fully grasped his own conceptual innovation with respect to natural law and the political consequences that follow from it, this fact explaining his continued use of the traditional terminology: "Hobbes speaks of the laws of nature because he has not fully emancipated himself from the medieval conception of natural law." David Gauthier, *The Logic of* Leviathan: *The Moral and Political Theory of Thomas Hobbes* (Oxford: Oxford University Press, 1969), 70.

23. As Jeffrey Barnouw observes, Hobbes's reconfiguration of natural law, specifically his detachment of it from "objective immutable determinations of good and evil, to be recognized by some infallible faculty," was considered "anathema to his contemporaries." Barnouw, "Reason as Reckoning," 51.

24. On this point see Arash Abizadeh, "Thomas Hobbes et le droit naturel," in *Droit naturel: Relancer l'histoire*, ed. Xavier Dijon (Brussels: Bruylant, 2008), 333; Loughlin, "The Political Jurisprudence of Thomas Hobbes," 12; Devin Stauffer, *Hobbes's Kingdom of Light: A Study of the Foundations of Modern Political Philosophy* (Chicago: University of Chicago Press, 2018), 222. Abizadeh nevertheless argues that despite jettisoning Aquinas's specific assumption of a natural human sociality and his teleological cosmology, Hobbesian natural law remains like the Thomist in that it is foundationally grounded in self-evident first principles: "If for Aquinas the first normative principle which grounds natural law is *good is to be done and pursued*, for Hobbes it is *desire and pursue your own good*." Abizadeh, *Hobbes and the Two Faces of Ethics*, 110. The ground of natural law for Hobbes is thus the universally rational desire to live a good and contented life: "Natural law dictates leaving the state of nature because a life permanently condemned to it would be—and can be *known* to be—either a miserable life not worth living, or a short life, or both." Abizadeh, 136. The potential for the political extension of this thin first principle will be elaborated on below.

25. Johan Sommerville thus observes generally that "one of his most characteristic techniques was to take commonly held views and, by introducing a few changes, employ them to reach unfamiliar conclusions." Johan P. Sommerville, *Thomas Hobbes: Political Ideas in Historical Context* (Basingstoke: Macmillan, 1992), 2.

26. Quoted in Steven Shapin and Simon Schaffer, Leviathan *and the Air-Pump: Hobbes, Boyle, and the Experimental Life* (Princeton, NJ: Princeton University Press, 1985), 118.

27. For Robin Douglass, this emphasis on peace is evidence that there is in fact one prepolitical moral value structuring Hobbes's political theory and that Hobbes thereby should not be characterized as a theorist of the autonomy of the political: "In so far as the autonomy of the political position can be attributed to Hobbes, it is most plausibly construed as meaning that all other moral values are subsumed under peace, the value at the heart of his politics." Robin Douglass, "Hobbes and Political Realism," *European Journal of Political Theory* 19, no. 2 (2020): 15.

28. Hobbes, *On the Citizen*, 2.1. For a critique of the logic underlying Hobbes's affirmation regarding the universal desire for self-preservation as natural necessity, see Paul Hurley, "The Many Appetites of Thomas Hobbes," *History of Philosophy Quarterly* 7, no. 4 (1990): 391–407.

29. Hobbes, *Leviathan, Volume Two*, 14, 198.

30. Hobbes, 16, 242. There are, however, some prominent readings of Hobbes that do interpret these laws as specifically divine commands. See, for example, Howard Warrender, *The Political Philosophy of Hobbes: His Theory of Obligation* (Oxford: Oxford University Press, 1957); F. C. Hood, *The Divine Politics of Thomas Hobbes: An Interpretation of* Leviathan (Oxford: Clarendon Press, 1964); A. E. Taylor, "The Ethical Doctrine of Hobbes," in *Hobbes Studies*, ed. K. C. Brown (Oxford: Basil Blackwell, 1965), 33–55; A. P. Martinich, *The Two Gods of* Leviathan: *Thomas Hobbes on Religion and Politics* (Cambridge: Cambridge University Press, 1992); Glenn Burgess, "On Hobbesian Resistance Theory," *Political Studies* 42, no. 1 (1994): 62–83; John Deigh, "Reason and Ethics in Hobbes's *Leviathan*," *Journal of the History of Philosophy* 34, no. 1 (1996): 33–60; Cooper, *Thomas Hobbes and the Natural Law*. Indeed, the passage quoted here from *Leviathan* 16 does continue with: "But yet if we consider the same Theoremes, as delivered in the word of God, that by right commandeth all things; then they are properly called Lawes." Hobbes, *Leviathan, Volume Two*, 16, 242. The evidence that we should consider the laws of nature in this way, however, given Hobbes's statements on the impossibility of so approaching divine will, is very scant. Furthermore, putting aside all the textual evidence that suggests the laws of nature cannot be read as divine commands, Iain Hampsher-Monk notes in addition that such a reading "is entirely inconsistent with a major thrust of *Leviathan*, which is to deny to religion any independent source of authority which might undermine the secular power." Hampsher-Monk, *A History of Modern Political Thought*, 31.

31. For example, Thomas Hobbes, *Thomas White's* De mundo *Examined*, trans. Harold Whitmore Jones (London: Bradford University Press, 1976), 38.4.

32. Thomas Hobbes, "A Dialogue between a Philosopher and a Student of the Common Laws of England," in *The English Works of Thomas Hobbes of Malmesbury, Volume Six*, edited by Sir William Molesworth (London: John Bohn, 1840), 38.

33. Hobbes, *Leviathan, Volume Two*, 15, 240. In Michael Lobban's words, "To act equitably in an inequitable world would be self-contradictory, since it would lead to one's destruction rather than to one's desired self-preservation." Lobban, "Thomas Hobbes and the Common Law," 44.

34. On this point see Gary B. Herbert, "Thomas Hobbes's Dialectic of Desire," in *The English Works of Thomas Hobbes of Malmesbury, Volume Six*, ed. Sir William Molesworth (London: John Bohn, 1840), 146.

35. Thomas Hobbes, *Behemoth, or the Long Parliament*, ed. Paul Seaward (Oxford: Clarendon Press, 2010), 195. Carl Schmitt, noting that Hobbes's account of law is concerned not with the latter's substantive content but rather its origin in the decision to institute it, goes so far as to maintain that all commonwealths are intrinsically dictatorships, the sovereign being that entity that dictates through exercising the will to decide. Carl Schmitt, *Dictatorship: From the Origin of the Modern Concept of Sovereignty to the Proletarian Class Struggle*, trans. Michael Hoelzl and Graham Ward (Cambridge: Polity, 2014), 17. Such a position perhaps minimizes the degree to which the sovereign's right to decide is authorized by the people and also the extent to which natural law minimally orients the direction of the decision, as will be discussed below.

36. Thomas Hobbes, "An Answer to a Book Published by Dr. Bramhall, Late Bishop of Derry; Called the 'Catching of the Leviathan,'" in *The English Works of Thomas Hobbes of Malmesbury, Volume Four*, edited by Sir William Molesworth (London: John Bohn, 1840), 377.

37. Hobbes, *On the Citizen*, 6.16. Referring to this passage, Evan Fox-Decent nevertheless plausibly writes that "the central terms have *some* meaning that is intelligible independently of civil law, but the civil law is necessary to narrow the scope of the terms so as to make them applicable to particular cases." Evan Fox-Decent, "Hobbes's Relational Theory," in *Hobbes and the Law*, ed. David Dyzenhaus and Thomas Poole (Cambridge: Cambridge University Press, 2012), 138. For an even stronger claim regarding the laws of nature as embodying substantive moral virtues see Bernard Gert, "The Law of Nature as the Moral Law," *Hobbes Studies* 1, no. 1 (1988): 26–44.

38. For examples of how the specific content of the empty laws of nature are filled see David Undersrud, "On Natural Law and Civil Law in the Political Philosophy of Hobbes," *History of Political Thought* 35, no. 4 (2014): 700–702.

39. Hobbes, *On the Citizen*, 6.16.

40. Hobbes, *The Elements of Law, Natural and Politic*, 2.10.8.

41. On this point see Jared Lucky, "'Strange and Deformed Births' in Hobbes's Civil Science," *History of Political Thought* 37, no. 4 (2016): 630–57.

42. See, for example, R. E. Ewin, *Virtues and Rights: The Moral Philosophy of Thomas Hobbes* (Boulder, CO: Westview Press, 1991), 129; John R. Visintainer, "Hobbes on Goodness and Pressure on the Sovereign," *Hobbes Studies* 12, no. 1 (1999): 32; Victoria Kahn, *Wayward Contracts: The Crisis of*

Political Obligation in England, 1640–1674 (Princeton, NJ: Princeton University Press, 2004), 137.

43. In Martin Bertman's words, "unlike the natural law theorist of the Thomistic sort, Hobbes doesn't organize a system of moral definitions as a standard or ideal to test the civil laws of a particular state. Instead, the civil laws are a kind of definition. They all have the same purpose of securing peace by means of providing rules." Martin A. Bertman, "Equity as Justice and Charity in Hobbes," in *Thomas Hobbes: De la métaphysique à la politique* (Paris: Librairie Philosophique J. Vrin, 1989), 112.

44. As Thomas Harvey notes, the moral order that human beings institute, to the extent that it does not lean on a natural foundation that delimits its form, is created "essentially *ex nihilo*." Thomas Harvey, "Hobbes's Voluntarist Theory of Morals," *Hobbes Studies* 22, no. 1 (2009): 50. See also Pat Moloney, "Leaving the Garden of Eden: Linguistic and Political Authority in Thomas Hobbes," *History of Political Thought* 18, no. 2 (1997): 266.

45. Nicholas Gooding and Kinch Hoekstra have recently challenged the positing of a radical gap between Aristotle and Hobbes on the question of politics, noting that "Aristotle and Hobbes *agree* that we need to establish political communities in order to best satisfy our natural needs and natural desires, and even that humans display a natural tendency to form such communities." Nicholas Gooding and Kinch Hoekstra, "Hobbes and Aristotle on the Foundation of Political Science," in *Hobbes's* On the Citizen, ed. Robin Douglass and Johan Olsthoorn (Cambridge: Cambridge University Press, 2020), 32. The authors go on to argue that Hobbes's rejection of humans as political animals pivots on the Aristotelian conception of political *philia* and its articulation of the relation between agreement and law.

46. Hobbes, *Leviathan, Volume Two*, 17, 260.

47. Hobbes, 15, 220.

48. Hence in *The Questions Concerning Liberty, Necessity, and Chance* Hobbes maintains that the superiority of human beings over animals is to be found primarily in the capacity for self-legislation that derives from the invention of speech: "Man excelleth beasts only in *making of rules to himself*, that is to say, in remembering, and in reasoning right upon that which he remembereth. They which do so deserve an honour above brute beasts." Hobbes, "The Questions Concerning Liberty, Necessity, and Chance," in *The English Works of Thomas Hobbes of Malmesbury, Volume Five*, edited by Sir William Molesworth (London: John Bohn, 1841), 186. Emphasis added.

49. Jacques Rancière, *Disagreement: Politics and Philosophy*, trans. Julie Rose (Minneapolis: University of Minnesota Press, 1999), 17.

50. Rancière, 16. Much as readers of Hobbes are hesitant to take fully seriously the latter's positing of natural equality, so too the majority of Rancière's readers, in the words of Rachel Magnusson, "simply would like to avoid the politics

of the equality of intelligences and all of its implications." Rachel Magnusson, "A Politics in Writing: Jacques Rancière and the Equality of Intelligences," in *Thinking Radical Democracy: The Return to Politics in Post-War France*, ed. Martin Breaugh et al. (Toronto: University of Toronto Press, 2015), 204.

51. Rancière, *Disagreement*, 29.
52. Rancière, 29–30.
53. Rancière, 77.
54. For a situation of Hobbes's thought in the context of the history of political thought's general obsession with unification and "becoming one," see John Grant, "'Becoming One': Visions of Political Unity from the Ancients to the Postmoderns," *Constellations* 21, no. 4 (2014): 575–88.
55. For Roberto Esposito, Hobbes's operation—the theoretical effort to cover up or mask the abyssal and chaotic nature of being through the construction of an exclusive artificial order of things—is a manifestation of nihilism (in the Heideggerian sense): "He is not a nihilistic thinker because he 'discovered' the essential void created by the withdrawal of the transcendental *veritas*, but because he 're-covered' it with another void intended to neutralize its dissolutive effects." Roberto Esposito, *Immunitas: The Protection and Negation of Life*, trans. Zakiya Hanofi (London: Polity, 2011), 86. The effacement of all sociality beyond that necessary to institute the commonwealth is that artificial void intended to occult or conceal the natural one. To this degree "the Leviathan-State coincides with the breaking of every communitarian bond, with the squelching of every social relation that is foreign to the vertical exchange of command-obedience." Roberto Esposito, *Communitas: The Origin and Destiny of Community*, trans. Timothy Campbell (Stanford, CA: Stanford University Press, 2010), 14.
56. See Bertman, "Justice and Contra-Natural Dissolution," 36. For a reading of Hobbes as wanting to complete Plato's project, the Hobbesian ideal of the state being interpreted as a Platonic one ruled by a philosophically inclined sovereign, see Craig, *The Platonian Leviathan* (Toronto: University of Toronto Press, 2010). See also David Johnston, "Plato, Hobbes, and the Science of Practical Reasoning," in *Thomas Hobbes and Political Theory*, ed. Mary G. Dietz (Lawrence: University Press of Kansas, 1990), 37–54; Karl Schuhmann, "Hobbes and the Political Thought of Plato and Aristotle," in *Selected Papers on Renaissance Philosophy and on Thomas Hobbes*, ed. Piet Steenbakkers and Cees Leijenhorst (Berlin: Springer-Science + Business Media, 2004), 191–207.
57. In the words of Michael Hardt and Antonio Negri, "the transcendence of the sovereign is founded not on an external theological support but only on the immanent logic of human relations." Hardt and Negri, *Empire* (Cambridge, MA: Harvard University Press, 2000), 84. For the authors, however, such an artificial transcendence, in which subjects authorize their own alienation via the mechanism of representation, can never be genuinely democratic. For them Hobbesian sovereignty must always be the substitution of one order of violence for another,

genuine pluralism being impossible in the face of sovereign monopolization of violence. Michael Hardt and Antonio Negri, *Multitude: War and Democracy in the Age of Empire* (New York: Penguin Press, 2004), 239. Needless to say, I do not find their reading adequately sensitive to the specificity of the exercise of sovereignty in a genuinely democratic commonwealth, the Hobbesian potential for which they ignore. As Gordon Hull notes, for Hardt and Negri, as well as for many other contemporary radical democratic political theorists, Hobbes is specifically counterposed with his reader Spinoza, the latter alone being seen as providing a philosophical ground for thinking democracy. In Hull's words, "If Spinoza is the hero of this narrative, Hobbes is the enemy revenant." Gordon Hull, *Hobbes and the Making of Modern Political Thought* (London: Continuum, 2009), 4. For just one of many contributions examining the affinities between Hobbes and Spinoza, see William Sacksteder, "How Much of Hobbes Might Spinoza Have Read?," *Southwestern Journal of Philosophy* 11, no. 2 (1990): 25–39.

58. See, for example, Hanna Pitkin, *The Concept of Representation* (Berkeley: University of California Press, 1967), 35; Sheldon Wolin, "Hobbes and the Culture of Despotism," in *Thomas Hobbes and Political Theory*, ed. Mary G. Dietz (Lawrence: University Press of Kansas, 1990), 33; Paul A. Rahe, *Republics Ancient and Modern, Volume II: New Modes and Orders in Early Modern Political Thought* (Chapel Hill: University of North Carolina Press, 1994), 157; Vickie B. Sullivan, *Machiavelli, Hobbes, and the Formation of a Liberal Republicanism in England* (Cambridge: Cambridge University Press, 2004), 83; Giuseppe Duso, "Hobbes et l'invention moderne du pouvoir," *Hobbes Studies* 27, no. 1 (2005): 40; Dick Howard, *The Primacy of the Political: A History of Political Thought From the Greeks to the French and American Revolutions* (New York: Columbia University Press, 2010), 226–27; Sheldon Wolin, "Hobbes and the Epic Tradition," in *Fugitive Democracy and Other Essays*, by Sheldon Wolin, ed. Nicholas Xenos (Princeton, NJ: Princeton University Press, 2016), 148. For the contrary suggestion, that the Hobbesian framework does not necessarily preclude active political participation, and may in fact depend on it, see, Alan Ryan, "Hobbes and Individualism," in *Perspectives on Thomas Hobbes*, ed. G. A. J. Rogers and Alan Ryan (Oxford: Clarendon Press, 1988), 105; Evan Oxman, "Hobbes on the Artificiality of (His Own) Authority," *Hobbes Studies* 31, no. 2 (2018): 188–211.

59. Yves Charles Zarka, "The Political Subject," in *Leviathan After 350 Years*, ed. Tom Sorell and Luc Foisneau, trans. Edward Hughes (Oxford: Oxford University Press, 2004), 177. See also George Shulman, "Metaphor and Modernization in the Political Thought of Thomas Hobbes," *Political Theory* 17, no. 3 (1989): 404. Tom Sorrel wonders whether under such conditions the subject may be considered a citizen in any meaningful sense of the term: "According to Aristotle, it is essential to being a citizen that one have a turn at holding political office and a hand in the state's judicial functions. A subject in Hobbes's sort of commonwealth fulfils the requirements of membership in the body politic

by obeying the sovereign, and definitely not by pressing into service a capacity for practical judgement and decision-making." Tom Sorell, *Hobbes* (London: Routledge & Kegan Paul, 1986), 123–24. For a contrary reading, suggesting that Hobbes produces a multifaceted and rich conception of citizenship within a commonwealth, see Raymond Polin, "Hobbes et le citoyen," in *Thomas Hobbes: Philosophie première, théorie de la science et politique*, ed. Yves Charles Zarka (Paris: Presses Universitaires de France, 1990), 327–37.

60. For an account of the various institutional means the sovereign may deploy to overcome the natural differentiation of desire and value, see Jean Pierre Marcos, "Figures et fonctions du tiers chez Hobbes," *Hobbes Studies* 11, no. 1 (1998): 13–32.

61. As Philippe Crignon puts it, "Because they are mutually differentiated, men have become strangers and opaque to one another; they struggle to know and understand each other." Philippe Crignon, "Diversité humaine et pluralisme: La reprise d'un thème hobbesien dans le libéralisme contemporain," in *Hobbes et le libéralisme*, ed. Yves Charles Zarka (Paris: Éditions Mimésis, 2016), 92.

62. For an example of a reading that resists the interpretation of the Hobbesian project in terms of "the unification of wills and the elimination of differences," see David Panagia, "Delicate Discriminations: Thomas Hobbes's Science of Politics," *Polity* 36, no. 1 (2003): 109. These two operations, however—"the unification of wills and the elimination of differences"—are very different, and although Hobbes seems to think that on a certain level the latter is possible through sovereign decisionism, the former is not. Hobbes never means to suggest that the process of authorization is intended to generate a literal homogenization of desire through the coalescence of the plurality of particular wills into a single one. Indeed, as Sharon Lloyd reminds us, he clearly criticizes Bramhall's contention that the direction of will is capable of being manipulated in such a way: "Hobbes repeatedly insists in his debate with Bramhall that we are not free to will what we will; our will is the product of our appetites and opinions, and the content of these appetites and opinions is determined not by our choice, but by our experience and natural constitution." S. A. Lloyd, "Authorization and Moral Responsibility in the Philosophy of Hobbes," *Hobbes Studies* 29, no. 2 (2016): 187.

63. Duncan Ivison, "The Secret History of Public Reason: Hobbes to Rawls," *History of Political Thought* 18, no. 1 (1997): 132. In this paper Ivison helpfully traces out the intellectual legacy of the Hobbesian conception of public reason.

64. Richard E. Flathman, "Hobbes: Premier Theorist of Authority," *Hobbes Studies* 10, no. 1 (1997): 19.

65. Richard E. Flathman, *Thomas Hobbes: Skepticism, Individuality, and Chastened Politics* (Lanham, MD: Rowman & Littlefield, 2002), 148.

66. For a representative interpretation of Hobbes as a command theorist of law who anticipates the legal positivist tradition, see Martin A. Bertman,

"Hobbes on the Character and Use of Civil Law," in *Hobbes oggi*, ed. Andrea Napoli and Guido Canziani (Milano: Franco Angeli, 1990), 159–76. For what H. L. A. Hart sees as the affinities between Hobbes's account and his own understanding of the minimum content of natural law, see H. L. A. Hart, *The Concept of Law* (Oxford: Clarendon Press, 1961), 191. For David Dyzenhaus's well-known statement on how the laws of nature militate against reading Hobbes as a command theorist or legal positivist, see David Dyzenhaus, "Hobbes on the Authority of the Law," in *Hobbes and the Law*, ed. David Dyzenhaus and Thomas Poole (Cambridge: Cambridge University Press, 2012), 186–209; David Dyzenhaus, "Hobbes and the Legitimacy of the Law," *Law and Philosophy* 20, no. 5 (2001): 461–98.

67. In the words of Sharon Lloyd, for whom Hobbes's natural law theory is fundamentally "self-effacing": "Natural law has supreme authority; but it directs us, first and foremost, to act as if legal positivism were true." Lloyd, *Morality in the Philosophy of Thomas Hobbes: Cases in the Law of Nature*, 280. See also Norberto Bobbio, "Natural Law and Civil Law in the Political Philosophy of Hobbes," in *Thomas Hobbes and the Natural Law Tradition*, trans. Daniela Gobetti (Chicago: University of Chicago Press, 1993), 114–48; Norberto Bobbio, "Hobbes and Natural Law Theory," in *Thomas Hobbes and the Natural Law Tradition*, trans. Daniela Gobetti (Chicago: University of Chicago Press, 1993), 149–71.

68. Abizadeh, *Hobbes and the Two Faces of Ethics*, 237. See also David Dyzenhaus, "How Hobbes Met the Hobbes Challenge," *Modern Law Review* 72, no. 3 (2009): 492–93; Fox-Decent, "Hobbes's Relational Theory," 130–31. For the claim that it is possible to read Hobbes both as a theorist of legal positivism and as affirming certain moral criteria delimiting the acceptable range of civil law, see Perez Zagorin, *Hobbes and the Law of Nature* (Princeton, NJ: Princeton University Press, 2009), 95.

69. See, for example, George Mace, *Locke, Hobbes, and the Federalist Papers* (Carbondale: Southern Illinois University Press, 1979), 59; Larry May, "Hobbes on Fidelity to Law," *Hobbes Studies* 5, no. 1 (1992): 77–89; Peter J. Steinberger, "Hobbesian Resistance," *American Journal of Political Science* 46, no. 4 (2002): 856–65; Eleanor Curran, *Reclaiming the Rights of the Hobbesian Subject* (Basingstoke: Palgrave Macmillan, 2007), 95–97; Susanne Sreedhar, *Hobbes on Resistance: Defying the Leviathan* (Cambridge: Cambridge University Press, 2010); Larry May, *Limiting Leviathan: Hobbes on Law and International Affairs* (Oxford: Oxford University Press, 2013); Christopher R. Hallenbrook, "Leviathan No More: The Right of Nature and the Limits of Sovereignty in Hobbes," *Review of Politics* 78, no. 2 (2016): 177–200; Abizadeh, *Hobbes and the Two Faces of Ethics*, 232; Susanne Sreedhar, "Interpreting Hobbes on Civil Liberties and Rights of Resistance," in *Interpreting Hobbes's Political Philosophy*, ed. S. A. Lloyd (Cambridge: Cambridge University Press, 2019), 141–55.

70. Hobbes, *Leviathan, Volume Two*, 21, 324.

71. Hobbes, 14, 198.

72. David van Mill, *Liberty, Rationality, and Agency in Hobbes* (Albany: State University of New York Press, 2001), 48. See also F. C. Hood, "The Change in Hobbes's Definition of Liberty," *Philosophical Quarterly* 17, no. 67 (1967): 150; Quentin Skinner, "Thomas Hobbes's Antiliberal Theory of Liberty," in *Liberalism without Illusions: Essays on Liberal Theory and the Political Vision*, ed. Bernard Yack (Chicago: University of Chicago Press, 1996), 154. For a statement on how Hobbes's scheme should be seen to correspond to the classical negative conception of liberty, see M. M. Goldsmith, "Hobbes on Liberty," *Hobbes Studies* 2, no. 1 (1989): 23–39.

73. Hobbes, *Leviathan, Volume Two*, 14, 198.

74. As Theodore Waldman articulates the idea: "Natural or original power refers to the abilities that a man has as an individual to obtain some future apparent good. It is a reflection of what he is as a creature. This is an amplification of his other statement on power in which he emphasized the inner capacity of an individual to move." Waldman, "Hobbes on the Generation of a Public Person," 71.

75. Hobbes, *Leviathan, Volume Two*, 5, 68.

76. Hobbes, 21, 324. Ralph Ross has characterized Hobbes's formulation here, of a free person as possessing both the liberty and the power to do what they would will, as "a condition that might be called effective freedom." Ralph Ross, "Some Puzzles in Hobbes," in *Thomas Hobbes in His Time*, ed. Ralph Ross, Herbert W. Schneider, and Theodore Waldman (Minneapolis: University of Minnesota Press, 1974), 44. On the essential connection of power and freedom for Hobbes see also Hood, "The Change in Hobbes's Definition of Liberty," 150; Skinner, "Thomas Hobbes's Antiliberal Theory of Liberty," 151–52; David James, "Hobbes's Argument for the 'Naturalness' and 'Necessity' of Colonization," *History of Political Thought* 38, no. 3 (2017): 444.

77. Hobbes, *Thomas White's* De mundo *Examined*, 33.2.

78. Hobbes, 33.3.

79. Hobbes, 33.4.

80. Thomas Hobbes, "Of Liberty and Necessity: A Treatise, Wherein All Controversy Concerning Predestination, Election, Free-Will, Grace, Merits, Reprobation, &c Is Fully Decided and Cleared," in *The English Works of Thomas Hobbes of Malmesbury, Volume Four*, edited by Sir William Molesworth (London: John Bohn, 1840), 240.

81. See, for example, Hobbes, "Of Liberty and Necessity," 247.

82. Hobbes, "The Questions Concerning Liberty, Necessity, and Chance," 154.

83. Hobbes, 372–73.

84. Hobbes, *Leviathan, Volume Two*, 21, 326.

85. Hobbes, *Thomas White's* De mundo *Examined*, 6.6.

86. Juhani Pietarinen, "Conatus as Active Power in Hobbes," *Hobbes Studies* 14, no. 1 (71–82): 71.

87. Pietarinen, 78.

88. Pietarinen, 78. On how this idea of active power remains in uneasy tension with various elements of Hobbes's first philosophy, see also Juhani Pietarinen, "Motion and Reason: Hobbes's Difficulties with the Idea of Active Power," in *The World as Active Power*, ed. Valtteri Viljanen and Juhani Pietarinen (Leiden: Brill, 2009), 185–212.

89. Hobbes, "Seven Philosophical Problems and Two Propositions of Geometry," in *The English Works of Thomas Hobbes of Malmesbury, Volume Seven*, ed. Sir William Molesworth (London: Longman, Brown, Green, and Longmans, 1845), 12.

90. Needless to say, however, human beings also share a set of additional universal faculties, such as curiosity, speech, and reason. Indeed, to the extent that they possess these capacities, they have a power and hence a freedom to do things that other beings cannot, the ability to deploy a nomenclature in order to construct propositions and syllogisms, for example, thus opening up a range of possible modes for the realization of their shared end. Hobbes, *Thomas White's De mundo Examined*, 37.8. Arash Abizadeh recognizes that Hobbes's concept of natural law includes an active power component that reveals something very specific about the being of the human: "Natural law includes the capacity to modify, by convention, the purely natural condition when the necessities of survival seem to require it. Human beings can in the final instance thereby act, by means of the expression of their will, because they have by natural right *an authority to modify*, that is say to create meaning. Humans are the intelligent and creative 'authors' of their acts." Abizadeh, "Thomas Hobbes et le droit naturel," 345. Natural law thus expresses the specifically human capacity to overcome the seemingly natural structure of the world and human life.

91. Hobbes, "On Man," in *Man and Citizen (De Homine and De Cive)*, trans. Charles T. Wood, T. S. K. Scott-Craig, and Bernard Gert (Indianapolis: Hackett, 1991), 48.

92. For differing statements on the extent to which Hobbes's civil science derives its normative force from a consideration of the facts of natural being see, for example, Herbert, "Thomas Hobbes's Dialectic of Desire," 144; Simone Goyard-Fabre, "Right and Anthropology in Hobbes's Philosophy," in *Thomas Hobbes: His View of Man*, ed. J. G. van der Bend (Amsterdam: Rodopi, 1982), 17–30; Martin A. Bertman, "Regulative and Constitutive Rules in Hobbes," in *Thomas Hobbes: His View of Man*, ed. J. G. van der Bend (Amsterdam: Rodopi, 1982), 14; Derek Reiners, "Biological Correctness: Thomas Hobbes's Natural Ethics," *Hobbes Studies* 21, no. 1 (2008): 63–83.

93. Pierre Garniron, "Hobbes dans les leçons d'histoire de la philosophie de Hegel," in *Thomas Hobbes : Philosophie première, théorie de la science et politique*, ed. Yves Charles Zarka (Paris: Presses Universitaires de France, 1990), 395.

94. Hobbes, *The Elements of Law, Natural and Politic*, 2.9.1.
95. Hobbes, 2.9.3.
96. Hobbes, 2.9.4.
97. Hobbes, 2.5.1.
98. Hobbes, 2.9.4.
99. For a reading detailing the extent to which Hobbes's concept of public safety should be seen as including an economic content, one sufficient enough to warrant identifying him as a political economist, see Tom Sorell, "Hobbes, Public Safety and Political Economy," in *International Political Theory after Hobbes: Analysis, Interpretation and Orientation*, ed. Raia Prokhovnik and Gabriella Slomp (Basingstoke: Palgrave Macmillan, 42–55). See also Lee Ward, "Equity and Political Economy in Thomas Hobbes," *American Journal of Political Science* 64, no. 4 (2020): 823–35. David Lay Williams has recently shown, furthermore, that Hobbes's egalitarianism extends well beyond mere sufficiency, it being concerned not just with ensuring an adequate standard of living for all, but addressing the social and psychological problems that result from the excessive concentration of wealth in the hands of a few. Ultimately the preservation of the commonwealth necessitates the minimization of economic inequality, which is to be achieved through active redistribution, education, and the restraint of economic elites. David Lay Williams, "Hobbes on Wealth, Poverty and Economic Inequality," *Hobbes Studies* 34, no. 1 (2021): 9–57.

100. As Rosamund Rhodes writes with reference to the principle of mutual accommodation, for example: "Reading Hobbes by keeping the importance of the fifth Law of Nature in focus, allows us to appreciate that it commands not only redistribution of such things as food and shelter, but also access to other goods that people could see as critically important to living well such as health care and education." Rosamund Rhodes, "Hobbes's Fifth Law of Nature and Its Implications," *Hobbes Studies* 22, no. 2 (2009): 156. See also Yoshinori Suzuki, "Thomas Hobbes on Social Welfare," *Hobbes Studies* 11, no. 1 (1998): 46–60. In Johan Olsthoorn's account, recognition of the sovereign's right to define just distribution in resources is sufficient to invalidate Macpherson's reading of Hobbes, distribution being irreducible to competitive market forces, as Macpherson assumes. Johan Olsthoorn, "Hobbes on Justice, Property Rights and Self-Ownership," *History of Political Thought* 36, no. 3 (2015): 479. For the contrary suggestion, that there is a certain counterstrain in Hobbes's thought affirming a right to property that exists prior to sovereign institution, see Benjamin B. Lopata, "Property Theory in Hobbes," *Political Theory* 1, no. 2 (1973): 203–18.

101. Hobbes, *Leviathan, Volume Two*, Introduction, 16.

102. Eleanor Curran calls the extended right to all that which is necessary for the preservation of a commodious life the right to "full preservation": "It includes the right not only to preserve our lives but also to the conditions that are necessary for basic human well-being or flourishing." Curran, *Reclaiming the Rights of the Hobbesian Subject*, 109.

103. Hobbes, *On the Citizen*, 13.4. Hence, as Raffaella Santi puts it, "The duty of the sovereign is to ensure not only that the people live, but live well. The *telos* of politics is thus constituted by safety and well-being." Raffaella Santi, "Thomas Hobbes, John Stuart Mill et la liberté," in *Hobbes et le libéralisme*, ed. Yves Charles Zarka (Paris: Éditions Mimésis, 2016), 64–65.

104. Hobbes, *On the Citizen*, 13.4.

105. Hobbes, *Leviathan, Volume Two*, 30, 520.

106. Hobbes, 30, 520.

107. Hobbes, 30, 520.

108. Hobbes, "A Dialogue between a Philosopher and a Student of the Common Laws of England," 70.

109. Hobbes, *Behemoth, or the Long Parliament*, 195. Joshua Cohen articulates the common skepticism regarding the likelihood of the sovereign respecting its obligation to advance the security of the subjects, on the basis of the recognition of the sovereign occupier's own particular interests and passions as a natural person: "We have no reason in general to expect the sovereign to conform to the terms of the sovereign's office—to ensure the 'safety of the people'—despite the natural law obligation to do so." Joshua Cohen, "Getting Past Hobbes," in *Hobbes Today: Insights for the 21st Century*, ed. S. A. Lloyd (Cambridge: Cambridge University Press, 2013), 14. According to one view, however, if the sovereign fails to maintain the commonwealth in a state in which the enjoyment of those things necessary to facilitate a contented life is not preserved, then the social contract is voided: by failing to maintain the safety of the people the sovereign demonstrates that it is not in fact sovereign, individuals thus being returned to a state of nature in full possession of their natural rights, and the problem identified is dissolved. See, for example, Peter J. Steinberger, "Hobbes, Rousseau, and the Modern Conception of the State," *Journal of Politics* 70, no. 3 (2008): 606–7.

110. Hobbes, *The Elements of Law, Natural and Politic*, 1.17.2.

111. Hobbes, 1.17.2. For an account of the ways in which Hobbes's absolute right to life may be conceptually extended to produce a wide range of subservient rights, see Renato Janine Ribeiro, "'Men of Feminine Courage': Thomas Hobbes and Life as a Right," *Hobbes Studies* 24, no. 1 (2011): 44–61.

112. Hobbes, *On the Citizen*, 3.14.

113. It should be noted that Quentin Skinner has suggested that after *Leviathan* Hobbes may have abandoned the idea of the true liberty of the subject, perhaps being persuaded by the criticisms levied by individuals like Robert Filmer. Quentin Skinner, "Historical Introduction," in *Writings on Common Law and Hereditary Right*, by Thomas Hobbes, ed. Alan Cromartie and Quentin Skinner (Oxford: Clarendon Press, 2005), 169. See Thomas Hobbes, "Questions Relative to Hereditary Right," in *Writings on Common Law and Hereditary Right*, ed. Alan Cromartie and Quentin Skinner (Oxford: Clarendon Press, 2005), 177–78.

114. Hobbes, *Leviathan, Volume Two*, 21, 336. As Eleanor Curran points out, the concept of the true liberty of the subjects cannot be comprehended if the idea of freedom is entirely reduced to the restrictive definition as the mere absence of impediments to motion. Eleanor Curran, "Blinded by the Light of Hohfeld: Hobbes's Notion of Liberty," *Jurisprudence* 1, no. 1 (2010): 95–97.

115. Hobbes, *Leviathan, Volume Two*, 21, 336–38.

116. Hobbes, 21, 336.

117. Sreedhar, *Hobbes on Resistance*, 53.

118. Richard Tuck, *Natural Rights Theories: Their Origins and Development* (Cambridge: Cambridge University Press, 1979), 122.

119. For example, according to Yves Charles Zarka the notion of the true liberty of subjects provides the foundation for the reconstruction of a specifically political subject within the Hobbesian framework, distinct from the more apparent deprived or nonpolitical subject. Zarka, "The Political Subject," 182.

120. Hobbes, *Leviathan, Volume Two*, 21, 338. Note, however, that Hobbes goes on to maintain that if the sovereign makes an offer of pardon to any such actor, then their participation in the resistance of the rest becomes immediately unjust, for through the pardon the threat to their well-being has been dissolved.

121. Sreedhar, *Hobbes on Resistance*, 139.

122. Sreedhar, 141–42. As Sreedhar is careful to emphasize, though, this Hobbesian right can only legitimate rebellion from necessity, not ideological rebellion. For further recognition of the significance of this particular passage within *Leviathan*, and how it reveals the possibility of translating Hobbes's individual right to self-defense into a political right to resist sovereign authority, see Burgess, "On Hobbesian Resistance Theory," 68–69; Lee Ward, "Thomas Hobbes and John Locke on a Liberal Right of Secession," *Political Research Quarterly* 70, no. 4 (2017): 878–81. For the contrary claim, one that rejects the possibility of such a translation, see Patricia Sheridan, "Resisting the Scaffold: Self-Preservation and Limits of Obligation in Hobbes's *Leviathan*," *Hobbes Studies* 24, no. 2 (2011): 137–57.

123. See, for example, Panagia, "Delicate Discriminations," 110.

124. Arash Abizadeh has noted the extent to which the Hobbesian sovereign can never possess the quantum of coercive power needed to rule on that basis alone and thus must also utilize a symbolic power interpreted in terms of charismatic authority. Arash Abizadeh, "The Representation of Hobbesian Sovereignty: *Leviathan* as Mythology," in *Hobbes Today: Insights for the 21st Century*, edited by S. A. Lloyd, 113–52 (Cambridge: Cambridge University Press, 2013). Sovereignty, to the extent that its foundation is largely symbolic, is intrinsically fragile. On the limitations of coercive force in this regard see also, for example, S. A. Lloyd, *Ideals as Interests in Hobbes's* Leviathan: *The Power of Mind over Matter* (Cambridge: Cambridge University Press, 1992); Sheldon Wolin, *Politics*

and Vision: Continuity and Innovation in Western Political Thought (Princeton, NJ: Princeton University Press, 2004), 232.

125. Hobbes, *Leviathan, Volume Two*, 30, 525. For a catalog of those principles that education aims to instill in subjects see Hobbes, 30, 524–30.

126. Patrick Craig, for example, criticizes Jacques Rancière on precisely this basis. Craig, "Jacques Rancière, Thomas Hobbes, and a Politics of the Part That Has No Part," *Theory & Event* 18, no. 1 (2015).

127. Indeed, such opposition need not even be self-consciously antagonistic. Within the context of the perception of a tension between *potentia* and *potestas* in Hobbes's later work—between power as a concrete and effective capacity and power as an authorized entitlement—Sandra Leonie Field writes that *Leviathan*'s "political ontology shows that the sovereign will face a constant need to maintain its power in the face of spontaneously emergent powers in the populace; such powers are a threat even when they have no seditious intent." Sandra Leonie Field, *Potentia: Hobbes and Spinoza on Power and Popular Politics* (Oxford: Oxford University Press, 2020), 109.

128. Hobbes, *The Elements of Law, Natural and Politic*, 1.17.4.

129. Hobbes, 1.17.14.

130. Hobbes, *Leviathan, Volume Two*, 15, 234–36.

131. Hobbes, 17, 258.

132. Hobbes, 15, 234. On this point see, for example, Peter Vanderschraaf, "Instituting the Hobbesian Commonwealth," *Pacific Philosophical Quarterly* 82, no. 3–4 (2001): 399; Ioannis Evrigenis, "The State of Nature," in *The Oxford Handbook of Hobbes*, ed. A. P. Martinich and Kinch Hoekstra (Oxford: Oxford University Press, 2016), 229. In the subsequent discussion, however, Hobbes is still unwilling to include any potential right to such self-government within his catalog of those inalienable ones whose subjective maintenance is required for commodious life. Hobbes, *Leviathan, Volume Two*, 15, 234–36.

133. Thomas Hobbes, *Leviathan, Volume Three: The English and Latin Texts (ii)*, ed. Noel Malcolm (Oxford: Clarendon Press, 2012), 36, 674. Emphasis added.

134. Such is noted by Giuseppe Sorgi, who provides the most comprehensive account of the extent and modes of political participation that Hobbes allows for in the commonwealth—and his usually negative judgments on them—of which I am aware. Sorgi writes that this chapter's statement of a natural human desire to participate in political decision-making "contains the germs of what will later be called direct democracy." Giuseppe Sorgi, *Hobbes Studies* 9, no. 1 (1996): 81.

135. Hobbes, *Leviathan, Volume Two*, 22, 348.

136. Hobbes, 22, 348.

137. Hobbes, 22, 350.

138. For an account of the logic behind Hobbes's supposed repudiation of his early concept of the body politic see Philippe Crignon, "Representation and the Person of the State," *Hobbes Studies* 31 (2018): 48–74.

139. Hobbes, *Leviathan, Volume Two*, 22, 350.
140. Hobbes, 22, 358.
141. Hobbes, 22, 358.
142. Hobbes, 22, 358–60.
143. Hobbes, 22, 358.
144. Hobbes, 22, 363.
145. Hobbes, 8, 108.
146. Hobbes, *On the Citizen*, 10.9.
147. Hobbes, 10.15.
148. Slomp, *Thomas Hobbes and the Political Philosophy of Glory*, 85.
149. Hobbes, "On Man," 62.
150. Slomp, *Thomas Hobbes and the Political Philosophy of Glory*, 91.
151. Hobbes, *On the Citizen*, 12.12.
152. Hobbes, *Leviathan, Volume Two*, 30, 540.
153. Hobbes, 19, 288.

154. The literature on these experiments is now quite large and increasingly growing. For just one short but instructive history of the incorporation of random selection into experiments in democratic innovation see Yves Sintomer, "From Deliberative to Radical Democracy? Sortition and Politics in the Twenty-First Century," *Politics & Society* 46, no. 3 (2018): 337–57. What is of particular note in Sintomer's account is the division of sortition-based mini-publics between those early ones that are assimilable to the logic of deliberative democracy, and later ones that affirm various principles of self-government and radical democracy.

155. Hobbes, *Leviathan, Volume Two*, 15, 232. Rosamund Rhodes has argued that *Leviathan*'s fifth law of nature requiring mutual accommodation is far more central to the overall Hobbesian project than has typically been recognized. Rhodes, "Hobbes's Fifth Law of Nature and Its Implications."

156. Hobbes, *Leviathan, Volume Two*, 15, 232.

157. R. E. Ewin gestures toward the principle of complaisance's implication in democratic life through stressing the political implications of toleration, different people being capable of living together peacefully so long as they share a commitment to certain decision procedures as means to negotiate disagreement. Ewin, *Virtues and Rights*, 204. On Hobbes as developing a theory of interpersonal relation grounded in mutual respect see Ron Replogle, "Personality and Society in Hobbes's *Leviathan*," *Polity* 19, no. 4 (1987): 570–94. As Danielle Allen observes, though, even if Hobbes's discussion of equity opens the door to a productive understanding of political life as grounded in such mutuality, he immediately endeavors to close this door as much as possible. Allen writes, "The signal discovery behind Hobbes's laws of nature, then, is this: *Reciprocity does not merely aid the conclusion of agreements that are achieved primarily through reason. Instead, it is one of the substantive questions at stake in all disputes within a consensually based political community.* But having made this discovery, Hobbes then foreclosed the

possibility of cultivating within citizens a culture of reciprocity. He abandoned the political possibilities inherent in citizenship for authoritarianism." Danielle S. Allen, *Talking to Strangers: Anxieties of Citizenship since Brown v. Brown of Education* (Chicago: University of Chicago Press, 2004), 97.

158. Hobbes, *On the Citizen*, 10.4.

159. Hobbes, 10.4.

160. Hobbes, 10.4.

161. Christopher Brooke, "Nonintrinsic Egalitarianism, from Hobbes to Rousseau," *Journal of Politics* 82, no. 4 (2020): 1408.

Bibliography

Abizadeh, Arash. "The Absence of Reference in Hobbes's Philosophy of Language." *Philosopher's Imprint* 15, no. 22 (2015): 1–17.
———. *Hobbes and the Two Faces of Ethics*. Cambridge: Cambridge University Press, 2018.
———. "Hobbes on Mind: Practical Deliberation, Reasoning, and Language." *Journal of the History of Philosophy* 55, no. 1 (2017): 1–34.
———. "The Representation of Hobbesian Sovereignty: *Leviathan* as Mythology." In *Hobbes Today: Insights for the 21st Century*, edited by S. A. Lloyd, 113–52. Cambridge: Cambridge University Press, 2013.
———. "Sovereign Jurisdiction, Territorial Rights, and Membership in Hobbes." In *The Oxford Handbook of Hobbes*, edited by A. P. Martinich and Kinch Hoekstra, 397–431. Oxford: Oxford University Press, 2016.
———. "Thomas Hobbes et le droit naturel." In *Droit naturel: Relancer l'histoire*, edited by Xavier Dijon, 331–78. Brussels: Bruylant, 2008.
Ahrensdorf, Peter J. "The Fear of Death and the Longing for Immortality: Hobbes and Thucydides on Human Nature and the Problem of Anarchy." *American Political Science Review* 94, no. 3 (2000): 579–93.
Airaksinen, Timo. "Hobbes on the Passions and Powerlessness." *Hobbes Studies* 6, no. 1 (1993): 80–104.
Allen, Danielle S. *Talking to Strangers: Anxieties of Citizenship since Brown v. Board of Education*. Chicago: University of Chicago Press, 2004.
Anonymous. "England's Miserie and Remedie in a Judicious Letter from an Utter-Barrister to His Speciall Friend, Concerning Leiutenant Col. Lilburn's Imprisonment in Newgate, Sept. 14 1645." In *Divine Right and Democracy: An Anthology of Political Writing in Stuart England*, edited by David Wootton, 276–82. Harmondsworth: Penguin Books, 1986.
———. "To the Right Honorable and Supreme Authority of This Nation, The Commons in Parliament Assembled." In *The English Levellers*, edited by Andrew Sharp, 77–84. Cambridge: Cambridge University Press, 1998.

Apeldoorn, Laurens van. "Reconsidering Hobbes's Account of Practical Deliberation." *Hobbes Studies* 25, no. 2 (2012): 143–65.
Apperley, Alan. "Hobbes on Democracy." *Politics* 19, no. 3 (1999): 165–71.
Arato, Andrew. *The Adventures of Constituent Power: Beyond Revolutions*. Cambridge: Cambridge University Press, 2017.
Aravamudan, Srinivas. "Hobbes and America." In *The Postcolonial Enlightenment: Eighteenth-Century Colonialism and Postcolonial Theory*, edited by Daniel Carey and Lynn Festa, 37–70. Oxford: Oxford University Press, 2009.
Arendt, Hannah. *The Origins of Totalitarianism*. San Diego: Harcourt, 1968.
Aristotle. *Politics*. Translated by C. D. C. Reeve. Indianapolis: Hackett, 1998.
Ashcraft, Richard. "Hobbes's Natural Man: A Study in Ideology Formation." *Journal of Politics* 33, no. 4 (1971): 1076–1117.
———. "Ideology and Class in Hobbes's Political Theory." *Political Theory* 6, no. 1 (1978): 27–62.
———. "Political Theory and Practical Action: A Reconsideration of Hobbes's State of Nature." *Hobbes Studies* 1, no. 1 (1988): 63–88.
Astorga, Omar. "Hobbes's Concept of Multitude." *Hobbes Studies* 24, no. 1 (2011): 5–14.
Ball, Terence. "Hobbes's Linguistic Turn." *Polity* 17, no. 4 (1985): 739–76.
Barnouw, Jeffrey. "Hobbes's Causal Account of Sensation." *Journal of the History of Philosophy* 18, no. 2 (1980): 115–30.
———. "Hobbes's Psychology of Thought: Endeavours, Purpose and Curiosity." *History of European Ideas* 10, no. 5 (1989): 519–45.
———. "Persuasion in Hobbes's *Leviathan*." *Hobbes Studies* 1, no. 1 (1988): 3–25.
———. "Reason as Reckoning: Hobbes's Natural Law as Right Reason." *Hobbes Studies* 21, no. 1 (2008): 38–62.
Baumgold, Deborah. "The Composition of Hobbes's *Elements of Law*." In *Contract Theory in Historical Context: Essays on Grotius, Hobbes, and Locke*, 105–28. Leiden: Brill, 2010.
———. "The Difficulties of Hobbes Interpretation." *Political Theory* 36, no. 6 (2008): 827–55.
———. "Hobbes's and Locke's Contract Theories: Political Not Metaphysical." In *Contract Theory in Historical Context: Essays on Grotius, Hobbes, and Locke*, 3–26. Leiden: Brill, 2010.
———. "Hobbes's Political Sensibility: The Menace of Political Ambition." In *Thomas Hobbes and Political Theory*, edited by Mary Dietz, 74–90. Lawrence: University Press of Kansas, 1990.
———. *Hobbes's Political Theory*. Cambridge: Cambridge University Press, 1988.
———. "When Hobbes Needed History." In *Contract Theory in Historical Context: Essays on Grotius, Hobbes, and Locke*, 53–73. Leiden: Brill, 2010.
Baumgold, Deborah, and Ryan Harding. "Excavating *On the Citizen*." In *Hobbes's On the Citizen*, edited by Robin Douglass and Johan Olsthoorn, 12–30. Cambridge: Cambridge University Press, 2020.

Baumrin, Bernard. "Hobbes's Egalitarianism." In *Thomas Hobbes: De la métaphysique à la politique*, edited by Martin Bertman and Michel Malherbe, 119–27. Paris: Librairie Philosophique J. Vrin, 1989.
Bejan, Teresa M. "Teaching the *Leviathan*: Thomas Hobbes on Education." *Oxford Review of Education* 36, no. 5 (2010): 607–26.
Berent, Moshe. "Hobbes and the 'Greek Tongues.'" *History of Political Thought* 17, no. 1 (1996): 36–59.
Bertman, Martin A. "*Conatus* in Hobbes' *De Corpore*." *Hobbes Studies* 14, no. 1 (2001): 25–39.
———. "Equality in Hobbes, with Reference to Aristotle." *Review of Politics* 38, no. 4 (1976): 534–44.
———. "Equity as Justice and Charity in Hobbes." In *Thomas Hobbes: De la métaphysique à la politique*, 33–46. Paris: Librairie Philosophique J. Vrin, 1989.
———. "God and Man: Action and Reference in Hobbes." *Hobbes Studies* 3, no. 1 (1990): 18–34.
———. "Hobbes and Performatives." *Critica: Revista Hispanoamericana de Filosofía* 10, no. 30 (1978): 41–53.
———. "Hobbes on Miracles (and God)." *Hobbes Studies* 20, no. 1 (2007): 40–62.
———. "Hobbes on the Character and Use of Civil Law." In *Hobbes oggi*, edited by Andrea Napoli and Guido Canziani, 159–76. Milano: Franco Angeli, 1990.
———. "Justice and Contra-Natural Dissolution." *Hobbes Studies* 10, no. 1 (1997): 23–37.
———. "The Natural Body and the Body Politic." *Philosophy & Social Criticism* 5, no. 1 (1978): 18–34.
———. "Regulative and Constitutive Rules in Hobbes." In *Thomas Hobbes: His View of Man*, edited by J. G. van der Bend, 9–15. Amsterdam: Rodopi, 1982.
———. "Semantics and Political Theory in Hobbes." *Hobbes Studies* 1, no. 1 (1988): 134–43.
Biletzki, Anat. *Talking Wolves: Thomas Hobbes on the Language of Politics and the Politics of Language*. Dordrecht: Kluwer Academic Publishers, 1997.
Blau, Adrian. "Extended Meaning and Understanding in the History of Ideas." *History and Theory* 58, no. 3 (2019): 342–59.
———. "History of Political Thought as Detective Work." *History of European Ideas* 41, no. 8 (2015): 1178–94.
———. "Methodologies of Interpreting Hobbes: Historical and Philosophical." In *Interpreting Hobbes's Political Philosophy*, edited by S. A. Lloyd, 10–28. Cambridge: Cambridge University Press, 2019.
———. "Reason, Deliberation, and the Passions." In *The Oxford Handbook of Hobbes*, edited by A. P. Martinich and Kinch Hoekstra, 195–220. Oxford: Oxford University Press, 2016.
———. "Textual Context in the History of Political Thought." *History of European Ideas* 45, no. 8 (2019): 1191–1210.

Bobbio, Norberto. "Hobbes and Natural Law Theory." In *Thomas Hobbes and the Natural Law Tradition*, translated by Daniela Gobetti, 149–71. Chicago: University of Chicago Press, 1993.

———. "Natural Law and Civil Law in the Political Philosophy of Hobbes." In *Thomas Hobbes and the Natural Law Tradition*, translated by Daniela Gobetti, 114–48. Chicago: University of Chicago Press, 1993.

Borrelli, Gianfranco. "Hobbes e la teoria moderna della democrazia rappresentanza assoluta e scambio politico." *Trimestre* 24, no. 3–4 (1991): 243–63.

Boss, Gilbert. "La doctrine libertine de Hobbes." *Hobbes Studies* 16, no. 1 (2003): 15–40.

———. "Raison et convention, ou la raison politique chez Hobbes." *Hobbes Studies* 9, no. 1 (1996): 55–70.

Boucher, Joanne. "The Erotic Political Philosophy of Thomas Hobbes." *Canadian Journal of Political Science* 49, no. 1 (2016): 89–105.

Bray, Michael. "The Hedges That Are Set: Hobbes and the Future of Politics." *Epoché: A Journal for the History of Philosophy* 11, no. 1 (2006): 173–200.

———. "Macpherson Restored? Hobbes and the Question of Social Origins." *History of Political Thought* 28, no. 1 (2007): 56–90.

Braybrooke, David. "A Note on Hobbesian Lessons on Bipartisanship." In *Hobbes Today: Insights for the 21st Century*, edited by S. A. Lloyd, 20–24. Cambridge: Cambridge University Press, 2013.

Brito Vieira, Mónica. *The Elements of Representation in Hobbes: Aesthetics, Theatre, Law, and Theology in the Construction of Hobbes's Theory of the State*. Leiden: Brill, 2009.

———. "'Leviathan' Contra 'Leviathan.'" *Journal of the History of Ideas* 76, no. 2 (2015): 271–88.

Brooke, Christopher. "Nonintrinsic Egalitarianism, from Hobbes to Rousseau." *Journal of Politics* 82, no. 4 (2020): 1406–17.

Brown, Clifford W., Jr, "Thucydides, Hobbes, and the Derivation of Anarchy." *History of Political Thought* 8, no. 1 (1987): 33–62.

———. "Thucydides, Hobbes and the Linear Causal Perspective." *History of Political Thought* 10, no. 2 (1989): 215–56.

Browning, Gary. "The Politics of Recognition: Life and Death Struggles in Hobbes and Hegel." *Hobbes Studies* 28, no. 1 (2015): 3–17.

Browning, Gary K., and Raia Prokhovnik. "Hobbes, Hegel and Modernity." *Hobbes Studies* 8, no. 1 (1995): 88–104.

Bull, Malcolm. "The Limits of Multitude." *New Left Review*, no. 35 (2005): 19–39.

Burgess, Glenn. "Contexts for the Writing and Publication of Hobbes's *Leviathan*." *History of Political Thought* 11, no. 4 (1990): 675–702.

———. "On Hobbesian Resistance Theory." *Political Studies* 42, no. 1 (1994): 62–83.

Butler, Ted. "Image, Rhetoric, and Politics in the Early Thomas Hobbes." *Journal of the History of Ideas* 67, no. 3 (2006): 465–87.
Byron, Michael. "Hobbes's Confounding Foole." In *Interpreting Hobbes's Political Philosophy*, edited by S. A. Lloyd, 206–22. Cambridge: Cambridge University Press, 2019.
———. *Submission and Subjection in* Leviathan: *Good Subjects in the Hobbesian Commonwealth*. Basingstoke: Palgrave Macmillan, 2015.
Campodonico, Angelo. "Secularization in Thomas Hobbes's Anthropology." In *Thomas Hobbes: His View of Man*, edited by J. G. van der Bend, 113–23. Amsterdam: Rodopi, 1982.
Cantalupo, Charles. *A Literary Leviathan: Thomas Hobbes's Masterpiece of Language*. Lewisburg, PA: Bucknell University Press, 1991.
Carmel, Elad. "'Philosophy, Therefore Is within Yourself': The Rational Potential in Hobbes's Theory." *Hobbes Studies* 31, no. 2 (2018): 166–87.
Carrive, Paulette. "Hobbes et les juristes de la Common Law." In *Thomas Hobbes: De la métaphysique à la politique*, edited by Martin Bertman and Michel Malherbe, 149–71. Paris: Librairie Philosophique J. Vrin, 1989.
Carter, Alan. "The Method in Hobbes' Madness." *Hobbes Studies* 12, no. 1 (1999): 72–89.
Castoriadis, Cornelius. *Ce qui fait la Grèce, 1: D'Homère à Héraclite*. Edited by Enrique Escobar, Myrto Gondicas, and Pascal Vernay. Paris: Seuil, 2004.
———. "The Greek Polis and the Creation of Democracy." In *Philosophy, Politics, Autonomy: Essays in Political Philosophy*, edited and translated by David Ames Curtis, 81–123 New York: Oxford University Press, 1991.
———. *La cité et les lois: Ce qui fait la Grèce, 2*. Edited by Enrique Escobar, Myrto Gondicas, and Pascal Vernay. Paris: Éditions du Seuil, 2008.
———. "La démocratie athénienne: Fausses et vraies questions." In *La montée de l'insignifiance: Les carrefours du labyrinthe, 4*, 220–33. Paris: Éditions du Seuil, 1996.
Chanteur, Janine. "Note sur les notions de 'peuple' et de 'multitude' chez Hobbes." In *Hobbes-Forschungen*, edited by Reinhart Koselleck and Roman Schnur, 223–35. Berlin: Duncker & Humbolt, 1969.
Chou, Chia-Yu. *Rethinking Hobbes and Kant: The Role and Consequences of Assumption in Political Theory*. London: Routledge, 2017.
Chwaszcza, Christine. "The Seat of Sovereignty: Hobbes on the Artificial Person of the Commonwealth or State." *Hobbes Studies* 25, no. 2 (2012): 123–42.
Cohen, Joshua. "Getting Past Hobbes." In *Hobbes Today: Insights for the 21st Century*, edited by S. A. Lloyd, 3–19. Cambridge: Cambridge University Press, 2013.
Coleman, Frank M. *Hobbes and America: Exploring the Constitutional Foundations*. Toronto: University of Toronto Press, 1977.

Coli, Daniela. "Hobbes's Revolution." In *Politics and the Passions: 1500–1850*, edited by Victoria Kahn, Neil Saccamano, and Daniela Coli, 75–92. Princeton, NJ: Princeton University Press, 2006.
Collins, Jeffrey R. *The Allegiance of Thomas Hobbes.* Oxford: Oxford University Press, 2005.
———. "Malcolm's *Leviathan*: Hobbes's 'Thing.'" *Modern Intellectual History* 12, no. 1 (2015): 95–120.
Condren, Conal. "On the Rhetorical Foundations of *Leviathan*." *History of Political Thought* 11, no. 4 (1990): 703–20.
Cooper, Julie E. "Thomas Hobbes on the Political Theorist's Vocation." *Historical Journal* 50, no. 3 (2007): 519–47.
———. "Vainglory, Modesty, and Political Agency in the Political Theory of Thomas Hobbes." *Review of Politics* 72, no. 2 (2010): 241–69.
Cooper, Kody W. *Thomas Hobbes and the Natural Law.* Notre Dame, IN: Notre Dame University Press, 2018.
Copp, David. "Hobbes on Artificial Persons and Collective Actions." *Philosophical Review* 89, no. 4 (1980): 579–606.
Courtland, Shane D. "Public Reason and the Hobbesian Dilemma." *Hobbes Studies* 20, no. 1 (2007): 63–92.
Craig, Leon Howard. *The Platonian* Leviathan. Toronto: University of Toronto Press, 2010.
Craig, Patrick. "Jacques Rancière, Thomas Hobbes, and a Politics of the Part That Has No Part." *Theory & Event* 18, no. 1 (2015).
Crepell, Ingrid. "The Democratic Element in Hobbes's 'Behemoth.'" In *Hobbes's Behemoth: Religion and Democracy*, edited by Tomaž Mastnak, 241–68. Exeter: Imprint Academic, 2009.
Crignon, Philippe. "Diversité humaine et pluralisme: La reprise d'un thème hobbesien dans le libéralisme contemporain." In *Hobbes et le libéralisme*, edited by Yves Charles Zarka, 75–102. Paris: Éditions Mimésis, 2016.
———. "Representation and the Person of the State." *Hobbes Studies* 31 (2018): 48–74.
Curran, Eleanor. "Blinded by the Light of Hohfeld: Hobbes's Notion of Liberty." *Jurisprudence* 1, no. 1 (2010): 85–104.
———. "Hobbes Comes Out for Equal Marriage." In *Hobbesian Applied Ethics and Public Policy*, edited by Shane D. Courtland, 161–78. London: Routledge, 2017.
———. "Hobbes on Equality: Context, Rhetoric, Argument." *Hobbes Studies* 25, no. 2 (2012): 166–87.
———. *Reclaiming the Rights of the Hobbesian Subject.* Basingstoke: Palgrave Macmillan, 2007.
Dallmayr, Fred. "Hobbes and Existentialism: Some Affinities." *Journal of Politics* 31, no. 3 (1969): 615–40.

Danford, John W. "The Problem of Language in Hobbes's Political Science." *Journal of Politics* 42, no. 1 (1980): 102–34.
Deigh, John. "Reason and Ethics in Hobbes's *Leviathan*." *Journal of the History of Philosophy* 34, no. 1 (1996): 33–60.
Deleule, Didier. "La fuite en avant : Une approche du chapitre 11 du *Léviathan*." In *Hobbes et le libéralisme*, edited by Yves Charles Zarka, 11–34. Paris: Éditions Mimésis, 2016.
Devine, Francis Edward. "Absolute Democracy or Indefeasible Right: Hobbes Versus Locke." *Journal of Politics* 37, no. 3 (1975): 736–68.
———. "Hobbes: The Theoretical Basis of Political Compromise." *Polity* 5, no. 1 (1972): 57–76.
Dietz, Mary G. "Hobbes's Subject as Citizen." In *Thomas Hobbes and Political Theory*, edited by Mary G. Dietz, 91–119. Lawrence: University Press of Kansas, 1990.
Douglass, Robin. "Authorization and Representation before *Leviathan*." *Hobbes Studies* 31, no. 1 (2018): 30–47.
———. "The Body Politic 'Is a Fictitious Body': Hobbes on Imagination and Fiction." *Hobbes Studies* 27, no. 2 (2014): 126–47.
———. "Hobbes and Political Realism." *European Journal of Political Theory* 19, no. 2 (2020): 250–69.
———. "Hobbes sur la représentation et la souveraineté." In *Les défis de la représentation: Langages, pratiques et figuration du gouvernement*, edited by Manuela Albertone and Dario Castiglione, 91–114. Paris: Classiques Garnier, 2018.
———. *Rousseau and Hobbes: Nature, Free Will, and the Passions*. Oxford: Oxford University Press, 2015.
———. "Thomas Hobbes's Changing Account of Liberty and Challenge to Republicanism." *History of Political Thought* 36, no. 2 (2015): 281–309.
Downes, Paul. *Hobbes, Sovereignty, and Early American Literature*. Cambridge: Cambridge University Press, 2015.
Duncan, Stewart. "Hobbes, Signification and Insignificant Names." *Hobbes Studies* 24, no. 2 (2011): 158–78.
Dungey, Nicholas. "Thomas Hobbes's Materialism, Language, and the Possibility of Politics." *Review of Politics* 70, no. 2 (2008): 190–220.
Duso, Giuseppe. "Hobbes et l'invention moderne du pouvoir." *Hobbes Studies* 27, no. 1 (2005): 28–45.
Dyzenhaus, David. "Hobbes and the Legitimacy of the Law." *Law and Philosophy* 20, no. 5 (2001): 461–98.
———. "Hobbes on the Authority of the Law." In *Hobbes and the Law*, edited by David Dyzenhaus and Thomas Poole, 186–209. Cambridge: Cambridge University Press, 2012.
———. "How Hobbes Met the Hobbes Challenge." *Modern Law Review* 72, no. 3 (2009): 488–506.

Epstein, Jeffrey H. *Democracy and Its Others*. New York: Bloomsbury, 2016.
Esposito, Roberto. *Communitas: The Origin and Destiny of Community*. Translated by Timothy Campbell. Stanford, CA: Stanford University Press, 2010.
———. *Immunitas: The Protection and Negation of Life*. Translated by Zakiya Hanofi. London: Polity, 2011.
Evrigenis, Ioannis. *Images of Anarchy: The Rhetoric and Science in Hobbes's State of Nature*. Cambridge: Cambridge University Press, 2014.
———. "The State of Nature." In *The Oxford Handbook of Hobbes*, edited by A. P. Martinich and Kinch Hoekstra, 221–41. Oxford: Oxford University Press, 2016.
Ewin, R. E. *Virtues and Rights: The Moral Philosophy of Thomas Hobbes*. Boulder, CO: Westview Press, 1991.
Feldman, Karen S. *Binding Words: Conscience and Rhetoric in Hobbes, Hegel, and Heidegger*. Evanston, IL: Northwestern University Press, 2006.
Fernández Peychaux, Diego A. "The Multitude in the Mirror: Hobbes on Power, Rhetoric, and Materialism." *Theory & Event* 21, no. 3 (2018): 652–72.
Field, Sandra Leonie. "Hobbes and Human Irrationality." *Global Discourse* 5, no. 2 (2015): 207–20.
———. "Hobbes and the Question of Power." *Journal of the History of Philosophy* 52, no. 1 (2014): 61–86.
———. *Potentia: Hobbes and Spinoza on Power and Popular Politics*. Oxford: Oxford University Press, 2020.
———. "Response to Critics." *European Hobbes Society Online Colloquium*, June 9, 2021. http://www.europeanhobbessociety.org/general/online-colloquium-5-reply-to-critics-by-sandra-leonie-field/.
Finn, Stephen J. *Thomas Hobbes and the Politics of Natural Philosophy*. London: Continuum, 2006.
Flathman, Richard E. "Hobbes: Premier Theorist of Authority." *Hobbes Studies* 10, no. 1 (1997): 3–22.
———. *Thomas Hobbes: Skepticism, Individuality, and Chastened Politics*. Lanham, MD: Rowman & Littlefield, 2002.
Fleming, Sean. "The Two Faces of Personhood: Hobbes, Corporate Agency and the Personality of the State." *European Journal of Political Theory* 20, no. 1 (2021): 5–26.
Flikshuh, Katrin. "Elusive Unity: The General Will in Hobbes and Kant." *Hobbes Studies* 25, no. 1 (2012): 21–42.
Foisneau, Luc. *Hobbes: La vie inquiète*. Paris: Gallimard, 2016.
———. "Les savants dans la cité." In *Thomas Hobbes: Philosophie première, théorie de la science politique*, edited by Yves Charles Zarka, 181–92. Paris: Presses Universitaires de France, 1990.
Forsyth, Murray. "Thomas Hobbes and the Constituent Power of the People." *Political Studies* 29, no. 2 (1981): 191–203.

Fox-Decent, Evan. "Hobbes's Relational Theory." In *Hobbes and the Law*, edited by David Dyzenhaus and Thomas Poole, 118–44. Cambridge: Cambridge University Press, 2012.
Frank, Jill. "Citizens, Slaves, and Foreigners." *American Political Science Review* 98, no. 1 (2004): 91–104.
Freund, Julien. "Le dieu mortel." In *Hobbes-Forschungen*, edited by Reinhart Koselleck and Roman Schnur, 9–31. Berlin: Duncker & Humbolt, 1969.
Frost, Samantha. "Faking It: Hobbes's Thinking Bodies and the Ethics of Dissimulation." *Political Theory* 29, no. 1 (2001): 30–57.
———. "Hobbes, Life, and the Politics of Self-Preservation." In *Interpreting Hobbes's Political Philosophy*, edited by S. A. Lloyd, 70–92. Cambridge: Cambridge University Press, 2019.
———. *Lessons from a Materialist Thinker: Hobbesian Reflections on Ethics and Politics*. Stanford, CA: Stanford University Press, 2008.
Funkenstein, Amos. *Theology and the Scientific Imagination: From the Middle Ages to the Seventeenth Century*. Princeton, NJ: Princeton University Press, 1986.
Garniron, Pierre. "Hobbes dans les leçons d'histoire de la philosophie de Hegel." In *Thomas Hobbes: Philosophie première, thèorie de la science et politique*, edited by Yves Charles Zarka, 391–412. Paris: Presses Universitaires de France, 1990.
Garsten, Bryan. "Religion and Representation in Hobbes." In *Leviathan*, by Thomas Hobbes, 519–46. edited by Ian Shapiro. New Haven, CT: Yale University Press, 2010.
Gauthier, David. "Public Reason." *Social Philosophy and Policy* 12, no. 1 (1995): 19–42.
———. *The Logic of* Leviathan: *The Moral and Political Theory of Thomas Hobbes*. Oxford: Oxford University Press, 1969.
Gert, Bernard. "Hobbes and Psychological Egoism." *Journal of the History of Ideas* 28, no. 4 (1967): 503–20.
———. "Hobbes on Language, Metaphysics, and Epistemology." *Hobbes Studies* 14, no. 1 (2001): 40–58.
———. *Hobbes: Prince of Peace*. Cambridge: Polity, 2010.
———. "Hobbes's Account of Reason and the Passions." In *Thomas Hobbes: De la métaphysique à la politique*, edited by Martin Bertman and Michel Malherbe, 83–92. Paris: Librairie Philosophique J. Vrin, 1989.
———. "Hobbes's Psychology." In *The Cambridge Companion to Hobbes*, edited by Tom Sorell, 157–74. Cambridge: Cambridge University Press, 1996.
———. "The Law of Nature as the Moral Law." *Hobbes Studies* 1, no. 1 (1988): 26–44.
Geuss, Raymond. *Changing the Subject: Philosophy from Socrates to Adorno*. Cambridge, MA: Harvard University Press, 2017.

Giamario, Patrick T. "The Laughing Body Politic: The Counter-Sovereign Politics of Hobbes's Theory of Laughter." *Political Research Quarterly* 69, no. 2 (2016): 309–19.
Giancotti, Emilia. "The Birth of Modern Materialism in Hobbes and Spinoza." In *The New Spinoza*, edited by Warren Montag and Ted Stoltze, 49–63. Minneapolis: University of Minnesota Press, 1997.
Glass, James M. "Hobbes and Narcissism: Pathology in the State of Nature." *Political Theory* 8, no. 3 (1980): 335–63.
Goldie, Mark. "The Reception of Hobbes." In *The Cambridge History of Political Thought, 1450–1700*, edited by J. H. Burns and Mark Goldie, 589–615. Cambridge: Cambridge University Press, 1991.
Goldsmith, M. M. "Hobbes on Liberty." *Hobbes Studies* 2, no. 1 (1989): 23–39.
———. *Hobbes's Science of Politics*. New York: Columbia University Press, 1966.
Gooding, Nicholas, and Kinch Hoekstra. "Hobbes and Aristotle on the Foundation of Political Science." In *Hobbes's On the Citizen*, edited by Robin Douglass and Johan Olsthoorn, 31–50. Cambridge: Cambridge University Press, 2020.
Goyard-Fabre, Simone. "La législation civile dans l'état-Léviathan." In *Thomas Hobbes: De la métaphysique à la politique*, edited by Martin Bertman and Michel Malherbe, 173–92. Paris: Librairie Philosophique J. Vrin, 1989.
———. *Le droit et la loi dans la philosophie de Thomas Hobbes*. Paris: Librarie C. Klincksieck, 1975.
———. "Right and Anthropology in Hobbes's Philosophy." In *Thomas Hobbes: His View of Man*, edited by J. G. van der Bend, 17–30. Amsterdam: Rodopi, 1982.
Grant, John. "'Becoming One': Visions of Political Unity from the Ancients to the Postmoderns." *Constellations* 21, no. 4 (2014): 575–88.
Green, Michael J. "Authorization and Political Authority in Hobbes." *Journal of the History of Philosophy* 53, no. 1 (2015): 25–47.
Halldenius, Lena. "Liberty, Law and *Leviathan*." *Theoria*, no. 131 (2012): 1–20.
Hallenbrook, Christopher R. "Leviathan No More: The Right of Nature and the Limits of Sovereignty in Hobbes." *Review of Politics* 78, no. 2 (2016): 177–200.
Hamilton, James J. "Hobbes the Royalist, Hobbes the Republican." *History of Political Thought* 30, no. 3 (2009): 411–54.
———. "The Origins of Hobbes's State of Nature." *Hobbes Studies* 26, no. 2 (2013): 152–70.
Hampsher-Monk, Iain. *A History of Modern Political Thought: Major Political Thinkers from Hobbes to Marx*. Oxford: Blackwell Publishers, 1992.
Hampton, Jean. *Hobbes and the Social Contract Tradition*. Cambridge: Cambridge University Press, 1986.

Hansen Soles, Deborah. *Strong Wits and Spider Webs: A Study in Hobbes's Philosophy of Language*. Aldeishot: Avebury, 1996.

Hanson, Donald W. "Reconsidering Hobbes's Conventionalism." *Review of Politics* 53, no. 4 (1991): 627–51.

———. "Science, Prudence, and Folly in Hobbes's Political Theory." *Political Theory* 21, no. 4 (1993): 643–64.

———. "Thomas Hobbes on 'Discourse' in Politics." *Polity* 24, no. 2 (1991): 199–226.

Hardt, Michael, and Antonio Negri. *Empire*. Cambridge, MA: Harvard University Press, 2000.

———. *Multitude: War and Democracy in the Age of Empire*. New York: Penguin Press, 2004.

Hart, H. L. A. *The Concept of Law*. Oxford: Clarendon Press, 1961.

Harvey, Thomas. "Hobbes's Voluntarist Theory of Morals." *Hobbes Studies* 22, no. 1 (2009): 49–69.

Hays, Peter. "Hobbes's Bourgeois Moderation." *Polity* 31, no. 1 (1998): 53–74.

Herbe, Karlfriedrich. "Au-delà de la citoyenneté: Hobbes et le problème de l'autorité." *Rivista di Storia della Filosofia* 59, no. 1 (2004): 219–25.

Herbert, Gary B. "The Non-Normative Nature of Hobbesian Natural Law." *Hobbes Studies* 22, no. 1 (2009): 3–28.

———. "Thomas Hobbes's Counterfeit Equality." *Southern Journal of Philosophy* 14, no. 3 (1973): 269–83.

———. "Thomas Hobbes's Dialectic of Desire." *New Scholasticism* 50, no. 2 (1976): 137–63.

Herzog, Annabel. "Hobbes and Corneille on Political Representation." *European Legacy* 14, no. 4 (2009): 379–89.

Herzog, Don. *Happy Slaves: A Critique of Consent Theory*. Chicago: University of Chicago Press, 1989.

Hillyer, Richard. "Keith Thomas's 'Definitive Refutation' of C. B. Macpherson: Revisiting 'The Social Origins of Hobbes's Political Thought.'" *Hobbes Studies* 15, no. 1 (2002): 32–44.

Hindess, Barry. *Discourses of Power: From Hobbes to Foucault*. Oxford: Blackwell Publishers, 1996.

Hobbes, Thomas. "An Answer to a Book Published by Dr. Bramhall, Late Bishop of Derry; Called the 'Catching of the Leviathan.'" In *The English Works of Thomas Hobbes of Malmesbury, Volume Four*, edited by Sir William Molesworth, 279–384. London: John Bohn, 1840.

———. *Behemoth, or the Long Parliament*. Edited by Paul Seaward. Oxford: Clarendon Press, 2010.

———. "Decameron physiologicum; or, Ten Dialogues of Natural Philosophy." In *The English Works of Thomas Hobbes of Malmesbury, Volume Seven*,

———. "A Dialogue between a Philosopher and a Student of the Common Laws of England." In *The English Works of Thomas Hobbes of Malmesbury, Volume Six*, edited by Sir William Molesworth, 1–160. London: John Bohn, 1840.

———. "A Discourse of Laws." edited by Noel B. Reynolds and Arlene W. Saxonhouse, 105–19. Chicago: University of Chicago Press, 1995.

———. "A Discourse of Rome." In *Three Discourses*, edited by Noel B. Reynolds and Arlene W. Saxonhouse, 71–102. Chicago: University of Chicago Press, 1995.

———. "A Discourse on the Beginning of Tacitus." In *Three Discourses*, edited by Noel B. Reynolds and Arlene W. Saxonhouse, 31–67. Chicago: University of Chicago Press, 1995.

———. *The Elements of Law, Natural and Politic*. Edited by Ferdinand Tönnies. London: Simpkin, Marshall, and Co., 1889.

———. "Elements of Philosophy. The First Section, Concerning Body." In *The English Works of Thomas Hobbes of Malmesbury, Volume One*, edited by Sir William Molesworth. London: John Bohn, 1839.

———. "An Historical Narration Concerning Heresy, and the Punishment Thereof." In *The English Works of Thomas Hobbes of Malmesbury, Volume Four*, edited by Sir William Molesworth, 385–408. London: John Bohn, 1840.

———. *Léviathan*. Translated by François Tricaud. Paris: Sirey, 1971.

———. *Leviathan, Volume Three: The English and Latin Texts (ii)*. Edited by Noel Malcolm. Oxford: Clarendon Press, 2012.

———. *Leviathan, Volume Two: The English and Latin Texts (i)*. Edited by Noel Malcolm. Oxford: Clarendon Press, 2012.

———. "Of Liberty and Necessity: A Treatise, Wherein All Controversy Concerning Predestination, Election, Free-Will, Grace, Merits, Reprobation, &c Is Fully Decided and Cleared." In *The English Works of Thomas Hobbes of Malmesbury, Volume Four*, edited by Sir William Molesworth, 229–78. London: John Bohn, 1840.

———. "Of the Life and History of Thucydides." In *The History of Thucydides, The English Works of Thomas Hobbes of Malmesbury, Volume Eight*, edited by Sir William Molesworth, xiii–xxxii. London: John Bohn, 1839.

———. "On Man." In *Man and Citizen (De Homine and De Cive)*, translated by Charles T. Wood, T. S. K. Scott-Craig, and Bernard Gert, 33–85. Indianapolis: Hackett, 1991.

———. *On the Citizen (De Cive)*. Edited and translated by Richard Tuck and Michael Silverthorne. Cambridge: Cambridge University Press, 1998.

———. "The Prose Life." In *The Elements of Law, Natural and Politic*, edited by J. C. A. Gaskin, 245–53. Oxford: Oxford University Press, 1994.

———. "The Questions Concerning Liberty, Necessity, and Chance." In *The English Works of Thomas Hobbes of Malmesbury, Volume Five*, edited by Sir William Molesworth. London: John Bohn, 1841.

———. "Questions Relative to Hereditary Right." In *Writings on Common Law and Hereditary Right*, edited by Alan Cromartie and Quentin Skinner, 177–78. Oxford: Clarendon Press, 2005.

———. "Seven Philosophical Problems and Two Propositions of Geometry." In *The English Works of Thomas Hobbes of Malmesbury, Volume Seven*, edited by Sir William Molesworth, 1–68. London: Longman, Brown, Green, and Longmans, 1845.

———. "Six Lessons to the Professors of the Mathematics." In *The English Works of Thomas Hobbes of Malmesbury, Volume Seven*, edited by Sir William Molesworth, 181–356. London: Longman, Brown, Green, and Longmans, 1845.

———. *Thomas White's De mundo Examined*. Translated by Harold Whitmore Jones. London: Bradford University Press, 1976.

———. "The Verse Life." In *The Elements of Law, Natural and Politic*, edited by J. C. A. Gaskin, 254–64. Oxford: Oxford University Press, 1994.

Hoekstra, Kinch. "The *De Facto* Turn in Hobbes's Political Philosophy." In *Leviathan After 350 Years*, edited by Tom Sorell and Luc Foisneau, 33–74. Oxford: Oxford University Press, 2004.

———. "Disarming the Prophets: Thomas Hobbes and Predictive Power." *Rivista di Storia della Filosofia* 59, no. 1 (2004): 97–153.

———. "The End of Philosophy (The Case of Hobbes)." *Proceedings of the Aristotelian Society* 106, no. 1 (2006): 25–62.

———. "Hobbes and the Foole." *Political Theory* 25, no. 5 (1997): 620–54.

———. "Hobbes on Law, Nature, and Reason." *Journal of the History of Philosophy* 41, no. 1 (2003): 111–20.

———. "Hobbesian Equality." In *Hobbes Today: Insights for the 21st Century*, edited by S. A. Lloyd, 76–112. Cambridge: Cambridge University Press, 2013.

———. "Hobbes's Thucydides." In *The Oxford Handbook of Hobbes*, edited by A. P. Martinich and Kinch Hoekstra, 547–74. Oxford: Oxford University Press, 2016.

———. "A Lion in the House: Hobbes and Democracy." In *Rethinking the Foundations of Modern Political Thought*, edited by Annabel Brett, James Tully, and Holly Hamilton-Bleakley, 191–218. Cambridge: Cambridge University Press, 2006.

Holman, Christopher. "Hobbes and the Tragedy of Democracy." *History of Political Thought* 40, no. 4 (2019): 649–75.

———. "'That Democratic Ink Must Be Wiped Away': Hobbes and the Normativity of Democracy." *Review of Politics* 83, no. 3 (2021): 305–28.

Holmes, Stephen. "Political Psychology in Hobbes's *Behemoth*." In *Thomas Hobbes and Political Theory*, edited by Mary G. Dietz, 120–52. Lawrence: University Press of Kansas, 1990.

Hood, F. C. "The Change in Hobbes's Definition of Liberty." *Philosophical Quarterly* 17, no. 67 (1967): 150–63.

———. *The Divine Politics of Thomas Hobbes: An Interpretation of* Leviathan. Oxford: Clarendon Press, 1964.

Howard, Dick. *The Primacy of the Political: A History of Political Thought From the Greeks to the French and American Revolutions*. New York: Columbia University Press, 2010.

Hoye, J. Matthew. "*Leviathan* against the City." *History of Political Thought* 41, no. 3 (2020): 419–49.

———. "Obligation and Sovereign Virtue in Hobbes's Leviathan." *Review of Politics* 79, no. 1 (2017): 23–47.

Hull, Gordon. "Building Better Citizens: Hobbes against the Ontological Illusion." *Epoché: A Journal for the History of Philosophy* 20, no. 1 (2015): 105–29.

———. *Hobbes and the Making of Modern Political Thought*. London: Continuum, 2009.

———. "Hobbes's Radical Nominalism." *Epoché: A Journal for the History of Philosophy* 11, no. 1 (2006): 201–23.

Hurley, Paul. "The Many Appetites of Thomas Hobbes." *History of Philosophy Quarterly* 7, no. 4 (1990): 391–407.

Ivison, Duncan. "The Secret History of Public Reason: Hobbes to Rawls." *History of Political Thought* 18, no. 1 (1997): 125–47.

Jackson, Michael. "Mushrooms, Like Men?" *Hobbes Studies* 13, no. 1 (2000): 46–57.

Jackson, Nicholas D. *Hobbes, Bramhall and the Politics of Liberty and Necessity: A Quarrel of the Civil Wars and Interregnum*. Cambridge: Cambridge University Press, 2007.

Jacobson, Norman. *Pride and Solace: The Functions and Limits of Political Theory*. Berkeley: University of California Press, 1978.

Jakonen, Mikko. "Multitude in Motion: Re-Readings of the Political Philosophy of Thomas Hobbes." Ph.D. diss. University of Jyväskylä, 2013.

———. "Needed But Unwanted: Thomas Hobbes's Warnings on the Dangers of Multitude, Populism and Democracy." *Las Torres de Lucca*, no. 9 (2016): 89–118.

———. "Thomas Hobbes on Revolution." *La Révolution Française*, no. 5 (2011): 1–26.

James, David. "Hobbes's Argument for the 'Naturalness' and 'Necessity' of Colonization." *History of Political Thought* 38, no. 3 (2017): 439–61.

Jaume, Lucien. "Hobbes and the Philosophical Sources of Liberalism." In *The Cambridge Companion to Hobbes's* Leviathan, edited by Patricia Springborg, 181–98. Cambridge: Cambridge University Press, 2007.

Jesseph, Douglas M. "Hobbes on the Foundations of Natural Philosophy." In *The Oxford Handbook of Hobbes*, edited by A. P. Martinich and Thomas Poole, 134–48. Oxford: Oxford University Press, 2016.

Johnson, Paul J. "Deduction and Dialectic in Hobbes's Theory of Civility." *Hobbes Studies* 4, no. 1 (1991): 96–114.

———. "Hobbes and the Wolf-Man." In *Thomas Hobbes: His View of Man*, edited by J. G. van der Bend, 31–44. Amsterdam: Rodopi, 1982.

———. "*Leviathan's* Audience." In *Thomas Hobbes: De la métaphysique à la politique*, 221–36. Paris: Librairie Philosophique J. Vrin, 1989.

Johnston, David. "Plato, Hobbes, and the Science of Practical Reasoning." In *Thomas Hobbes and Political Theory*, edited by Mary G. Dietz, 37–54. Lawrence: University Press of Kansas, 1990.

———. *The Rhetoric of Leviathan: Thomas Hobbes and the Politics of Cultural Transformation*. Princeton, NJ: Princeton University Press, 1986.

Kahn, Victoria. *Rhetoric, Prudence, and Skepticism in the Renaissance*. Ithaca, NY: Cornell University Press, 1985.

———. *Wayward Contracts: The Crisis of Political Obligation in England, 1640–1674*. Princeton, NJ: Princeton University Press, 2004.

Kapust, Daniel J. "The Problem of Flattery and Hobbes's Institutional Defense of Monarchy." *Journal of Politics* 73, no. 3 (2011): 680–91.

Kapust, Daniel J., and Brandon P. Turner. "Democratical Gentlemen and the Lust for Mastery: Status, Ambition, and the Language of Liberty in Hobbes's Political Thought." *Political Theory* 41, no. 4 (2013): 648–75.

Karskens, Machiel. "Hobbes's Mechanistic Theory of Science, and Its Role in His Anthropology." In *Thomas Hobbes: His View of Man*, edited by J. G. van der Bend, 45–56. Amsterdam: Rodopi, 1982.

Kavka, Gregory S. *Hobbesian Moral and Political Theory*. Princeton, NJ: Princeton University Press, 1986.

———. "Some Neglected Liberal Aspects of Hobbes's Philosophy." *Hobbes Studies* 1, no. 1 (1988): 89–018.

Kidder, Joel. "Acknowledgements of Equals: Hobbes's Ninth Law of Nature." *Philosophical Quarterly* 33, no. 131 (1983): 133–46.

Kitanov, Severin V. "Happiness in a Mechanistic Universe: Thomas Hobbes on the Nature and Attainability of Happiness." *Hobbes Studies* 24, no. 2 (2011): 117–36.

Klimchuk, Dennis. "Hobbes on Equity." In *Hobbes and the Law*, edited by David Dyzenhaus and Thomas Poole, 165–85. Cambridge: Cambridge University Press, 2012.

Klosko, George, and Daryl Rice. "Thucydides and Hobbes's State of Nature." *History of Political Thought* 6, no. 3 (1985): 405–9.

Kramer, Matthew M. *Hobbes and the Paradoxes of Political Origins*. Basingstoke: Macmillan Press, 1997.

Kraynak, Robert P. *History and Modernity in the Thought of Thomas Hobbes*. Ithaca, NY: Cornell University Press, 1990.

———. "Hobbes's *Behemoth* and the Argument for Absolutism." *American Political Science Review* 76, no. 4 (1982): 837–47.

Krom, Michael P. "Vain Philosophy, the Schools and Civil Philosophy." *Hobbes Studies* 20, no. 1 (2007): 93–119.

Kronman, Anthony K. "The Concept of an Author and the Unity of the Commonwealth in Hobbes's *Leviathan*." *Journal of the History of Philosophy* 18, no. 2 (1980): 159–75.

Krook, Dorothea. "Thomas Hobbes's Doctrine of Meaning and Truth." *Philosophy* 31, no. 116 (1956): 3–22.

Lawton, Rob, and Helen Pringle. "A Life Well Lost? Hobbes and Self-Preservation." *Hobbes Studies* 6, no. 1 (1993): 58–79.

LeBuffe, Michael. "Motivation, Reason, and the Good in *On the Citizen*." In *Hobbes's* On the Citizen, edited by Robin Douglass and Johan Olsthoorn, 89–107. Cambridge: Cambridge University Press, 2020.

Leibniz, Gottfried Wilhelm. *Philosophical Papers and Letters*. Edited and translated by Leroy E. Loemker. Dordrecht: Kluwer Academic Publishers, 1989.

Leijenhorst, Cees. "Sense and Nonsense about Sense: Hobbes and Aristotle on Sense Perception and Imagination." In *The Cambridge Companion to Hobbes's* Leviathan, edited by Patricia Springborg, 82–108. Cambridge: Cambridge University Press, 2007.

Levy, Fritz. "The Background of Hobbes's *Behemoth*." In *The Historical Imagination in Early Modern Britain: History, Rhetoric, and Fiction, 1500–1800*, edited by Donald R. Kelley and David Harris Sacks, 243–68. Cambridge: Cambridge University Press, 1997.

Lindsay, Adam. "'Pretenders of a Vile and Unmanly Disposition': Thomas Hobbes and the Fiction of Constituent Power." *Political Theory* 47, no. 4 (2019): 475–99.

Lister, Andrew. "Skepticism and Pluralism in Thomas Hobbes's Political Thought." *History of Political Thought* 29, no. 1 (1998): 35–60.

Lloyd, S. A. "Authorization and Moral Responsibility in the Philosophy of Hobbes." *Hobbes Studies* 29, no. 2 (2016): 169–88.

———. "By Force or Wiles: Women in the Hobbesian Hunt for Allies and Authority." *Hobbes Studies* 33, no. 1 (2020): 5–28.

———. *Ideals as Interests in Hobbes's* Leviathan: *The Power of Mind over Matter*. Cambridge: Cambridge University Press, 1992.

———. *Morality in the Philosophy of Thomas Hobbes: Cases in the Law of Nature*. Cambridge: Cambridge University Press, 2009.

Lobban, Michael. "Thomas Hobbes and the Common Law." In *Hobbes and the Law*, edited by David Dyzenhaus and Thomas Poole, 39–67. Cambridge: Cambridge University Press, 2012.

Lopata, Benjamin B. "Property Theory in Hobbes." *Political Theory* 1, no. 2 (1973): 203–18.
Loughlin, Martin. "The Political Jurisprudence of Thomas Hobbes." In *Hobbes and the Law*, edited by David Dyzenhaus and Thomas Poole, 5–21. Cambridge: Cambridge University Press, 2012.
Lucky, Jared. "'Strange and Deformed Births' in Hobbes's Civil Science." *History of Political Thought* 37, no. 4 (2016): 630–57.
Lukac de Stier, María L. "The Notion of Good in Hobbes's System." *Hobbes Studies* 15, no. 1 (2002): 87–99.
Lukes, Steven. "Methodological Individualism Reconsidered." *British Journal of Sociology* 19, no. 2 (1968): 119–29.
Lund, William R. "Hobbes on Opinion, Private Judgment and Civil War." *History of Political Thought* 13, no. 1 (1992): 51–72.
———. "Neither 'Behemoth' nor 'Leviathan': Explaining Hobbes's Illiberal Politics." In *Hobbes and Behemoth: Religion and Democracy*, edited by Tomaž Mastnak, 269–93. Exeter: Imprint Academic, 2009.
Mace, George. *Locke, Hobbes, and the Federalist Papers*. Carbondale: Southern Illinois University Press, 1979.
MacGillivrary, Royce. "Thomas Hobbes's History of the English Civil War: A Study of Behemoth." *Journal of the History of Ideas* 31, no. 2 (1970): 179–98.
MacMillan, Alissa. "Conditioned to Believe: Hobbes on Religion, Education, and Social Context." *Hobbes Studies* 30, no. 2 (2017): 156–77.
Macpherson, C. B. "Hobbes's Bourgeois Man." In *Hobbes Studies*, edited by K. C. Brown, 169–83. Oxford: Basil Blackwell, 1965.
———. *The Political Theory of Possessive Individualism*. Oxford: Oxford University Press, 1962.
Magnusson, Rachel. "A Politics in Writing: Jacques Rancière and the Equality of Intelligences." In *Thinking Radical Democracy: The Return to Politics in Post-War France*, edited by Martin Breaugh, Christopher Holman, Rachel Magnusson, Paul Mazzocchi, and Devin Penner, 189–209. Toronto: University of Toronto Press, 2015.
Malcolm, Noel. "General Introduction." In *Leviathan, Volume One: Editorial Introduction*, by Thomas Hobbes, 1–195. edited by Noel Malcolm. Oxford: Clarendon Press, 2012.
———. "Hobbes and Spinoza." In *Aspects of Hobbes*, 27–52. Oxford: Oxford University Press, 2002.
———. "Hobbes and the European Republic of Letters." In *Aspects of Hobbes*, 457–545. Oxford: Oxford University Press, 2002.
———. "Hobbes and the Royal Society." In *Aspects of Hobbes*, 317–35. Oxford: Oxford University Press, 2002.
———. "Hobbes, Sandys, and the Virginia Company." In *Aspects of Hobbes*, 53–79. Oxford: Oxford University Press, 2002.

———. "Hobbes's Science of Politics and His Theory of Science." In *Aspects of Hobbes*, 145–57. Oxford: Oxford University Press, 2002.

———. "Thomas Hobbes: Liberal Illiberal." *Journal of the British Academy*, no. 4 (2016): 113–36.

———. "The Title Page of *Leviathan*, Seen in a Curious Perspective." In *Aspects of Hobbes*, 200–233. Oxford: Oxford University Press, 2002.

Malherbe, Michel. "Hobbes et la doctrine de l'accident." *Hobbes Studies* 1, no. 1 (1988): 45–62.

Manent, Pierre. *An Intellectual History of Liberalism*. Translated by Rebecca Balinski. Princeton, NJ: Princeton University Press, 1995.

———. *Naissances de la politique moderne*. Paris: Gallimard, 2007.

Manin, Bernard. *The Principles of Representative Government*. Cambridge: Cambridge University Press, 1997.

Mansfield, Harvey C. "Hobbes and the Science of Indirect Government." *American Political Science Review* 65, no. 1 (1971): 97–110.

Marcos, Jean Pierre. "Figures et fonctions du tiers chez Hobbes." *Hobbes Studies* 11, no. 1 (1998): 13–32.

Martel, James. "The Radical Promise of Thomas Hobbes: The Road Not Taken in Liberal Theory." *Theory & Event* 4, no. 2 (2000).

———. "The Spectacle of the Leviathan: Thomas Hobbes, Guy Debord, and Walter Benjamin." *Law, Culture, and the Humanities* 2, no. 1 (2006): 67–90.

———. *Subverting the Leviathan: Reading Thomas Hobbes as a Radical Democrat*. New York: Columbia University Press, 2007.

Martens, Stephanie B. *The Americas in Early Modern Political Theory*. New York: Palgrave Macmillan, 2016.

Martinich, A. P. "Authorization and Representation in Hobbes's *Leviathan*." In *The Oxford Handbook of Hobbes*, edited by A. P. Martinich and Kinch Hoekstra, 315–38. Oxford: Oxford University Press, 2016.

———. *Hobbes*. New York: Routledge, 2005.

———. *Hobbes: A Biography*. Cambridge: Cambridge University Press, 1999.

———. *Hobbes's Political Philosophy: Interpretation and Interpretations*. Oxford: Oxford University Press, 2021.

———. "Hobbes's Reply to Republicanism." *Rivista di Storia della Filosofia* 59, no. 1 (2004): 227–39.

———. *The Two Gods of Leviathan: Thomas Hobbes on Religion and Politics*. Cambridge: Cambridge University Press, 1992.

Mastnak, Tomaž. "Godly Democracy." In *Hobbes's Behemoth: Religion and Democracy*, edited by Tomaž Mastnak, 210–40. Exeter: Imprint Academic, 2009.

Matheron, Alexandre. "The Theoretical Function of Democracy in Spinoza and Hobbes." In *The New Spinoza*, edited by Warren Montag and Ted Stoltze, 207–17. Minneapolis: University of Minnesota Press, 1997.

Mathie, William. "Commentary on Professor May's 'Hobbes on Equality and Justice.'" In *Hobbes's "Science of Natural Justice,"* edited by Craig Walton and Paul J. Johnson, 253–56. Dordrecht: Kluwer, 1987.

———. "Justice and Equity: An Inquiry into the Meaning and Role of Equity in the Hobbesian Account of Justice and Politics." In *Hobbes's "Science of Natural Justice,"* edited by Craig Walton and Paul J. Johnson, 257–76. Dordrecht: Kluwer, 1987.

May, Larry. "Hobbes on Equity and Justice." In *Hobbes's "Science of Natural Justice,"* edited by Craig Walton and Paul J. Johnson, 241–52. Dordrecht: Kluwer, 1987.

———. "Hobbes on Fidelity to Law." *Hobbes Studies* 5, no. 1 (1992): 77–89.

———. *Limiting Leviathan: Hobbes on Law and International Affairs*. Oxford: Oxford University Press, 2013.

McClure, Christopher Scott. *Hobbes and the Artifice of Eternity*. Cambridge: Cambridge University Press, 2016.

McNeilly, F. S. *The Anatomy of Leviathan*. London: Macmillan & Co., 1968.

McQueen, Alison. "Mosaic Leviathan: Religion and Rhetoric in Hobbes's Political Thought." In *Hobbes on Politics and Religion*, edited by Laurens van Apeldoorn and Robin Douglass, 116–34. Oxford: Oxford University Press, 2018.

Meiksins Wood, Ellen. *Citizens to Lords: A Social History of Western Political Thought from Antiquity to the Late Middle Ages*. London: Verso, 2008.

———. *Liberty and Property: A Social History of Western Political Thought from Renaissance to Enlightenment*. London: Verso, 2012.

Michaelis, Loralea. "Hobbes's Modern Prometheus: A Political Philosophy for an Uncertain Future." *Canadian Journal of Political Science* 40, no. 1 (2007): 101–27.

Miller, Ted H. "The Uniqueness of *Leviathan*: Authorizing Poets, Philosophers, and Sovereigns." In Leviathan *After 350 Years*, edited by Tom Sorell and Luc Foisneau, 75–104. Oxford: Oxford University Press, 2004.

Mills, Charles W. *The Racial Contract*. Ithaca, NY: Cornell University Press, 1997.

Minogue, Kenneth. "From Precision to Peace: Hobbes and Political Language." *Hobbes Studies* 3, no. 1 (1990): 75–88.

Mitchell, Joshua. "Hobbes and the Equality of All." *Political Theory* 21, no. 1 (1993): 78–100.

Moffitt, John F., and Santiago Sebastián. *O Brave New People: The European Invention of the American Indian*. Albuquerque: University of New Mexico Press, 1998.

Moloney, Pat. "Hobbes, Savagery, and International Anarchy." *American Journal of Political Science* 105, no. 1 (2011): 189–204.

———. "Leaving the Garden of Eden: Linguistic and Political Authority in Thomas Hobbes." *History of Political Thought* 18, no. 2 (1997): 242–66.

Murphy, Mark C. "Was Hobbes a Legal Positivist?" *Ethics* 105, no. 4 (1995): 846–73.

Nacol, Emily C. *An Age of Risk: Politics and Economy in Early Modern Britain*. Princeton, NJ: Princeton University Press, 2016.

Negri, Antonio. *The Savage Anomaly: The Power of Spinoza's Metaphysics and Politics*. Translated by Michael Hardt. Minneapolis: University of Minnesota Press, 1991.

Nerney, Gayne. "The Hobbesian Argument for Human Equality." *Southern Journal of Philosophy* 24, no. 4 (1986): 561–76.

———. "*Homo notans*: Marks, Signs, and Imagination." *Hobbes Studies* 4, no. 1 (1991): 53–75.

Nichols, Robert Lee. "Realizing the Social Contract: The Case of Colonialism and Indigenous Peoples." *Contemporary Political Theory* 4, no. 1 (2005): 42–62.

Oakeshott, Michael. "Introduction to *Leviathan*." In *Hobbes on Civil Association*, 1–74. Oxford: Basil Blackwell, 1975.

Ober, Josiah. *The Athenian Revolution: Essays on Ancient Greek Democracy and Political Theory*. Princeton, NJ: Princeton University Press, 1996.

———. "The Original Meaning of 'Democracy': Capacity to Do Things, Not Majority Rule." *Constellations* 15, no. 1 (2008): 3–9.

Odzuck, Eva. "'Not a Woman-Hater,' 'No Rapist,' or Even Inventor of 'the Sensitive Male'? Feminist Interpretations of Hobbes's Political Theory and Their Relevance for Hobbes Studies." In *Interpreting Hobbes's Political Philosophy*, edited by S. A. Lloyd, 223–41. Cambridge: Cambridge University Press, 2019.

Odzuck, Eva Helene. "'I Professed to Write Not All to All': Diversified Communication in Thomas Hobbes's Political Philosophy." *Hobbes Studies* 30 (2017): 123–55.

O'Gorman, Ned. "Hobbes, Desire, and the Democratization of Rhetoric." *Advances in the History of Rhetoric* 16, no. 1 (2013): 1–28.

Olsthoorn, Johan. "Hobbes on Justice, Property Rights and Self-Ownership." *History of Political Thought* 36, no. 3 (2015): 471–98.

———. "Hobbes's Account of Distributive Justice as Equity." *British Journal for the History of Philosophy* 21, no. 1 (2013): 13–13.

———. "Leviathan, Inc.: Hobbes on the Nature and Person of the State." *History of European Ideas* 47, no. 1 (2021): 17–32.

———. "On the Absence of Moral Goodness in Hobbes's Ethics." *Journal of Ethics* 24, no. 2 (2020): 241–66.

Orwin, Clifford. "On the Sovereign Authorization." *Political Theory* 3, no. 1 (1976): 26–44.

Overton, Richard. "An Arrow Against All Tyrants and Tyranny . . ." In *The English Levellers*, edited by Andrew Sharp, 54–69. Cambridge: Cambridge University Press, 1998.

———. "A Remonstrance of Many Thousand Citizens and Other Freeborn People of England to Their Own House of Commons . . ." In *The English Levellers*, edited by Andrew Sharp, 33–53. Cambridge: Cambridge University Press, 1998.

Oxman, Evan. "Hobbes on the Artificiality of (His Own) Authority." *Hobbes Studies* 31, no. 2 (2018): 188–211.

Pacchi, Arrigo. "Hobbes and the Passions." *Topoi* 6, no. 2 (1987): 111–19.

Paden, Roger. "Hobbesian Deliberators." *Hobbes Studies* 7, no. 1 (1994): 28–43.

Paganini, Gianni. "Hobbes e lo scetticismo continentale." *Rivista di Storia della Filosofia* 59, no. 1 (2004): 303–28.

———. "Hobbes's Philosophical Method and the Passion of Curiosity." In *Interpreting Hobbes's Political Philosophy*, edited by S. A. Lloyd, 50–69. Cambridge: Cambridge University Press, 2019.

———. "How Far Can a 'Radical' Philosopher Go? Thomas Hobbes's Paradox of Gender Relations and One Possible Solution." *Hobbes Studies* 33, no. 1 (2020): 29–53.

Panagia, David. "Delicate Discriminations: Thomas Hobbes's Science of Politics." *Polity* 36, no. 1 (2003): 91–114.

Parietti, Guido. "Hobbes on Teleology and Reason." *European Journal of Philosophy* 25, no. 4 (2017): 1107–31.

Parker, Henry. *Some Few Observations upon His Majesties Late Answer to the Declaration or Remonstance Sic of the Lords and Commons of the 19 of May, 1642*. London: s.n., 1642.

Parkin, Jon. "The Reception of Hobbes's *Leviathan*." In *The Cambridge Companion to Hobbes's Leviathan*, edited by Patricia Springborg, 441–59. Cambridge: Cambridge University Press, 2007.

Pateman, Carole. *The Sexual Contract*. Stanford, CA: Stanford University Press, 1988.

Patton, Paul. "Nietzsche and Hobbes." *International Studies in Philosophy* 33, no. 3 (2001): 99–116.

Paul, Joanne. "Council, Command and Crisis." *Hobbes Studies* 28, no. 2 (2015): 107–31.

Pettit, Philip. "Liberty and *Leviathan*." *Politics, Philosophy and Economics* 4, no. 1 (2005): 131–51.

———. *Made with Words: Hobbes on Language, Mind, and Politics*. Princeton, NJ: Princeton University Press, 2008.

Pietarinen, Juhani. "*Conatus* as Active Power in Hobbes." *Hobbes Studies* 14, no. 1 (71–82): 2001.

---. "Motion and Reason: Hobbes's Difficulties with the Idea of Active Power." In *The World as Active Power*, edited by Valtteri Viljanen and Juhani Pietarinen, 185–212. Leiden: Brill, 2009.
Pitkin, Hanna. *The Concept of Representation*. Berkeley: University of California Press, 1967.
---. "Hobbes's Concept of Representation—I." *American Political Science Review* 58, no. 2 (1964): 328–40.
---. "Hobbes's Concept of Representation—II." *American Political Science Review* 58, no. 4 (1964): 902–18.
Polin, Raymond. "Hobbes et le citoyen." In *Thomas Hobbes: Philosophie première, théorie de la science et politique*, edited by Yves Charles Zarka, 327–37. Paris: Presses Universitaires de France, 1990.
---. *Politique et philosophie chez Thomas Hobbes*. Paris: Presses Universitaires de France, 1953.
Poole, Thomas. "Hobbes on Law and Prerogative." In *Hobbes and the Law*, edited by David Dyzenhaus and Thomas Poole, 68–96. Cambridge: Cambridge University Press, 2012.
Prokhovnik, Raia. "Hobbes, Sovereignty, and Politics: Rethinking International Political Space." In *International Political Theory after Hobbes: Analysis, Interpretation and Orientation*, edited by Raia Prokhovnik and Gabriella Slomp, 189–212. Basingstoke: Palgrave Macmillan, 2010.
---. "Hobbes's Artifice as Social Construction." *Hobbes Studies* 18, no. 1 (2005): 74–94.
---. *Rhetoric and Philosophy in Hobbes's* Leviathan. New York: Garland Publishing, 1991.
Rahe, Paul A. *Against Throne and Altar: Machiavelli and Political Theory under the English Republic*. Cambridge: Cambridge University Press, 2008.
---. *Republics Ancient and Modern, Volume II: New Modes and Orders in Early Modern Political Thought*. Chapel Hill: University of North Carolina Press, 1994.
Rancière, Jacques. *Disagreement: Politics and Philosophy*. Translated by Julie Rose. Minneapolis: University of Minnesota Press, 1999.
Rapaczynski, Andrzej. *Nature and Politics: Liberalism in the Philosophies of Hobbes, Locke and Rousseau*. Ithaca, NY: Cornell University Press, 1987.
Raylor, Timothy. *Philosophy, Rhetoric, and Thomas Hobbes*. Oxford: Oxford University Press, 2018.
Rayner, Jeremy. "Hobbes and the Rhetoricians." *Hobbes Studies* 4, no. 1 (1991): 76–95.
Reiners, Derek. "Biological Correctness: Thomas Hobbes's Natural Ethics." *Hobbes Studies* 21, no. 1 (2008): 63–83.
Remer, Gary. "Hobbes, the Rhetorical Tradition, and Toleration." *Review of Politics* 54, no. 1 (1992): 5–33.

Replogle, Ron. "Personality and Society in Hobbes's *Leviathan*." *Polity* 19, no. 4 (1987): 570–94.
Rhodes, Rosamund. "Hobbes's Fifth Law of Nature and Its Implications." *Hobbes Studies* 22, no. 2 (2009): 144–59.
Ribeiro, Renato Janine. "'Men of Feminine Courage': Thomas Hobbes and Life as a Right." *Hobbes Studies* 24, no. 1 (2011): 44–61.
Ridge, Michael. "Hobbesian Public Reason." *Ethics* 108, no. 3 (1998): 538–68.
Ristroph, Alice. "Criminal Law for Humans." In *Hobbes and the Law*, edited by David Dyzenhaus and Thomas Poole, 97–117. Cambridge: Cambridge University Press, 2012.
Robin, Corey. *Fear: The History of a Political Idea*. Oxford: Oxford University Press, 2004.
Rogers, G. A. J. "Hobbes and His Contemporaries." In *The Cambridge Companion to Hobbes's Leviathan*, edited by Patricia Springborg, 413–40. Cambridge: Cambridge University Press, 2007.
Ross, George MacDonald. *Starting with Hobbes*. New York: Continuum, 2009.
Ross, Ralph. "Some Puzzles in Hobbes." In *Thomas Hobbes in His Time*, edited by Ralph Ross, Herbert W. Schneider, and Theodore Waldman, 42–60. Minneapolis: University of Minnesota Press, 1974.
Rudolph, Ross. "Hobbes et la psychologie morale: l'obligation et la vertu." In *Thomas Hobbes: Philosophie première, théorie de la science et politique*, edited by Yves Charles Zarka, 247–63. Paris: Presses Universitaires de France, 1990.
———. "The Micro-Foundations of Hobbes's Political Theory." *Hobbes Studies* 4, no. 1 (1991): 34–52.
Runciman, David. "Hobbes's Theory of Representation: Anti-Democratic or Proto-Democratic?" In *Political Representation*, edited by Ian Shapiro, Susan C. Stokes, Elisabeth Jean Wood, and Alexander S. Kirshner, 15–34. Cambridge: Cambridge University Press, 2010.
———. *Pluralism and the Personality of the State*. Cambridge: Cambridge University Press, 2009.
———. *Political Hypocrisy: The Mask of Power from Hobbes to Orwell and Beyond*. Princeton, NJ: Princeton University Press, 2008.
———. "The Sovereign." In *The Oxford Handbook of Hobbes*, edited by A. P. Martinich and Kinch Hoekstra, 359–77. Oxford: Oxford University Press, 2016.
———. "What Kind of Person Is Hobbes's State? A Reply to Skinner." *Journal of Political Philosophy* 8, no. 2 (2000): 268–78.
Ryan, Alan. "Hobbes and Individualism." In *Perspectives on Thomas Hobbes*, edited by G. A. J. Rogers and Alan Ryan, 81–105. Oxford: Clarendon Press, 1988.
———. "Hobbes's Political Philosophy." In *The Cambridge Companion to Hobbes*, edited by Tom Sorell, 208–45. Cambridge: Cambridge University Press, 1996.

———. *The Philosophy of the Social Sciences*. London: Macmillan Press, 1970.
Sacksteder, William. "Hobbes: Man the Maker." In *Thomas Hobbes: His View of Man*, edited by J. G. van der Bend, 77–88. Amsterdam: Rodopi, 1982.
———. "Hobbes's Science of Human Nature." *Hobbes Studies* 3, no. 1 (1990): 35–53.
———. "How Much of Hobbes Might Spinoza Have Read?" *Southwestern Journal of Philosophy* 11, no. 2 (1990): 25–39.
———. "Man the Artificer: Notes on Animals, Humans and Machines in Hobbes." *Southern Journal of Philosophy* 22, no. 1 (1984): 105–21.
Sagar, Paul. "Of Mushrooms and Method: History and the Family in Hobbes's Science of Politics." *European Journal of Political Theory* 14, no. 1 (2015): 98–117.
———. "What Is the Leviathan?" *Hobbes Studies* 31, no. 1 (2018): 73–92.
Santi, Raffaella. "Thomas Hobbes, John Stuart Mill et la liberté." In *Hobbes et le libéralisme*, edited by Yves Charles Zarka, 51–74. Paris: Éditions Mimésis, 2016.
Saxonhouse, Arlene W. "Hobbes and the Beginnings of Modern Political Thought." In *Three Discourses*, by Thomas Hobbes, 123–54. edited by Noel B. Reynolds and Arlene W. Saxonhouse. Chicago: University of Chicago Press, 1995.
Schlatter, Richard. "Thomas Hobbes and Thucydides." *Journal of the History of Ideas* 6, no. 3 (1945): 350–62.
Schmitt, Carl. *Dictatorship: From the Origin of the Modern Concept of Sovereignty to the Proletarian Class Struggle*. Translated by Michael Hoelzl and Graham Ward. Cambridge: Polity, 2014.
Schuhmann, Karl. "Hobbes and the Political Thought of Plato and Aristotle." In *Selected Papers on Renaissance Philosophy and on Thomas Hobbes*, edited by Piet Steenbakkers and Cees Leijenhorst, 191–207. Berlin: Springer-Science + Business Media, 2004.
———. "Skinner's Hobbes." *British Journal for the History of Philosophy* 6, no. 1 (1998): 115–25.
Schwartzberg, Melissa. *Democracy and Legal Change*. Cambridge: Cambridge University Press, 2007.
Shapin, Steven, and Simon Schaffer. Leviathan *and the Air-Pump: Hobbes, Boyle, and the Experimental Life*. Princeton, NJ: Princeton University Press, 1985.
Sheridan, Patricia. "Resisting the Scaffold: Self-Preservation and Limits of Obligation in Hobbes's *Leviathan*." *Hobbes Studies* 24, no. 2 (2011): 137–57.
Shulman, George. "Hobbes, Puritans, and Promethean Politics." *Political Theory* 16, no. 3 (1988): 426–43.
———. "Metaphor and Modernization in the Political Thought of Thomas Hobbes." *Political Theory* 17, no. 3 (1989): 392–416.
Sintomer, Yves. "From Deliberative to Radical Democracy? Sortition and Politics in the Twenty-First Century." *Politics & Society* 46, no. 3 (2018): 337–57.

Skinner, Daniel. "Political Theory beyond the Rhetoric-Reason Divide: Hobbes, Semantic Indeterminacy, and Political Order." *Review of Politics* 73, no. 4 (2011): 561–80.

Skinner, Quentin. "The Context of Hobbes's Theory of Political Obligation." In *Visions of Politics, Volume 3: Hobbes and Civil Science*, 265–86. Cambridge: Cambridge University Press, 2002.

———. *From Humanism to Hobbes: Studies in Politics and Rhetoric*. Cambridge: Cambridge University Press, 2018.

———. "Historical Introduction." In *Writings on Common Law and Hereditary Right*, by Thomas Hobbes, 159–76. edited by Alan Cromartie and Quentin Skinner. Oxford: Clarendon Press, 2005.

———. "Hobbes and His Disciples in France and England." In *Visions of Politics, Volume 3: Hobbes and Civil Science*, 308–23. Cambridge: Cambridge University Press, 2002.

———. *Hobbes and Republican Liberty*. Cambridge: Cambridge University Press, 2008.

———. "Hobbes and the *Studia Humanitatis*." In *Visions of Politics, Volume 3: Hobbes and Civil Science*, 38–65. Cambridge: Cambridge University Press, 2002.

———. "Hobbes on Persons, Authors and Representatives." In *The Cambridge Companion to Hobbes's* Leviathan, 157–80. Cambridge: Cambridge University Press, 2007.

———. "Hobbes on Representation." *European Journal of Philosophy* 13, no. 2 (2005): 155–84.

———. "Hobbes on Rhetoric and the Construction of Morality." In *Visions of Politics, Volume 3: Hobbes and Civil Science*, 87–141. Cambridge: Cambridge University Press, 2002.

———. *Reason and Rhetoric in the Philosophy of Hobbes*. Cambridge: Cambridge University Press, 1996.

———. "Thomas Hobbes's Antiliberal Theory of Liberty." In *Liberalism without Illusions: Essays on Liberal Theory and the Political Vision*, edited by Bernard Yack, 149–69. Chicago: University of Chicago Press, 1996.

Slomp, Gabriella. "Hobbes, Thucydides and the Three Greatest Things." *History of Political Thought* 11, no. 4 (1990): 565–86.

———. "On Ambition, Greed, and Fear." In *Hobbes's* Behemoth*: Religion and Democracy*, edited by Tomaž Mastnak, 129–47. Exeter: Imprint Academic, 2009.

———. "The Politics of Motion and the Motion of Politics." In *International Political Theory after Hobbes: Analysis, Interpretation and Orientation*, edited by Raia Prokhovnik and Gabriella Slomp, 18–41. Basingstoke: Palgrave Macmillan, 2000.

———. *Thomas Hobbes and the Political Philosophy of Glory*. Basingstoke: Macmillan Press, 2000.

Smith, Bruce J. *The Sense of Injustice and the Origin of Modern Democracy.* Rochester, NY: University of Rochester Press, 2018.
Smith, Sophie. "Democracy and the Body Politic from Aristotle to Hobbes." *Political Theory* 46, no. 2 (2018): 167–96.
Smith, Travis D. "On the Fourth Law of Nature." *Hobbes Studies* 16, no. 1 (2003): 84–94.
Sommerville, Johan P. "Hobbes and Independency." *Rivista di Storia della filosofia* 59, no. 1 (2004): 155–73.
———. *Thomas Hobbes: Political Ideas in Historical Context.* Basingstoke: Macmillan, 1992.
Sorell, Tom. *Hobbes.* London: Routledge & Kegan Paul, 1986.
———. "Hobbes, Public Safety and Political Economy." In *International Political Theory after Hobbes: Analysis, Interpretation and Orientation,* edited by Raia Prokhovnik and Gabriella Slomp. Basingstoke: Palgrave Macmillan, 42–55.
———. "Law and Equity in Hobbes." *Critical Review of International Social and Political Philosophy* 19, no. 1 (2016): 29–46.
———. "The Normative and the Explanatory in Hobbes's Political Philosophy." *Rivista di Storia della Filosofia* 59, no. 1 (2004): 205–17.
Sorgi, Giuseppe. "Hobbes on 'Bodies Politic.'" *Hobbes Studies* 9, no. 1 (1996): 71–87.
Spragens, Thomas A. *The Politics of Motion: The World of Thomas Hobbes.* Lexington: University Press of Kentucky, 1973.
Springborg, Patricia. "*Leviathan,* Mythic History, and National Historiography." In *The Historical Imagination in Early Modern Britain: History, Rhetoric, and Fiction, 1500–1800,* edited by Donald R. Kelley and David Harris Sacks, 267–97. Cambridge: Cambridge University Press.
Sreedhar, Susanne. *Hobbes on Resistance: Defying the Leviathan.* Cambridge: Cambridge University Press, 2010.
———. "Interpreting Hobbes on Civil Liberties and Rights of Resistance." In *Interpreting Hobbes's Political Philosophy,* edited by S. A. Lloyd, 141–55. Cambridge: Cambridge University Press, 2019.
Stanlick, Nancy A. "Hobbesian Friendship: Valuing Others for Oneself." *Journal of Social Philosophy* 33, no. 3 (2002): 345–59.
Stanton, Timothy. "Hobbes and Locke on Natural Law and Jesus Christ." *History of Political Thought* 29, no. 1 (2008): 65–88.
Stauffer, Devin. *Hobbes's Kingdom of Light: A Study of the Foundations of Modern Political Philosophy.* Chicago: University of Chicago Press, 2018.
Steinberger, Peter J. "Hobbes, Rousseau, and the Modern Conception of the State." *Journal of Politics* 70, no. 3 (2008): 595–611.
———. "Hobbesian Resistance." *American Journal of Political Science* 46, no. 4 (2002): 856–65.
Steinmetz, Alicia. "Hobbes and the Politics of Translation." *Political Theory* 49, no. 1 (2021): 83–108.

Strauss, Leo. *The Political Philosophy of Hobbes: Its Basis and Genesis.* Chicago: Chicago University Press, 1952.
Strong, Tracy B. "Glory and the Law in Hobbes." *European Journal of Political Theory* 16, no. 1 (2017): 61–76.
———. "How to Write Scripture: Words, Authority, and Politics in Thomas Hobbes." *Critical Inquiry* 20, no. 1 (1993): 128–59.
Sullivan, Vickie B. *Machiavelli, Hobbes, and the Formation of a Liberal Republicanism in England.* Cambridge: Cambridge University Press, 2004.
Suzuki, Yoshinori. "Thomas Hobbes on Social Welfare." *Hobbes Studies* 11, no. 1 (1998): 46–60.
Tabb, Kathryn. "The Fate of Nebuchadnezzar: Curiosity and Human Nature in Hobbes." *Hobbes Studies* 27, no. 1 (2014): 13–34.
Taylor, A. E. "The Ethical Doctrine of Hobbes." In *Hobbes Studies*, edited by K. C. Brown, 33–55. Oxford: Basil Blackwell, 1965.
Taylor, Quentin. "Leviathan Bound; or the Re-Education of Thomas Hobbes." *Hobbes Studies* 22, no. 2 (2009): 123–42.
Thomas, Keith. "The Social Origins of Hobbes's Political Thought." In *Hobbes Studies*, edited by K. C. Brown, 185–236. Oxford: Basil Blackwell, 1965.
Townshend, Jules. "Hobbes as Possessive Individualist: Interrogating the C. B. Macpherson Thesis." *Hobbes Studies* 12, no. 1 (1999): 52–71.
Trainor, Brian. "Hobbes, Skinner, and the Person of the State." *Hobbes Studies* 14, no. 1 (2001): 59–70.
Trigg, Christopher. "Drones, Hobbes, and Liberal Enchantment." *Political Theology* 19, no. 7 (2018): 553–71.
Tuck, Richard. "Democratic Sovereignty and Democratic Government: The Sleeping Sovereign." In *Popular Sovereignty in Historical Perspective*, edited by Richard Bourke and Quentin Skinner, 115–41. Cambridge: Cambridge University Press, 2016.
———. *Hobbes.* Oxford: Oxford University Press, 1989.
———. "Hobbes and Democracy." In *Rethinking the Foundations of Modern Political Thought*, edited by Annabel Brett, James Tully, and Holly Hamilton-Bleakley, 171–90. Cambridge: Cambridge University Press, 2006.
———. *Natural Rights Theories: Their Origins and Development.* Cambridge: Cambridge University Press, 1979.
———. *Philosophy and Government, 1572–1651.* Cambridge: Cambridge University Press, 1993.
———. *The Rights of War and Peace: Political Thought and the International Order from Grotius to Kant.* Oxford: Oxford University Press, 1991.
———. *The Sleeping Sovereign: The Invention of Modern Democracy.* Cambridge: Cambridge University Press, 2015.
———. "The Utopianism of *Leviathan*." In Leviathan *After 350 Years*, edited by Tom Sorell and Luc Foisneau, 125–38. Oxford: Oxford University Press, 2004.

Undersrud, David. "On Natural Law and Civil Law in the Political Philosophy of Hobbes." *History of Political Thought* 35, no. 4 (2014): 683–716.

Urbinati, Nadia. *Democracy Disfigured: Opinion, Truth, and the People.* Cambridge: Harvard University Press, 2014.

Vanden Houten, Art. "Prudence in Hobbes's Political Philosophy." *History of Political Thought* 33, no. 2 (2002): 266–87.

Vanderschraaf, Peter. "Instituting the Hobbesian Commonwealth." *Pacific Philosophical Quarterly* 82, no. 3–4 (2001): 383–405.

van Mill, David. *Liberty, Rationality, and Agency in Hobbes.* Albany: State University of New York Press, 2001.

Vaughan, Geoffrey M. "The Audiences of 'Behemoth' and the Politics of Conversation." In *Hobbes's Behemoth: Religion and Democracy*, edited by Tomaž Mastnak, 170–85. Exeter: Imprint Academic, 2009.

———. *Behemoth Teaches Leviathan: Thomas Hobbes or Political Education.* Lanham, MD: Lexington Books, 2002.

Villey, Michel. "Le droit de l'individu chez Hobbes." In *Hobbes-Forschungen*, edited by Reinhart Koselleck and Roman Schnur, 173–97. Berlin: Duncker & Humbolt, 1969.

Vinx, Lars. "Hobbes on Civic Liberty and the Rule of Law." In *Hobbes and the Law*, edited by David Dyzenhaus and Thomas Poole, 145–64. Cambridge: Cambridge University Press, 2012.

Virno, Paolo. *A Grammar of the Multitude: For an Analysis of Contemporary Forms of Life.* Translated by Isabella Bertoletti, James Cascaito, and Andrea Casson. Los Angeles: Semiotext(e), 2004.

Visintainer, John R. "Hobbes on Goodness and Pressure on the Sovereign." *Hobbes Studies* 12, no. 1 (1999): 26–32.

Voisset-Veysseyre, Cécile. "The Wolf Motif in the Hobbesian Text." *Hobbes Studies* 23, no. 2 (2010): 124–38.

Waldman, Theodore. "Hobbes on the Generation of a Public Person." In *Thomas Hobbes in His Time*, edited by Ralph Ross, Herbert W. Schneider, and Theodore Waldman, 61–83. Minneapolis: University of Minnesota Press, 1974.

Walton, Craig. "The *Philosophia Prima* of Thomas Hobbes." In *Thomas Hobbes in His Time*, edited by Ralph Ross, Herbert W. Schneider, and Theodore Waldman, 31–41. Minneapolis: University of Minnesota Press, 1974.

Ward, Lee. "Equity and Political Economy in Thomas Hobbes." *American Journal of Political Science* 64, no. 4 (2020): 823–35.

———. "Thomas Hobbes and John Locke on a Liberal Right of Secession." *Political Research Quarterly* 70, no. 4 (2017): 876–88.

Warrender, Howard. *The Political Philosophy of Hobbes: His Theory of Obligation.* Oxford: Oxford University Press, 1957.

Watkins, J. W. N. *Hobbes's System of Ideas.* London: Hutchinson & Co., 1965.

———. "Philosophy and Politics in Hobbes." In *Hobbes Studies*, edited by K. C. Brown, 237–62. Oxford: Basil Blackwell, 1965.
Weithman, Paul. "Hobbes on Persons and Authorization." In *Interpreting Hobbes's Political Philosophy*, edited by S. A. Lloyd, 173–90. Cambridge: Cambridge University Press, 2019.
Wetters, Kirk. *The Opinion System: Impasses of the Public Sphere from Hobbes to Habermas*. New York: Fordham University Press, 2008.
Whelan, Frederick G. "Language and Its Abuses in Hobbes's Political Philosophy." *American Political Science Review* 75, no. 1 (1981): 59–75.
Whiteside, Kerry H. "Hobbes's Ultranominalist Critique of Natural Right." *Polity* 20, no. 3 (1988): 457–78.
Williams, David Lay. "Hobbes on Wealth, Poverty and Economic Inequality." *Hobbes Studies* 34, no. 1 (2021): 9–57.
Willms, Bernard. "La politique comme philosophie première: Hobbes penseur radical de la politique." In *Thomas Hobbes: Philosophie première, théorie de la science et politique*, edited by Yves Charles Zarka, 91–104. Paris: Presses Universitaires de France, 1990.
———. "Liberty as *conditio humana*." In *Thomas Hobbes: His View of Man*, edited by J. G. van der Bend, 99–11. Amsterdam: Rodopi, 1982.
Wolin, Sheldon. "Hobbes and the Culture of Despotism." In *Thomas Hobbes and Political Theory*, edited by Mary G. Dietz, 9–36. Lawrence: University Press of Kansas, 1990.
———. "Hobbes and the Epic Tradition." In *Fugitive Democracy and Other Essays*, by Sheldon Wolin, 117–48. edited by Nicholas Xenos. Princeton, NJ: Princeton University Press, 2016.
———. *Politics and Vision: Continuity and Innovation in Western Political Thought*. Princeton, NJ: Princeton University Press, 2004.
Wood, Neal. "Thomas Hobbes and the Crisis of the English Aristocracy." *History of Political Thought* 1, no. 3 (1980): 437–52.
Wootton, David. *Power, Pleasure, and Profit: Insatiable Appetites from Machiavelli to Madison*. Cambridge: Belknap Press, 2018.
Wright, Joanne H., and Nancy J. Hirschmann. "Introduction: The Many Faces of 'Mr. Hobs.'" In *Feminist Interpretations of Thomas Hobbes*, edited by Nancy J. Hirschmann and Joanne H. Wright, 1–17. University Park: Pennsylvania State University Press, 2012.
Zagorin, Perez. *Hobbes and the Law of Nature*. Princeton, NJ: Princeton University Press, 2009.
Zarka, Yves Charles. "Aspects sémantiques, syntaxiques et pragmatiques de le théorie du langage chez Hobbes." In *Thomas Hobbes de la métaphysique à la politique*, edited by Martin Bertman and Michel Malherbe, 33–46. Paris: Librairie Philosophique J. Vrin, 1989.

———. "Droit de resistance et droit penal chez Hobbes." In *Hobbes oggi*, edited by Andrea Napoli and Guido Canziani, 177–96. Milano: Franco Angeli, 1990.
———. *Hobbes and Modern Political Thought*. Translated by James Griffith. Edinburgh: Edinburgh University Press, 1995.
———, ed. *Hobbes et le libéralisme*. Paris: Éditions Mimésis, 2016.
———. *La décision métaphysique de Hobbes: Conditions de la politique*. Paris: Librairie Philosophique J. Vrin, 1987.
———. "Liberté, nécessité, hasard: La théorie générale de l'événement chez Hobbes." *Rivista di Storia della Filosofia* 59, no. 1 (2004): 249–61.
———. "The Political Subject." In Leviathan *After 350 Years*, edited by Tom Sorell and Luc Foisneau, translated by Edward Hughes, 167–82. Oxford: Oxford University Press, 2004.

Index

Abizadeh, Arash, 69, 121–122, 154–155, 203n5, 212n92, 214n101, 223n76, 245n131, 253n24, 262n90, 265n124
absolutism
  aristocracy and, 30
  characteristics of democracy and, 5, 29–31
  deliberation and, 30
  Leviathan and, 30
  modern democratic theory and, 3, 5
  monarchy and, 29
  nominalism and, 225–226n88
  reason and, 242n89, 249n170
  sovereignty and, 29–31
absurd speech, 5–6, 119, 156, 224n85
accommodation, 175, 263n100, 267n154
administration of democracy, 23–31
Agrippa, 33
Allen, Danielle, 267n157
alterity. *See* diversity
anthropology. *See* philosophical anthropology
Anti-White (Hobbes), 84, 86, 124, 156, 217n12
Arato, Andrew, 213n100
aristocracy
  absolutism and, 30
  Aristotelianism and, 31
  characteristics of democracy and, 33, 51–54, 68, 192n3
  De Cive and, 31
  definition of, 18, 22, 31
  deliberation and, 54
  election in, 31
  Elements of Law and, 40, 54, 99, 175
  equality and, 11, 102, 105–108, 128–130, 176, 185
  Leviathan and, 210n63
  modern democratic theory and, 31
  monarchy and, 176
  normativity of democracy and, 178
  obedience and, 209n53
  orators and, 33, 51–54
  originary democratic moment and, 23, 31, 50, 54, 99, 175
  parliamentarian thought and, 52–53
  participation and, 51
  sovereignty and, 18, 27
  unitary will and, 18, 22
Aristotelianism
  aristocracy and, 31
  characteristics of democracy and, 42, 50, 194n35, 201n126
  civil war and, 58
  contingency and, 83
  equality and, 102–103, 107–108, 127, 166, 234n8

Aristotelianism (continued)
  liberty and, 42, 50, 58
  natural law and, 12, 149, 158, 252n19, 253n24, 256n43
  philosophical anthropology and, 97–98, 145, 149, 256n45
  politics and, 149, 256n45
  psychological egoism and, 98
  reason and, 103
  sense perception and, 221n56
  sovereignty and, 258–259n59
  teleology and, 78, 83
  women and, 103
artificial persons. See persons
assemblies. See characteristics of democracy; critique of democracy
Athenian democracy
  chaos of, 77, 139–140
  characteristics of democracy and, 50
  critique of democracy and, 32–33, 77, 139–140, 184
  hubris of, 33, 77, 139, 184
  liberty and, 58
  modern democratic theory and, 139–140
  normativity of democracy and, 184
  openness of world and, 139–140
authorization
  alienation and, 202n1, 202n3
  diversity and, 70
  Leviathan and, 3, 10, 46–47, 59–67, 69–71, 170, 182, 202n1, 213n99, 215n111, 216n112
  multitude and, 3, 63–65, 69
  natural law and, 146
  nominalism and, 4
  normativity of democracy and, 60–61, 67
  originary democratic moment and, 66–71
  participation and, 67, 170
  persons and, 62–66, 211n85, 212n93
  reason and, 118
  representation and, 3, 62, 65, 67–68, 203n5, 211n85
  social contract and, 202n3
  sovereignty and, 3, 46–47, 61–66, 69, 202n3, 212n92
  unitary will and, 3, 64–69, 213n99, 259n62

Ball, Terence, 223n68
Barnouw, Jeffrey, 198n84, 244n121, 253n23
Baumgold, Deborah, 47, 209n56, 216n111, 225n88
Baumrin, Bernard, 239n59
Behemoth (Hobbes)
  audience of, 241n79
  civil war in, 53–54
  democratical gentlemen in, 52–54, 60, 101–102
  eloquence in, 36
  equality in, 115, 132
  liberty in, 52
  natural law in, 148
  obedience in, 202n127
  oligarchy in, 53
  orators in, 52
  parliamentarian thought in, 53
  reason in, 248n169
  scriptural interpretation in, 134
  writing of, 241n79, 249n180
Bejan, Teresa, 241n76
Benjamin, Walter, 222n61
Berent, Moshe, 201n126
Bertman, Martin, 198n77, 219n22, 230n136, 256n43
Blau, Adrian, 204n10
Bobbio, Norberto, 155
Borrelli, Gianfranco, 3
Boss, Gilbert, 229n132, 233n151

Bramhall, John, 57, 82, 93, 97, 127, 148, 157, 227n109, 259n62
Bray, Michael, 220n40
Braybrooke, David, 194n35
Brooke, Christopher, 177
Byron, Michael, 220n45

Carmel, Elad, 240n72
Carrive, Paulette, 246n146
Castoriadis, Cornelius, 6–7, 139, 217n6, 250n1
Chanteur, Janine, 192n11, 193n18
characteristics of democracy. *See also* equality; openness of world
   absolutism and, 5, 29–31
   administration and, 23–31
   aristocracy and, 33, 51–54, 68, 192n3
   Aristotelianism and, 42, 50, 194n35, 201n126
   Athenian democracy and, 50
   civil war and, 53–54
   command distinguished from counsel in, 37–38
   conflict inherent in democracy and, 18, 41–43, 45, 49, 75, 151, 181–182, 199n92
   counsels and, 32, 35, 37–38
   De Cive and, 19, 28, 31
   definition of democracy through, 2, 8–10, 18, 22–26, 28, 50, 192n3, 207n34
   deliberation and, 9, 11, 13, 19, 24, 30, 35–39
   dissolution of democracy and, 24, 30
   Elements of Law and, 18–19, 27–28
   eloquence and, 37–38
   equality and, 11, 108, 110, 185
   institutional spaces and, 24–25, 28, 50–51, 75, 167–168
   Leviathan and, 18–19, 30
   liberty and, 7, 12, 50, 54
   modern democratic theory and, 25–26, 192n3
   monarchy and, 33–34
   multitude and, 8–9, 19–20, 24, 26, 50, 200–201n118
   natural law and, 12–13
   normativity of democracy and, 2, 7–9, 12, 18–19
   openness of world and, 102, 139–140
   orators and, 51–52
   originary democratic moment and, 10, 23–25, 50, 99
   overview of, 2, 6–13, 17–19
   participation and, 6, 10, 19, 24, 28–31, 48, 50–52, 76–77
   persons and, 20–24, 33, 51
   recall of officials and, 28–29
   representation and, 3–4, 214n101
   role of democracy in Hobbes's thought and, 2, 6–13, 18, 32, 43, 47–48, 71, 75, 174, 182
   self-institution and, 6–7, 10, 76–77
   self-limitation and, 33–34
   social contract and, 23
   sovereignty and, 8, 13, 17–18, 24–31, 50–51
   unitary will and, 19–23, 26, 35–36, 50
Chou, Chia-Yu, 236–237n21
Cicero, 5, 119
civil law. *See also* natural law
   diversity and, 99
   equality and, 107
   justice and, 118, 129, 169
   liberty and, 56–58, 178
   natural law and, 129, 141, 146–149, 154–155, 160–161, 256n43
   obedience and, 58, 118, 154–155
   participation and, 178
   sovereignty and, 57, 167

302 | Index

civil science
  critique of democracy and, 32, 43, 182
  De Cive in, 48
  disagreement and, 153–154
  diversity and, 152–153, 177
  Elements of Law and, 48
  equality and, 106, 108, 115
  geometry and, 191n32
  internalization of, 163
  liberty and, 162
  limits of natural knowledge and, 77–81
  modern democratic theory and, 3–5
  nominalism and, 89–90
  normativity of democracy and, 8, 48, 173–174, 191n32
  ontological materialism and, 80
  philosophical anthropology and, 84, 115
  philosophy and, 80
  reason and, 35, 153
  repolitization of, 154
  role of democracy in, 2, 8–9, 18, 43, 47–48, 75, 174, 182
  sense perception and, 84–85
  sovereignty and, 8
civil war
  Aristotelianism and, 58
  Behemoth and, 53–54
  characteristics of democracy and, 53–54
  critique of democracy and, 31, 41–42
  De Cive and, 42, 183
  deliberation and, 41, 53–54
  Elements of Law and, 42
  English Civil War, 46, 53, 182–183
  Leviathan and, 41, 46, 53, 66
  liberty and, 58
  multitude and, 41
Cohen, Joshua, 264n109

Coke, Edward, 128, 211n74
Collins, Jeffrey, 189n6
commonwealths. *See* aristocracy; characteristics of democracy; monarchy; sovereignty
complete understanding, 81, 84, 125–126, 139
contingency. *See* openness of world
Cooper, Kody, 252n19
Craig, Leon, 31, 104, 192n5
Craig, Patrick, 200n118
creativity, 95–100
Crepell, Ingrid, 248n169
Crignon, Philippe, 259n61
Critical Theory, 185
critique of democracy. *See also* development of Hobbes's thought
  ancient precursors to, 1–2, 32–33, 49
  Athenian democracy and, 32–33, 77, 139–140, 184
  civil science and, 32, 43, 182
  civil war and, 31, 41–42
  conflict inherent in democracy and, 7, 9, 11–12, 34, 41–43, 45, 49, 75, 151, 181–182, 199n92
  consistency of, 2, 6–13, 18, 32, 43, 47–48, 71, 75, 174, 182
  counsels and, 37–38
  as counterfigure, 2, 8–9
  deliberation and, 6–7, 9, 11–12, 35–43, 49, 51, 143, 172, 181–182, 186, 199n92
  diversity and, 33, 37, 40, 42, 172
  eloquence and, 6, 9, 36–38, 52, 143, 177, 182
  flattery and, 33–35
  hubris and, 7, 31–36, 77
  liberty and, 42–43, 49–50
  madness of democracy and, 38–43, 151, 172, 181, 199n106

Index | 303

modern democratic theory and, 45, 173–174
monarchy and, 32, 34–36
most undesirable authority, democracy as, 32, 34, 39–41, 47, 49, 71, 173
multitude and, 37–43
normativity of democracy and, 32, 48, 71, 141, 143, 170
openness of world and, 7, 36
orators and, 32–34, 51–52
overview of, 6–12, 32–33
participation and, 169–173
passions and, 6–7, 9, 36–40, 172
persons and, 34, 40
philosophical anthropology and, 172–173
reason and, 9, 36–43, 172
reinstating of what democracy was designed to overcome, 18–19, 40–41, 151–152
rejection of, 143, 173, 177, 186
self-limitation and, 6–7, 9, 12, 33–34, 36
sovereignty and, 6–9, 31–32, 41–42, 172–173, 181
unitary will and, 4–5, 20, 33, 35–36, 41, 45, 49
curiosity, 122–126, 150, 178, 244n121
Curran, Eleanor, 263n102, 265n114

Debord, Guy, 222n61
"Decameron Physiologicum" (Hobbes), 83
De Cive (Hobbes)
    administration in, 23, 26, 29
    aristocracy in, 31
    characteristics of democracy in, 19, 28, 31
    civil science in, 48
    civil war in, 42, 183
    deliberation in, 38
    development of Hobbes's thought in, 48, 55, 68–71, 169–170, 182
    diversity in, 111
    eloquence in, 36–38
    equality in, 106–108, 111
    liberty in, 9–10, 48–49, 54–60
    monarchy in, 8
    multitude in, 19–23, 26
    natural law in, 122, 142–143, 148, 160–161
    normativity of democracy in, 9–10, 54–55, 58–61, 68, 169–170, 183
    openness of world in, 96–97
    originary democratic moment in, 10, 12–13, 23, 60, 69–71, 169–170, 182, 209n56
    participation in, 12, 24, 54–59, 142, 165–166, 169–170, 186
    passions in, 10, 38
    persons in, 19–23, 68
    philosophical anthropology in, 97
    philosophy in, 75–76
    public safety in, 160–161
    reason in, 122, 241n85
    representation in, 69–70
    sovereignty in, 10, 25–26, 29, 45–46, 60, 63, 69–70
De Corpore (Hobbes), 75–77, 82, 104, 114, 158
definition of democracy. *See* characteristics of democracy
De Homine (Hobbes), 40, 61, 80, 92, 94–95, 114, 132, 171
Deleule, Didier, 229n122
deliberation
    absolutism and, 30
    action and, 121
    aristocracy and, 54
    characteristics of democracy and, 9, 11, 13, 19, 24, 30, 35–39
    civil war and, 41, 53–54

deliberation *(continued)*
  critique of democracy and, 6–7, 9, 11–12, 35–43, 49, 51, 143, 172, 181–182, 186, 199n92
  De Cive and, 38
  definition of, 121
  eloquence and, 9, 37, 59
  equality and, 9, 11–12
  flattery and, 35
  good and evil and, 121
  happiness and, 122–126
  liberty and, 157–158
  madness and, 121–122
  modern democratic theory and, 173–174
  monarchy and, 35–36
  participation and, 51, 172–173
  passions and, 6–7, 9, 36–40, 121–122
  philosophical anthropology and, 122–126
  reason and, 6–7, 11, 36, 38–40, 121–122
  self-limitation and, 6–7, 12
  sovereignty and, 9
  unitary will and, 9, 19, 36
democracy. *See* Athenian democracy; characteristics of democracy; critique of democracy; Hobbesian Democracy; modern democratic theory; normativity of democracy
democratical gentlemen, 52–54, 60, 101–102
democratical Hobbesians, 3–5
democratic imaginary. *See* characteristics of democracy
desires. *See* passions
development of Hobbes's thought
  critique of democracy and, 47–49, 71, 75, 182
  De Cive and, 48, 55, 68–71, 169–170, 182
  disappearance of democracy and, 66–71
  Elements of Law and, 9, 46–48, 71, 182–183, 213n96
  Leviathan and, 9, 45–48, 53, 55–58, 66–71, 166–167, 170, 182–183, 202n1, 202n3, 210n63, 213n96, 214n103
  liberty and, 49–50, 55–57
  normativity of democracy and, 48, 71, 75, 169, 182
  participation and, 48, 164–173, 177–178
  role of democracy in, 2, 6–13, 18, 32, 43, 47–48, 71, 75, 174, 182
Devine, Francis Edward, 251n8
A Dialogue between a Philosopher and a Student of the Common Law of England (Hobbes), 127–128, 147
"A Discourse on the Beginning of Tacitus" (Hobbes), 49, 99
diversity
  authorization and, 70
  civil law and, 99
  civil science and, 152–153, 177
  critique of democracy and, 33, 37, 40, 42, 172
  De Cive and, 111
  Elements of Law and, 90, 111
  equality and, 11, 105–106, 111–112, 119–120, 130–131, 176–177, 184–185, 267–268n157
  good and evil and, 91–92
  happiness and, 125–126
  natural law and, 142, 144–146, 149, 152–153, 165
  nominalism and, 89–90
  ontological materialism and, 11, 232n143
  openness of world and, 10, 95–100, 177
  participation and, 170–171

passions and, 89–96, 111
philosophical anthropology and, 96, 171
philosophy and, 80, 117
reason and, 116–122, 127–128
self-institution and, 11
sense perception and, 86–90
social-historical context of, 95–100
sovereignty and, 5, 36, 67, 99
speech and, 89–90, 93–94
toleration and, 267n157
unitary will and, 33, 36, 96, 259n62
dogmatici, 96, 143
Douglass, Robin, 215n106, 215n111, 222n67, 254n27
Downes, Paul, 4
Dungey, Nicholas, 232n143
Dutch republican tradition, 2
Dyzenhaus, David, 260n66

The Elements of Law (Hobbes)
administration in, 23, 27–28
aristocracy in, 40, 54, 99, 175
characteristics of democracy in, 18–19, 27–28
civil law in, 149
civil science in, 48
civil war in, 42, 46
development of Hobbes's thought in, 9, 46–48, 71, 182–183, 213n96
diversity in, 90, 111
dogmatici in, 96–97
equality in, 85, 106–108, 110–111
justice in, 110
liberty in, 9, 48–55, 57–59, 165
mathematici in, 96
multitude in, 19–23
natural law in, 143, 149, 160–161, 252n14
normativity of democracy in, 9, 51, 175, 183

originary democratic moment in, 23–24, 28, 50, 54, 60, 71, 99, 182, 213n96, 216n112
participation in, 9, 49–54, 59, 167–168
passions in, 40
persons in, 19–23
power in, 85, 232n141
public safety in, 160–161
sense perception in, 85–86
sovereignty in, 27–28, 45–46, 63, 159–160
writing of, 9
eloquence. *See also* speech
characteristics of democracy and, 37–38
critique of democracy and, 6, 9, 36–38, 52, 143, 177, 182
De Cive and, 36–38
deliberation and, 9, 37, 59
forms of, 36–37
opinion and, 37
participation and, 51
passions and, 37–38, 172, 182
reason and, 36–37, 143, 182
English Civil War, 46, 53, 182–183
Epstein, Jeffrey, 229n132
equality
aristocracy and, 11, 102, 105–108, 128–130, 176, 185
Aristotelianism and, 102–103, 107–108, 127, 166, 234n8
Behemoth and, 115, 132
characteristics of democracy and, 11, 108, 110, 185
civil law and, 107
civil science and, 106, 108, 115
De Cive and, 106–108, 111
deliberation and, 9, 11–12
diversity and, 11, 105–106, 111–112, 119–120, 130–131, 176–177, 184–185, 267–268n157

equality (continued)
  equality-in-difference, 11, 106, 112, 141, 150, 176, 178
  error and, 112, 132
  happiness and, 123–126
  indigenous peoples and, 103–104
  of intelligences, 19, 102–107, 110–116, 126–127, 130, 135, 150–151
  judgment and, 131–132
  justice and, 108–110, 135, 238n38
  legal right and, 109–110
  Leviathan and, 106–109, 120, 129–130
  liberty and, 110, 141
  madness and, 131
  modern democratic theory and, 150–151, 175
  multitude and, 132
  natural equality, 11, 75, 103–109, 111, 164, 166, 176, 185
  natural law and, 106–111, 164
  nominalism and, 11, 112
  normativity of democracy and, 102–103, 140–141, 150, 175–176, 234n4
  ontological materialism and, 11
  participation and, 164, 166
  passions and, 111, 114
  pedagogy and, 114–116
  political competency and, 128–130
  political inequality and, 107–108, 176
  positive substance of, 111
  practice of, 126–135
  reason and, 11, 103–107, 110–120, 126–130
  reciprocity and, 267–268n157
  rejection of all titles and, 102, 105–108, 128–130, 185
  scriptural interpretation and, 133–134
  sense perception and, 112–113, 131
  sovereignty and, 105–106, 176–177
  speech and, 112–113
  state of nature and, 102
  women and, 103
  worth of individuals and, 128–130
error, 5, 112, 115, 119, 121, 132
Esposito, Roberto, 257n55
ethical preference for democracy. *See* normativity of democracy
Ewin, R. E., 267n157

Field, Sandra Leonie, 195n45, 207n34, 231n141, 249n170, 266n127
Finn, Stephen, 225–226n88
Flathman, Richard, 4, 153–154, 220n46
Flikshuh, Katrin, 215n111
Foisneau, Luc, 28, 199n92
foresight, 120, 122–123, 126
forms of commonwealth. *See* aristocracy; characteristics of democracy; monarchy
Forsyth, Murray, 213n99
Fox-Decent, Evan, 255n37
Frank, Jill, 234n8
freedom. *See* liberty
Frost, Samantha, 84, 223n71, 231n141

Garsten, Bryan, 203n5
Gauthier, David, 55, 241–242n89, 253n22
geometry, 79–80, 113, 191n32
Gert, Bernard, 199n106, 200n116
Geuss, Raymond, 221n51
Giancotti, Emilia, 218n14, 222n63
glory, 32, 59, 129, 169–171
Goldie, Mark, 187n3
Goldsmith, M. M., 213n97, 215n111, 226n98

good and evil, 90–92, 97, 116–117, 121, 146, 159, 244n117
Gooding, Nicholas, 256n45
Green, Michael J., 202n3

Hamilton, James, 210n62
Hampsher-Monk, Iain, 218n15, 252n14
Hampton, Jean, 195n62
Hansen, Donald, 249n171
happiness, 122–126, 160, 178, 245n132
Harding, Ryan, 209n56
Hardt, Michael, 257–258n57
Harvey, Thomas, 256n44
Herbe, Karlfriedrich, 210n63
Herbert, Gary, 232n143
Herzog, Don, 132, 207n37
Hesiod, 139, 250n1
Hirschmann, Nancy, 103
Hobbesian Democracy. *See also* development of Hobbes's thought
  anatomy of democracy and, 5–6
  defense of, 2, 173–179
  modern democratic theory contrasted with, 1 13, 26, 45, 75, 154–155, 173–175, 181, 183, 187n3
  nominalism and, 178
  overview of, 2–8, 173–179
  summary of contents on, 8–13
Hoekstra, Kinch, 3, 105, 189n6, 197n71, 243n98, 256n45
Horae Subsecivae (Hobbes), 99
House of Commons, 52
House of Lords, 53
Hoye, J. Matthew, 213n96, 248n159
hubris
  Athenian democracy and, 33, 77, 139, 184
  critique of democracy and, 7, 31–36, 77

monarchy and, 198n77
multitude and, 7, 31–36
openness of world and, 7, 36
persons and, 33
philosophy and, 117
reason and, 117
self-institution and, 77
self-limitation and, 7, 33, 36, 198n77
Hull, Gordon, 234n4, 258n57
human diversity. *See* diversity
human equality. *See* equality

imagination, 85, 87–88, 90, 94–95, 105, 112, 130, 222n67
institutional spaces of democracy, 24–25, 28, 50–51, 75, 167–168
intelligences, equality of, 19, 102–107, 110–116, 126–127, 130, 135, 150–151

Jakonen, Mikko, 41, 191n2, 193n18, 200n117
Jesseph, Douglas, 217n13
Johnson, Paul, 228n120, 240n76
Johnston, David, 240n71
justice. *See also* natural law
  civil law and, 118, 129, 169
  distributive justice, 109–110, 238n48
  Elements of Law and, 110
  equality and, 108–110, 135, 238n38
  law and, 173
  Leviathan and, 109–110, 150, 173
  social contract and, 108
  sovereignty and, 108

Kahn, Victoria, 99, 219n36
Kapust, Daniel, 35, 198n89, 206n25
Kitanov, Severin, 245n132
knowledge, limits of natural, 77–84

308 | Index

Kraynak, Robert, 201n126
Krom, Michael, 224–225n85

law. *See* civil law; natural law; sovereignty
Lawton, Robert, 244n117
LeBuffe, Michael, 241n85
Leijenhorst, Cees, 221n56
Leveller political thought, 60, 201n122
Leviathan (Hobbes)
  absolutism in, 30
  aristocracy in, 210n63
  audience of, 240n76
  authorization in, 3, 10, 46–47, 59–67, 69–71, 170, 182, 202n1, 213n99, 215n111, 216n112
  characteristics of democracy in, 18–19, 30
  civil war in, 41, 46, 53, 66
  command distinguished from counsel in, 37–38
  curiosity in, 123
  development of Hobbes's thought in, 9, 45–48, 53, 55–58, 66–71, 166–167, 170, 182–183, 202n1, 202n3, 210n63, 213n96, 214n103
  editions of, 58, 61, 66, 214n103
  emergence of communal bodies in, 99
  equality in, 106–109, 120, 129–130
  happiness in, 123, 125
  historical context of, 46, 68, 182, 189n6
  justice in, 109–110, 150, 173, 175
  language of democracy dropped from, 66–71
  legal right in, 109–110
  liberty in, 55–58, 155, 161, 264n113
  madness in, 39
  modern democratic theory and, 173–174
  motion in, 90
  multitude in, 3, 37–38
  natural law in, 142, 144, 146, 150, 175
  nonsovereign political entities in, 99
  normativity of democracy in, 48, 60–61, 175, 183
  openness of world in, 96
  originary democratic moment in, 10, 12–13, 48, 66–71, 170, 182–183, 213n96, 213n99, 215n111, 216n112
  participatory desire in, 68, 142, 164–173, 178, 186
  passions in, 126, 171
  persons in, 60–62, 65
  prudence in, 123
  public safety in, 160–161
  reason in, 113
  representation in, 10, 46–47, 59–66, 182
  rhetorical techniques of, 53
  Roman Empire in, 30
  sense perception in, 86, 90
  sovereignty in, 18, 30, 45–47, 64–66, 160, 167, 266n127
  summum bonum in, 245n131
  writing of, 9, 45–46, 240n76
liberalism. *See* modern democratic theory
liberty
  as absence of impediments, 10, 40, 48, 55–57, 155–156, 183
  ancient precursors to, 57–58, 207n37
  Aristotelianism and, 42, 50, 58
  Athenian democracy and, 58
  Behemoth and, 52

characteristics of democracy and, 7, 12, 50, 54
civic freedom and, 48, 55–58, 169
civil law and, 56–58, 178
civil science and, 162
civil war and, 58
critique of democracy and, 42–43, 49–50
De Cive and, 9–10, 48–49, 54–60
definition of, 49–50, 55, 155–156
deliberation and, 157–158
development of Hobbes's thought and, 49–50, 55–57
Elements of Law and, 9, 48–55, 57–59, 165
equality and, 110, 141
Leviathan and, 55–58, 155, 161, 264n113
motion and, 10, 40, 48, 55–57, 155–156, 183
natural freedom, 57, 147, 156–157, 161
natural law and, 142, 154–165, 186
necessity and, 157–158
normativity of democracy and, 9–10, 12, 55–59, 141
orators and, 52
participation and, 9, 48, 50–51, 55–59, 178
philosophical anthropology and, 155–157, 262n90
power and, 154–159, 164
republican conception of, 57
self-limitation and, 6–7
sovereignty and, 50, 58, 161–163, 208n51
true liberty, 12, 110, 141–142, 159–165, 169, 178, 186, 264n113

limits of natural knowledge, 77–84
Lloyd, Sharon, 155, 259n62, 260n67
Locke, John, 213n100
Lukes, Steven, 227n111
Luther, Martin, 249n179

Machiavelli, Niccolò, 42, 97, 201n125
MacMillan, Alissa, 227n106
Macpherson, C. B., 231n140, 263n100
madness
 critique of democracy and, 38–43, 151, 172, 181, 199n106
 definition of, 121, 172, 181
 deliberation and, 121–122
 equality and, 131
 good and evil and, 121
 Leviathan and, 39
 passions and, 39–40, 121–122
 reason and, 39–40, 121–122, 172
 self-limitation and, 172
Malcolm, Noel, 103, 187n2, 213n98, 246n148
Martel, James, 4, 222n61, 225n88
Martinich, A. P., 196–197n71, 216n113, 236n15
Mastnak, Tomaž, 206n25, 207n33
materialism. *See* ontological materialism
May, Larry, 108, 191n1
mechanics of sovereign institution. *See* sovereignty
memory, 113, 120, 123–124
mental discourse, 87, 120–121
methodological individualism, 94, 98, 227n111
Mill, David van, 194n35, 250n7
Mills, Charles, 236n14
Minogue, Kenneth, 252n17

310 | Index

modern democratic theory
  absolutism and, 3, 5
  accommodation and, 175
  administration and, 25–26
  aristocracy and, 31
  Athenian democracy and, 139–140
  characteristics of democracy and, 25–26, 192n3
  civil science and, 3–5
  critique of democracy and, 45, 173–174
  deliberation and, 173–174
  democratical Hobbesians in, 3–5, 200n116
  equality and, 150–151, 175
  Hobbesian Democracy contrasted with, 1–13, 26, 45, 75, 173–175, 181, 183, 187n3
  Leviathan and, 173–174
  liberal pluralist Hobbesians in, 4
  limits of, 7
  lottocratic structures in, 174
  mini-publics in, 173–174
  normativity of democracy and, 48
  radical democracy in, 4, 150–151, 163, 258n57, 267n154
Moffitt, John F., 235n13
monarchy
  absolutism and, 29
  aristocracy and, 176
  characteristics of democracy and, 33–34
  critique of democracy and, 32, 34–36
  De Cive and, 8
  definition of, 18, 34
  deliberation and, 35–36
  flattery and, 34–35
  Hobbes's preference for, 3, 8–9, 32, 35–36, 153, 173–175, 198n90
  hubris and, 198n77
  limitations on, 28–29, 34

  natural law and, 153
  originary democratic moment and, 23, 50, 99
  participation and, 172–173
  persons and, 29, 35, 61
  philosophical anthropology and, 172–173
  reason and, 35
  sovereignty and, 8–9, 18, 25, 29, 35, 61, 153
  temporary monarchs, 28–29
  tyranny and, 18, 34
  unitary will and, 8–9, 18, 22, 29, 35–36
motion, 10, 40, 48, 55–57, 78, 85–86, 90–92, 142, 155–156, 183
multitude
  administration and, 26–27
  authorization and, 3, 63–65, 69
  characteristics of democracy and, 8–9, 19–20, 24, 26, 50, 200–201n118
  civil war and, 41
  consent of majority and, 26–27
  counsels and, 37–38
  critique of democracy and, 37–43
  De Cive and, 19–23, 26
  definition of, 20–21, 194n26
  Elements of Law and, 19–23
  equality and, 132
  hubris and, 7, 31–36
  Leviathan and, 3, 37–38
  originary democratic moment and, 8, 19, 24, 41, 64–67
  persons and, 3, 20–23, 64–67, 192n12
  problem of, 8, 19, 41, 63–64
  reason and, 37–38
  sovereignty and, 8, 18, 20–23, 26–27, 63–66
  unitary will and, 20–23, 26–27, 63–65, 69, 193n18

natural law. *See also* justice
  antipolitics and, 142, 149–154
  Aristotelian-Thomist tradition in, 12, 149, 158, 252n19, 253n24, 256n43
  authorization and, 146
  Behemoth and, 148
  characteristics of democracy and, 12–13
  civil law and, 129, 141, 146–149, 154–155, 160–161, 256n43
  critique of, 143–149
  De Cive and, 122, 142–143, 148, 160–161
  definition of, 146–147
  disagreement on, 143–144
  diversity and, 142, 144–146, 149, 152–153, 165
  dogmatici and, 143, 186
  Elements of Law and, 143, 149, 160–161, 252n14
  equality and, 106–111, 164
  good and evil and, 146, 159
  Leviathan and, 142, 144, 146, 150, 175
  liberty and, 142, 154–165, 186
  minimal content of, 12, 142, 148–149, 158–159, 186
  monarchy and, 153
  motion and, 142
  normativity of democracy and, 12, 141, 143, 150, 154, 155, 186
  obedience and, 154–155
  openness of world and, 12, 99–100, 141, 143–148, 150, 186
  participation and, 142–143, 164–173
  philosophical anthropology and, 145–146, 149–150, 262n90
  politics and, 149–154, 163, 254n27
  positive law and, 144, 148
  power and, 154–159
  public safety and, 160–161, 164–165
  reason and, 141, 146
  reconstruction of, 143–149
  self-institution and, 141
  self-preservation and, 13, 58, 141, 146–148, 151–152, 159–160, 162, 177–178, 186
  sovereignty and, 12–13, 141–142, 151–155, 159–160
natural persons. *See* persons
natural philosophy. *See* ontological materialism
necessity, 10, 41, 50–51, 82–84, 87, 157–158
Negri, Antonio, 257–258n57
nominalism. *See also* speech
  absolutism and, 225–226n88
  authorization and, 4
  civil science and, 89–90
  diversity and, 89–90
  equality and, 11, 112
  Hobbesian Democracy and, 178
  normativity of democracy and, 225n88
  reason and, 118
  sense perception and, 88
  sovereignty and, 99, 118
  speech and, 88–89, 118
  ultranominalism, 88, 224nn80–81
normativity of democracy
  accommodation and, 175
  aristocracy and, 178
  Athenian democracy and, 184
  authorization and, 60–61, 67
  characteristics of democracy and, 2, 7–9, 12, 18–19
  civil science and, 8, 48, 173–174, 191n32
  critique of democracy and, 32, 48, 71, 141, 143, 170
  De Cive and, 9–10, 54–55, 58–61, 68, 169–170, 183

312 | Index

normativity of democracy *(continued)*
  development of Hobbes's thought
    and, 48, 71, 75, 169, 182
  Elements of Law and, 9, 51, 175, 183
  equality and, 102–103, 140–141,
    150, 175–176, 234n4
  ethical preference for democracy
    and, 2, 10, 12, 143, 154,
    164–165, 183, 185
  Leviathan and, 48, 60–61, 175, 183
  liberty and, 9–10, 12, 55–59, 141
  modern democratic theory and, 48
  natural law and, 12, 141, 143, 150,
    154, 155, 186
  nominalism and, 225n88
  openness of world and, 101,
    140–141, 184
  originary democratic moment and,
    48, 54–55, 59–61, 67–71, 183
  parliamentary thought and, 60, 67
  participation and, 9, 51, 54–55,
    58–59, 67, 143, 164–173, 185,
    186
  persons and, 60–61, 68
  public safety and, 155
  self-institution and, 102
  sovereignty and, 48, 60–61, 67–68

obedience
  Behemoth and, 202n127
  civil law and, 58, 118, 154–155
  natural law and, 154–155
  reason and, 148
  sovereignty and, 148, 154–155,
    209n52
Ober, Josiah, 140
Observations (Parker), 101
"Of Liberty and Necessity" (Hobbes),
  83, 122
O'Gorman, Ned, 198n87
Olsthoorn, Johan, 212n93, 238n48,
  238n51, 239n54, 241n84

ontological conditions for democracy.
  See equality; openness of world
ontological materialism
  accident defined in, 77–78
  antifoundationalism of, 78
  bodies defined in, 77–78
  civil science and, 80
  definition of, 76
  diversity and, 11, 232n143
  dynamism of, 78
  equality and, 11
  essence redefined in, 78
  limits of natural knowledge and,
    77–81
  methodology of, 79
  motion and, 78
  necessity and, 10, 84, 157–158
  openness of world and, 10, 76, 78,
    184
  overview of, 76–78
  philosophical anthropology and,
    84–85
  self-institution and, 10–11, 76–80
  singularity of individuals in, 77,
    84, 183–184
  teleology absent in, 10, 76, 78,
    184
openness of world
  accidental origins of communal
    bodies and, 99
  Athenian democracy and, 139–
    140
  causation and, 82–84
  characteristics of democracy and,
    102, 139–140
  complete understanding and, 81,
    84, 125–126, 139
  critique of democracy and, 7, 36
  De Cive and, 96–97
  definition of, 81–82
  democratical gentlemen and,
    101–102

diversity and, 10, 95–100, 177
hubris and, 7, 36
Leviathan and, 96
limits of natural knowledge and, 77–84
motion and, 83
natural law and, 12, 99–100, 141, 143–148, 150, 186
necessity and, 82–84
nihilism and, 257n55
normativity of democracy and, 101, 140–141, 184
ontological materialism and, 10, 76, 78, 184
originary democratic moment and, 99
parliamentarian thought and, 101–102
passions and, 95–96
philosophical anthropology and, 97–99
psychological egoism and, 98
self-institution and, 76–77, 99–100, 102
self-limitation and, 6–7, 184
sense perception and, 83
sovereignty and, 41–42, 97–100, 151–152, 229n132, 257–258n57
state of nature and, 97–100
teleology and, 10, 76, 78, 83, 97–98, 151
unitary will and, 36, 67
orators
 aristocracy and, 33, 51–54
 Behemoth and, 52
 characteristics of democracy and, 51–52
 critique of democracy and, 32–34, 51–52
 liberty and, 52
 participation and, 51, 54
 sovereignty and, 52–53

originary democratic moment
 aristocracy and, 23, 31, 50, 54, 99, 175
 authorization and, 66–71
 characteristics of democracy and, 10, 23–25, 50, 99
 De Cive and, 10, 12–13, 23, 60, 69–71, 169–170, 182, 209n56
 disappearance of language of, 66–71
 Elements of Law and, 23–24, 28, 50, 54, 60, 71, 99, 182, 213n96, 216n112
 Leviathan and, 10, 12–13, 48, 66–71, 170, 182–183, 213n96, 213n99, 215n111, 216n112
 monarchy and, 23, 50, 99
 multitude and, 8, 19, 24, 41, 64–67
 normativity of democracy and, 48, 54–55, 59–61, 67–71, 183
 openness of world and, 99
Orwin, Clifford, 215n111
Overton, Richard, 201n122

Paden, Roger, 243–244n115
Paganini, Gianni, 123
Parker, Henry, 101, 211n83, 247–248n158
parliamentarian thought, 52–53, 60, 67, 101–102, 182, 207n34, 211n83, 247–248n158
participation
 aristocracy and, 51
 authorization and, 67, 170
 characteristics of democracy and, 6, 10, 19, 24, 28–31, 48, 50–52, 76–77
 civil law and, 178
 critique of democracy and, 169–173
 De Cive and, 12, 24, 54–59, 142, 165–166, 169–170, 186

participation *(continued)*
  deliberation and, 51, 172–173
  development of Hobbes's thought and, 48, 164–173, 177–178
  diversity and, 170–171
  Elements of Law and, 9, 49–54, 59, 167–168
  eloquence and, 51
  equality and, 164, 166
  Leviathan and, 68, 142, 164–173, 178, 186
  liberty and, 9, 48, 50–51, 55–59, 178
  monarchy and, 172–173
  natural law and, 142–143, 164–173
  normativity of democracy and, 9, 51, 54–55, 58–59, 67, 143, 164–173, 185, 186
  orators and, 51, 54
  participatory desire, 59, 68, 142, 164–173, 177–178, 186
  philosophical anthropology and, 165–166, 171–172
  self-institution and, 76–77
  sense perception and, 170–171
  sovereignty and, 31, 172–173
passions
  critique of democracy and, 6–7, 9, 36–40, 172
  De Cive and, 10, 38
  definition of, 40, 114
  deliberation and, 6–7, 9, 36–40, 121–122
  diversity and, 89–96, 111
  Elements of Law and, 40
  eloquence and, 37–38, 172, 182
  equality and, 111, 114
  happiness and, 125–126
  Leviathan and, 126, 171
  madness and, 39–40
  openness of world and, 95–96
  philosophical anthropology and, 171
  philosophy and, 117
  reason and, 9, 36–43, 114
  vainglory and, 32, 59, 129, 169–171
Pateman, Carole, 103
Paul, Joanne, 247n158
perception. *See* sense perception
persons
  artificial persons, 22, 45–46, 61–62, 64–65, 212nn92–93, 214n101
  authorization and, 62–66, 211n85, 212n93
  characteristics of democracy and, 20–24, 33, 51
  confusion surrounding use of, 21
  critique of democracy and, 34, 40
  De Cive and, 19–23, 68
  definition of, 21
  Elements of Law and, 19–23
  hubris and, 33
  Leviathan and, 60–62, 65
  monarchy and, 29, 35, 61
  multitude and, 3, 20–23, 64–67, 192n12
  normativity of democracy and, 60–61, 68
  religion and, 203n5
  representation and, 61–62, 65–68
  signification of, 21, 61
  sovereignty and, 4, 18, 20–22, 26, 45–47, 60–61, 65, 192n4, 212n92, 215n106, 264n109
  unitary will and, 18–22, 35, 65
Pettit, Philip, 68, 209n52
philosophical anthropology
  Aristotelianism and, 97–98, 145, 149, 256n45
  civil science and, 84, 115
  creativity and, 95–100
  critique of democracy and, 172–173
  curiosity and, 122–126, 150, 178, 244n121

Index | 315

De Cive and, 97
deliberation and, 122–126
diversity and, 96, 171
error and, 112
imagination and, 85, 87–88, 90, 94–95, 105, 112, 130, 222n67
liberty and, 155–157, 262n90
mental discourse and, 87, 120–121
monarchy and, 172–173
natural law and, 145–146, 149–150, 262n90
ontological materialism and, 84–85
openness of world and, 97–99
overview of, 75
participation and, 165–166, 171–172
passions and, 171
power and, 232n141
psychological egoism and, 98
sense perception and, 84–89
sociality of humanity and, 1, 10, 96–99, 145, 165–166, 172–173, 232n141
theatricality and, 210n69
universal human nature denied in, 85
philosophy. *See also* Aristotelianism; ontological materialism
ancient philosophy, 95, 117
authority and, 95
civil science and, 80
De Cive and, 75–76
definition of, 75–76, 191n32
disagreement in, 80, 117
dispositions and, 94
diversity and, 80, 117
division of, 76
dogma in, 97
geometry and, 79–80
good and evil and, 97
hubris and, 117
intelligence and, 113–115

limits of natural knowledge and, 77–81
mathematics and, 79
methodological individualism in, 79–80, 94, 98, 227n111
moral philosophy, 76, 97, 108, 114–115, 117, 145, 175
passions and, 117
religion contrasted with, 134
scholastic philosophy, 5
self-institution and, 76
sense perception and, 113
socialization and, 114–115
speech and, 89, 119
true philosophy, 79, 89, 114, 224–225n85
truth and, 79–80
Pietarinen, Juhani, 158
Pitkin, Hanna, 46
Platonism, 103, 151–152
pluralism, 4, 153–154, 258n57
Polin, Raymond, 233n154
political science. *See* civil science
Politics (Aristotle), 58, 107
power. *See also* sovereignty
development of Hobbes's thought and, 231–232n141
Elements of Law and, 85, 232n141
happiness and, 125
liberty and, 154–159, 164
natural law and, 154–159
philosophical anthropology and, 232n141
sense perception and, 85–86
practical reason, 11, 120, 126, 251n7
Pringle, Helen, 244n117
Prokhovnik, Raia, 251n8
propositional truth, 79, 112–114
"The Prose Life" (Hobbes), 32, 49, 115
prudence, 119–120, 123–126
public safety, 155, 160–161, 164–165, 263n99

316 | Index

Puritanism, 197n76

The Questions Concerning Liberty, Necessity, and Chance (Hobbes), 121, 256n48

Rahe, Paul, 198n90
Rancière, Jacques, 150–151, 256n50
Rapaczynski, Andrzej, 239n59
reason
　absolutism and, 242n89, 249n170
　Aristotelianism and, 103
　authorization and, 118
　autonomy and, 250–251n7
　Behemoth and, 248n169
　civil science and, 35, 153
　critique of democracy and, 9, 36–43, 172
　De Cive and, 122, 241n85
　definition of, 113, 116–117, 122
　deliberation and, 6–7, 11, 36, 38–40, 121–122
　diversity and, 116–122, 127–128
　eloquence and, 36–37, 143, 182
　equality and, 11, 103–107, 110–120, 126–130
　good and evil and, 116–117
　hubris and, 117
　intelligences and, 102–107, 110–117
　lack of universal form of, 118
　Leviathan and, 113
　madness and, 39–40, 121–122, 172
　monarchy and, 35
　multitude and, 37–38
　natural law and, 141, 146
　natural reason, 110–116, 122, 127–128, 150, 240n72
　nominalism and, 118
　obedience and, 148
　passions and, 9, 36–43, 114
　pedagogy and, 114–116
　plurality of, 116–122
　practical reason, 11, 120, 126, 251n7
　public reason, 117, 242n89
　right reason, 79, 114, 117–118, 122, 146, 153, 177, 241n85
　sense perception and, 86–87
　socialization and, 113–114, 127–128
　sovereignty and, 118, 242n89
　speech and, 113, 117–118
　truth and, 113–114
religion, 58, 133–134, 203n5, 222n61
representation
　authorization and, 3, 62, 65, 67–68, 203n5, 211n85
　characteristics of democracy and, 3–4, 214n101
　De Cive and, 69–70
　Leviathan and, 10, 46–47, 59–66, 182
　mechanics of, 66
　persons and, 61–62, 65–68
　sovereignty and, 3–4, 65–66, 67, 212n92
　unitary will and, 20, 67–68
resistance to sovereignty, 22, 47, 55, 58, 155, 162–163
revolution, 53, 60, 189n6
rhetoric. *See* deliberation; eloquence
Rhodes, Rosamund, 263n100
Ristroph, Alice, 221n55
Roman Empire, 27, 30, 95, 97, 168
Ross, Ralph, 261n76
Rudolph, Ross, 228n119
Rump Parliament, 53
Runciman, David, 3, 65, 192n3, 211n85

Sacksteder, William, 221n58
Sagar, Paul, 212n93
Santi, Raffaella, 264n103

Schmitt, Carl, 255n35
Schoolmen, 127
Schumann, Karl, 234n6
Schwartzberg, Melissa, 201n122
science, civil. *See* civil science
scientific knowledge, limits of, 77–81
Sebastián, Santiago, 235n13
self-institution
   artifice and, 99–100
   characteristics of democracy and, 6–7, 10, 76–77
   diversity and, 11
   history as creation and, 100
   hubris and, 77
   natural law and, 141
   normativity of democracy and, 102
   ontological materialism and, 10–11, 76–80
   openness of world and, 76–77, 99–100, 102
   participation and, 76–77
   philosophy and, 76
self-limitation
   characteristics of democracy and, 33–34
   critique of democracy and, 6–7, 9, 12, 33–34, 36
   deliberation and, 6–7, 12
   hubris and, 7, 33, 36, 198n77
   liberty and, 6–7
   madness and, 172
   openness of world and, 6–7, 184
self-preservation, 13, 58, 141, 146–148, 151–152, 159–160, 162, 177–178, 186
sense perception
   Aristotelianism and, 221n56
   civil science and, 84–85
   diversity and, 86–87, 89–90
   Elements of Law and, 85–86
   equality and, 112–113, 131
   essence and, 85–86
   great deception of, 85
   as indirect representation, 85–88, 90
   Leviathan and, 86, 90
   limits of natural knowledge and, 83–84
   motion and, 85–86, 90–91
   nominalism and, 88
   openness of world and, 83
   participation and, 170–171
   philosophical anthropology of, 84–89
   philosophy and, 113
   power and, 85–86
   reason and, 86–87
   singularity of individuals in, 84–85
   speech and, 86–90
Shulman, George, 197n76
signification. *See* speech
Skinner, Quentin, 46, 53, 57, 101, 191n33, 204n9, 205n18, 212n94, 248n158, 264n113
Slomp, Gabriella, 171, 218n21, 227–228n114, 227n101
social contract, 23, 103, 108, 202n3
social-historical alterity. *See* diversity
sociality of humanity, 1, 10, 96–99, 145, 165–166, 172–173, 232n141
Sommerville, Johan, 189n6, 253n25
Sorgi, Giuseppe, 266n134
Sorrel, Tom, 92–93, 258n59
sovereignty. *See also* power
   absolutism and, 29–31
   accidental origins of communal bodies and, 99
   acquisition and, 216n113
   administration and, 25–29
   aristocracy and, 18, 27
   Aristotelianism and, 258–259n59
   authorization and, 3, 46–47, 61–66, 69, 202n3, 212n92
   characteristics of democracy and, 8, 13, 17–18, 24–31, 50–51

sovereignty (*continued*)
  civil law and, 57, 167
  civil science and, 8
  critique of democracy and, 6–9, 31–32, 41–42, 172–173, 181
  De Cive and, 10, 25–26, 29, 45–46, 60, 63, 69–70
  deliberation and, 9
  diversity and, 5, 36, 67, 99
  Elements of Law and, 27–28, 45–46, 63, 159–160
  equality and, 105–106, 176–177
  imagination and, 222n67
  justice and, 108
  just law and, 118, 173
  Leviathan and, 18, 30, 45–47, 64–66, 160, 167, 266n127
  liberty and, 50, 58, 161–163, 208n51
  monarchy and, 8–9, 18, 25, 29, 35, 61, 153
  multitude and, 8, 18, 20–23, 26–27, 63–66
  natural law and, 12–13, 141–142, 151–155, 159–160
  nominalism and, 99, 118
  normativity of democracy and, 48, 60–61, 67–68
  obedience and, 148, 154–155, 209n52
  openness of world and, 41–42, 97–100, 151–152, 229n132, 257–258n57
  orators and, 52–53
  originary democracy moment and, 10, 23, 67–68
  participation and, 31, 172–173
  pedagogy and, 115
  persons and, 4, 18, 20–22, 26, 45–47, 60–61, 65, 192n4, 212n92, 215n106, 264n109
  primary duty of, 159–160, 162–163
  public safety and, 159–160, 162–163
  reason and, 118, 242n89
  representation and, 3–4, 46–47, 65–66, 67, 212n92
  resistance to, 22, 47, 55, 58, 155, 162–163
  scriptural interpretation and, 133–134
  self-preservation and, 13, 58, 141, 146–148, 151–152, 159–160, 162, 177–178, 186
  sleeping sovereign image, 4, 25
  social contract and, 23, 103, 108, 202n3
  speech and, 117–118, 223n68
  state of nature and, 99
  unitary will and, 18, 20–21, 26, 35, 67

speech. *See also* eloquence; nominalism
  absurd speech, 5–6, 119, 156, 224n85
  abuses of, 113
  common names, 88–89, 93
  definitions and, 119
  dispositions and, 94–95
  diversity and, 89–90, 93–94
  equality and, 112–113
  geometry and, 113
  grounds for generation of, 89
  inconstancy of language and, 93–94
  motion and, 90
  naming and, 5, 18, 86, 88–91, 93–94, 122–123, 150, 223n76
  nominalism and, 88–89, 118
  philosophy and, 89, 119
  propositional truth and, 112–114
  prudence and, 122–123
  reason and, 113, 117–118
  sense perception and, 86–90

signification and, 5, 21, 56, 61, 89, 93, 113, 117–119, 127, 133, 141, 146
singularity of individuals and, 88–89
socialization and, 93–95
sovereignty and, 117–118, 223n68
universal names, 88–90
Spragen, Thomas, 78
Sreedhar, Susanne, 162–163, 265n122
state of nature, 97–100, 102, 200n117, 208n43, 231n139, 236n14, 264n109
Stier, María Lukac de, 229n123
Strauss, Leo, 234n4
Strong, Tracy, 249n179

teleology, 10, 76, 78, 83, 97–98, 151
Thomist tradition of natural law, 12, 149, 158, 252n19, 253n24, 256n43
Thucydides, 32–33, 49, 197n71
titles, rejection of all, 102, 105–108, 128–130, 185
truth, 79–80, 112–114
Tuck, Richard, 3, 24–26, 28, 98, 192n12, 194nn36–37, 195n45, 246n148

unitary will
  aristocracy and, 18, 22
  authorization and, 3, 64–69, 213n99, 259n62
  characteristics of democracy and, 19–23, 26, 35–36, 50
  critique of democracy and, 4–5, 20, 33, 35–36, 41, 45, 49
  deliberation and, 9, 19, 36
  diversity and, 33, 36, 96, 259n62
  monarchy and, 8–9, 18, 22, 29, 35–36
  multitude and, 20–23, 26–27, 63–65, 69, 193n18
  openness of world and, 36, 67
  persons and, 18–22, 35, 65
  representation and, 20, 67–68
  sovereignty and, 18, 20–21, 26, 35, 67

vainglory, 32, 59, 129, 169–171
Vanden Houten, Art, 243n106
Vaughan, Geoffrey, 241n79
"The Verse Life" (Hobbes), 32, 49
Vieira, Mónica Brito, 40, 210n69, 211n73, 214n103
Virno, Paolo, 193n13, 200n118

Waldman, Theodore, 230n135, 261n74
Wallis, John, 146
war, civil. *See* civil war
Watkins, J. W. N., 226n98
Weithman, Paul, 211n74
White, Thomas, 79
will, unitary. *See* unitary will
Williams, David Lay, 263n99
Willms, Bernard, 208n43, 249n171
Wolin, Sheldon, 248n159
women, 103, 235n10
Wood, Ellen, 204n9
words. *See* speech
Wright, Joanne, 103

Zagorin, Perez, 208n51
Zarka, Yves Charles, 97, 152, 202n1, 215n111, 219n32, 223n68

www.ingramcontent.com/pod-product-compliance
Ingram Content Group UK Ltd.
Pitfield, Milton Keynes, MK11 3LW, UK
UKHW041923140426
5217IPUK00014B/292